The European Macroeconomy

Growth, Integration and Cycles 1500–1913

Lee A. Craig

Professor of Economics, North Carolina State University and Research Economist at the National Bureau of Economic Research, USA

Douglas Fisher

Professor of Economics, North Carolina State University, USA

Edward Elgar
Cheltenham, UK • Northampton, MA, USA

Published by
Edward Elgar Publishing Limited
Glensanda House
Montpellier Parade
Cheltenham
Glos GL50 1UA
UK

Edward Elgar Publishing, Inc.
136 West Street
Suite 202
Northampton
Massachusetts 01060
USA

A catalogue record for this book
is available from the British Library

Library of Congress Cataloguing in Publication Data
Craig, Lee A.
    The European macroeconomy : growth and integration 1500–1913 / Lee
A. Craig, Douglas Fisher.
    Includes index.
    1. Europe—Economic conditions.   2. Industries—Europe—History.
3. Capitalism—Europe—History.   4. Europe—Economic integration—
History.   I. Craig, Lee A. (Lee Allan), 1960–   .   II. Fisher,
Douglas, 1934–   .   III. Title.
HC240.C68   2000
330.94—dc21   99–31597
                                                                          CIP

ISBN 1 85278 643 4

Typeset by Manton Typesetters, Louth, Lincolnshire, UK.
Printed and bound in Great Britain by Bookcraft (Bath) Ltd.

Contents

Figures

Tables

Preface

The general purpose of this study is to describe the growth and economic integration of the European economy between 1500 and 1913. We have picked the date 1500 somewhat arbitrarily, to be sure, but it seems reasonable for us to assert that by that date the simultaneous expansion of international trade and the rise of the nation state marked a national or *macro*economic progress that spilled across the borders of the existing and future nations of Europe in an irreversible fashion. Similarly, 1913 is a natural stopping date, as much of the modern shape of the European economy was in place; while, at the same time, the subsequent political developments can accurately be said to have ushered in a new regime.

Obviously, these dates are not intended to suggest that growth and integration were not important prior to 1500 nor that economic developments after 1913 have not altered the economic map of Europe; however, before 1500 growth rates (in real terms) were not rapid by modern standards, to begin with, and the degree of integration was also comparatively small in 1500. After that date one can speak of world markets in many raw materials and consumer goods and, certainly, of substantial capital (and even labour) flows across national borders. Also, there seems to be a discontinuity in the rate of overall economic growth after that date.

We survey, with considerable illustration, much of the existing work on these broad themes, but, we should emphasize, we attempt to minimize both the specifics of the academic controversies surrounding some issues and the technical details – statistical and otherwise – around which many of these controversies revolve. We do so in order to present a consistent and coherent set of findings to a general audience. Necessarily, this work represents our views as to what is important in a truly vast literature. The reader should note, especially, that further documentation is available in two detailed studies from which parts of this volume have been drawn (Fisher, 1992; and Craig and Fisher, 1997).

In Part I we address the role of macroeconomics in the study of economic history. In Chapter 1, we deal with general methodological issues. This material involves a discussion of how markets worked in this period, the role of money in the developing European economy, and several sections describing our theoretical framework (with respect to growth, cycles and integration).

These themes run throughout the rest of the volume. In this first part we also feel that an historical review, running toward political economy, is in order. The reason is that in this period, national (macroeconomic) policies – for example, trade policy – were formulated and certain national institutions, such as central banks, first emerged. Indeed, the basis of national income accounts, which is grist for the macroeconomist's mill, arises with the nation state. Much of this political material, and its implications for macroeconomic studies of the growth of the European economy, is contained in Chapter 2.

The formal macroeconomic material begins in Part II, covering the period from 1500 to 1750. This period features the great Elizabethan boom, the persistent inflation known as the 'price revolution' and a period of general enrichment of the European economy through the growth of agriculture, manufacturing and trade. This period also features the arrival of mercantilism as a guiding national policy. While the data are not really adequate to provide a full macroeconomic analysis, we are able to offer a considerable amount of narrative material and many suggestions, partly guided by the theoretical framework developed in Chapter 1. In all of this, our basic purpose is to establish some preliminary generalizations about growth rates and business cycles and to provide material on the integration of European product and capital markets.

In Part III, we turn to the period of the industrial revolution (roughly 1750 to 1850). At this point we have available some broad indices of economic performance, and so we can explore in some detail the macroeconomic character of an emerging European economy. This exploration involves a discussion of growth, cycles and the further integration of this economy. In Part IV, finally, we consider the period from 1850 to 1913. We believe that the voluminous national data that are available here strongly support the notion that this is an economically integrated community (by 1913) and that much can be gained by analysing it in this fashion. Again, we are interested in growth and cycles, but even these topics are considered from an integrated perspective. Finally, Chapter 13 contains our conclusions; here we consider it important to present both a summary of our findings and a summary of the many qualifications we have scattered throughout the study.

We thank our former colleague Theresa A. Spencer with whom we collaborated on several projects, some of which are noted in the text; she also assisted in the early work on this volume. In addition, Kristin Morgan provided efficient secretarial support.

Finally, we dedicate this volume to the memory of Robert E. Gallman – a great scholar, a good colleague, and a dear friend. We wish that he were still here to show us, if just once more, our errors and how to correct them.

PART I

The Foundations of Macroeconomics in an
Historical Context

1. Macroeconomics and economic history

1. GENERAL THESES

In this chapter we establish the main themes of the volume, make clear our methodological preferences and provide a general overview of the work. Broadly speaking, our main objective is to explore the accelerating growth and increasing integration of the European economy from 1500 to 1913.[1] In the presentation of the main arguments and supporting evidence, we employ the methodology and quantitative techniques of modern economics. One does not need to be dogmatic about such an approach, but it does seem likely that from AD1500, economic agents can be discussed as if they were profit-and-utility maximizers operating under constraints that they perceived (however imperfectly).[2] One also can argue that economic agents in this period performed their calculations with as effective a 'model' – and with as accurate an information set – as the times (and again the agents' constraints) permitted. Thus, while we emphasize the macroeconomic (or aggregate) performance of the emerging European nation states in this study, our views are firmly founded in the behavior of individual economic agents (that is, in microeconomics).

As discussed in the Preface, this volume consists of four major parts. In Chapter 2, we review the political integration of the countries covered in this survey. The primary purposes of the discussion of political integration is to establish the date at which modern nation states emerged and to suggest ways that their political integration contributed to their economic integration, especially near the end of the period. Another purpose of Chapter 2 arises because the method of analysis in this study – macroeconomics – is often very ahistorical both in its abstraction and in its use of aggregate data. The use of economic aggregates requires that, to a certain extent at least, the nation state be the unit of focus. Thus the discussion of the political integration of the European states emphasizes important aspects of their political development during the period 1500–1913. The aspects of most concern involve the political unification of nations, the economic dimensions of that unification and early economic policies. These policies include taxation, the regulation of trade and financial markets and the creation of central banks. Finally, in Chapter 2 we are also interested in how certain political institutions evolved in this period, pointing the way to greater integration on at least some fronts. Perhaps the most important example of these political developments is the emergence of elected bodies to replace divine-right monarchs.

Part II covers the growth of the market before 1750. In Chapter 3, we consider population growth and its role in the economic development of the West in the period 1500 to 1750. We also consider the contribution of agriculture. We consider these topics together because population change and overall economic growth are tied largely to the agricultural sector, but we also focus on agriculture because this period contains the 'agricultural revolution', although certainly other periods can also lay claim to that title.[3] The pronounced agricultural progress of the time both stimulated and responded to the growth of knowledge (a part of human capital development) and real economic growth. The agricultural sector also operated as a supplier of products to industry and commerce in several ways.[4] By the late seventeenth century, there were strong indications of vigorous growth and by the mid-eighteenth century, the pressure was so great that dramatic changes had already occurred to produce a strong agricultural component to more rapid growth across much of Europe. Even so, the agricultural sector is of gradually diminishing relative importance in this period.

Chapter 4 discusses the development of the European financial community from 1500 to 1750. The beginning of this period coincides with the so-called 'price revolution', the general increase in Western European price levels (from around 1500 to 1618). This inflation was associated with the inflow of silver (and, to a lesser extent, gold) from the New World and the evidence we review suggests that inflation spread rapidly across Europe at this time. Quite naturally, we feel that this event, particularly as interpreted by the quantity theory of money which was first put forward at this time, suggests that prices were sufficiently flexible and that the European economies were sufficiently integrated to bring about this 'price integration'. As the seventeenth century wore on, central banks began to appear and commercial banking began to develop activities that characterize the industry to this day. The emergence of central banks was a consequence, largely, of the development of nation states, while the growth of commercial banking can be attributed to the emergence of central banks and to the growth of commerce and industry, both nationally and internationally. We close Chapter 4 with a discussion of the surprisingly large financial interaction among nations by 1750.

International trade is at the center of the economic expansion of this period and most probably grew at rates that exceeded those in agriculture and domestic industry; we discuss trade and early manufacturing in Chapter 5. Trade is important for many reasons, including the substantial profits that played an important role in the early stage of the industrial revolution. We show that European trade generally expanded in this period and it diversified considerably to provide a broad foundation for growth in other sectors. Chapter 5 also contains details and some macroeconomic generalizations relating to the beginnings of industrialization before its late eighteenth-century acceleration. We will examine the possibility that there was a noticeable expansion in Elizabethan times that leveled off somewhat in the seventeenth century. We conclude Chapter 5 by considering the role that mercantilism might have played in these developments.

Chapter 6 unites the previous three chapters by identifying growth rates and business cycles between 1500 and 1750, to the extent possible. The sketchiness of the data preclude any deep analysis of cyclical phenomena, but there are sufficiently rich narrative and empirical accounts to provide us with some tentative generalizations. We also use standard growth models aggressively in order to try to establish bounds on the growth rates of different countries in this period.

In Part III of this study, we focus on what is sometimes called the 'first industrial revolution' in Europe; this era covers the period from 1750 to 1850. In our presentation, we discuss events on a country-by-country basis, beginning with Britain in Chapter 7. In Chapter 8, we single out a set of countries – Belgium, France, the German states and later Germany – whose entrepreneurs and central governments responded relatively quickly to the economic opportunities that emerged during the late eighteenth and early nineteenth centuries. The countries discussed in Chapter 9 were somewhat slower to industrialize, and include Austria–Hungary, the Scandinavian countries, the Netherlands, Italy and the Iberian countries. In both Chapters 8 and 9 we will be most interested in relative growth rates and in the business cycle history, as these matters can be gleaned from the historical record. We pursue these matters partly because we are interested in establishing the degree of real integration across these economies and because growth experiences and cross-country cycles are indicators of integration. Much of our information is derived in a non-statistical way in this part of the study, but there is surprising similarity of these events across countries, particularly after 1790, at least putting aside the weather-pest-induced agricultural crises that were often relatively local in character.

In Part IV, we turn to the post-1850 period. We find that by 1850, Europe is well integrated economically. Not even labour markets can be said to be limited to national borders, as the evidence on migration – from country to country, from farm to city, and from Europe to America and back – attests. We go over this material, and the by-now-abundant data on population growth in Chapter 10, which also presents broad figures on economic growth for all countries for which such data exist (for 1850 to 1913). These data take the form of industrial production indices, output data (GNP and related measures) and exports. What we see is that the growth rates of these series are remarkably similar across countries and convergence toward the U.K. economy is apparent for many of these countries.

Chapter 11, then, considers the financial aspects of economic growth in this later period. Just as with Chapter 4, the focus is on the (further) development of central banks and commercial banking systems after 1850, but there are new elements in this period, with central bank accommodation and cooperation during financial crises and the successful operation of the gold standard being among the most important. There are also much better data available, so that a serious attempt can be made to provide a statistical gauge of the degree of financial integration at this time.

In Chapter 12 we turn our attention to what might be termed the 'international business cycle'. Here we present a summary of a rapidly growing literature that attempts to explain how industrial nations came to share cyclical experiences in this period. Indeed, as measured by their 'phase coincidence' and various other statistics, by 1913 many of the more developed of the European countries appear to be in almost perfect lock step from this point of view.[5] Finally, in Chapter 13, we look at the whole 1500 to 1913 period, quantitatively as far as possible, in order to illustrate the remarkable changes that occurred. We divide this material into real, financial and cyclical aspects and examine the changing nature of the growth and integration of Europe. The purpose, of course, is to provide an overview of the study, but there are conclusions offered in this chapter that are hard to see in the shorter segments studied in the earlier chapters.

Before we turn to the material discussed above, however, it is worth taking a moment to discuss in general terms a few of the key economic concepts around which the remaining chapters revolve. These concepts include the market, money, economic growth, business cycles and integration or convergence. Each is discussed below.

2.   THE MARKET

The principal character in the economic story presented in this study is the *market*. A market is an institutional arrangement in which goods and services are exchanged through the activities of buyers and sellers. A necessary precondition for markets to emerge is the opportunity for specialization in production and the use of markets to allocate goods is a consequence of this specialization. The evolution of markets in Western Europe, from the harvest festival to the village fair to specialized trading through intermediaries, provided an increasingly efficient arrangement by which individuals took advantage of the opportunities to specialize in production and distribution. While it is arguable that vestiges of 'command' and 'customary' economies survived beyond the middle ages (and indeed mark some economic activity today), it is surely reasonable to argue that by 1500 much of the economic activity of Western Europe had been transformed into a loose system of markets in which participants were bound together by mutual dependence; in this network domestic and international commerce flourished.

A market *system* or economy is one that is characterized by specialization, competition and price flexibility in its markets. A degree of specialization is the *sine qua non* for the trade that is conducted in the market. Self-interest – that is to say 'gain' – is the motivating force behind specialization, constrained as usual by opportunity costs, themselves the basis of rational economic decisions. Competition – produced by sufficient buyers and sellers so that no economic agent can substantially influence the market – and optimizing behavior on the part of market participants are the driving forces in a market economy. The price mechanism is the means of coordinating the activities of these market participants. In the market, or through the activities of information-producing intermediaries (such as commercial banks), consumers and suppliers acquire information about quantities, qualities and prices and allocate their resources in order to maximize their net benefits (utility or profits). Initially incompatible plans between buyers and sellers become mutually compatible over time by self-interested adjustments in relative prices, again constrained by opportunity costs.

Clearly, price flexibility and the economics of information are important elements of the market.[6] Importantly, in the period 1500–1913, as markets and financial institutions developed relatively rapidly by historical comparison, the market system grew and spread economically valuable information. In fact, to the extent that information is introduced in a competitive environment, it is likely to dominate other sorts of information, derived from barter or even from 'non-market' techniques (for example, astrology or divine revelation). Market-generated information dominates because it reflects the value of the marginal decisions of traders in actual markets and, no doubt, because it is more amenable to verification by economic agents. In short, it provides a reliable signal.

The importance of the simultaneous substitution of the price signal for other means of information and the participation in markets that coincided with specialization in production and distribution cannot be overstated. Indeed, much of the economic growth experienced since early modern times resulted from these processes, which de Vries (1994) characterizes as part of the *industrious* revolution. The increasing use of markets for the allocation of economic resources had a number of benefits. In particular, the resulting specialization yielded more output per unit of input, which in turn provided greater returns for the owners of the resources employed in these markets. Increased efficiency, in effect, freed resources for other uses, with those uses being determined by market forces.[7] In addition to its effects on aggregate output, there were other aspects to this revolution. As the quantity of trade expanded, so did its sophistication and part of the increasing sophistication of trade included the expanded use of media of exchange such as money.

3.   MONEY

The financial services industry grows when certain economic agents (for example, the suppliers of financial intermediation) perceive the opportunity to profit by creating a medium of exchange and a safe and profitable store of value, while certain other economic agents (the demanders of intermediation products) also perceive gains from the increased services, in the form of a reduction in transactions costs and an increase in security (and in interest payments). In a market system like that described above, the existence of a generally-accepted money also facilitates decision-making because it provides a unit of account in which to measure values. However, once money is established, economic agents will also need to distinguish relative from absolute (that is, money) prices. This last aspect is an inevitable characteristic of monetization that produces some of the costs of the money system to economic agents. Generally speaking, the costs arise when a monetary event of some magnitude arrives unexpectedly. In the 1500 to 1750 period, for example, there are costs associated with debasements of the currency, inflation associated with the inflow of specie from the New World (as discussed in Chapter 4) and with financial panics. We added the proviso about such events being unexpected here simply because, if economic agents anticipated an event, they would do their best to avoid its consequences.

The potential effects on real economic activity from changes in the quantity and quality of money suggest there are positive externalities from 'sound' money, which provides one reason the state often enters into the money-supplying industry. A monetary system, to the extent that it is run in a socially suboptimal way by private agents, will be associated with uncertainty and perhaps even temporary lapses into less efficient (barter) systems. A government, if it can stabilize the production of money and effectively supervise the money-producing (banking) industry, may be able to limit these effects, although the record of governments in this respect is far from perfect. Another, and historically perhaps more powerful, motivation for the state's entry into the money business is the opportunity for the state to profit directly from money creation – that is, the government can gain what are known as 'seigniorage' profits as the producers of currency (just as they had long done at the mint, where they pressed coins for a fee).

There is another way the government can profit by controlling the money-production mechanism. The state can levy a particularly devious tax on money holders and on the holders of obligations written in money (that is, nominal) terms by occasionally and *unexpectedly* permitting the supply of money to grow more rapidly than the demand. This action generally produces inflation and reduces the real value of the government's outstanding debts.[8] Of course the government's objective in unleashing inflation could well be benevolent, as in its attempts to finance activities with significant social benefits. Furthermore, money creation may also be the government's only realistic option – as in the case of reducing war-produced debts that cannot easily be paid off in any other way because of, for example, political constraints.[9] In fact, central banks were often created specifically to fund the affairs of state and by carrying government debt as an asset to support their liabilities (e.g. currency), they effectively monetize that debt. We discuss some examples of this in later chapters of this study.

Putting aside the ambiguities about governments, the above discussion leads us to think of money as extending the market economy along an economically useful – that is, more efficient – path.[10] The monetary history of the 1500–1913 period suggests that the major developments of the monetary industry were such that practically all markets and regions eventually participated in the monetary network. The money industry is not necessarily presumed to be a leader in growth in this period; rather it is part of a financial sector that grows and develops along with other sectors in a rapidly changing (domestic and international) market economy. In particular, it often seems to be an increasingly effective facilitator, rather than a freestanding engine, of economic growth.[11] For readers with a penchant for metaphors, we offer the view of the real sector of the economy as an engine and money as a lubricant.

Often in historical studies much is made of the institutional constraints on optimizing behaviour, and with good reason. Indeed, as we shall see below, there are quite a few examples of such situations, many of which involve the activities of the state, but, if we are to understand how and when costly and relatively inefficient institutional structures collapsed or were altered over time, it seems important to appreciate that rational economic agents would have been working to bring about the downfall of such structures. For example, the enclosure movement in England that eliminated open-field agriculture (see Chapter 3) had begun long before the process was formalized by Parliament in the late eighteenth century. A further example is provided by the commercial revolution, to which we referred above, which was itself evident before the era in question even began. Indeed, this centuries-long process extended money and credit (and commerce) throughout the Western economies (and subsequently to their imperial outposts) and this increase in commerce was primarily a private sector development. Even so, the state blessed and helped finance endeavors it supported (such as exploration and conquest), even though such broad government developmental policies as there were (notably mercantilism) often fell victim to policy ineffectiveness at some point.

The monetary and financial policies that did work, in the limited way that theory suggests is possible, could well have been the unanticipated ones. A good example would be the sudden devaluations, debasements or extraordinary credit demands that tended to coincide with wars.[12] Influences that would not work, in the sense of inspiring more or less effort from economic agents, are the many gradual and easily predictable events, whether government-inspired or not, that are the subject of much of the written history of this period.[13] In any event, during the period in question each of the European nation states established financial systems that spread and controlled the money supply. As we argue in subsequent chapters, this process played an important role in supporting real economic growth.

4.   GROWTH

While we do not emphasize formal growth models in this study, a few notes will help the reader to follow the argument in later chapters. In standard economic growth models either the demand side or the supply side induces growth. The supply-side model is built on an aggregate production function and is generally employed under the assumptions that prices are flexible and markets are competitive and operated by economic agents who are rational.[14] A general result of the model is that the economy (in dynamic equilibrium) will tend to grow at the augmented rate of growth of the labour force (see Phelps, 1965).[15] This feature is particularly useful in discussing growth in this period, because the items just mentioned – especially labor supply, technical change and the rate of investment – are the most often mentioned topics in the historical literature.

Under certain circumstances, the conditions required for the framework just discussed could easily fail to hold. For example, suppose that consumption is actually growing at a slower rate than population because some economic agents are simply unable to borrow and consume according to their expected lifetime income because of the effects of credit rationing. The modern literature refers to this phenomenon as 'liquidity-constrained consumption behavior' and it is very likely to have been a factor in the economies of the period we are studying, if only because lending institutions were undeveloped, at least by modern standards, and were, in any case, not available to all potential borrowers. Indeed, it clearly holds for certain segments of the population even in modern economies. Liquidity constraints, then, would limit overall growth and the actual historical experience of these countries would deviate from that predicted by the growth model.

The foregoing is a description of a supply-side growth model. While in dynamic equilibrium the demand side of the economy will grow at the same rate as the supply side, there are some clear advantages to laying out the characteristics of a demand-side growth model. One is that the data often exist for work on the demand side but not on the supply side. The demand side of an economy refers to the spending activities of broad categories of economic agents – consumers, investors and the government in particular (in a closed economy). If net investment is positive in equilibrium, then the economy will grow (since, by definition, its capital stock will be growing). In dynamic equilibrium, then, one version of the model (the well-known Harrod–Domar growth model) concludes that the growth rate of the economy depends directly on the ratio of savings to real income and on the marginal efficiency of capital – that is, the change in real income with respect to a change in the capital stock (investment). This conclusion betrays the model's Keynesian origins, but, even so, it is a general enough framework to be employed effectively in historical studies. One reason we might employ a demand-side rather than a supply-side model is that with the former it would be possible to explore the determinants of growth when one has investment data but not capital stock data, a situation that frequently occurs.

5. CYCLES

The competitive model of the economy is based on economic freedom and the profit motive. A free market would allocate resources so that production would adjust to consumer demand, output would grow through savings and capital accumulation, income would be distributed among social classes according to the value markets place on the productive capacities of the inputs, and the same principles would apply to both domestic and international economic relationships. However, when events deviate from this scenario or when the above phenomena do not combine to produce a situation precisely consistent with the full employment of workers and capital, then the result is periodic deviations from long-run equilibrium. These deviations characterize the business cycle.

In the modern literature we speak of a 'shock-persistence' mechanism that can generate the irregular cyclical experiences that we have observed over the long history of the business cycle. The shocks that generate the downturns of these cycles are assumed to be unanticipated, since the effects of anticipated shocks can be avoided to some extent, and these unanticipated shocks can be real or monetary, though their relative importance and the relationship between the two sources are very much open questions. Examples of real shocks include wars and agricultural disasters; examples of monetary ones include unexpected debasement of the currency or financial panics that result in significant financial and sometimes real distress.[16]

Once in motion, the business cycle is spread out over time by the actions of economic agents; a popular term for this is the cycle's 'persistence'. This persistence is influenced by the time it takes individuals to react to the shock, by ingrained consumption and investment patterns and by the inflexibility of economic institutions. Among the list of the latter are restrictions on prices and the legal insistence that nominal contracts be honored, but some of the persistence in the economic system results from individuals who are attempting to spread their purchases (and thus the effects of shocks) over time.

A typical downturn, then and now, begins with a shock – a crop failure, for example – that produces a reaction by consumers, investors or the government in the form of a reduction of spending. During the period of decline of a typical recession, inventories accumulate, unemployment grows and demand appears insufficient for the quantity of goods that producers would like to supply. Recovery, then, typically commences when inventory restocking becomes necessary or for a multitude of other reasons that are often specific to each cycle. Note that in an economy that is typically growing, the seeds of recovery exist in the underlying growth rate itself – in, that is to say, the actions of businessmen and consumers who correctly anticipate a return to something like the *usual* growth rate of the economy.

6. INTEGRATION

European countries started at different levels of aggregate economic and per capita output in 1500, experienced different paths of growth and arrived at different junctions in 1913.[17] Even so, we feel that economic integration and convergence of per capita output were generally increasing in this period, and that by 1913 many countries that were on the (economic) periphery in 1500 had been drawn into the international economic community. The terms integration, convergence and catching up are frequently used in the social sciences in general and in economics in particular, and it is not clear to us that the terms are always used to mean the same thing; therefore, we now turn to a review of these concepts.

The literature that has emerged from the studies of integration in the social sciences recognizes two broad components of national integration, each of which contains a number of more specific aspects. The first of these broad components is territorial integration and the second is social integration. In this volume, we focus on *territorial integration*, which can be thought of as the physical linking or consolidation of a region or regions.[18] One way in which this integration occurs is through transregional transportation and communication systems. In these cases, topography – that is, physical geography – plays an important role. Economic factors come into play in territorial integration when the exchange of goods, populations, capital and technology occurs across regions. Territorial integration also includes political integration, which would involve the recognition of and submission to a common ruling hierarchy in some minimum level of political, social and economic activities. Indeed, the nature of Europe's economic integration over the past two centuries depends crucially on the earlier political integration of the individual European nation states; however, the economic aspects of territorial integration can also be transnational.

There is a vast literature on economic integration that is summarized in Craig and Fisher (1997, Chap. 2). What is of interest to us in this study are the means by which integration is achieved. One of the first to write explicitly on this topic was Heckscher (1935), who views integration primarily as a process that is promoted through the elimination of internal (and external) barriers to trade. Recent work on the trends in the growth of per capita output or incomes across nations extends Heckscher's analysis. In this more recent literature the tendency of countries with relatively low per capita output to grow faster than countries with higher living standards is referred to as 'catching up' and 'convergence',[19] and like Heckscher these contemporary scholars view integration as a process rather than a state.

There are several noteworthy recent examples of empirical studies of this type of convergence. Williamson (1996 and 1998) emphasizes the role of 'globalization', by which he means the erosion of barriers to and thus the expansion of international labor and capital flows. While the results he presents reflect mainly the labor flows, Collins and Williamson (1999) offer similar findings for capital flows.[20] In the context of our discussion of various meanings of the term 'economic integration', one can think of these studies as demonstrating the processes of a particular type of integration, which ultimately resulted in convergence; whereas, what we offer in this volume is a multidimensional view of the meaning of convergence itself. Our view tends to focus more on the institutional arrangements by which various countries 'caught up' or converged on the economic leader or leader(s).

Before considering the patterns of convergence and non-convergence identified in the literature, it is useful to consider why some countries initially lagged behind others. In 1500, to pick an arbitrary starting point, the economies of certain countries – England and Spain, for example – differed from others – the German states, for example – in ways that generated a faster rate of growth for the former as a result of technological change, trade and population growth. As time went by, the key 'initial conditions' for subsequent growth changed, and some richer nations fell to lower rungs of the economic ladder (relatively speaking), while others rose. (The reversal of the positions of Spain and Germany in this period provides just such an example.) To complicate matters, any discussion of the convergence of nations must deal with the fact that some of the resources generated by growth could be directed toward revising the initial conditions. These changes could be the result of government action (for example, through development policies), could be driven by the market or could be the result of technological change (itself a market process).

In discussing convergence, one needs to consider more than the growth of per capita income or output. One thing to bear in mind, and much is made of this in the literature, is that resource endowments, preferences and technologies differ across nations. Even so, as the markets for goods, materials, capital and technical knowledge expand, a nation's dependence on its own resources diminishes. This relaxing of constraints plays an important role in understanding the growth of Europe in the period 1500 to 1750. In addition, one might mention differences in the degree of financial sophistication and differences of entrepreneurial spirit as important influences here, as Gerschenkron (1962 and 1970) certainly does.

It should be apparent to this point that convergence (and catching up) describe processes by which economies evolve over time and that an important element of the path of their evolution is their economic position relative to that of other economies at any particular point in time. The problem one encounters is that, as it is often presented in the literature, this material does not explicitly address the issue of *economic integration* – that is, the process by which individual economies become part of a larger whole. It is one of the purposes of this study to examine changes in the extent or degree of integration over time in Western Europe. In subsequent chapters, we examine the extent to which changes in the aggregate economic activity in one country affect aggregate economic activity in another during this long period and we seek the sources of these interactions.

Without getting too far ahead of our story, we note at this point that we believe that Europe, at least, has been quite 'global' for some time, and much of what follows in the subsequent chapters develops evidence for this view. That is, the developed world in this period appears highly and increasingly 'integrated' in the various ways that we will measure this concept, and we think that is what the modern literature is referring to when it speaks of 'the global economy' of our own time. The reader should thus be aware that in this study we are thinking of globalization as a *process* with no particular geographical dimensions.

NOTES

1. When we say 'Europe' in this context, we mean the nation states of central and western Europe, with the exception of the Balkans and a few smaller states.
2. The starting date is arbitrary, of course, but is it worth noting that by 1500 the effects of the so-called 'commercial revolution' (which included such technological innovations as double-entry bookkeeping, bills of exchange, and insurance) were well known throughout the West and reflect formal calculations that are consistent with our assertion of optimizing behavior.
3. In particular the transformation of *homo sapien* from hunter to settled agriculturalist *c.* 10,000 BC, the mechanization of western agriculture in the nineteenth century and the application of scientific principles to agriculture in the present century have all been referred to in the literature as 'revolutions'.
4. The processing of raw agricultural products into semi-finished or finished goods was an important industry, and much of the shipping trade and early modern finance were tied to moving agricultural commodities; for more detail, see Chapter 3.
5. Phase coincidence refers to the situation in which two or more countries are in the same phase of their business cycles.
6. The tendency of prices to fluctuate with the relative scarcity of goods is as old as exchange itself and was recognized by the ancients. The absence of such flexibility is typically the result of actions by the state or some other ruling body (e.g. a guild, the village elders) with enforcement capabilities – that is, by command.
7. But there certainly were costs, as well. These included a reduction in leisure, increased family instability, and, according to contemporaries, an increase in 'vice'. For a discussion of this issue, see de Vries (1994, pp. 259–61).
8. As an instrument of public policy, early modern regimes typically inflated by debasement or 'calling down' the currency – that is by reducing the precious metal content of a standard unit of coinage.
9. We are, here, thinking of France just before the Revolution or Germany after the First World War.
10. We mean here 'economic efficiency' – that is, more net real output will result from a monetized economy than would otherwise be the case, *ceteris paribus*.
11. Indeed, below we discuss evidence that suggests the growth of real output *caused* the growth of the financial sector rather than the other way around. There are, however, cases in which the financial sector was clearly in the lead, especially between 1850 and 1914, in France, Germany and possibly Italy.
12. A specific example is provided by the abandonment of convertibility by the British government (by the Bank of England) in 1791 in the face of the large credit needs of the war effort at the time.
13. A good example would be the mercantilistic tariff policies designed to protect infant industries that seem never to have grown up. In this case, comparative advantage simply undermined the policy in the form of lower cost alternatives that were smuggled in or were sold in other markets (and which provide a benchmark for the resources wasted by the mercantilistic schemes).
14. While strict satisfaction of these conditions is unlikely for any particular time period, it is arguable that partial conformance to these assumptions will permit one to use the model in a general way.
15. That is, if the labor supply grows at a rate of $\alpha+\beta$, where β represents the effect of 'augmentation' (technical change) on labor supply and α represents the growth rate of the labor force itself, then this rate is common to the growth rates of consumption, the capital stock and the rate of investment, in dynamic equilibrium.
16. The financial panic may, of course, have real or financial causes, and so could be, in many cases, an indicator of the underlying shock rather than the shock itself.
17. Maddison (1991) and Craig and Fisher (1997) offer estimates of real output per capita for a large set of European countries as far back as 1820 and Maddison (1982) reports

comparable figures for the United Kingdom, France, and the Netherlands from 1700. Otherwise, there are few readily comparable aggregate output figures prior to the twentieth century.

18. For a discussion of social integration, see Craig and Fisher (1997, Chap. 2).
19. See for example, Abramovitz (1986) and Barro and Sala-i-Martin (1992).
20. More theoretical treatment of these issues can be found in O'Rourke and Williamson (1994) and O'Rourke et al. (1994).

2. Political integration and economic change in early modern Europe

1. INTRODUCTION

In Chapter 1, we defined political integration as the recognition of a common ruling hierarchy. Clearly, following this definition, the nation states of Europe were not *collectively* politically integrated by 1913. More important for our purposes is the fact that political integration was essentially completed *within* the European nation states in the 1500–1913 period. In many ways, as we shall argue elsewhere in this study, economic integration across national boundaries never totally respected the political structure of Europe, whether local, national, or transnational. However, one must be careful not to leap from this assertion to the proposition that national borders denote inappropriate boundaries in the study of economic integration, and for several reasons we do not make that leap. For one thing, this volume is a macroeconomic history and must deal with aggregate variables. Among the most important of these are real gross national product, the price level, the money supply, international trade data and population, all of which are collected nationally. National political units also determine the structure of banking systems; they set import quotas and tariffs; they subsidize particular industries; they establish tax systems and they control central banks. We argue that for many, though certainly not all, issues relating to economic growth and development the nation state is actually the relevant economic unit of reference. Of course, many important factors contribute to economic growth – human capital, technological innovation and natural resources – and these are distributed in ways that often ignore national boundaries – mineral deposits offer a good example. Furthermore, the theme of this book involves the establishment of higher economic 'authorities', some of which were discussed in the previous chapter, that ultimately created a pan-European economy; so, although our primary focus is on national aggregates, we recognize the potential problems of using such data.

We also argued in Chapter 1 that economic conditions at any point in time can influence the subsequent path of development and in this chapter we review several instances in which economic change was associated with the 'initial conditions' that marked the early modern European states. In particular we focus on political integration (consolidation, really) and we note the connection between political integration and economic development, focusing on three important issues: the rise of the middle class and its attempts to seize control of taxation and public expenditures, the evolution of transportation and trade networks (not the least of which were the global empires established by several states) and the advent and development of financial institutions and markets. Necessarily, then, there is a strong political flavor to this chapter, since in 1500 divine-right monarchs were the rule, while in 1913 they were not.

2. TAXATION, THE MIDDLE CLASS AND THE EARLY MODERN STATE

The growth of trade and the accompanying relative decline of the manorial system in the late Middle Ages led to the growth of urban areas. The merchants, artisans and manufacturers who collectively made up that amorphous body we have come to refer to as the middle class formed the dominant economic (and later political) groups in these locales. The growth of the middle class and the emergence of the nation state are inextricably linked during the early modern era. This link resulted partly from the strained relationship between early modern monarchs and the middle class. For one thing, the wealth generated by manufactures and trade was valued by rulers because it allowed them to expand their tax bases, which in turn allowed them to consolidate, expand and perpetuate their rule. For another, extracting the taxes from the creators of mercantile wealth became increasingly difficult as the merchants and manufacturers organized and employed their resources to enlarge their economic and political influence while reducing that of their rulers.

It is also true that from the point of view of the growing middle class, the monarchy offered both privilege and grief. On the one hand the crown either granted or at least recognized certain privileges in connection with some especially attractive trade and manufacturing opportunities. On the other hand, in return for these privileges, the crown was prepared to demand a sizeable share of the profits generated by these activities. Eventually, of course, these tensions were resolved by the demise of monarchical control of the finances of state in every western country, but in the early modern period this process was still unfolding and the rising nation states had dramatically different experiences in this respect.

The formation of the separate kingdoms and later nation states of England and France was still very much an open issue at the end of the Middle Ages. In 1337, seeking the consolidation of the two crowns, England's Edward III proclaimed himself King of France while visiting his lands there, thus precipitating the Hundred Years War. Although in the traditional narratives of the era much is made of Edward's ancient feudal claims as the provocation for the Hundred Years War,[1] the immediate cause of his campaign in France was more narrowly economic and involved the interests of English wool producers, who were the primary suppliers of wool to the Flemish textile manufacturers and merchants. The conflict over control of the Flemish textile regions largely centered around the allegiance of, and thus the tax revenues generated by, the thriving middle class in that region. During the century leading up to the conflict, the wool industry in Flanders and the surrounding territories represented one of the most dynamic economic forces in Europe, rivaled only by the diverse economic interests of the Italian city-states. (In fact profits from the Flemish wool industry were lent to the English Crown through the intermediation of Florentine bankers!) The resulting gains from trade led to an alliance between English wool producers and the Flemish textile magnates, most of whom belonged to the nascent middle class and all of whom were nominally subjects of the King of France.

The Flemish, however, often chafed at their treatment at the hands of the French Crown. Armed conflict between Flemish textile workers and French knights erupted in 1302 and again in 1327. In those conflicts the manufacturers and merchants had sided with their French rulers, but in the 1330s France's Philip VI pushed for closer economic and political ties with the increasingly prosperous Flemish urban areas, partly because they were among the wealthiest regions of his kingdom and thus especially able to generate tax revenues for the consolidation and expansion of that kingdom. French assertion of political control over the increasingly independent (and wealthy) textile towns (particularly Bruges and Ghent) drove the manufacturers, led by Jacob van Artevelde, to rebellion. The merchants turned to England for support, which Edward gladly supplied, thus touching off the Hundred Years War. This turn of events illustrates the ability of the nascent middle class to leverage their growing wealth in order to play one crown off against another in the quest for the control over the tax base.

Although the English Crown had sought to exploit the tensions accompanying a rising middle class in fourteenth-century Flanders, in the seventeenth century similar tensions in England revolutionized the political economy of the West. The conflict between Parliament and the Stuarts that marked the English Civil War resulted in the two most significant (at least from an economic perspective) political achievements of the early modern era, namely the perpetuation of Parliament's right to approve new taxes and the establishment in 1689 of a constitutional monarchy.[2] Parliament's right to approve new taxes (1340), which dated from the Hundred Years War (and Edward's demand for revenue to pursue his campaigns in France), was important because Parliament ultimately reflected the interests of those who would be taxed. Indeed, the establishment of a constitutional monarchy more clearly delineated the separate interests and responsibilities of both the ruler and the ruled, and made the perpetuation of the former's reign dependent upon recognition of the prerogatives of the latter. Together these two achievements allowed the rising British middle class to pursue its economic self-interest relatively unencumbered, at least by Continental standards. The spirit of enterprise inherent in the rising mercantile and manufacturing classes contributed to rising rates of economic growth. In turn, the growing British economy allowed Parliament to carve out a larger role for the government in meeting national objectives (economic and political), without, except possibly in wartime, unleashing the negative influence of the crowding-out of private investment expenditure.

In order to understand the role political developments played in Britain's subsequent economic growth, it is helpful to contrast it with the Continental powers at that time. In Britain a stable political system based on individual freedom ensured the property rights of the growing middle class, which in turn invested its financial and human capital in industry and trade and in an increasingly productive agricultural sector. Indeed, perhaps the most notable property issue of the era was the ever-broadening enclosure movement, which, by increasing the private return to agricultural innovation, contributed to the agricultural revolution in England (see Chapter 3). The English political system thus protected and rewarded capital accumulation and economic innovation. At the same time English domestic prosperity provided a growing tax base to be tapped by Parliament and the Crown to further national policies.

In the sixteenth century Habsburg Spain was the pre-eminent Continental power and the first to establish a great overseas empire, while in the seventeenth century the United Provinces carved out a global empire; however, eventually both the Spanish and the Dutch proved unable to protect their empires (and their positions atop the European economic ladder) from British encroachment. Then in 1713, Louis XIV succeeded in placing a Bourbon on the Spanish throne (by the Treaty of Utrecht), and France again became Britain's dominant Continental adversary. Like England a century earlier, France eventually had to come to terms with the tension between the Crown and those who made up its potential tax base. As we noted above, the early dynastic conflict had turned on the consolidation of the English and French thrones. Now the issue was European dominance and the tools were military and economic, with the mercantilist policies of Louis XIV (reign 1643–1715) and his English rivals dominating the economic arena. In this conflict, leaders of both countries acted as if the economic growth and political advances by their rivals necessarily meant the decline of their own influence. The wars most notable for this combination of political and economic interests are those that involved the attempt to place a Bourbon on the vacant Spanish throne in 1701, an attempt that, although ultimately successful, expended a great deal of French resources; the support of Austria (by Louis XV) against Prussia in the Seven Years War; and the struggle over who was to dominate the North American and Caribbean trade (over much of the latter half of the eighteenth century).

During these conflicts, French living standards were probably surpassed only by those in England and the Low Countries. While the French probably maintained their relative position over the next century or so, they never really challenged the British for economic supremacy in this respect. On this point, it is customary to mark two related factors: the wars (through the Napoleonic era) that were both expensive and ultimately unsuccessful for the French and the difficulties of financing the activities of the French government (in peace and war). These two factors hampered French economic development relative to that of Britain throughout the period.

As our discussion of the English Civil War reveals, the conflict between the British Parliament and the Stuarts culminated in the latters' expulsion, the creation of a constitutional monarchy and the protection of Parliament's prerogatives with respect to taxation. No such conflict emerged in France before the Revolution, and rather than go to an elected assembly, hat in hand, the Bourbons financed their reign through the recognition of local monopolies (enforced by the guilds) in return for tax revenues. In addition the offices responsible for the collection, disbursement and borrowing of revenues were all for sale (or at least for rent). Thus, the French kings of the seventeenth and eighteenth centuries financed a series of military and domestic projects by utilizing a taxing mechanism that probably inhibited the growth of the economy. In addition to being inefficient, this approach was unsuccessful, because it did not yield sufficient revenues to cover all of the Crown's spending projects, and, like other early modern monarchies, the Bourbon's resorted to extensive borrowing. It was their effort to finance the large war expenditures that resulted in the transfer of wealth from taxpayers to borrowers; the interest rate burdens accompanying those efforts finally drove the monarchy to the financial brink. Although Louis XVI tried, almost from the beginning of his reign, to reform the tax system, most notably during Turgot's tenure as minister of finance, the monarchy's finances limped along for more than a decade after Turgot's dismissal in 1777. In 1789, then, Louis called the Estates-General to consider reform. This act merely resulted in providing a venue for the expression of a common discontent, and in the chaos that ensued, the *ancien régime* was destroyed.

3.   TRADE AND THE EARLY MODERN STATE

Spain was the archetypal Great Power; it was the first major European state to achieve political integration along the lines of its current national boundaries; along with Portugal, which it eventually absorbed during this period, it was the first to establish and maintain an overseas empire. At the dawn of the early modern age it was *the* military (and soon-to-be economic) power of the West. By the mid-nineteenth century, however, Spain's days of political glory were long gone and Spain could be counted among western Europe's poorer countries. It is interesting to consider further this change in fortune for a country that, through its overseas exploration, must be considered one of the founders of the modern world order.

The Muslim encroachment in western Europe reached its high-water mark in Iberia, and much of Spanish history in the late Middle Ages is dominated by Christian efforts to reconquer the peninsula. By the fifteenth century, however, the Moors had been driven back until their last Iberian possession was Granada. In the north, the union of Ferdinand of Aragon and Isabella, of Castile (1469) ultimately resulted in a united Spain that had a well-known expansionist orientation. They further consolidated their rule through their conquest of Granada in 1492, and immediately sought a place in the rapidly growing effort to discover and claim new lands. The successful addition of overseas territory meant that the Spanish Empire and the Habsburg-dominated Holy Roman Empire were Europe's two most powerful monarchies at the dawn of the early modern era. The marriage of the Habsburg ruler Maximilian's son, Philip, to Juana, the heiress of Castile and Aragon in 1496, united the House of Habsburg and the Spanish Crown. Philip and Juana's son, Charles, became King of Spain as Charles I in 1516 and Holy Roman Emperor as Charles V in 1519. As Emperor, Charles ruled the greatest empire the West had known since the days of Charlemagne, spanning the continent from the Iberian peninsula to the plains of Hungary. This empire lasted only a generation, however, for by family compact the Austrian and Spanish holdings were separated upon Charles' abdication in 1556. The eastern realm, including the hereditary Habsburg lands in Austria and the recently acquired lands of Bohemia, Hungary, and Croatia went to Charles' brother, Ferdinand. The Spanish Crown, including the Spanish Netherlands, passed to Charles' son, Philip II.

Philip, a devout catholic, zealously supported the Counter-Reformation, and among his subjects the Dutch proved to be the most intransigent. England's Elizabeth I, whose father, Henry VIII, had separated the Church of England from that of Rome, supported the Dutch in their struggles against Philip, waging a naval war (Crown-supported piracy, really) against Spain. When Elizabeth ordered the execution of Mary Stuart, the Catholic claimant to the English Crown in 1588, Philip responded by sending the Armada against England. Although weather and Spanish blunders had as much to do with the repulse of the Armada as English seamanship and technology, the event showed just how far England had come as an economic and military power, largely on the strength of its merchant fleet; it was also somewhat of a turning point for the Spanish, as Spain's *relative* economic and military decline began shortly thereafter.

The staples of the early modern Spanish economy included specie (primarily silver), which was extracted and imported from Spain's imperial holdings, and wool, which was produced domestically. Although these two activities generated a great deal of Spain's wealth during the early modern era, and although they engendered envy and various degrees of imitation among Spain's early modern competitors, in the end the means by which both activities were carried out contributed to Spain's relative economic and military decline. Spanish policies in the New World were particularly misguided from an economic perspective. Rather than promote economic development which would expand the tax base and provide revenues indefinitely, Spanish conquerors for the most part plundered the New World in the quest for specie. The specie provided a windfall gain to the throne and to the entrepreneurs who financed and participated in its discovery and extraction, but from a public policy perspective, it was not without its complications. The resulting inflation undermined nominal contracts, while in Spain a persistent balance of payments deficit arose that was the result of the rising demand for foreign products. Indeed, the inflation *itself* contributed to the specie outflow as individuals (and the Crown) sought the cheaper prices and greater variety in the expanding world markets of the time.

Once Spanish expenditures outgrew the New World's ability to cover them, the Crown actually turned to borrowing sums that ultimately strained its fiscal machinery. The defense of the Empire that generated this wealth and its expansion at the expense of European rivals, along with the significant costs of Spanish involvement in the Counter-Reformation, led directly to the financial insolvency of the Spanish Crown, and it has been argued that this in turn contributed to Spain's decline as a great power.[3] While borrowing is not, *per se*, a harmful act by governments, borrowing beyond the capacity to service the debt is. Such borrowing can, and probably did, crowd out private domestic investment, thus actually handicapping Spain's economic growth, though this is not the only way in which it was harmful. While borrowing to build ships that end up at the bottom of the Atlantic is not conducive to economic growth, it may not be as costly in the long run as the failure to ensure property rights and to establish free trade zones. In any case, the occasional forced refinancing of its loans ruined the Spanish Crown's credit rating, which restricted subsequent borrowing for investment in public goods.

Accompanying the disruption of Spanish capital markets was the Crown's counterproductive domestic agricultural policy. The production of wool was controlled by the sheepherders' guild – the Mesta. Although the Mesta, which also included sheep owners, had been established in 1273, it grew in importance with the consolidation of the crowns of Aragon and Castile and the emergence of a unified Spain at the end of the fifteenth century. Spanish wool, provided by the renowned Merino sheep, was the finest on the Continent, and during the sixteenth century a great deal of it was consumed in the expanding European textile industry, particularly in the Spanish Netherlands. The growing demand for Spanish wool provided part of the revenues which, if invested in domestic industry or the modernization of Spanish agriculture, might have contributed to Spain's membership among the early industrializing countries. This did not happen for a variety of reasons, some political and some economic.

For one thing, there were costs imposed on Spanish economic growth by the specialization in wool production, which resulted in part from the special treatment the Mesta received from the Crown. Because the sheep were herded from the mountains to the lowlands every winter and back in the summer, they could be easily taxed, as could the wool when it was exported. The Crown chose to use such taxes to contribute to the financing of the expansion of its global empire, and in exchange granted common grazing rights to the Mesta. During the next three centuries, as other countries increasingly enclosed agricultural land, thereby granting property rights to private farmers, Spain perpetuated the common property rights of the Mesta, which itself was not disbanded until 1836. Thus Spanish agriculture, and the economy more generally, did not experience the agricultural transformation that occurred elsewhere in western Europe in the sixteenth and seventeenth centuries. There actually was an effective model on which to base their agricultural policy, for the Moors had developed a highly efficient agriculture during the late Middle Ages, marked by state-of-the-art irrigation. By contrast, the system of great estates, landlords (the church being the largest) and tenant farming that sprang up after the expulsion of the Moors after 1492 proved less efficient. With the knowledge gleaned from several centuries of economic history, it seems clear that calculated public policies contributed to Spain's relative decline as an economic power. Even so, there are many other factors to consider, including the notion that the above-mentioned policies were the best that could have been designed for the Spanish conditions of the time.[4] These include a decline in Mediterranean influence, an arid and mountainous country and a slowly growing stock of human capital.

Public policies associated with trade and the rise of the modern nation state were prominent in northern Europe as well. The Catholic–Protestant split in the Holy Roman Empire played an important role in the progress of Germany's political integration, for it was within the Empire that the Reformation dawned, and it was largely the division of Germanic peoples between the Protestant and Catholic Churches that ultimately divided the Empire politically as well. Although there had been earlier rebellions against the Roman Church, in 1517 Luther's nailing of his 95 theses to the door of the church at Wittenberg, which was a church of the Imperial Court, created a schism in the Church that remains to this day. The economic, political and social consequences of that historic incident were so pervasive and monumental that they defy a concise description. In terms of Germany's political integration, however, both the short and long-run implications are quite clear. Wars, both great and insignificant, were waged between Catholic and schismatic German princes and their various European supporters, not always with regard to religion, for the next century and a half. The last of these wars, the Thirty Years War, was the most destructive. The war, which ended in 1648, left the lands that eventually formed the German Reich economically damaged, and the peace that followed left them politically fragmented.

Perhaps the most familiar historical landmark of the economic development among the northern and western German states was the *Hansa*, though it was by no means the most progressive from an economic perspective. North German cities had formed *Hansas* (literally, associations) since the thirteenth century. These associations were typically trading agreements among cities with the objective of obtaining and protecting trading privileges, especially the creation and enforcement of monopolies over the trade in particular goods, such as fish, naval stores and iron. The formal chartering of the most famous *Hansa*, often called the Hanseatic League, occurred in 1367 when 77 German towns banded together to protect the herring monopoly from the encroachment of the King of Denmark. In this conflict they defeated the Danes, an event that actually marked the high-water point of the League.

Because the *Hansa* was essentially a trading cartel it led to an inefficient allocation of resources and created an incentive for individual members to cheat on the others. The resources that went into enforcing and protecting the cartel could have been employed in more economically productive ways. In addition, the League never established a system of credit among its members, despite the obvious incentives to do so.[5] In any case, with the shift in world trade that resulted from the discovery of new territories and the establishment of overseas empires, the dynamic focus of northern European trade shifted to the Atlantic, in particular to the Dutch and English ports, and by the middle of the sixteenth century the League was neither an economic nor a political power on a European scale, although the ports were still important regional trading centers.

More essential to the economic development of the early modern German states, though perhaps less well established in the historical literature than the

Hansa, were the banking establishments in Augsburg and Nuremberg. The Fugger family of Augsburg was the first great banking house to challenge the financial control of the Italians. By the sixteenth century, the Fuggers had made Augsburg the financial center of Europe. Unfortunately, their choice of clients turned out to be poor – the largest of these were the Spanish Habsburgs, whose inability to pay their loans was matched only by their demand for more credit, and who ultimately drove the Fuggers to insolvency. The rise of the Dutch following their independence from Spain in the seventeenth century ended German financial dominance, and the Thirty Years War also contributed to their relative decline. Still, the Rhenish states prospered during the following century, and by the mid-eighteenth century they contained some of the most economically advanced regions on the Continent.

As noted, the *Hansas* were trading cartels that in the course of defending and enforcing their privileges and hegemony had acquired an important character of the nation state – namely, the resort to organized violence to support their position. Thus they occupied an intermediate ground between rulers who specialized in the affairs of state, including the perpetuation of their prerogatives through violence, and the rising middle class that specialized in trade and early industry. Quite naturally, these two forms of geopolitical organization – the state as an extension of the trading cartel and the state as a public-goods-providing monopolist with a comparative advantage in violence – came into conflict, and eventually it was the nation state that emerged as the more successful of the two.

The economic powers of the late Middle Ages – the Italian City States, German trading cities and Flemish textile regions – all depended to a certain extent on advantages offered by a favorable geographic location. The Italians were well situated to finance the East–West trade; the German trading cities could control the trade along a number of important river valleys of central Europe, and the Flemish textile producers profited from access to English wool just across the Channel and from large consumer markets to their immediate north and south. The Scandinavian states of Denmark, Norway and Sweden did not enjoy the same locational advantages. They were not located on good trade routes nor was their climate as conducive to agriculture, which might have provided the exports for trade with the proto-industrial centers to the south. Thus the Scandinavians never managed to be at the top of Europe's economic ladder by either aggregate or per-capita measures during the early modern era, and even by the middle of the nineteenth century they were clearly below the great powers, though the economic situation varied from one Scandinavian state to another.

By the Union of Kalmar (1397) the crowns of all three Scandinavian countries were united under Margaret of Denmark. The union lasted for almost a century and a half, during which time the Crown was relatively weak, being dominated on the one hand by the economic and military power of the *Hansa* and on the other by the domestic political power of the nobility. These two forces led to a permanent rupture in the political integration of Scandinavia in 1523. The joint ruler at that time, Christian II, formed a political alliance with the merchants in the Baltic trading towns. This arrangement caused a rebellion by the nobility and the Church, and in the confusion that followed the top administrator of the kingdom, Gustavus (I) Vasa, defected from the Union and established the independent Kingdom of Sweden. While Denmark was racked by civil war, Gustavus went to war against Lübeck – one of, if not the, most powerful of the *Hansa* cities – and broke the *Hansa's* Baltic monopoly forever. This victory marked the beginning of Sweden's rise and 200-year reign as the most powerful economic and military force in the Baltic.

Like most of the conflicts, both great and small, that we have reviewed in this chapter, Sweden's subsequent involvement in the Thirty Years War reflected a number of issues – economic, political and religious. With respect to religion, Scandinavia had largely converted to Lutheranism in the sixteenth century; so Sweden's ruler, Gustavus Adolphus, helped defend the north German (Protestant) princes against the (Catholic) Imperial forces. Politically, Swedish interests were threatened by the Emperor's granting of the Duchy of Mecklenburg to Albert of Wallenstein, an Imperial commander (and a Catholic). Economically, the Swedish mercantile (middle class) interests were concerned about the possible repercussions for the Baltic trade if the Emperor were to subjugate the north German princes. Having earlier defeated the *Hansa*, they did not relish the thought of a restored German trading association backed by a strong Imperial military force.

These objectives and concerns led Gustavus Adolphus to align with France against the Empire. Although a Catholic power, France, practicing *realpolitik* before the word was coined, aligned with Sweden to further her own position at Imperial expense.[6] Gustavus Adolphus died in battle in 1632, but for his earlier triumphs and the subsequent victories of his generals, the Treaty of Westphalia granted West Pomerania, Bremen–Verden and Wismar to Sweden, thus extending Swedish authority into the Continent. This achievement marked the high-water point of Swedish power.

Sweden's rise as a major political power resulted from the conflict over control of the Baltic trade, but its relative decline as an economic and military power, which began in the eighteenth century during the reign of Charles XII, resulted from visions of imperial grandeur. Russia, Poland, Denmark and, eventually, Prussia all challenged Sweden's territorial gains of the previous century. The various disputes arising from Swedish expansionism culminated in the Great Northern War (1700–21), which proved disastrous for Sweden. In the end Sweden lost almost all of its territory on the southern and eastern

Baltic coasts, leaving it with essentially the territory comprising modern Sweden and Finland. The territorial losses of the eighteenth and nineteenth centuries were a blow to the country's prestige, security and resource base as well as to the Crown's tax base, but more importantly for Sweden's economic development, the wars were a significant waste of national wealth, and the Crown, which had earlier lived off its conquests, ended up paying several large indemnities to the victors.

The histories of these countries illustrate the role of trade in the founding of the modern state. The expansionist vision of the combined crowns of Castile and Aragon led to the creation of an international empire, the economic underpinning of which was the flow of commodities from the periphery to the center. Further north, the battle between the *Hansa* and the Swedish Crown represents the climax of the mercantile city-state as a dominant form of social, political and economic organization. After the sixteenth century, the *Hansa* and other regional bodies were replaced by the nation state, which possessed a broader tax base and offered a potentially larger and more diverse set of public goods, not the least of which was the ability to support trade with other states. This power, as it was linked with the rising merchant classes both politically and economically, resulted in increasingly complex designs to foster growth and, of course, to the search for government-sponsored economic rents. Trade was at the center of these early efforts and modern practices in this respect do not differ in any important way from the techniques in common use by the end of the mercantilist era in, say, 1776.

4.   FINANCE AND THE EARLY MODERN STATE

In the Middle Ages, the city states of Genoa and Venice were the centers of the East–West trade in the Mediterranean and thus were established as the leading economic powers of Europe.[7] One of the keys to this power was credit, and the primary instrument was the bill of exchange – essentially an IOU drawn against commodities, (de Roover, 1953). These bills provided three fundamental services in facilitating the growth of trade. First, because barter was an inherently inefficient means of exchange, traders resorted to the use of various media to facilitate exchange; since time immemorial commodity monies (largely gold and silver) had served as the primary media, because they were judged to have intrinsic value. As the volume of trade grew, however, the quantity of specie required to finance transactions grew to the point at which transferring it was both quite costly and dangerous, and the amount of specie in circulation was not always sufficient to carry on trade without costly adjustments in prices. The bill of exchange represented a claim on specie that could itself be traded in lieu of the precious metals.

Second, as Neal (1991) explains in a more modern context, traders often faced the situation of an imbalance between accounts payable and accounts receivable. When this occurred they could either borrow, if accounts payable lagged behind accounts receivable, by selling a bill, or they could lend, if accounts receivable lagged behind accounts payable, by purchasing a bill. This facility was not available in earlier trading systems. Finally, in order to take advantage of scale economies in shipping, traders had to buy in quantities that often strained their immediate financial capacity. Thus they often required short-term credit until their goods could be sold. Bills of exchange also fulfilled this role. It was in the marketing and clearing of such bills that the Italians specialized, and to broaden the market in these financial instruments they established what we might call 'branches' in major trading centers throughout Europe. These banking syndicates were primarily the creation of a number of great banking families, such as the Bardi, Peruzzi, and Medici of Florence.

By the fifteenth century the territory that became modern Italy consisted of more than a dozen republics, duchies and kingdoms, the most important being the republics of Venice and Florence, the Duchy of Milan, the Papal States and the Kingdom of Naples. During the next hundred years these states produced what is arguably the greatest accumulation of writers, poets, musicians, painters and architects the West had seen since Periclean Athens two millennia earlier. This Renaissance in Western thought and expression coincided with the high-water mark of Italian economic influence. Indeed a good deal of artistic expression was financed by Italian trading magnates who expressed their gratefulness for God's bounty by commissioning works of art in His honor.

Among these states, Venice was the dominant economic power, unchallenged since her eclipse of Genoa in the previous century.[8] Two threats, one from the east and one from the west, eventually led to the decline of Venice. In the east, Portugal and Spain sought to circumvent Italian domination of the trade in Asian luxuries (and the ever increasing belligerence of the Ottoman Turks) by finding either a western or southern sea route to the Orient.[9] Their success weakened not only Venice's but also all of the other Italian states' longstanding advantage in the financing of both the final legs of that trade and the exchange of goods throughout Europe. In the east the Ottoman Turks proceeded into Central Europe after the fall of Constantinople (1453), and their advance through the Balkans brought them into conflict with the Venetians. The resulting series of wars during the subsequent century were expensive and economically unproductive for Venice.

In fact, the relative shift in European trade from the Levant and points further east to the Atlantic ended forever Italian dominance in European economic affairs. To compete in the realm of the early modern great powers required some combination of a large tax base and the political infrastructure to exploit it. In fact, some politically successful states – for example, Spain, France and Austria – had access to large tax bases; others – England and the United Provinces – found success in efficiently exploiting relatively smaller bases. But Venice, a city-state after all, could not muster the revenue if its armies were not successful, and so it slipped away, speaking relatively. In fact, by the end of the eighteenth century Venice was no longer a significant economic influence in either trade or finance. As went Venice, so went the other Italian city-states until, really, the end of the nineteenth century, following unification

Whereas the Italian states underwent relative economic decline and remained politically fragmented until the nineteenth century, the relative economic status of the Dutch owed much to the timing and nature of their political integration, which like so much of subsequent European history resulted as an outgrowth of the Protestant Reformation. During and shortly after the Hundred Years War the 'Low Countries' (roughly the modern states of Belgium and the Netherlands) became allied with the Duchy of Burgundy, primarily through dynastic marriage and a number of territorial cessions. Upon the death of the Burgundian Duke Charles (the Bold) in 1477, the territory was separated from France through the marriage of Charles' daughter, Mary, to the future Habsburg Emperor, Maximilian. By Habsburg family compact, these lands became part of the Kingdom of Spain upon the accession of Maximilian's grandson, Charles I (later, Emperor Charles V), to that throne in 1516. The Dutch openly resented Habsburg rule, especially so after the Reformation. The combination of what the Dutch (and Belgians) considered to be confiscatory taxes, including forced loans (see below) to finance Spanish imperial expansion and the Spanish persecution of Dutch Protestants, led to open revolt in 1568, which was formalized among the northern (Dutch) provinces by the Union of Utrecht in 1579. Drawing on their economic wealth, the Dutch, with help from the English, prosecuted a series of successful campaigns for independence, which they declared as the United Provinces of the Dutch Republic in 1581. Sporadic fighting went on until the Twelve Years Truce ended the conflict in 1609. By then the Dutch had achieved *de facto* independence, and Spain finally recognized full independence of the United Provinces with the Treaty of Westphalia in 1648.

In the same year that the truce between the Netherlands and Spain was declared (1609), the Bank of Amsterdam was founded. The timing and structure of the bank's charter were directly related to the Netherlands' separation from Spain. Prior to the revolt, Antwerp had been the financial center of the region, but in 1557 Philip II, Charles' heir, forcibly lengthened the terms of a number of large loans, the funds for which had been largely raised in Antwerp, and a decade later his governor imposed new direct taxes. During the revolt, and especially after the subsequent success of the northern provinces in securing independence, much economic activity moved north, farther from direct Spanish control, and Amsterdam became the region's financial center.

The Bank of Amsterdam was a central part of the Dutch rise in the financial world. It was founded as a deposit bank at the behest of importers who complained about the costs of determining the value of the plethora of currencies they encountered in the course of their business.[10] By decreeing that all bills of exchange above a certain value be paid at the Bank of Amsterdam with liabilities of the bank, the city gave it a *de facto* monopoly on the payment of bills of exchange in Amsterdam. The bank was, and remained almost exclusively, a deposit bank until the late eighteenth century when it was driven to insolvency by unsuccessful loans to the Dutch East India Company. By all accounts the Bank of Amsterdam was a great success and, together with several other Dutch banks chartered along the same lines, it contributed to the Netherlands' pre-eminent position in seventeenth-century European finance.[11]

Independence from Spain did not, however, necessarily mean national political integration. Although the head of state, or *Statthalter*, was granted to the head of the House of Orange, the Dutch state was subordinate to the individual provinces, and this often resulted in the provision of a lower level of public goods, such as national defense, than was provided by her larger neighbors and rivals, though certainly the Dutch were more successful in defending themselves than their Belgian neighbors. Individually and collectively, the United Provinces had a representative government dominated at the local, provincial and national level by the Regents, a political entity that drew its members almost exclusively from the economic elites. Though limited to an oligarchy that by today's standards looks like little more than a prosperous clique, it was nonetheless a nascent republic surrounded by divine-right monarchies, with the notable exception of England's constitutional monarchs (from 1689).[12] Furthermore, by resorting to an excise tax the Dutch had the most modern tax system in early modern Europe. Early Dutch economic prosperity and growth resulted from the fact that the United Provinces had both a representative system of government and one that was dominated by individuals with commercial, rather than landed interests.

In other respects as well the United Provinces can be viewed as the first modern state. Its economy was based on finance, trade and a proto-industrial textile industry rather than agriculture, even though Dutch agriculture was possibly the most technologically advanced in the world. With the exception of the key Italian city-states and a few German towns, the Dutch had the most sophisticated financial markets in early modern Europe, and as the Atlantic trade outgrew that of the Mediterranean and the Rhine, the Netherlands replaced Italy and Germany as the financial center of Europe. As noted, the

Bank of Amsterdam contributed to this shift, and the creations of the earlier commercial revolution, which included such innovations as banking, discounting bills of exchange, insurance and double-entry bookkeeping, flourished in the Netherlands. The agricultural revolution also played a significant role in modernizing the Dutch economy. Land drainage, crop rotation, introduction of root crops and fertilizers were all part of Dutch agricultural practice before they were widely adopted elsewhere, and the resulting rise in agricultural productivity contributed to the development of other sectors of the economy, just as it did in England.

Their position atop Europe's seventeenth-century economic ladder, geographical situation and mercantilistic theories of national wealth led the Dutch to pursue an overseas empire. The objective was to procure lands that could produce staples that would either be marketed directly or processed into finished products. There were two problems, however. The net gains from such activity were exaggerated by the mercantilist-thinking governments of the time and the other great powers sought the same lands, products and markets. This latter problem brought the Dutch into conflict with the British in a series of seventeenth and eighteenth-century wars. In these wars, the Dutch enjoyed a number of military successes, but in the end they emerged as the permanently weaker of the two powers. Their relatively subordinate status resulted partly from their failure to dominate the British militarily, partly because of their relatively small resource base and partly because of Great Britain's manufacturing and commercial success before the industrial revolution. The loss of parts of their empire and an end to the expansion of that empire cost the Dutch much in direct profits, but more important perhaps was the shift of Europe's financial axis to London. The British also had a more diversified natural resource base, including excellent coal deposits, iron ore, lead, tin and copper, and they had considerably more land for agricultural expansion and livestock production.

Despite these differences, the Dutch political and economic systems provided an average standard of living that was surpassed only by the British during the seventeenth and eighteenth centuries. Furthermore, the Dutch Republic still prospered relative to its better-endowed Continental neighbors because of its liberal institutions and its strong commercial structure. Even after the industrial revolution spread to the Continent and the size of the Dutch manufacturing sector waned relative to its larger neighbors, the Dutch maintained their per capita standing, though by aggregate measures the Dutch could no longer be said to be among the dominant economic powers.

As we noted above, London eventually became Europe's financial center, and the expression that sterling was 'as good as gold' derives from the security of the value of claims against the British financial sector. It is no accident that central banking in England, in the form of sterling's defender –

the Bank of England – emerged during the turmoil of the seventeenth century. The creation of the Bank resulted from a fundamental principle of public finance: because there are often short-run increases in the demand by governments for resources imposed by unforeseeable circumstances such as war, and because increased taxes are politically dangerous and, to be sure, create hardships for the taxpayers, governments have always sought ways to smooth the supply of tax revenues over time in the face of their fluctuating demand for those revenues. The obvious solution is to borrow the money and pay it back with future revenues. After Parliament had disposed of the Stuarts, who on occasion repudiated large debts and who frequently resorted to arbitrary and unpopular taxing schemes, it discovered that its credit was no better than that of the Stuart's. In a war with France over the restoration of James II, Parliament's resources were actually limited to the personal wealth of its members and its ability to directly wrest tax revenues from the populace. In order to restore the government's credibility and to facilitate these transactions, Parliament created the Bank of England (1694) – a private bank with public interests. Thereafter, it was to this anchor that the British financial market, which became the world's greatest, was fastened.

Despite its mid-nineteenth century pre-eminence, the United Kingdom's role as the dominant economic power in Europe simply could not have been predicted with any certainty a century or more earlier. Portugal, Spain, the United Provinces and France had developed prosperous trading empires before the English, but each had come into conflict with England and been defeated militarily and eclipsed economically. Since Tudor times, the primary objective of English foreign policy had been, and would continue to be, the prevention of Continental hegemony by a single power. As England grew into Great Britain and later the United Kingdom, it successfully utilized its economic might in trade, finance and manufacturing to support its geopolitical objectives. The Empire, in turn, paid handsomely in some cases and it is this interaction – between economics and politics, really – that helped launch the United Kingdom into the Industrial Revolution. At the center of all this was world trade, which came to be dominated by the United Kingdom.

5.   CONCLUSIONS

Our summary of the political integration of western European countries has paid somewhat less attention to the influence of political on economic events than is common in the literature. Partly this reflects the recent literature, which has downgraded the long-run economic effects of Spanish silver, European imperialism, the French Revolution and, above all else, mercantilism on economic outcomes. We will be developing these themes in succeeding chapters, but for now we want to summarize those political aspects that do appear to have had a strong influence on the pre-industrial economies of early modern Europe.

By far the most important of these aspects is the political unification in European countries that was achieved by 1500. While several countries had uncompleted political agendas in the nineteenth century, Sweden, Spain, France, Austria, England and Portugal were essentially integrated in 1500, and several other countries were close behind. This unified structure stabilized the protection of property rights and provided an effective tax base for the construction of social overhead capital and for the production of public goods. It also provided an incentive to manage the development of the financial system – partly for purposes of obtaining access to credit markets – and, this too enhanced the development of the economy. What we feel we have to explain in the remainder of this study is how these countries grew – and grew together – and the aforementioned topics strike us as helping to explain this remarkable outcome. While many historians choose to emphasize the political machinations of the leaders of these countries and the obvious waste of resources that accompanied their efforts to expand their hegemony, we think this is less important than the economic issues that we have outlined above. The outcome was for broad economic growth over this period that brought each of these countries, in its own way, into a thriving pan-European economy by the early nineteenth century, *at the latest*.

NOTES

1. The territorial disputes between England and France were aggravated by the fact that Edward's mother, Isabella, was the daughter of the former French king, Philip IV. Isabella's brother, Charles IV, the last direct descendent of the Capetian line, ascended the throne, rather than Edward, under what became known as the Salic Law, when on Charles' death an assembly of barons declared 'no woman or her son could succeed to the monarchy'. This maneuver resulted in the accession of Philip VI and the establishment of the Valois dynasty.
2. The literature contains numerous comparative studies of early modern England and France. Our interpretation is the same as North's (1981). For a recent summary see Landes (1994).
3. Kennedy (1987) uses Spain's relative economic decline as a template for the shifting economic and political fortunes of subsequent European powers. While we generally agree with his conclusions regarding Spain, as our explanations elsewhere in this chapter reveal, we feel that each country had its own macroeconomic circumstances that contributed to its path of economic development.
4. We have presented the traditional interpretation of the Mesta's effect on Spanish economic development; see, for example, Klein (1920), and for a summary North (1981). For a different view of the Mesta, see Nugent and Sanchez (1989).
5. Kindleberger (1993, p. 46) cites the absence of credit markets among the members of the *Hansa* as an example of market failure. The suppression of banking by excluding non-League citizens from residence may well have been a means of enforcing the cartel. This policy was especially damaging because it denied German merchants access to the Italian bankers, who were at the time the acknowledged leaders of European finance.

6. Denmark, as it turned out, fought against the Empire before Sweden but accepted a truce before Gustavus Adolphus entered the conflict; the Danes later turned against Sweden only to be defeated.
7. For a discussion of the political dimensions of the financial connections between the Italian city-states and the East–West trade, see Norwich (1996).
8. For a history of the rise of these states, see Luzatto (1963).
9. The Ottoman advance into Europe in the fourteenth century was a combination of their alliance with the Byzantine Emperor, John Cantacuzene, who enlisted their aid against competing claimants, and the abatement of the Mongol threat to the Turks' eastern flank.
10. According to Kindleberger, prior to the creation of the Bank of Amsterdam, there were 14 mints in the United Provinces alone (1993, p. 50).
11. Perhaps the best English-language study of the role of the Bank of Amsterdam in seventeenth-century European finance is that of Barbour (1963).
12. It is noteworthy that England's first constitutional monarch, William I, was the Prince of Orange and thus *Statthalter* of the United Provinces.

PART II

The Growth of the European Market Economy
1500–1750

3. Population growth and agricultural change before the industrial revolution

1. INTRODUCTION

In Chapter 1 we noted that population growth is inextricably linked with the overall rate of economic growth and therefore any review of the pre-industrial European economy would naturally include an analysis of population growth. The population growth rate for Europe as a whole accelerated after 1450, decelerated in the seventeenth century, but was still positive in every country between 1500 and 1750. In our discussion of population in Section 2, we consider some of the causes of these trends, although this is not our emphasis; rather, most of our attention is directed toward the possible consequences of population growth. In this respect, our focus is on macroeconomic topics and, so we are mainly interested in the role of population growth in aiding or thwarting overall economic growth. The reader will appreciate that a good deal of this discussion concerns matters that are controversial. In view of the state of the data, matters will surely remain that way, although we certainly hope to help clarify and illustrate the issues.

Population growth was closely related to the behavior of agricultural output in this period, and so in Section 3 we describe the general progress of European agriculture up to 1750. One obvious reason for the association of population growth with agricultural growth is the practice in the literature of estimating agricultural growth rates from population growth rates. We believe this practice has outlived its usefulness and we take some pains to explain why we think so. More important for this chapter, however, is the fact that during this period agriculture is the dominant sector of the economy by standard indicators, such as the value of output or the share of the labor force; thus obtaining a better understanding of both agricultural output and agricultural productivity is important if one is to understand overall growth.

The concluding section of this chapter contains a first pass at the controversial topic of the 'standard of living' in early modern Europe. We are only interested in the macroeconomic aspects of this topic, and there are not enough data for a large (empirical) literature to have developed on the pre-industrial economy. Even so, we will look at some data on real wages that yield a pessimistic view of the period and also consider the detailed historical record for individual countries looking for clues as to how the various segments of the population fared. While we undertake no original empirical work on the question, we will, at various points in the chapter, foreshadow some work in Chapter 6, where we argue that the body of empirical evidence suggests that per capita agricultural output (as well as aggregate per capita output) rose in this period for most countries.

Before we turn to the discussion of population, agriculture and the standard of living, the reader should note that these subjects, and the large number of specific issues that must be addressed under each of them, are closely related. Population change is a function of human fertility and mortality, which in turn are dependent on a population's material well-being and health – that is, on its standard of living. The standard of living, in turn, is a function of economic output and its distribution, which in this era was largely determined in the agricultural sector. So, we are not talking about separate subjects but rather a single subject viewed from different vantage points.

2.   POPULATION GROWTH IN EARLY MODERN EUROPE

We begin with a set of data that shows just how general the population growth was in this period. Table 3.1 illustrates population data up to 1760 and provides average annual compounded growth rates. Broadly speaking, the table shows positive population growth for all countries for all periods, with only Belgium in the sixteenth century and Spain in the seventeenth showing slightly declining populations and Germany and Italy in the seventeenth century showing zero growth. A second broad generalization is that population grew more slowly in the seventeenth century than in the sixteenth, probably because of the adverse effects of the Thirty Years War and the epidemic diseases of the time, especially in the 1660s, 1670s and 1680s. Finally, for all but the United Kingdom and the Netherlands, population growth accelerated in the first 60 years of the eighteenth century.[1]

We have already conjectured that population growth rates could establish a floor for the rate of growth of real output for these countries.[2] Following that logic, we can claim that economic growth was widespread in Western Europe in this period, even in the seventeenth century, which is often considered to have been a period of economic stagnation.[3] We have little basis on which to establish an overall growth rate of real output, of course, but given other evidence (as, for example, the extensive narrative and empirical evidence for England in the sixteenth century), there must have been periods when overall growth rates of the economy exceeded a half of one per cent per year. Indeed, by the end of the period in 1750, some countries probably experienced annual growth rates of real output between one-half and one per cent.[4] We emphasize

Table 3.1   Population in Europe 1500–1760

	Population ('000s)				Annual Growth Rate (Century) %		
	1500	1600	1700	1760	16th	17th	1700–1760
Austria	1,420	1,800	2,100	2,778	0.24	0.15	0.47
Belgium	1,500	1,400	2,000	2,530	–0.07	0.36	0.39
Denmark	600	650	700	820	0.08	0.07	0.26
Finland	150	200	250	490	0.29	0.22	1.12
France	16,400	18,200	21,120	25,246	0.10	0.15	0.30
Germany	12,000	15,000	15,000	18,310	0.22	0.00	0.33
Italy	10,500	13,300	13,300	16,900	0.24	0.00	0.40
Netherlands	950	1,500	1,900	1,960	0.46	0.24	0.05
Norway	300	400	500	687	0.29	0.22	0.53
Portugal	1,200	1,796	2,000	2,457*	0.40	0.11	0.41
Spain	7,500	8,685	8,621	9,580*	0.15	–0.01	0.21
Sweden	550	760	1,260	1,916	0.32	0.50	0.70
Switzerland	800	1,000	1,200	1,480	0.22	0.18	0.35
U.K.	4,400	6,800	9,273	11,069	0.44	0.31	0.30
Total	58,270	71,491	79,224	96,223	0.20	0.10	0.32

Note: * 1750. Figures are for subsequent national boundaries.

Sources: All but Portugal and Spain are from Maddison (1982); Portugal and Spain are derived from Bairoch, Batou and Chevre (1988).

this conclusion because there are some who disparage pre-industrial economic growth. This evidence suggests that most of (Western) Europe experienced real economic growth throughout much of the 1500–1750 period.

The rate of population growth is arithmetically equal to the birth rate less the death rate plus the rate of net migration; thus, ignoring migration for the time being, rising fertility rates and falling death rates provide us with our broad causal categories and both occurred at times in this period. We note that the prevailing view (see Flinn, 1981) is that fertility rates were subject to much less fluctuation than death rates prior to modern times; however, fertility rates were certainly capable of great fluctuations, especially under the influence of fluctuations in mortality. Death rates are, of course, affected by economic factors – and by medical and other health factors, which themselves are related to economic factors – and so economic growth, which undoubtedly accelerated around 1700, probably produced a downward trend in the average death rate, although this is not easy to document.[5] The level and distribution of income and wealth play important roles in understanding the behavior of death rates, because privation can lead to death directly as well as through increased susceptibility to disease.[6]

Fertility, too, has its economic side, for children are, after all, partly consumption and partly investment goods. As investment goods, given the high rate of infant mortality of the time, much of the emphasis would have been on rapid production, but as consumption goods, it is not obvious that the quantity of children is not (to some) an inferior good, the demand for which is adversely affected as per capita incomes rise.[7] It is not out of the question to suggest that both of these phenomena had roles to play throughout this period.

The English data provide us with a closer look at the population experience of a prospering European economy; these data are drawn from Wrigley and Schofield (1981).[8] In Figure 3.1 we show the population figures themselves along with the 'proximate' determinants: the crude birth rate and the crude death rate. The population is measured in millions (on the right hand axis) and the two rates in number per thousand (on the left hand axis). The population series shows a general increase, with a marked period of expansion from 1541 to around 1600. Indeed, from 1541 to 1601, there were 23 years when English population grew faster than 1 per cent per year.[9] In contrast, there was a decline running from 1658 to 1686, an era which included wars with Spain and the Netherlands and concluded on the eve of the Glorious Revolution. This decline was so severe that it took 30 years, from 1686 until 1717, for the population to reach its 1658 level. After a brief relapse beginning in 1729, population growth started to accelerate and continued to do so to 1750 (and beyond, for that matter). Over the entire period (approximately 200 years) population roughly doubled, yielding an average annual compounded rate of growth of approximately 0.33 per cent.

Figure 3.1 shows periodic spikes associated with outbreaks of plague, which represents the primary disease agent in the dramatic demographic events of the early modern era, especially until the late seventeenth century (see Flinn, 1981). From the early eighteenth century, however, the plague appeared only sporadically in Europe; the last major outbreaks occurred in northern Europe in 1710–11 and in a few Mediterranean ports thereafter – Marseilles (1720), Palermo (1743) and Cadiz (1800). Interestingly, there was still no correct theory of the plague when it died out. Explanations of why the plague disappeared in Europe (it remained in the Ottoman Empire until the late nineteenth century) often emphasize the role of governments, including clearing away the dead, enforcing isolation, and removing some of the penalties of being isolated, such as the obtaining of food. In addition, economic

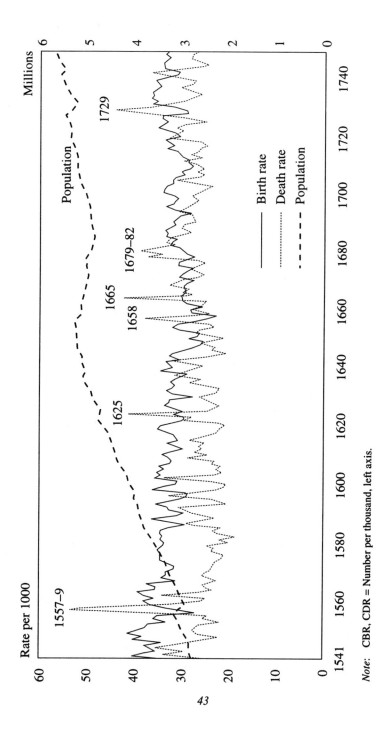

Note: CBR, CDR = Number per thousand, left axis.

Figure 3.1 English population statistics 1541–1750

43

growth itself may have contributed to the development of better sanitation, better diets (see below) and increased poor relief. Finally, there are biological and ecological explanations of the disappearance of the plague, including the accumulation of protective antibodies by the human and/or rat populations and change in the bacillus itself. But having noted all of these possibilities, it is still not obvious why the plague died out.[10]

With the decline of the incidence of plague, other diseases increased in prominence; these included louse-borne typhus, typhoid fever and dysentery. Also, the diseases of measles and smallpox, which had been around for centuries, were leading killers of early modern populations. As with plague, these diseases became less prominent over time for several reasons. First, famine associated with agricultural crises, which themselves were generally weather-related, became less significant as agricultural productivity increased and the distribution of agricultural staples improved as transportation and communication improved (see below). Secondly, rising incomes led to better (and more certain) diets, better personal and public sanitation and better housing; all of this worked to insulate human populations from the various early modern diseases. Finally, the tendency of the endemic diseases, such as smallpox and measles, to become childhood diseases through the biology of the virus (Kunitz, 1983) or the propensity of human populations to become resistant to such diseases (McNeill, 1976) relieved the pressure they put on mortality rates.

In general terms, then, population showed an upward trend in this period, with a leveling in the late seventeenth century. In England, for example, the crude birthrate series displays a downward trend to around 1660 and an upward trend thereafter. Since the birthrate may be influenced by agricultural production, the reversal of trend in 1660 suggests that this might be the beginning of the agricultural revolution in England, though this point is much contested in the literature.[11] For the crude death rate series, there appears to be a slight downward trend until around 1580, an upward drift for the next century and then a resumption of the downward drift until the end of the period. Overall, 1541 to 1750, there is no noticeable trend, however, in the English data.

With regard to the influence of population growth on economic activity, the natural thing for an economist to do is to look at the effects of population growth on the demand and supply sides of the economy. With regard to the demand side, the most obvious influence is that there are more mouths to feed. In addition, 'broader' markets may arise as a result of population growth and this provides for economic opportunities across many sectors, provided that the supply side responds appropriately.[12] Indeed, the economic opportunities might arise in the form of economies of scale, which may explain, at least partly, why we see the development of larger-scale farming, shipping networks and so forth throughout the period (with more than a hint of acceleration at the end). There may also be scale economies in the provision of certain public goods (Boserup, 1965), like a navy to protect imperial trading outposts and sea lanes. In addition, population growth increases the demand for governmental services, not only for aid in distribution, public sanitation and the like, but also because governments of countries with growing populations have, potentially, growing armies and navies. With respect to the service sector, the growth of cities in this period, stimulated largely by the growth of commerce and early industry, put pressure on governments to provide more infrastructure – for example docks and roads – and to deal with the growing problems of poverty, disease, sanitation and public order. Finally, the demands of a growing population can force change in a society's social and political institutions. We are, after all, dealing with the period that began with the Reformation and culminated with the industrial and agricultural revolutions as well as an expansion in representative government.

With regard to the supply side, the most obvious effect of population growth is on the supply of human capital. In the absence of changes in labor force participation rates, the labor force will grow at the rate of growth of the population, and this is the most obvious influence of a growing population on the supply side. Population growth also affects the other factors of production. If the economy is growing along an equilibrium path, then the profit rate will tend not to change as population grows – as a result of competition among the owners of capital – but behind this result is an equivalent rise of the quantity of capital and output. By putting the matter this way, we remind the reader that our discussion logically implies that the quantity of capital was essentially endogenous in this period, and was driven by the real growth rate, itself the result of population growth and technological change.

Population growth, of course, can be excessive, at least in the sense that it can be detrimental to economic growth, especially in the short run. In particular, it is likely that an economy that has long had a slow population growth rate would have some difficulties with a rate of growth that is significantly accelerated, especially in the short run, partly because the transition to a higher rate would typically feature larger groups of those elements of the population least likely to contribute to economic output – children and the aged.[13] Even rapid population growth has its positive 'supply-side' benefits, however, for, in the long run, it could stimulate the introduction of labor-using (and land- and capital-saving) technology that could be superior to the technology in use at the onset of the rapid growth.[14] Of course a growing population could also exert downward pressure on growth by, in effect, eating its capital – that is, if at low income levels consumption is a sufficiently large share of expenditure as to produce an inadequate amount of savings and investment, then future growth will be less than it could have been with lower rates of population growth. This situation has certainly occurred from time to time throughout history and is observed in our own time in developing economies. We want to emphasize here, however, that it is our view that over the course of the early modern era the long-run rates of growth of European population and real economic output became positive and remained that way. Given the history of economic change during this era, and much of what we document in the remainder of this as well as subsequent chapters, it is difficult for us to conclude that early modern population growth served as a brake on economic growth.

3.   AGRICULTURE

Although the agricultural sector of each country is of gradually diminishing relative importance during the early modern era, there was a burgeoning international trade in raw, semi-finished and processed agricultural products (see Chapter 4 below); furthermore, there was, by comparison with earlier times, a tremendous growth in agricultural output in this period. Here we address the contribution of agricultural progress to overall economic growth. This question is complicated by the lack of accurate (or in many cases any) figures on agricultural output and productivity before the nineteenth century. Before turning to those data that are available, we consider the salient features of the qualitative changes in early modern European agriculture – features that often have been referred to as 'revolutionary'.[15] In England, for example, which was one of the more advanced agricultural countries in Europe,[16] per capita agricultural output grew by roughly 0.32 per cent per annum between 1660 and 1740 (Jackson, 1985, p. 346).[17] Such a figure must have represented a substantial discontinuity in the history of European agriculture.

Broadly speaking, output can grow because more inputs – that is, land, labor and capital – are employed or because the inputs are employed more productively (or some combination of the two). Thus agricultural output could have increased through any combination of the employment of more farm workers, perhaps working longer hours, more farm land, more implements or through technological change that increased the productivity of these agricultural inputs. The available information suggests that all of these forces were at work in early modern European agriculture.

The effort to expand acreage and production during the fifteenth and sixteenth centuries was prompted by favorable trends in the demand for agricultural products, which was reflected in the upward movement in farm prices relative to all other prices as well as to the growth in population described above.[18] Among the things that farmers could and did do was to develop marginal farmland. The land development of the sixteenth and seventeenth centuries was particularly concerned with drainage and irrigation. There was nothing new in this, but the scale of operation was now much larger than before. Sullivan's (1985) work on English agricultural patents shows that before 1780 the largest number of patents was associated with surface drainage and the irrigation of land. The drainage of marshes and land formerly under sea water were highly capital-intensive enterprises and were found on the Continent as well as in Zealand, Holland, Friesland, and in the English Fens. In addition, the development of the rice culture in the Po Valley of Northern Italy proceeded at the same time.

The (non-land) capital stock also expanded during the early modern era. This expansion largely consisted of the growth of the stock of draught animals and mechanical implements. It is worth noting here the subtle differences between an invention, a technological innovation and an increase in the capital stock. For example, the seed drill was invented in this period. After it became known, farmers adopted it (an innovation in farming); this necessarily involved them in a capital expenditure. In the following discussion we are mostly talking about the adoption of existing (or marginally improved) technology on existing farms.

In the seventeenth and eighteenth centuries a number of farm implements were invented. Most of these were used in grain cultivation and were thus most profitably employed on open flat terrain where plots were not separated from one another and where the ground was relatively free from stones. In Western Europe, the small size of many farms, the diversity of the soil, the terrain and the type of crops grown inhibited the use of these innovations. While in England most of the patented inventions or innovations took place in the processing stage of grain production (Sullivan, 1985), several were in the soil preparation and planting stages as well. Among the innovations in processing were threshing blocks (conical blocks revolving around an axle), versions of which were found in sixteenth-century Italy and in eighteenth-century Denmark, Sweden, Northern Netherlands, southwest France and Austria. In Holland the winnowing mill was introduced (from China) and greatly improved separation of the grain from the chaff. Among the innovations in soil preparation and planting were improved plows and the seed drill for example. In addition, the cultivator or horse-drawn hoe was developed during this era.

One innovation that increased the value of the capital stock was the growing use of the horse. Horses could be driven at a substantially faster pace than oxen but at a higher capital outlay. Apparently the financial capital was available and the pay-off sufficient to justify this major investment. Although horses were in wide use centuries earlier, the shoulder collar having been perfected by AD900 (Mokyr, 1990, p. 38), prior to the early modern era,

horses were largely used in hauling and there seems to have been an acceleration in their employment in agriculture during this period. Although we have
little in the way of reliable information concerning the growth of inputs for
the continental economies, data for Great Britain suggest that during the
eighteenth century land and capital inputs combined probably increased by
roughly 30 per cent or about 0.25 per cent per year (Allen, 1994, Table 5.4).
So, together with the other developments discussed below, these technological advances were disseminated and gradually adopted, particularly on large
farms, and they contributed to an increase in agricultural output over the
period.

   Although the long-run trend of agriculture's share of the labor force was
downward across much of Europe, the actual number of workers in the
agricultural sector often either grew or remained relatively constant over
fairly long periods until relatively late in the nineteenth century. Indeed,
figures reported in Allen (1994, Table 5.3) indicate that between 1700 and
1851 the British agricultural labor force grew by 0.10 per cent per annum,
though the pace of growth was uneven. For example, there was a slight
decline in the British labor input in the eighteenth century – about 0.05 per
cent per year – but the number of English and Welsh farm workers began to
grow again after 1800. Furthermore, figures reported by de Vries (1984,
pp. 170–72) show that the agricultural labor force of the Netherlands – arguably Europe's most agriculturally advanced nation – may have been growing
at between 0.25 and 0.50 per cent per year between the mid-seventeenth and
mid-eighteenth centuries. Note that such evidence contrasts with the traditional view that agricultural modernization 'freed' farm labor for industrial
employment.[19] The *slow* decline and in some cases actual increase in the
agricultural labor force during the early modern era resulted from the fact
that much of the agricultural revolution was labor-intensive, a subject about
which we say more below.

   While increases in inputs suggest one source of the growth of early modern
agricultural output, changes in output that cannot be explained by changes in
the quantity of inputs are typically attributed to changes in total factor productivity (TFP), which accordingly, embodies technological change and a number
of other important economic factors, such as improvements in human capital
or the quality of land or capital not captured in the measures of quantities of
these inputs. For example, a person-hour will likely yield more output if it
represents an educated worker or an acre of land will be more productive if it
has had nitrogen restored to it.[20] Estimates of the average annual compounded
growth of TFP for Great Britain during the eighteenth century fall within the
range of 0.1 to 0.6 per cent (Allen, 1994, Table 5.5). Although these figures
may seem low by subsequent experience,[21] they are definitely high compared
to those prevailing for western agriculture before 1500.

In addition to TFP growth, it was possible to expand production by changing the organizational structure of the agricultural sector. At the head of the list was the enclosure of open fields with its potential for taking advantage of economies of scale and the elimination of the adverse economic incentives associated with the commons.[22] The system of enclosures first appeared in England in the Middle Ages where small peasant holdings and common fields were absorbed and consolidated by large landholders and were enclosed with fences or hedges. In subsequent centuries this process and formal Acts of Parliament led to the enclosure of most English farm land. According to Wordie (1983), during the sixteenth and seventeenth centuries, the share of English farmland enclosed rose from roughly 45 per cent to over 70 per cent. England was a leader in this activity, but the practice was widespread across Europe, especially after the 1550s. During the eighteenth century large landowners in Burgundy surrounded their estates with railings. In Germany the *Bauernlegn* were enclosures by which large landowners combined several farmsteads and removed the farmhouses from them. So, although much of the discussion in the literature focuses on the English experience, enclosure took place across western and central Europe, for similar reasons.

Enclosure had at least four effects on agricultural productivity. First, the elimination of open field farming in small strips also eliminated communal management of crop choice and rotations.[23] On an enclosed farm the individual farmer was free to choose his crop portfolio and rotation; this clearly could (and did) produce more efficient combinations, and ambitious farmers were more likely to achieve better combinations. Second, an owner-operator of an enclosed farm was the sole claimant to any net returns from improvements to the farm and this provided a clearer incentive to make capital improvements both on and off the land itself (irrigation ditches, canals, roads). Third, the elimination of the commons and common grazing rights provided individual farmers with an opportunity to improve their livestock holdings through selective breeding; under the commons, such procedures would have been constrained to some extent by the need to achieve community consensus. Finally, enclosure provided the opportunity for the further consolidation of arable land through outright purchase or the elimination of long-term leases that existed under the open-field system; thus enclosure contributed to the creation of larger estates, which in turn offered the aforementioned economics of scale in production.[24]

Each of the effects just mentioned contributed to gains in agricultural output, though the size of the combined effect remains a relatively controversial subject among historians. The figures and sources cited by Wordie (1983, pp. 503–5) suggest that the contribution to output from enclosure was substantial, perhaps as high as 24 per cent in the seventeenth century, and such a figure is consistent with yield comparisons from the late eighteenth century reported by Turner (1986); however more recent summaries, such as those offered by Allen (1994) and Clark (1993), suggest that the net contribution to output growth was much lower than that, perhaps as low as 3 per cent after 1700 (Allen, 1994, p. 118).[25] Indeed, by increasing the private return to farming, the most important aggregate effect of this activity may have been to provide an incentive to bring more land into production.[26]

Related to enclosure were the changes in crop rotation; specifically, farmers increasingly relied on legumes (such as clover, sainfoin and lucerne), root crops (including the turnip and swedes) and improved grasses (such as ryegrass) to supplement the classic cereal crops – wheat, barley, rye and oats. The leguminous plants provided fodder for livestock and fixed nitrogen in the soil. The root crops served as fodder as well, but they also tended to break up heavy soils and required a good deal of hoeing and manuring, which in turn disrupted the weed cycle and provided fertilizer, respectively. Together these crops allowed the farmer to keep more livestock and to stall-feed stock, which in turn yielded more manure to be used as fertilizer resulting in higher crop yields. During the sixteenth century and through to the eighteenth these new crops were adopted across northern Europe (but especially in Flanders, Brabant, Zealand, Holland, Friesland, the Rhineland, Nassau, the Palatinate and Baden). The introduction of these crops allowed the farmer to eliminate the fallow cycle of the three-field system (a typical rotation would have been winter wheat or rye, spring barley and fallow), which was fairly common across northern Europe by the late Middle Ages. During the early modern era, this system was replaced by more complicated patterns that eliminated fallow. Perhaps the best known of these so-called 'convertible' rotations, the Norfolk system, included four crops with no fallow: wheat, turnips, barley and clover and/or ryegrass. Although known earlier, this and similar rotations came to be much more generally employed in this period.

These types of improvement typically increased yields, that is, output per unit of land. Although a substantial quantity of yield data exists, it is difficult to draw general conclusions because such data come from specific plots of land in particular years. Still, efforts have been made to determine long-run trends in yields more generally. For example, Gregory Clark estimates that in the two centuries between 1400–49 and 1561–1649 English wheat yields grew very little – from 13.0 to 13.6 bushels per acre or (using the midpoints of the ranges) 0.03 per cent per year; however, between 1561–1649 and 1650–1733 average yields increased to 18.9 bushels per acre or 3.8 per cent per year (Clark, 1991, p. 456).[27] This growth subsided substantially in the first two-thirds of the eighteenth century – probably to something like 0.30 to 0.50 per cent per annum (Clark, 1991, p. 456; Turner, 1982, p. 504; Overton, 1984, p. 246)[28] – but both the levels and the growth rates were still high by pre-1600 standards.

In addition to the changes in crop production, there were dramatic changes in the quantity, quality and diversity of livestock produced by early modern European farmers. The commons created disincentives for improving the care, feeding and breeding of livestock; enclosure eliminated these disincentives and the result was a dramatic increase in the production of meat and dairy products. The introduction of fodder crops into the rotation and the increased attention to selective breeding led to greater fleece production as well as to higher milk yields and slaughter weights. Using two different techniques for calculating agricultural output, Allen (1994, Table 5.1) shows that meat and dairy production grew around one per cent per year during the eighteenth century, which was roughly 50 per cent faster than the growth of grain production, which itself grew rapidly by historical comparison.

If one assumes that the labor force grew at roughly the rate of population growth and that there was little or no change in output per worker, then population growth would correspond with the growth of agricultural output. This approach, employed by Jones (1981) for England, suggests that population growth rate numbers can serve directly as an index to agricultural output, in effect; thus, for the 1500 to 1800 period, Jones arrives at the growth rates shown in Table 3.2.[29]

These figures suggest an acceleration of growth after 1700 and thus offer a starting point for any subsequent analysis of agricultural performance during this era. By tying agricultural growth to population growth, however, the standard of living – proxied here by output per capita – is assumed constant, as is the effect of technical change and innovation on agricultural productivity. These factors, accordingly, did no more than permit agricultural output to keep up with population, again, *by assumption*.

Interestingly, the pre-1700 growth rates for total output are roughly equivalent to those reported by Clark (1993) for output *per worker* for the entire period 1300–1850! If both Jones' and Clarks' figures are accurate, then mathematically, it must be that labor force growth was exactly zero. Yet labor

Table 3.2   Estimates of early growth rates in England

Period	Growth of Total Output %	Average Annual Compounded Rate of Growth %
1500–1600	25–37	0.27
1600–1700	25–36	0.27
1700–1800	61	0.48
1500–1800	176	0.34

Note: Where a range is offered, we have used the midpoint to calculate rates of growth.

force figures reported by Allen (1994) indicate that the agricultural labor force was growing by roughly 0.10 per cent per year after 1700; these different observations cannot be reconciled, of course. Furthermore, as we noted above, many of the changes associated with the agricultural revolution were actually labor-intensive and brought forth an increase in the number of agricultural workers. Therefore, to try to reconcile these differences, we need to explore the sources and timing of pre-industrial agricultural growth in more detail.

Recent estimates of output per agricultural worker for a number of countries for the nineteenth century allow us to estimate productivity levels around 1800 and in some cases growth rates for the eighteenth century. Table 3.3 contains these estimates. The two sets of figures for Great Britain and France illustrate the fundamental difference between two competing views of agricultural change during the eighteenth century, at least in Western Europe. The estimates labeled Method A were generated by projecting Clark's (1993, Table 4.1) figure for Great Britain backwards using rates of growth of output and agricultural workers derived from Allen (1994, Tables 5.3 and 5.5). We obtained the French estimates from Allen's (1994, p. 96) claim that British agricultural workers were 15 per cent more productive than French workers in 1700 and 33 per cent more productive in 1800. By this method, agricultural productivity growth in eighteenth-century Britain does seem somewhat

Table 3.3   Agricultural output per worker 1700–1850

	Bushels of Wheat Equivalents per Worker		Average Annual Compounded Rate of Growth %
	c. 1700	*c.* 1800	
Method A			
Great Britain	83	194	0.85
France	55	146	0.71
Method B			
Great Britain	207	240	0.15
France	180	180	0.00
Other Estimates			
Austria–Hungary	50	63	0.24
Germany	50	76	0.43
Netherlands	104	115	0.10
Sweden	50	70	0.22

revolutionary, particularly when compared to the population-based figures for earlier periods reported above.

The estimates derived via Method B tell a different story, however. Here, again, we used Clark's nineteenth-century productivity measure, but we projected those figures backward using the productivity growth rates between 1770–80 and 1850 reported in Clark (1993, Table 4.4), which he derives using the relative prices of inputs and outputs. These estimates indicate that productivity growth in British agriculture between 1700 and 1770–80 was essentially zero; thus, the vast majority of the growth in British agricultural productivity between 1300 and 1850 occurred *before* not after 1700! Clark's conclusion would place grain output per British agricultural worker at 240 bushels in 1700. This estimate would be roughly three times that derived using Method A, and would place British agricultural productivity at almost twice what it was in the Netherlands in 1700 (see below). Since the Netherlands was by all accounts an advanced agricultural country (if not the *most* advanced country), this position is difficult to defend. We have taken the liberty of modifying it somewhat by using Allen's claim, which was noted above, concerning the relative productivity of British and French agricultural workers to derive the Method B estimates for 1700.

This approach – that is, Method B – yields a much lower and certainly not revolutionary growth rate for British agriculture (0. 15 per cent per annum) and no growth for French agricultural productivity, but the level estimates still seem quite high given our estimates for the other European countries. For example, it still leaves the average British farm worker twice as productive as one in the Netherlands in both 1700 and 1800, a scenario that is inconsistent with contemporary accounts of the economic and agricultural development of the two countries. On net, it is probably not unreasonable to consider the growth rates resulting from the two approaches as upper and lower bounds on the growth in productivity in eighteenth-century British and French agriculture and the British figures, at least, would seem to be roughly consistent with Allen's (1999) summary of the agricultural revolution in England. Turning to the other Continental countries in the table, it seems not unreasonable, given the narrative accounts of European agriculture, to compare the productivity of Austria–Hungary, Germany and Sweden in 1700 with that of France.[30] Since parts of northern France were quite modern by the standards of the day, we have used 90 per cent of the French figure (Method A) as the base for the other Continental countries in 1700. Including the figures for the Netherlands, which are derived from de Vries (1984), we see the growth of output relative to the labor input was robust by the standards of the day across Europe. Furthermore, by 1800 even the more economically backward countries of Austria–Hungary, Germany and Sweden had agricultural labor forces that were roughly 50 per cent more productive than those of fourteenth century England, though timing the growth of productivity between the two periods is quite difficult.

In this section we have considered only the supply side of early modern agriculture. On the demand side population growth and urbanization proceeded over long periods, gradually widening the market for agricultural production and creating a climate that was favorable to enclosure and other innovations. Essentially the changes that were taking place in agriculture were the same kinds that would be taking place in industry and commerce. Specifically the increase in the share of agricultural output that ultimately ended up as marketable surplus induced farmers to become more concerned with producing for a regional and national market than they had before. There was also an increase in specialization in the appearance of the professional farmer who was willing to apply scientific knowledge and experimentation to activities and institutions that were formerly more regulated by traditional methods. As we noted at the beginning of this chapter, however, these innovations are related to that amorphous concept the 'standard of living' to which we now turn.

4. THE STANDARD OF LIVING BEFORE THE INDUSTRIAL REVOLUTION

The standard of living controversy is arguably the most hotly contested issue in the entire economic-history literature. While much of the debate focuses on the post-1750 period and revolves around the effects of the Industrial Revolution on living standards, the economic changes we described above may well have affected pre-industrial living standards. Broadly speaking, there are two main areas of research on this topic. The first involves the behavior of average measures of economic well-being, such as real wages or per capita income and/or output. As we have seen, for much of the period between 1500 and 1750 output was probably growing faster than population for most of Europe, *though not much faster*, and there is occasional evidence of substantial deviation from that long-term trend.[31] The second topic around which the standard of living debate revolves is the distribution of income and wealth, which, as we show below is not unrelated to movements in per capita measures of living standards. In the era before national income accounting, of course, we cannot deal with the distribution of income directly.

A reasonable way to proceed under the circumstances is to use real-wage data to measure living standards since effects on the real wage could run in the same direction as effects on the distribution itself, under certain conditions. To see this point, consider the formula for a two-factor distribution between capital (K) and labor (L), as in

$$1 = w(L/y) + r(K/y) \equiv S_L + S_K \tag{3.1}$$

where w and r are the real wage and interest rate, respectively. Thus S_L is the share of income (y) going to labor and S_K is the share going to capital. If the productivity of labor (y/L) is constant, then it follows that a $S_L/w > 0$; further, since w is the ratio of nominal wages (W) to the price level (P), for 'sticky' wages, $S_L/P < 0$. To illustrate how this would work in practice, and using Spain as an example, consider Hamilton's (1934, p. 274–5) argument that

> Since Spain was predominantly an agricultural country with little or no industry beyond the handicraft stage, the volume of employment probably varied within narrow limits ... Hence perfect index numbers of wages would gauge the money incomes of the men who worked for hire with tolerable certainty and in conjunction with index numbers of the cost of living would crudely measure changes in real wages.

A detailed and generally consistent picture of the behavior of real wages in early modern Europe can be obtained from the work of Phelps Brown and Hopkins (1956, 1957 and 1959) and Wrigley and Schofield (1981). While some of the real wage series graphed in Figure 3.2 do not cover the entire period from 1501 to 1750, some do. In any case, the patterns are fairly easy to discern. (Note that all series are based at 1501 = 1.000.) We will discuss the characteristics of these data at various points below.

The most striking thing about Figure 3.2 is the decline in real wages during most of the sixteenth century. Indeed, as the figures in Table 3.4 demonstrate, the declines possibly were experienced across Europe and were quite substantial. If taken literally, and this has been done in some of the literature using the real wage as a proxy for living standards, except in Germany, European workers at the end of the sixteenth century enjoyed only 40 per cent of the living standards at the beginning of the century, and even in Germany real wages were declining by about 0.45 per cent per year on average. One is surprised, indeed, to find England conforming to this pattern since this includes the period sometimes referred to as the 'Great Elizabethan Boom'.

Another noticeable feature of the data in Figure 3.2 is that over the 150 years after 1600 (for three countries) real wages either rose (Germany, England) or remained roughly constant (Austria). Nevertheless, by 1745–50, even in the countries in which wages in general rose, workers did not see real wages back at the 1500 level. Two sequential questions then arise. The first concerns whether or not we accept the real wage data as an accurate reflection of early modern living standards. If so, then the second question concerns the causes of the long-run decline in real wages.

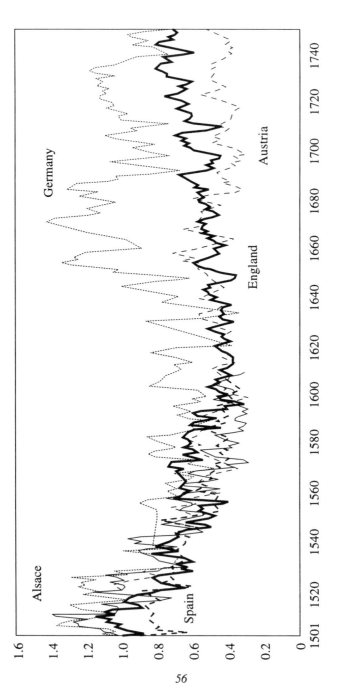

Figure 3.2   Real wages in Europe 1501–1750

Table 3.4   Index of real wages, 1500 = 1.000

	1595–1604	1740–1750
Alsace	0.391	—
Austria	0.400	0.428
England	0.429	0.720
Germany	0.628	0.858
Spain	0.391	—

Let us concentrate on the period of decline. Phelps Brown and Hopkins (1959) note that while at the time there was little notice of the phenomenon, subsequent research certainly did not miss it. They cite Malthus (1826) and Clapham (1949) for England, and Nef (1937) for France among others. Phelps Brown and Hopkins are, to be sure, concerned with the possibility that the calculations are biased downward; they offer the idea that it was because real wages had actually fallen from a 'very high' level in the fifteenth century, but we think this would be small comfort to someone with a life expectancy of 40 years who spent his entire life in the period of decline (in 100 years, there were two and a half of these generations). Phelps Brown and Hopkins go on to suggest that it was the day laborer who felt the full force of this 'price revolution'. Actually, one is hard-pressed to find any other period like this in history and we are now obliged to consider the strength of these explanations.

One obvious possible explanation for the declining real wage is the behavior of population. If population grew relatively rapidly in the sixteenth century, then there could have been upward pressure on commodity prices – that is, an increase in the demand for commodities relative to their supply – and a downward pressure on real wages – that is, an increase in the supply of labor relative to its demand.[32] Here it is not so much that population (and thus the labor force) grew faster than in the fifteenth (or seventeenth) century, but that it grew faster than the early modern economy could absorb at constant prices.

Among the five countries whose wages we consider, the United Kingdom had the fastest growing population and Spain the slowest; the others were near the European average in the sixteenth century, and the population growth of each was higher than in the subsequent century. The problem with this view can be seen in the English population figures, for in Figure 3.1 we see what appears to be a steady rise in population after 1541 until 1658, a rise that is only marred by sudden increases in the death rate. Only if output and jobs increased faster for some reason after 1600 (as Phelps Brown and Hopkins suggest may have happened), so that the population rise of that particular period did not put pressure on resources, could we explain this apparent contradiction between population growth and the trend in real wages.

Be that as it may, there is another strand to the population argument that is also capable of verification to some extent. Broadly, this version involves the argument that the inflation of the Price Revolution of the time produced a steadily falling real wage and this in turn produced, by means of a 'profit-inflation', a greater volume of saving than was in some sense economically optimal. Thus, interest rates, the quantities of capital and labor, and income (in terms of Equation 3.1, r, K, y and L) all rose and to maintain the relationship among these variables, (that is, the equality in Equation 3.1), real wages must have fallen (Clough and Rapp, 1975). In some accounts of this process, as already noted, the causal agent is relatively rapid population growth that simultaneously produces the upward pressure on commodity prices, which show up as inflation and the fall in real wages (with the latter usually *lagging behind* the inflation). Other accounts of this real wage effect emphasize the monetary causes of inflation, but retain the wage-lag part of the argument.[33] Certainly any lag in the adjustment of wages to consumer prices would presumably result in lower living standards for workers.

Two more recent tests of the 'population-misery' hypothesis for Great Britain are found in Lee (1973) and Lindert (1985). Lee regresses real wages on a trend variable (a demand-cum-productivity proxy) and population and finds that the former raises real wages and the latter lowers them. Lindert reruns the tests over the 1546 to 1800 period, using a non-linear version (time, time squared and the logarithms of real wages and population) and again finds the negative effect of population on real wages. It is particularly interesting that in one of Lindert's tests, where lagged prices (to represent unexpected changes in prices) were included, the population and demand proxies were swamped by a *negative* effect of lagged prices on real wages. This result is rejected by Lindert who goes on to consider how population growth itself might have induced price level changes (via its direct effect on the velocity of money).

Now we turn to questions concerning the adequacy of the real wage data that were discussed above. The real wage that appears there is a statistical artifact, being the ratio of separately calculated nominal wages and the price level, and is only as good as its components. The price level – that is, the denominator of the real wage indices – used in this research is a fixed-weight index. As such, it must rely on market baskets of goods that are defined at a point in time. Unfortunately, there are very few data here, and virtually no time-series aspect to the market basket employed in this literature. The implication is that substitution effects will be confused with income effects (which are what the price index hopes to capture). The direction of this bias is generally upward for the Laspeyres index that is generally used in these studies.[34] Increases in the quality of the products in the basket, not accounted for by changes in the weights, would also lead to an upward bias in the measure of the price level. However, there is little one can do about these matters without data that are simply unlikely ever to be available, and for some purposes, such as broad comparisons across countries, such biases might be only a nuisance.

Of more importance, we feel, is the state of the nominal wage data. In modern times, nominal wages are determined in competitive markets and real wages are calculated by economists. The market-determined nominal wages fluctuate considerably (as do the real wages) for they, not the real wages, are the 'price' that is negotiated in the market (in the first instance). For the period we are considering (and onward as we shall see in Chapters 7 and 8) the data on nominal wages are handled (by economists) as if official or reported nominal wages are actually market nominal wages. Most unusually, for the early modern era, *the nominal wage thus measured rarely changes* and sometimes goes as much as 40 years without changing at all! If we are to accept the nominal wages used in these studies at face value, we must put aside arguments that there were other nominal wages (invisible to the researcher) or that payment was rendered 'in kind' or in adjustments to working hours and conditions (also largely invisible to the researcher). The alternative is to say that markets then were simply unlike those today, and thus did not respond to changes in other market conditions, and thus that the nominal wage did not change over time.

When one reviews the underlying nominal wage data, what stands out is the infrequency of changes in the nominal wage rates . Of course, this point is not the same thing as infrequency of observation, but the infrequency of change is startling. In the English data there appear to be only ten changes in the series, which therefore consists of ten 'observations' in the 250 years of the sample. Thus, these data are remarkable in admitting of so little adjustment in nominal wage payments for such long periods of time.

While we have no immediate practical solution to the problem, we cannot resist observing that acceptance of these constant nominal wages as market wages implies (since both demand and supply must have been shifting frequently in this period) that the labor market was in a perpetual state of disequilibrium, at least in the short run (until people died or were born in adequate numbers). Furthermore, other evidence to be discussed in Chapters 4, 5 and 6 suggests that only the labor market had this characteristic. In all other markets, bargains were struck in nominal terms and markets appear to have been reasonably competitive, especially in product and capital markets. Thus, it is clear that the primary data used for interpreting the behavior of the standard of living in early modern Europe are not particularly reliable for that purpose. Perhaps this is not altogether surprising, since the standard of living really consists of a vector of characteristics, and it would be very difficult to map that vector into a single number regardless of the quality of the underlying data; this comment, also applies to modern work on the problem. For some purposes then, one might consider the growth in agricultural production and productivity and population growth as more general indicators of the progress of the early modern living standards, though, again, these offer little in the way of details concerning the distribution of the fruits of that progress.

Because of the absence of national income and product accounts for the early modern era, our discussion to this point has focused primarily on the levels and trends of average real wages and so we have said relatively little concerning the distribution of income or wealth. In fact there are two types of information that provide some evidence on these questions. The first type of evidence reflecting the distribution of the product is the pay structure by skill and/or occupation. While this is a controversial issue after 1750, during the first half of the eighteenth century the evidence for Britain suggests that the skill premium declined slightly between 1710 and 1737 and then rose slowly thereafter (Williamson, 1982). The second type of evidence on distribution involves biological measures of well-being, such as the mean adult height of a population .[35] Interestingly, data on the heights of British recruits increased during the latter part of the cycle covering the distribution of wages above – that is the post-1737 part (Floud and Harris, 1997). This observation offers modest additional support for amelioration of inequality on the eve of industrialization and is consistent with the wage compression accompanied by economic growth discussed above.

Of course there were other aspects of early modern economic change that affected the living standard. For example, de Vries (1994) discusses the increases in hours worked and workplace intensity that preceded the Industrial Revolution. In conjunction with the unreliable real wage data, this observation would suggest a decline in early modern living standards; in the absence of evidence on declining real wages, it might even suggest that family incomes rose! Indeed, as we saw in our discussion of agriculture, the changes readily adopted by early modern farmers were often those that increased total hours worked and the intensity of effort, and they most likely raised farm income. It is possible that one of the enhancing effects of technological change on early modern living standards was to provide workers with more opportunities above their reservation wage – that is more *total* time – even *if* the return per *unit of time*, the real wage, fell. This is hardly the standard interpretation of the evidence reported above, but then the standard interpretation leads to a question: Why was there not a social revolution? This interpretation suggests an answer: Early modernity, for all of its faults, left us better off.

5. SUMMARY

The early modern period was marked by long-run population growth, economic growth, agricultural progress and declining real wages. The reasons for population growth seem to vary from period to period with the 'natural' influences of disease, famine, war and occasional general poverty giving way, as the eighteenth century unfolded, to a more consistent pattern of growth, as death rates fell modestly while fertility rates rose, sometimes dramatically. The decline of death rates was caused, at least in part, by the disappearance of major epidemics and an improvement in the European food supply; this latter improvement and the increased fertility were no doubt associated with more rapid economic growth itself to some extent – though this growth occurred with tremendous deviations from the trend (see Chapter 6). As the data in Table 3.1 suggest, this experience was common to a broad slice of Western Europe, so the door is clearly open for equally broad generalizations.

With respect to agriculture, we speculated that the steady agricultural progress of the time was the result of the growth of inputs and technological change, the latter largely associated with the introduction of new crops and rotations in association with the improvement of livestock. These changes had a broader interaction with overall economic growth, providing both stimulus and response to real and human capital development as well as serving as a supplier of products to industry and commerce. This conclusion is not controversial. By the early seventeenth century, there were signs of vigorous agricultural growth, at least by earlier standards, and by the mid-eighteenth century, something like a revolution had already occurred. Although aggregate measures of inputs and outputs (and thus total factor productivity) before 1750 are rare, after 1700 output per farm worker and per capita probably grew at a fairly robust pace, again by historical comparison, across much of western and central Europe. In addition, the diversity and the quality – in terms of nutrition – of the food supply improved with the growth of livestock products, and the reliability of the food supply improved with the transportation network.

Not every observer sees the situation in this light, of course, and pessimistic conclusions are easy to find, particularly in the literature concerning living standards. Here the reliance on measures of the real wage tend to yield a strongly negative view of the trends in living standards of early modern wage earners. We have raised some questions concerning the way in which the data on early modern wages have been used to generate trends in real wages but, perhaps more importantly, we challenge the traditional interpretation of the wage data. It is not only possible but logical and consistent with behavior in our own time that a falling real wage accompanied by the opportunity to work more hours over the course of the year could produce an improvement in the economic well-being of early modern workers. The disincentives to effort in pre-modern agriculture and the constraints placed on time in pre-modern industry can themselves be interpreted as constraining upward pressure on Western living standards. Despite the grousing of generations of scholars, early modern workers pursued the opportunities offered by a life-style that involved more work at sustained levels of intensity for what may have even been a declining wage. While this choice may have unambiguously lowered the quality of life per unit of time on the job, it provided for a richer life away from the job. The economic history of the intervening centuries suggests that such a choice has enriched most of us.

NOTES

1. The U.K.'s eighteenth-century expansion begins just after 1750. The reader should note at this point that throughout this volume we have tried to maintain the formal distinctions between England, Great Britain, and the United Kingdom; however, three things make such an effort difficult. First, we occasionally refer to data series or periods that include two or more of those political entities. Second, since this is a survey of the literature, we are often at the mercy of the secondary sources, which frequently either take little notice of the distinctions or find them unimportant. Finally, there are several instances in which contemporary scholars have constructed series based on subsequent political boundaries for years before those boundaries were drawn.
2. See the section entitled 'Growth' in Chapter 1.
3. We consider the long-run trends and cyclical behavior of output in Chapter 6.
4. In Great Britain, which was quite possibly the fastest-growing economy in the eighteenth century, the average annual rate of growth of various measures of per capita income range from 0.30–0.44 from 1700 to 1760 and 0.17–0.52 for 1760 to 1800 (Mokyr, 1993, Table 1.1).
5. Evidence presented in Weir (1984) indicates that in England and France crude death rates fell by about 25 per cent or more between 1740 and 1800, with most of the decline coming before 1750, though the steepness of this decline is slightly misleading, because, as Post (1984) explains, the early 1740s witnessed the last great famine-disease cycle in western Europe. Post argues that dysentery was the chief culprit in the 1740s.
6. For an excellent recent summary of both the issues involved and the literature on this subject, see Steckel (1995).
7. An important work on this subject is Becker and Tomes (1976).
8. The population experience of the European states varied dramatically both cross-sectionally and in the short run. Thus, with a few notable exceptions, such as the fertility response to mortality, generalizations are difficult to support; however, the longer-run trends are clearer and more consistent across countries.
9. This period has sometimes been characterized in the literature as 'the Elizabethan boom' in England. The growth rate of real output may well have exceeded 1 per cent during this period. We discuss this further in Chapter 6.
10. It has even been suggested that the changing makeup of the rat population might have led to the declining incidence of the plague (Deane, 1979). Although we hesitate to push our knowledge of rodentia too far, it seems that *Rattus norvegicus*, the brown or Norwegian rat, proved a more efficient forager than his displaced cousin, *Rattus rattus*, the black rat, whose fleas carried the plague. As the former was less of a house dweller than the latter, the plague nexus was disrupted.

11. See, for example, Clark (1992 and 1993) and the discussion below.
12. Here, we mean that the supply side responds in a profit-maximizing way to the economic incentives that arise from the increase in the number of consumers and in their purchasing power.
13. The rate of natural increase of a population is the birth rate less the death rate. An increase in fertility leads directly to an increase in the number of infants. Similarly, since infants, children and the elderly had the highest death rates, reductions in mortality typically led to an increase in the size of those groups.
14. It is often argued that such growth – and the relative migration of the labor force from agricultural to manufacturing pursuits – helped drive the British industrial revolution (see Deane, 1979). We say relatively, because, paradoxically, as we note below, the agricultural revolution on net probably had a labor-using dimension.
15. A great deal of controversy exists concerning the timing of the productivity growth typically referred to as the 'agricultural revolution'. Though we avoid entering this battle, the interested reader should consult Chambers and Mingay (1966), Kerridge (1967), Clark (1993), and Allen (1994).
16. Though it was not the most advanced; that distinction belonged to the Low Countries.
17. Of course there was tremendous variation across regions and over time within a particular country, as Outhwaite (1986) shows.
18. Indeed, Sullivan (1985, p. 313) estimates that for England between 1661 and 1850 the elasticity of agricultural patents with respect to population was 3.10 and with respect to relative food prices it was 1.55.
19. Crafts (1978 and 1980) notes that the relevant measurement is the decline of the share of the labor force in agriculture – about 0.70 per cent per year in eighteenth-century England (1980, p. 154). He estimates that the income elasticity of food was relatively large – in the neighborhood of 0.7 – and this worked to dampen the labor-release effect.
20. For a more detailed discussion concerning the interpretation of TFP, see Abramovitz (1993).
21. TFP growth in British agriculture between 1800 and 1850 was probably greater than 1.1 per cent per year.
22. Many of the improvements associated with enclosure could have been achieved in the open field system *if* there were sufficient coordination and cooperation among local farmers; indeed there were examples of such efforts, but they were not ubiquitous (see Turner, 1986).
23. McCloskey (1972) persuasively argues that open-field agriculture was a form of insurance against the effects of climatic disaster; however, the expansion of agricultural markets, improvements in transportation, and the institutional shifts associated with property rights in land led to the death of the open-field system (see Allen, 1988; Hoyle, 1990; Turner, 1986; and Wordie, 1983).
24. What we are trying to emphasize here are the effects of the open-field system – and especially of its 'common' property rights – on the costs of transactions involved with agricultural improvements. Eliminate the open-field system, and the transactions can go forward, unencumbered by the transactions costs associated with communal decision making.
25. McCloskey puts the figure at 'roughly 13 per cent' (1975, p. 160), and Wordie notes that this 'figure is probably nearer to the truth' (1983, p. 504) than the upper bound estimates reported above.
26. It has also been argued that enclosure affected population growth and the supply of labor. For example, Philpot (1975) argues that by eliminating the commons and improving the health of animals and the human food supply, enclosure both disrupted the animal–human disease nexus and made the human population better able to fight disease by improving its access to nutrition. Turner (1976) challenges Philpot's analysis and conclusions. In addition, Crafts (1978) challenges the view, expressed by Chambers (1953), that enclosure did not 'free' rural labor for industrial pursuits.
27. These calculations are based on a yield of 28 bushels per acre in 1860, which is consistent with estimates reported in Turner (1982, p. 504).

28. Though the yield data reported in Overton (1990) are considerably more cyclical than this summary suggests.
29. These numbers are drawn by Jones directly from population estimates, but not the populations estimates reported above, although they are amended by trade figures after 1700.
30. Figures reported by Clark (1987) suggests that the productivity of agricultural labor in Austria-Hungary in the early nineteenth century was comparable to that of England *c.* 1300!
31. Biological measures of the standard of living offer an avenue for exploring the interaction between mean measures of output, such as output per capita, and their distribution. Although this literature has focused primarily on living standards after 1750, there is some evidence on earlier periods. For a review, see Steckel (1995).
32. Although, strictly speaking, these are relative price changes, they would tend to show a decline in the real wage index given the way in which price indices (and thus inflation) are calculated. We provide a more comprehensive discussion of inflation during this period in Chapter 4.
33. Such accounts are difficult to verify with any of the data we have at our disposal in view of the paucity of nominal wage rate data. See the discussion below.
34. Loschky (1980) questions the use of the Laspeyres index for the reason stated in the text and attempts some recalculations based on Paasche (fixed weight) and chained price indices. He finds that real wages calculated using these indices did not fall as much as reported by Phelps Brown and Hopkins. These claims are disputed (and modified) in a reply by Lydall and Phelps Brown (1982).
35. Mean adult height reflects net nutrition during the key periods of growth – infancy and early adolescence for *Homo sapiens*. In conjunction with more traditional economic indicators it can provide some evidence on the distribution of those indicators.

4. Inflation, the quantity theory of money and the banking system

1. INTRODUCTION

In this chapter we consider the role played by early modern finance in the discontinuity in real growth that occurred during the sixteenth and seventeenth centuries. We argue that this discontinuity was *associated with* the 'price revolution', a century-and-a-quarter long rise in Western European price levels that had its roots in the importation of gold and silver (specie) from the European powers' New World colonies. Although the linkages are complex, the quest for overseas treasure in the sixteenth and seventeenth centuries was clearly associated with an economic expansion in Western Europe. More generally, what we show in this chapter is that the monetary system of Western Europe changed from a metallic coinage in 1500, with relatively little financial intermediation, to one where, by 1750, functioning banking systems (and even central banks) existed in a number of important countries, and the use of financial institutions and financial instruments had expanded remarkably.

The next section of this chapter reviews and analyses the price revolution. Here we investigate evidence that suggests an international payments system was in place and that a *de facto* commodity standard operated more or less as the specie flow mechanism would suggest, with closely correlated international price levels and a close association between money and the price level on a domestic level. Our explanation for this system relies on the quantity theory of money, which not coincidentally was developed at this time, but we also document and discuss competing theories of the causes of inflation to some extent. In Section 3 we extend the data to the end of the period (1750), utilizing additionally some further money stock data. There we note that while from 1500 to around 1620 European prices generally rose, after 1620 (to 1750) there is no discernible trend in the price level data for various countries. Although there is no trend, the price behavior is interesting all the same, particularly during the Thirty Years War. Furthermore, as we shall see in Chapter 6, these data are useful for helping to detect cyclical patterns in the pre-industrial economy.

In Section 4 we address the second main task of this chapter which is to document the rise of both commercial and central banking. Banks, at least as we think of them today, were a creation of the late medieval Italian city states and from the dawn of the early modern age banking was an increasingly familiar activity throughout Western Europe, although certainly not in its modern limited liability form. For the most part, the main surge of banking in Europe occurs after 1750, but central banking goes back to the early seventeenth century and, in any event, what happened across most of Europe after 1750 has its roots in the period we are considering. We also tie our material to the development of the nation state, as discussed in Chapter 2, because it is reasonable to argue that central banks arise and banking systems expand after a nation's political unity has been established. Indeed, this explains why we will continue to investigate the links of banking with overall growth right through Part IV of this study.

Banks, to continue, are the creations of entrepreneurs in the first instance (though a government charter may be required), while the central bank, although it often began as a private bank, is more obviously a creation of the government. From the inception of central banks, these distinctions were blurred and the consequences were not always fortunate, at least for economic growth, both because of the conflict between private and public interests and because of the use (at times) of central banks to achieve political objectives inconsistent with monetary and financial stability. The latter problem is with us to this day, of course. Central bank behavior, too, will be part of the story of early business cycles, to be discussed in Chapter 6. Finally, we note that while central banks existed prior to 1750, we do not find many instances in which they behaved like modern central banks – that is, they did not operate as a lender of last resort and they did not try to control the monetary base through open market operations. This observation removes much of the macroeconomic interest from the subject, and, accordingly, we are appropriately brief.

2.   THE PRICE REVOLUTION (1500–1618)[1]

From the early sixteenth to the mid-seventeenth century, the price levels of most European countries rose erratically, but with an unmistakable upward drift of between 1 and 2 per cent per year. Although the overall influence of this long inflation on real activity remains in dispute, it is clear that one important input was the considerable inflow of specie (at that time, mostly silver) from the American colonies. This flow was at its strongest from the early sixteenth century until the onset of the Thirty Years War (1618) and thus coincides with the long upward drift in prices.[2] What is particularly striking about this event – recognizing that the point of impact of the inflow of specie from the Americas was for the most part Spain – is the roughly parallel rise of

Spanish and other European price levels. The exact date when inflation begins varies somewhat from country to country, but in the period of the most rapid inflow of New World specie from 1500 to 1618, most countries in Europe experienced a roughly parallel rise in their average prices, occasionally punctuated, to be sure, by frequently non-coincident sharp spikes and dips in the measured price level. This is certainly true for the five countries – Spain, England, Alsace (France), Germany, and Austria – for which we have annual data for the entire period.

Figure 4.1 shows the price level data for the period 1500 to 1618 (taken from Phelps Brown and Hopkins, 1956, 1957 and 1959); we also include a (smoothed) French money supply series (the solid line) as calculated by Glassman and Redish (1985). We have picked 1618 as the terminal date because, as we will explain below, the upward trend in the price series disappears at that point, and other factors, notably the financial aspects of the Thirty Years War, need to be considered. It is abundantly clear that these price data (and the money series) all show a similar upward drift. The unusual episodes (the 'spikes' in the price data) differ quite a bit – with the British and Alsatian price levels showing greater volatility – but the common upward drift is unmistakable. The Spanish price index (not identified in the figure) is the darker dotted line. Note that the French money supply is remarkably stable compared to all of the price series, no doubt because the monetary series was smoothed when it was constructed. Below we explain how the behavior of these series is consistent with the quantity theory of money, but for now we continue our survey of the empirical material.

Another way to grasp the relationship among the trends shown in Figure 4.1 is to calculate the growth rates for these series, as in Table 4.1. These calculations show the narrow range for the estimated trends in these data, with the growth rates of price levels between 1.25 per cent and 1.64 per cent per year, and with the French money stock growing just below the lower bound of this range.

Other statistics suggesting a large amount of interaction are the correlation coefficients across these countries; these are reported in Table 4.2. The correlations among the prices in the table are very high (they are, of course, trend-dominated). None is below 0. 91, and the correlations of all of the price series with the French money supply are equally high. What is important about these findings is that, since these are annual data and since the correlations are across countries, the suggestion is that money and prices adjusted quite rapidly *internationally*. Since these are prices in product markets, this finding attests to the integration of product markets and to the flexibility of money prices in this period. Both of these characteristics, if acceptable, are very important to the interpretation of what caused this situation and to any discussion of the possible integration of European product markets.[3]

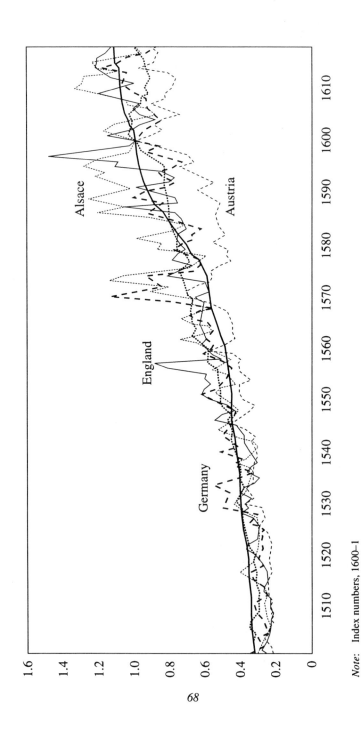

Note: Index numbers, 1600–1

Figure 4.1 European prices and money 1501–1618

Table 4.1   Annual compounded growth rates of price levels (and French money) 1501–1618

Alsace	1.64
Austria	1.34
England	1.56
Germany	1.29
Spain	1.25
French Money	1.24

Note: These rates were calculated by the regression of the natural log of the series on trend.

Table 4.2   Correlations among the logarithms of the price levels and French money* 1501–1618

	Alsace	Austria	England	Germany	Spain	French money
Alsace	—	0.93	0.93	0.95	0.94	0.94
Austria		—	0.94	0.95	0.95	0.94
England			—	0.92	0.96	0.94
Germany				—	0.93	0.91
Spain					—	0.96

Note: * The logs smooth the data and slightly elevate the correlations.

The standard explanation of the price rise, ignoring potential complications for the moment, is the classical quantity theory of money, buttressed by the international specie-flow mechanism. The early modern era was one of 'hard money' primarily, and economic agents held their liquid reserves in silver (and gold) when possible, and otherwise in coins struck from other metals or in inventories of (other) readily marketable commodities. In fact the monetary bases of European countries in this period consisted of silver-dominated metallic coins, whether in the hands of individuals or dealers in financial instruments (that is, in early 'banks').[4] The coinage was often legitimized by the government (or other agents) through minting operations that earned 'seigniorage' profits. These imposed a fairly uniform standard on any particular coinage, at least in the long run. In the short run, however, debasement and counterfeiting were real hazards. In view of the absence of any really firm governmental control over the quantity or quality of the coinage, the market effectively determined its value – that is, different political units had different coinages at different times (varying in content, quality, reliability and so forth), and pounds, livres, florins, ducats and such, all circulated side by side at rates determined by market forces – in effect by the estimated market value of the silver content of the minted money.[5]

In this hard-money world, the relatively large flow of precious metals from the New World into Spain (and sometimes into other countries) was a significant event, at least in strictly monetary terms. The institutional nature of the process is documented in an extensive modern literature that begins with Hamilton (1934). We offer the Spanish situation as an example. The Spanish Crown dictated that the New World specie be coined at the imperial mint at Seville. The Crown taxed the specie at roughly 20 per cent (the so-called 'imperial fifth') and extracted seigniorage rents from the rest,[6] but whether the resulting coinage ended up in the hands of the Crown or private traders, much of it eventually filtered throughout Europe, the Levant and the Far East to finance Spain's various military expeditions and balance of payments deficits. In the simplest terms, the money supply grew faster than real economic activity and the result was a general increase in prices – in a word, inflation.

The general idea can be illustrated with the equation of exchange, here given as Equation 4.1.

$$MV = Py \qquad (4.1)$$

In this equation, which must hold strictly by definition in a monetary economy, M is the stock of money and V is 'velocity'; that is, V is the number of times the average unit of money is spent in a period of time. On the right hand side is the money value of spending over the same period of time – that is, the product of the price level, P, and the level of real output, y, which would be analogous to the nominal value of gross domestic product in modern national accounting systems. If specie enters a country such as Spain, it is quickly taken to the mint for coinage, or dispersed as bullion (and ornament) in other ways. We generally refer to the arrival of specie taken to the mint as an addition to the 'monetary base' of the country; when it is converted into money, M in Equation 4.1 rises. If payment habits change relatively slowly, and if real income grows relatively slowly – that is, if velocity and real income remain roughly constant – then the price level will rise.[7] The data presented above may well illustrate such a situation in the sixteenth century; we say 'may', because, of course, there are no data for V or y during this era, so we cannot prove that this is correct.

Certainly, Spanish prices generally rose during this period. More important for the purposes of this section is that other European price levels also generally rose throughout the period (as did the French money supply). The international version of the quantity theory of money, as we have described it, begins with the reaction of international trade in response to price differences among nations. In particular, if Spanish prices are greater than those in other countries, then Spanish citizens will buy internationally traded commodities abroad, and foreigners (from the Spanish viewpoint) will cease to buy Spanish commodities. The result is a balance of payments deficit for Spain, which is closed by the export of specie from Spain to the other countries.[8] The result is that the monetary base of the specie-receiving country expands and, according to the quantity theory of money, so does the price level. In the short run, it is usually argued, there could be real effects (positive) on the receiving country from the monetary injection, but in the long run only a price level response will be noticeable. The latter proposition is often referred to as that of the 'long-run neutrality' of money (in the quantity theory).

Although it provides a logically consistent and plausible explanation of the price revolution, the quantity theory of money has been rejected by some scholars. The most widely accepted contrasting theory to the quantity theory argues that prices are not driven by specie (which, at most, establishes a floor for the price level) but by the actions of monopolists (or governments), who take advantage of their market power to raise prices. Modern proponents of this theory point to substantial sixteenth- and seventeenth-century opinion that favored monopolistic and other non-competitive techniques as the typical pricing behavior in European product and factor markets. Hamilton (1934) mentions the activities of middlemen (wholesalers, really), who were often accused of charging higher prices by illegal means. Usury is also often mentioned in this context; so are the activities of foreign capitalists, depopulation, vagrancy, luxury, the flagrant idleness of women and even the effect of shortages of goods caused by shipping so many supplies to the New World.[9] Such arguments were not confined to Spain. For example, speaking of Belgian prices, Verlinden, Craeybeckx, and Scholliers (1972) dismiss the quantity theory of money (in the short run) in favor of numerous local disruptions traceable to the activities of monopolists. They point out that, 'In the eyes of contemporaries, including the government, monopolies were ... the main if not the only cause of high prices (1972, p. 68).' In England, bad harvests, speculation, middlemen, government spending and monopolies were often-heard complaints, and product-related cost-push explanations were also put forward frequently.[10] In France, Malestroit (in 1566) favored civil unrest, bad harvests, the loss of labor after famines and bullion *exports* as inducers of inflation; this last argument was countered by Jean Bodin (in 1568), who put forward the first publicly recorded statement of the quantity theory of money (as described above). In the French case 'by general acclaim Bodin emerged the winner in the dispute (Spooner, 1972, p. 90).'[11] Even so, it seems that outside France neither laymen nor politicians seem to have been much taken with the quantity theory at least until after 1600.

Ultimately, the main cause of the long-run European inflation is an empirical issue. The first issue raised by the quantity theory concerns whether

Spanish specie reached European markets in sufficient volume to raise prices generally over time. That Spanish specie entered the channels of European trade is clear; Artur Attman argues that 'the precious metals imported from America via Seville, Cadiz and Lisbon were largely distributed from the Iberian peninsula to the main arteries of world trade (1986, p. 7).' But he then argues that a large volume of specie moved through Europe to the Baltic, the Levant and Asia.[12] Obviously, though, a considerable amount of specie was retained in Europe, with, as Attman says, the surplus period ending around 1620.[13]

A second issue concerning the validity of the quantity theory is that the known episodes of monetary importation into particular countries do not match the timing of the known inflations very well. Hamilton (1934), for example, remarks on significant inflation in Spain *before* the price revolution. Doughty (1975) makes the same point with respect to England. Cipolla locates the Italian price crest in 1551-60, but the inflow of specie apparently was substantial only after 1570 (by which time the Italian inflation had subsided). He explains the price rise in Italy in terms of the rebuilding after 'the war that had reigned there throughout the first half of the century (1972, p. 45)'. The stimulus is apparently some kind of cost-push influence that may also have been associated with what is sometimes called 'profit inflation'.[14] Finally, Hammarström (1957) argues that Swedish prices do not share the broad European experience (as this experience is described above).[15]

Generally speaking, the arguments that other episodes of inflation antedated the appearance of New World specie are surely irrelevant, since we do not have information on the production of whatever money was used in that earlier period. It would be like arguing that the widespread inflation of the late 1970s could not have been caused by contemporary monetary policy, because there had already been inflation in the 1940s. Furthermore, specie would not necessarily have to actually flow into a particular country for that country's prices to be influenced by the increase in the *world* money supply, as suggested by the 'monetary approach to the balance of payments' (Craig et al., 1995). In fact, if sellers in the domestic market recognized the price increases in foreign markets, then they could raise domestic prices without anything actually flowing between the two countries except information.

Of the remaining propositions designed to refute the quantity theory, a main contender is the 'monopoly' argument. The proponents of this argument sometimes appear to confuse the price level with changes in the price level (inflation). If a monopoly replaces competitive firms, the price of the monopolized good will rise, but the existence of monopoly in and of itself will have no effect on subsequent price increases. Remember that the general inflation persisted for over a hundred years! To argue that monopolies caused this phenomenon, one would have to argue that not only did monopoly power emerge in the early sixteenth century, thus raising prices, but that it continued to grow steadily, exerting upward pressure on prices throughout the sixteenth and early seventeenth centuries; it then stopped and remained constant over the next hundred years or so. There is no evidence that such a pattern of industrial concentration characterized early modern Europe. Indeed as markets grew beyond regional and national borders, national governments attempted to reduce the growing competition in international trade via restrictive legislation. In short, national 'monopolies' were eroded in this period of increasing trade, thus weakening any inflationary pressure from this source.

Finally the remaining contender is basically a 'demand-pull' explanation of the price revolution that sometimes is tied up with a related concern over the possibility of a sustained rise in the velocity of money in this period. The demand-pull theory (expounded, for example, by Clough and Rapp (1975)), argues that an increase in the demand for money accompanying the expansion of European economic activity produced the rise in prices and a simultaneous pressure for exploration (in order to increase the stock of money). Population growth is sometimes linked to this particular proposition as an additional source of pressure on prices.[16] The first modern proponent of the more general population thesis is Elsas (1935), and a key finding is that agricultural prices rose more than the prices of manufactured products (see also Phelps Brown and Hopkins, 1957 and 1959, and Postan, 1959). This change in relative prices is generally attributed to population increases exceeding the productive capabilities of the agricultural sector. Ramsey (1963) also puts the issue in these terms, allowing, however, that specie inflows did have something to do with inflation. In addition, Doughty (1975) mentions the relationship between population and agriculture for England, favoring the influence of increases in the demand for food (frustrated by an inelastic supply). We should note, though, that the population growth rate during this period was roughly half the inflation rate at about 0.6 of 1 per cent per year.[17] Furthermore, if real growth rates (in y in Equation 4.1) were positive, say at 0.5 per cent per year, then as a matter of arithmetic, money must have played a substantial role in the growth of prices or velocity must have risen at a phenomenal rate for a century! In any case, we have also suggested in Chapter 3 that agricultural output grew faster than population throughout the early modern period, suggesting that what we might be looking at is a rise in the demand for agricultural products which would be responsible for a rise in the *relative* price of agricultural products, without having any necessary influence on the price *level*.[18]

We need to underscore the point just made. What we are saying is that a straightforward counter-argument to the population theory is simply that whether or not the inflation is evenly spaced in all sectors, the general causal agent for the level of prices can still be money. Relative prices can and do change during periods of inflation (Flynn, 1978). The effect of population, that is to say, would likely be on *relative* prices without necessarily having anything to do with the *absolute* price level; in fact, this is mostly a matter of constructing effective measures of inflation.[19] McCloskey (1972, p. 1333) points out, 'the central flaw in the revisionist argument is that it repeatedly uses the theory of relative prices as a theory of absolute prices.' It needs to be underscored, then, that the monetary explanation of inflation clearly can encompass changes in relative prices, which is not always clearly understood by opponents of the quantity theory of money.

A related argument involving increases in velocity comes into play from time to time. Looking back to Equation 4.1, we have already pointed out that a rise in velocity, other things being equal, would produce a rise in the price level; thus, the general idea is quite defensible, just arguing from the 'equation of exchange' perspective. In fact, we don't know if there was a rise in velocity in this period. Miskimin (1975) suggests that the frequency of transactions from a given money stock increases as the urban economic activity grows relative to rural activity. This argument is sensible given the reduction of distance involved in the typical trade. Gould (1964) and Lindert (1985) also take this view.[20] There are, however, three problems with the velocity argument. First, urban growth is suggestive of economic growth in general. Thus in our view the rise of *V* is associated with a rise in *y* in this period; the latter would dampen the inflation caused by the former. Second, we do not have actual data on velocity which may, after all, not have changed at all. If we had data for *y* and *M*, then we could sort this out, calculating velocity as a residual (after all, we do have price data). That is what we do today; however, attempts to measure velocity by measures of urbanization run into the first objection. Furthermore, we do not know how great the production of 'competing monies' was in the period. These substitutes for money would have lowered velocity (as they do now) by enabling more transactions on a given base of hard money (see Bordo, 1986). We should note, in addition, that velocity arguments of inflation do not have many adherents for periods when we do have more adequate data (from, say, 1850 to the present). Also, it is worth noting that velocity would have to have been rising at 1 to 2 per cent per year, which, for over 100 years, would produce a substantial change. In any case, it is not obvious why velocity would rise at all in a world in which the specie-backing of financial liabilities was substantial. Quite simply, we don't know how fast money stocks grew, but it is quite possible that they outpaced inflation, in effect providing enough real money to feed the increasing demand. Indeed, for all we know, velocity fell in this period, as the 'moneyness' of the economy expanded more rapidly than real economic output![21]

Let us recap this rather complicated discussion. Putting aside the facts about inflation and the interactions among national price levels, most of this section has featured an important debate over the causes of inflation. During the period of the price revolution a very modern-sounding debate emerged; we say 'modern-sounding' because many points still made in the twentieth century appeared at that time. We believe, however, that it is no more likely then than now that the inflation rate was driven by anything other than the rate of growth of the money supply. The evidence and the linkages are there, no other theory deals as well with the century-long inflation and, almost as important, after the upward trend in the money growth rate fell, so did the trend in the inflation rate.

3. PRICES FROM 1618 TO 1750[22]

From 1618 to 1648 the Thirty Years War raged on the Continent in a series of campaigns that at one time or another involved every major European power. Although often referred to as a war of religion, in fact the causes and consequences of the war involved political disputes as much as, if not more than, doctrinal ones. In either case, much of the fighting was done in what is modern-day Germany, and the bloodshed and property damage there were considerable. From the point of view of the macroeconomist, two questions are at the top of the list. How were these campaigns financed? And what were the repercussions for the growth and inflation rates of the respective countries? Although few data are readily available to address these questions directly, we do have information concerning inflation rates. These data may suggest answers to other questions as well. In Figure 4.2, we show the price levels (on an annual basis) for the same countries listed in Figure 4.1. Two things are remarkable about the price series; they are very volatile and, across the entire period, they show no trend.[23] The latter is remarkable because the gold and silver inflow into Europe from the Americas continued in this period; indeed, the estimated French money supply, not shown in the graph, grew rapidly in the 1640s (see Glassman and Redish, 1985), though this was a deflationary period in Alsace.

States have three means of finance at their disposal: taxation, borrowing and inflation.[24] With the notable exception of Spain, the Spanish Netherlands and the United Provinces, which were in revolt against Spain, early modern princes generally found it difficult to borrow the large sums required to finance war.[25] Furthermore, because of the low-yield and relatively inflexible mechanisms typically employed for raising taxes at the time,[26] the extraordinary nature of wartime expenditures made inflation an appealing option, and the result was the inflation of 1619–1623, which, as Figure 4.2 shows, was quite pronounced for the countries of the Holy Roman Empire included there. This period is often referred to as the *Kipper- und Wipperzeit*, literally the

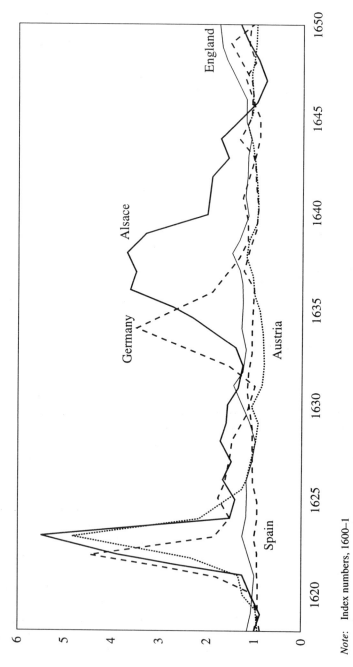

Note: Index numbers, 1600–1

Figure 4.2   European price levels 1618–1650

'clipping and seesawing time'. In an age of hard money, seigniorage – profit from the mint – was basically a tax on the creation of money resulting from the state's ability to monopolize the activity. One way to increase the seigniorage was to coin more money from a given quantity of specie.[27] Of course this ultimately leads to a depreciation of the coinage as holders of the now-debased coins try to exchange them in a neighboring principality for non-debased coins. In an age when ascertaining the metal content of a coin was relatively costly, an unanticipated debasement yielded seigniorage to the debasing prince at a cost to the unsuspecting traders in neighboring principalities. Once the debasement is widely recognized, however, two things happen: the price of the debased coins among moneychangers and merchants falls and the neighboring princes, attempting to reverse the outflow of 'good' money and inflow of bad, 'call down' their currencies and a general inflation ensues.

This then is the process by which the constituent states of the Empire generated inflation of the order of 40 per cent per annum during the *Kipper-und Wipperzeit* period. Note from Figure 4.2 that neither Spain, which had superior access to credit via Antwerp, nor England, which at this stage was not engaged in the conflict in any significant way, experienced inflation. Note also that the rapid inflation ended abruptly in 1623, which corresponds with the agreement among several of the major Imperial princes to return to the minting standards established by the Imperial Ordinance of 1559.

Two later bouts of inflation during this era were associated with specific regions and events. The dramatic rise of prices in Germany during the early 1630s coincided with the 'Swedish' phase of the war. While we do not have direct evidence concerning the source of the corresponding inflation, three pieces of information suggest that the German inflation also had a 'Swedish' phase. First, the price indices illustrated in Figure 4.2 are based an a relatively small number of commodities and, because the war was fought largely on German soil, it is possible that the spike represents a real supply shock caused by the disruption of the war. Second, assuming that at least some of the spike in prices during the first half of the 1630s was a monetary phenomenon, the cause may lie in Swedish public policies. Swedish war expenditures in Germany were extraordinary – roughly ten times the normal state budget (Parker, 1987, p. 134) and it would not be surprising if at least some of this expenditure was covered by an adulterated coinage.[28] Finally, more than any other power, Sweden's coinage was copper-based, and the period in question coincided with a substantial depreciation in the silver price of copper. Taken together, then, these observations suggest some combination of real shocks, local taxation through confiscation and devaluation as potential causes of the inflation.

From 1650 to 1750, annual price levels are only available for three countries, England, Germany and Austria. The English series has no discernible trend, while the other two series appear to drift upward, with different starting dates for the upward movement.[29] We show the three annual series in Figure 4.3 to drive home a point – namely that each of these countries experienced different inflationary and deflationary periods once the price revolution had runs its course (let us assert, by 1618). In particular, while the German and Austrian prices were correlated moderately (at 0.56), neither of these series was correlated at all with English prices. Note, though, that the fact that the trends are so similar in these series after 1618 attests to a long-run norm that must have been influenced by the world production of precious metals (since all of these countries had metallic-based money stocks). In the short run, however, there was little coordination, apparently from 1618 until the classical gold standard was put in place, just after 1870. As we shall see in Part IV of this volume, during the period of the gold standard, price levels once again conformed closely across the European countries.

While the specific inflationary episodes discussed above are interesting, it is also worth noting that the price levels show no general trend between 1618 and 1650 and perhaps a slight upward trend thereafter. Although the production of the New World gold and silver (and with it Spain's fortunes) declined substantially after 1630, total world gold production continued to grow during the period, and both world and the New World production accelerated after 1700. Referring again to the equation of exchange (Equation 4.1 above), there are three possible explanations for the unresponsiveness of European prices to these forces. First, it has been argued that the direct remittance of specie to Asia from the New World grew by roughly a factor of 2.75 between 1600 and 1750 and this was considerably faster than the specie flows into Spain and (later) Portugal combined (Attman, 1986, p. 33). Thus the growth of the *European* money supply may well have slowed relative to real economic growth. Second, despite the continued, albeit slower, growth of the money supply, velocity may have fallen during this period. As noted above, we have argued elsewhere that a decline in the velocity may be associated historically with the expansion of the 'moneyness' of the economy, which itself is an indicator of early economic growth. Such a process may well have been present between 1618 and 1750, but given the conflicting evidence on velocity discussed above, we hesitate to push this point very far. Finally, it is likely that real economic growth was rapid enough to help alleviate any inflationary pressure on prices produced by the rate of growth of the money supply.

For the period as a whole, then, we conclude that the quantity theory of money probably explains both the general trends in prices and specific episodes in which there were substantial deviations from those trends. While this conclusion may be somewhat controversial among some parties for whom certain events suggest particular local causes not related to the quantity

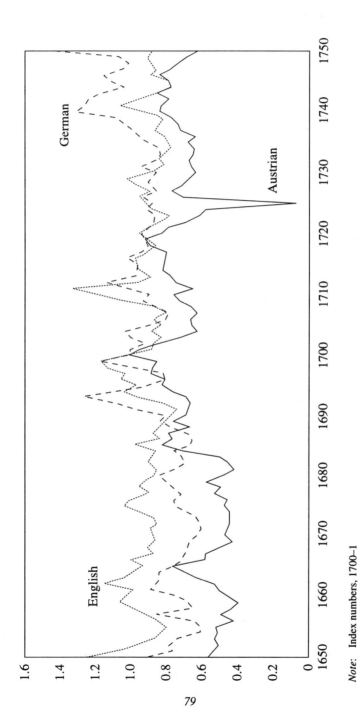

Note: Index numbers, 1700–1

Figure 4.3 Austrian, English, and German prices 1650–1750

theory, we think that the evidence presented above is strong enough to infer a pervasive role for the quantity theory.

4.   BANKING BEFORE 1750

There exists a plethora of descriptive titles for institutions engaged in financial intermediation in Western history. In his *Financial History of Western Europe* Charles Kindleberger lists 14 descriptive names of the various financial institutions (1982, p. 44).[30] He notes that some of these institutions maintained distinct titles but engaged in similar activities, while others went by the same title but performed quite different functions. By the word 'bank' we normally mean private institutions that create and in some cases issue liabilities against the assets of third parties in the process of providing what we might loosely call 'financial intermediation' products.[31] Broadly speaking, we place these institutions into five categories based on their primary functions. These include: (1) merchant banks and discount houses, which were primarily engaged in handling bills, typically though not exclusively, secured by commodities; (2) commercial banks, which accepted (initially only) deposits, issued liabilities and made loans of various types; (3) mutual savings banks and building societies, which specialized in small deposits, mortgages and small loans; (4) *crédit-mobilier* banks and investment banks, which were engaged in the underwriting of securities; and (5) mixed or universal banks that performed some combination or all of the above. Obviously, this list is neither exhaustive nor are the categories mutually exclusive, since, for example, commercial banks made mortgage loans and *crédit-mobilier* banks issued liabilities. Also, note that we have not classified these institutions by their type of ownership – that is, whether they were tightly held, joint-stock and/or limited liability organizations; rather, we have concentrated on their financial products. Finally, we should add that the numerical ordering of the categories roughly approximates the chronological evolution of banking: merchant banking financed the Age of Discovery; deposit banks emerged at that time and commercial and savings banks grew in importance in the late eighteenth and early nineteenth centuries; *crédit-mobilier* banks developed in the mid-nineteenth century; and universal banks dominated much of late-nineteenth century finance. In some form or another, all of these types of banking exist today.

The evolution of private (as opposed to central) banking followed several paths, which are related to the various financial activities discussed above. The early money changers (who had a bench or *banca*) dealt primarily in the exchange of currencies, with no element of credit involved. Eventually these dealers became exchange bankers – who remitted funds – and/or deposit bankers – who transferred funds locally and sometimes made loans. A second avenue into banking was through the short-run financing of foreign trade. With the development of the bill of exchange, it became possible for merchants to export or import, rather than to do both. Before long, some traders developed into dealers in bills of exchange. Because time elapsed between the time the bill was drawn and when it was paid a market emerged for discounting – essentially, the extension of short-term credit. These early merchant bankers, eventually, drifted into some of the other functions of banking.[32]

In this period, early modern banks spread geographically; indeed, this spread is associated with a spread of their product line. Long before the sixteenth century, international merchants and bankers were emerging in the Tuscan towns of Florence, Sienna and Lucca and later in Venice and Genoa.[33] Initially the lending was local, but over time Italian bankers became skilled in transferring monies in support of international trade. Eventually, Italian banks spread throughout Europe, especially into France, Belgium, Holland, England and Germany. Among their operations were loans to the various crowned heads of Europe, usually on security (jewels or tax assignments). By the fifteenth century, German bankers from the towns of Augsburg, Nuremburg and Regensburg emerged and were dominant in the North, largely on the basis of Bavarian silver deposits and the trade in woolens, silks and spices. They also lent to crowned heads of state – notably the Habsburgs – but a number of large loans went bad in the sixteenth century and these particular banks declined. From the sixteenth century onward, merchant (and deposit) banking was well established across most of Western and Central Europe, with Italian and German banks still in evidence in the finance of international trade.

We pursue the subsequent development of banking in later chapters, but before leaving the topic for now, it is worth recalling that central banking actually emerged at this time. For reasons discussed in Chapter 2, the evolution of central banking, in its early years, is indistinguishable from the development of private banking (and the modern nation state for that matter), with the main difference being the restrictive charters that were designed to provide both a measure of financial security for depositors and to maintain order in the financial sector. Two of the first banks chartered by a government for public use were the Bank of Barcelona (1401) and the Bank of St. George, Genoa (1407). In 1587, after debating the abolition of all private banking (because of failures), Venice established the Bank of the Rialto and later the Giro Bank (clearing bank) in 1619. These two banks undertook the public functions of transferring money and clearing mercantile payments, while providing financing to the government. The Banks of Amsterdam (1609), Hamburg (1619) and Nuremburg (1621) were then modeled after the earlier deposit and transfer banks of Venice. These banks provided money-changing, safe deposit and overdraft protection; they also accepted cheques and converted a number of currencies to a standard 'bank money' – that is, into liabilities of the bank; however, none issued banknotes and none were by charter permitted to offer loans.[34]

Historically, central or national banks were *specifically* created or reorganized to handle or facilitate the accounts of the states that chartered them, usually through the extension of credit. In time, European central banks gradually came to undertake their modern role of controling the money supply and serving as a lender of last resort. Of course, a good deal of the change occurred after the period we are currently considering. The Bank of Stockholm, organized in 1656, was divided from the beginning into two departments (an exchange bank and a lending bank) and is arguably the forerunner of the modern central bank. In 1661 this bank issued the first bank notes (currency) in Europe; these were based on reserves of copper and this probably explains why its notes were superior to coin, since the relative price of copper was such that large weights were required for even modest transactions. In 1668, the Bank of Stockholm became the Bank of Sweden when it was taken over by the state; it is, accordingly, the oldest still functioning central bank in the world.

The only other European central bank established before 1750 was the Bank of England. After several decades of internal political upheaval and wars with the Dutch and the French, the Crown's finances were, shall we say, unsteady. The Bank of England was chartered by Parliament in 1694 specifically to advance a loan to William I to make war on France. It was a private bank with public functions and was given the power to issue notes, buy and sell bullion, discount bills and make loans. It was divided into an issue department and a banking department, a division that exists to this day. The former department issued bank notes against reserves, while the latter handled the other traditional banking functions. The initial capital of the bank was lent to the government and this, as well as subsequent commercial loans, dominated the asset side of its balance sheet.

In the history of banking, the early importance of the Bank of England lies in the concentration of the various functions of banking under one roof, including deposit, transfer, issue, advance and discount. Adding to the Bank's importance, these services were offered to the state as well as to the business community. The Bank of England also acted as custodian of the nation's gold reserves and was responsible for maintaining a sound monetary system as far as possible. Its working funds were obtained by taking deposits in exchange for notes, which were issued against 100 per cent reserves, except those issued against government loans! Thus the creation of the bank allowed the money supply to grow with government debt as a reserve and any subsequent increase in debt could result in an increase in the circulation of notes. To the extent that this process caused the money stock to grow more rapidly than real economic activity, inflation resulted (*ceteris paribus*) with the side effect of reducing the real value of the government's outstanding debt. Interestingly, this 'monetization' of the national debt is one of the most prominent legacies of early central banking and continues to influence central banking in the twentieth century.

With respect to the other functions of central banks – controlling the money supply and operating as a lender of last resort – early central banks were influenced by three considerations. One was the acquisition of a monopoly of note issue; another was the restraint imposed by the metallic standard of the day, specifically in maintaining a convertible currency; and a third was a legislated constraint on note issue (such as a reserve requirement). Little controversy surrounds the acquisition of a monopoly of note issue – a bank either did or did not have it. In most cases such monopolies were obtained in the nineteenth century; by 1913 almost every central bank in Europe had a monopoly of the note issue (Craig and Fisher, 1997). As for serving as a lender of last resort, before a central bank could perform such a role its directors had to reconcile this function with the fact that they were, in most cases, directors of a privately-owned institution with a public role. In fact, with respect to the lender of last resort function, it was not until well after 1750 that this aspect of central banking was understood, appreciated and, for that matter, pursued. When it was recognized at any time, it was typically pursued through the amelioration of the effects of financial panics. We will discuss this in our cyclical reviews in later chapters in this study.

Early modern banking emerged from trade. We have argued elsewhere in this volume (and Adam Smith, among others, preceded us in that argument) that the expansion of trade was an important component of early modern growth. Did the expansion of the financial sector cause, in some sense, the expansion of trade, or was it the other way around? For our purposes, it does not really matter. At the level of generality we are forced to employ, the important feature is the logical link between the two. However, our work in other historical periods leads us to conclude that a not illogical sequence might go something like this: the expanding markets and emergence of the nation-state at the end of the middle ages led to the quest for empire and overseas treasure, which in turn fostered a growth in the intermediaries to handle the resulting transactions and contributed to a general European inflation (because of the success in obtaining specie). Once the foundations of international trading empires had been established, there was no going back. Subsequent tides of specie ebbed and flowed but labor and capital followed the inexorable growth of economic activity beyond the manor.

5.   CONCLUSIONS

It is easy to lose the influence of the financial sector amidst the stirring stories of what happened in the political and real sectors of the European economy before 1750. Traditionally, most attention has been paid to the price revolution, simply because it coincided with and was the result of European expansion internationally. However, more mundane matters were probably more important in the long run, at least in terms of establishing the foundations of modern economic growth. Most notable among these was the development of commercial banking into forms recognizable to us at the end of the twentieth century.

What drove both banking and real developments, and strongly influenced the political changes in the period, were rapidly evolving national and international marketplaces. The entrepreneurs who were behind this activity needed financial facilities as their activities outstripped their own means, and thus the important precursors to the modern global capital markets can be found dotting the European landscape of this time. Banking, that is to say, while aggressive and innovative during this period, was driven by economic activity rather than the converse. This observation does not minimize the role of financial activity, in our view, but places it in its rightful place as a vital part of the incredibly dynamic, and increasingly international, economic community over the two and a half centuries before the industrial revolution.

The price revolution, then, and the resulting argument about what caused inflation, is almost a sideshow. It is certainly true that the energetic search for specie motivated a good deal of economic activity of the speculative sort during this period, and it was also true that gold and silver swelled the monetary bases of most European countries, but at the same time it is also true – and possibly ironic – that the country that gained the most treasure – Spain – actually gained the least in real terms when the dust had finally settled on the price revolution. As to the dispute itself, little more needs to be said. The protagonists had their day in court (literally), and then the whole business was turned over to the historians of economic thought until the twentieth century, when the possibility of running an independent monetary policy that favored unemployment over inflation became a reality. In a small way, we are contributing to that discussion, but persistent inflation of the sort we are used to now did not exist at any time in the period of our study, except during the price revolution. We will, though, refer to the quantity theory of money again, for we have war finances and the gold standard to consider in later chapters.

NOTES

1. For considerably more detail on the event, the literature, and further empirical tests, see Fisher (1989).
2. According to Vilar (1977), at its peak the New World generated 300 tons of silver a year of which 170 tons were shipped directly to Europe. Calculations from figures reported in Kindleberger (1982, p. 27) indicate that the gold price of silver fell by almost 50 per cent during the hundred years following 1550.
3. We say 'if acceptable' because trend-dominated data such as these can produce misleadingly high correlations.
4. Transactions were also conducted via bills of exchange and the liabilities of deposit banks. The former were typically drawn against commodities and cleared through merchant banking houses, while the latter were deposits maintained by merchants specifically for such transactions. Bank notes were not common until much later, the Swedish Riksbank being the first European bank to issue liabilities in the form of bank notes (1661).
5. This phenomenon created profit opportunities for those with knowledge of the value of the various coins in circulation – literally, money changers.
6. These were the general rules. There were myriad exceptions and the actual fate of any particular load of bullion might have deviated substantially from this course. See Hamilton (1934) for the details.
7. By 'relatively slowly' we only mean 'substantially slower than the growth of the money stock'.
8. This scenario would hold so long as exchange rates were not flexible. Exchange rates would be fixed so long as countries on a single commodity standard, say silver, did not alter the specie content of their coins. Of course, if a country's coinage were bimetallic or if two countries maintained different commodity standards, say one gold and the other silver, then exchange rates might fluctuate with the market prices of the two commodities. Finally, debasement would devalue a country's coinage and thus alter its exchange rate.
9. See the more comprehensive lists in Hamilton (1934) and Flynn (1978).
10. See, for example, Outhwaite (1982).
11. Actually, the quantity theory had been put forward in Spain by Azpilcueta de Navarro (in 1556); furthermore, it was well established in Spain by the end of the century. See the references and discussion in Flynn (1978) and in Grice-Hutchinson (1952).
12. In fact, Kindleberger (1982, p. 27) points out that a good deal of Spanish silver was shipped *directly* from the New World to the Far East.
13. We also note that Attman may have underestimated the flow from the New World, which certainly *could* imply that even greater quantities were retained in Europe.
14. One reason profits might be 'inflated' is that wages might lag behind profits. The profit inflation argument (with reference to the period of the price revolution) occurs in Keynes (1930, pp. 152–63); Nef (1937) considers its relevance to English and French experience during the same period. See also Outhwaite (1982).
15. This observation may be accurate, but since Hammarstrom has no information on specie inflows, her statement cannot be taken as a refutation of the quantity theory, since if specie did not enter Sweden, prices would not rise!
16. The general increase in economic activity and population growth are often connected with the growing urbanization (as well as each other) of the period. See, for example, Goldstone (1984) and below.
17. Using the annual numbers for England in Wrigley and Schofield (1981), a regression of Log (Population) on trend for 1541–85 yields a compound growth rate of 0.60 per cent (when inflation was 1.30 per cent). For the 1586 to 1618 period population growth continued at 0.60 while inflation was 1.06 per cent.
18. An example in modern times of a similar phenomenon is the rapid rise in medical 'prices' in many developed countries.
19. Also see Flynn (1986). If the price index actually employed is not a chained index (such as a Divisia), then it is conceivable that it will capture the changes in relative prices

incorrectly. A fixed-weight index such as the commonly-used Laspeyres is subject to this problem (it is only absolutely correct when relative prices do not change at all; see Hicks (1946)). The indices discussed in this section are all fixed-weight Laspeyres indices and hence could give credence to relative-price effects that would not turn up in a chained index.

20. A central problem in this literature arises because of the apparent misconception that the quantity theory of money requires a constant velocity; it does not. As Friedman (1956) points out, all that is actually required is that the demand for money be stable (or, equivalently, that the velocity function be stable) for the main propositions of the quantity theory to go through.

21. We have offered a similar explanation for the generally falling velocities of the Western economies in the nineteenth century (Craig and Fisher, 1997).

22. Much of the material in this section is indebted to the discussion in Parker (1987).

23. The lack of trend also shows up in Dutch prices (van Stuijvenberg and de Vrijer, 1982), although these are available only as 10-year averages.

24. Ricardian equivalence suggests that in the long run, or present values, these options are equivalent – that is, borrowing is just future taxation (whether the taxation is by a lump sum tax or an inflation rate). Having noted this, we are willing to acknowledge that these options might yield different effects in the short run, especially in that they appear to alter incentives at the margin (if only to evade the taxes).

25. Credit may have been available *at some price* but in most cases the risk premia associated with war loans were high enough to make other means of finance more appealing.

26. Early modern European rulers were not absolute monarchs. Most had to include estates in decisions concerning major changes in the tax system.

27. This discussion of the *Kipper- und Wipperzeit* is largely based on Kindleberger (1991).

28. It is worth noting, though, that a substantial proportion of this was 'borrowed' from the soldiers in the field by simply deferring their compensation. This situation led to the mutiny of 1633, which was resolved by granting local commanders the right to settle arrears through direct – i.e. local German – 'contributions'. This was essentially 'a license to plunder' (Parker, 1987, p. 135).

29. Again, the Dutch figures also show no trend (van Stuijvenberg and de Vrijer, 1982).

30. These include merchant, private, exchange, deposit, discount, public, court, joint stock, mixed, industrial, investment, universal, *crédit mobilier*, and *banques d'affaires*. One could add mutual credit societies, building associations and postal banks among others.

31. Thus, we exclude pawnbrokers, money changers and goldsmiths from whose activities modern banking is typically, though erroneously, thought to have emerged.

32. These activities are explained in more detail in Neal (1994). The activities of goldsmiths, who accepted deposits, discounted commercial bills and eventually provided credit, also led to banking, but this was a later transformation, rather than part of the origin of modern banking, as is often presumed. In the late Middle Ages and the early modern era, the typical avenue to banking was through trade.

33. See for example the essays by Sombart, Luzatto, de Roover, and Usher in Lane and Riemersma (1953).

34. The Bank of Amsterdam made loans anyway, carrying the loans to both the city of Amsterdam and the Dutch East India Company on its books from time to time. In addition, a loan bank operated alongside the Bank of Hamburg.

5. Trade, industry and mercantilism 1500–1750

1. INTRODUCTION

Trade, both domestic and international, lies at the center of the economic expansion in this long period. Indeed, to the extent that the growth rates of international trade exceeded those in agriculture and industry, we could think of trade as a leading sector.[1] Although much of the more colorful historiography of the era emphasizes the trade in spices, silks and other exotic (by European standards) luxuries, the products shipped – locally, regionally and internationally – were primarily agricultural, including wine, timber, grain and either cloth or the materials for making cloth. Both the composition and patterns of country-specific trade are often easy to misread. On this point we agree with Brenner (1972) who argues that while, when one market died out (for whatever reason), new ones typically emerged, this process was not one of substitution but rather a direct response to the generally rising levels of real income and to the existence of many new products available throughout the West. Furthermore, the resulting expansion in trade followed the significant technological changes in shipping and finance of the preceding centuries. In the next section we survey the large body of material on the behavior of trade flows and the causal relationships between trade and the macroeconomic development of the major trading countries.[2]

In Chapter 4, we discussed the work of the quantity theorists; it turns out that many of these same economists were also *mercantilists*, at least to the extent that they extolled the virtues of a balance of trade surplus, and so at about the same time we see the early stirrings of what became, a century later, something like a school of (economic) thought with a legislative programme designed to enhance a nation's wealth. The enactment of this programme – mainly in Britain and France but also in several other countries – produced a legislative record that we consider in Section 3. We also review some modern debates over the role of mercantilism and, especially, consider the views of Keynes, who saw some elements of his own macroeconomic theories in these earlier writings, which, somewhat inconsistently, tended to be influenced by the specie-flow mechanism of the quantity theory of money.

With respect to industry or manufacturing, this era predates the formation of the factory in particular and the industrial revolution more generally. In Section 4 we emphasize Europe's pre-industrial foundations. Among these foundations were the development of a transportation infrastructure (including roads, bridges, waterways and ports) and the expansion of particular product lines (such as timber and coal); the evolution of pre-industrial technology in important industries (such as textiles and metallurgy) and the development of a proto-industrial workforce. In one sense, as we noted in Chapter 1, trade is the most fundamental of economic concepts, and as such, these topics may not seem particularly dramatic; however, coupled with the expansion of capital and the development of capital markets, these developments did, after all constitute the foundation of the much more rapid industrialization of the eighteenth century.

2.   TRADE AND COMMERCE

Perhaps the principal hypothesis concerning the growth of European trade during the early modern period is the notion that it dominated, and thus in some sense led, overall economic growth. Indeed in some of the literature trade is seen as playing such a major role that it can hardly be overestimated in terms of its contribution as an essential precursor of the Industrial Revolution. Marx claimed that modern capitalism was the product of the Renaissance and the New World discoveries. 'For', in Mantoux's words, 'the sudden growth of trade together with the increase in currency and of wealth, completely changed the economic life of western nations (1983 [1928], p. 35)'. The growth in trade that occurred during this period had both quantitative and qualitative aspects. The quantitative changes reflected a rise in the volume of international trading and was important because it made possible greater specialization within the European economy. The qualitative change reflected the extension of the price system – that is, the systematic use of pricing schemes based on the principles of supply and demand – rather than on autarky, command and/or tradition, which were more important in the medieval economy. Arguably, elements of the price system were in place since time immemorial, but there is also little doubt that what Hicks (1969) calls 'market penetration' increased its hold substantially in the centuries immediately preceding the industrial revolution.

Before examining the details of the growth in trade, it is important to consider the consequences of this growth. These include the development of specialized traders – the merchant class – and the expansion of urban communities. Through trading networks, organized and maintained by merchants, urban industry drew raw materials from a multitude of geographically dispersed mines, forests, farms and grazing lands. In return, industry distributed its products to increasingly distant users through other trading networks. In reference to English trade, Deane (1979, pp. 69–70) claims,

> ... it created a demand for the products of British industry; [it] gave access to raw materials; it helped to create an institutional structure and a business ethic which was to prove almost as effective in promoting the home-trade as it had been for the foreign trade; [it] was a prime cause of the growth of large towns and industrial centres ...

Trade also generated substantial profits, some of which were turned to other uses, and through specialization trade helped promote the growth of the incomes of every country it touched. In any event, the development of European trade and commerce from 1500 to 1750 is generally quite spectacular, for the period saw the actualization of economic gains foreshadowed in the earlier 'commercial revolution' and the contemporaneous 'age of discovery'.[3]

Early modern European explorers went forth in the name of the monarch who financed them, with the blessing of the Church and in search of economic treasure – hence the expression 'God, Gold and Glory'. In the end much of the glory tended to perish with the discoverers themselves,[4] and the authority of God's representatives on earth was challenged by the Reformation and deposed, at least in secular matters, by the modern nation state.[5] The quest for treasure, however, left social, political and economic legacies with which we still contend today.

It is hard to imagine the subsequent developments in exploration and trade and the resulting changes, economic and otherwise, in the absence of the technological changes in ocean shipping that had occurred in the two centuries prior to 1500.[6] The carvel construction technique, sternpost rudder, lateen sail and astrolabe were all developed or widely adopted in the fourteenth and fifteenth centuries. From 1500 the use of the full-rigged ship expanded; this development was accompanied by the rapid increase in size (from around 100 tons early in the fifteenth century to about 300–500 tons and more by the middle of the sixteenth century) and by the specialization in commerce, as opposed to the combined military and commercial roles of many earlier ships.[7]

In the period to 1700 these innovations in commercial shipping culminated in the development of the Dutch *fluyt*. This ship had short masts and small sails and made extensive use of pulleys and blocks to economize on labor (and increase lifting power). These devices were certainly not new, but they caught hold commercially in this particular vessel. Although the *fluyt* was slow, it was inexpensive to operate and for two centuries it dominated the important short-haul trade in Western Europe.[8] Otherwise the period saw steady improvements in the design and handling of ships and, as the fleets grew, the further development of ships designed to deal with particular products or markets. Another major innovation, and one that is frequently overlooked, was the advancement of cartography and the resulting emergence of more reliable maps. Finally, improvements in waterways (canals and rivers) and in ports kept pace and some monumental projects were undertaken in this period, such as the French canals of the seventeenth century.

Despite the importance of the creation of a worldwide sea-trading network, the full significance of intra-European trade has been obscured in the literature by the emphasis on the growth of overseas trade; indeed, quantitatively the intra-European trade is much larger than the overseas trade and deserves more emphasis than it has typically been accorded.[9] Even before the great voyages of discovery, Europe had developed a very extensive trade in commodities. The economics of this situation are easy to understand. In order for a good, X, to be profitably shipped from point A to point B, the price of X in B must be greater than its price in A, and this difference must be greater than the cost of shipping X from A to B. Since shipping costs typically varied directly with the volume and/or weight of the good, only those goods with relatively high value-to-volume or weight ratios would be shipped over long distances. A review of early modern European trading patterns confirms this observation. Bulky goods, conversely, would travel locally.

In the fifteenth century the Mediterranean region maintained trade routes running eastward by land and sea to the Orient and northwards by sea around Iberia, or by river or mountain passes to central and western Europe.[10] Mediterranean exports included foodstuffs, the most prominent of which were salt and salted victuals, olive oil, wine, cheese, dried grapes and sugar. Southern Italy and southern Spain were the principal sources of oil, while Cyprus and Crete produced wines that sold all over the Mediterranean. Exports of raw materials included wool and cotton (a re-export, that was grown in the Near East). Spanish wool, generally considered the finest in the world, was shipped to northwest Europe and northern Italy for processing. Among the minerals, copper, tin and lead were established items of trade and largely imported.[11] Copper was imported overland from central Europe and exported regionally in Venetian ships, while England was the chief source of lead and tin. The various manufactures of Mediterranean cities also found widespread markets: Italian textiles, Milanese armor, Venetian soap and glassware, Genoese paper and Spanish leather and silver goods were in demand both inside and outside the region. Perhaps the richest trade of all was the Venetian trade in imported spices. Trade with the East brought spices to the Mediterranean world together with Chinese and Persian silks, Indian calicoes, and precious stones. From Venice the spices were distributed to northern Italy, across the Alps to southern Germany, by sea to Marseilles and France, to Spanish cities and through the Straits to western and northern Europe.

Central Europe was another important trading region. It contained a relatively dense concentration of towns and considerable proto-industry. Also, the region had some of Europe's richest silver and copper deposits and was traversed by a network of roads and rivers; of the latter, the Danube and the Rhine and their tributaries were arguably the most important arteries of trade. German silver and later copper flowed towards both Italy and the Low Countries. Over time, the market became focused more and more upon Antwerp, whose prosperity rested upon a commercial alliance between Portuguese spices, German silver and copper and specie from the New World. Other commodities eventually became a major part of trade; these included cloth, canvas, linen, (all largely produced or at least processed in the Low Countries) and hops and grain.

Because it played such an important role in the early modern economy, we pause for a moment to expound on the European grain trade. Although succinctly characterizing such a complex phenomenon is impossible, there are a few macro-dimensions worth considering.[12] First and, perhaps most obviously, guided by prices, grain tended to flow from one region to another. On a day-to-day, or at least seasonal, basis this meant grain flowed from countryside to town, but it also meant that from season to season, or year to year, grain might flow from one countryside to another or from one countryside to the towns surrounding another. Second, despite the ongoing transregional trade, the production and consumption of various grains displayed a strong regional character. Oats tended to dominate diets and production as one went from south to north, with wheat dominating in the other direction, and the importance of rye grew relative to wheat and oats as one went from west to east. Barley was most common north of a line running from northwest to southeast through central Europe. Third, after controlling for these strong regional tendencies, wheat was the grain that was most closely correlated with income.[13]

The Northern European region consists of the territories running from the northern coast of the Netherlands to the Baltic. Initially the Dutch and the *Hanse* merchants dominated trade in this area until the end of the seventeenth century when the English, Scots and Scandinavians began to obtain an increasing share. In this region, we can distinguish between two trades, one seaborne, one overland, both of them in bulky goods for everyday use. Seaborne trade consisted of trade in grain, salt and salt fish, woolen cloth and furs, flax, hemp, timber and other forest products, iron and copper. Overland transport was mainly cattle which went from Denmark to the principal markets in northern Germany. The Baltic itself was the primary source of grain and salt herring in northern Europe. Indeed, demand for grain was generated by the growing population of western Europe, especially the Netherlands, which at this time included the territories that eventually became

Belgium, including the Principality of Liège, one of the most advanced manufacturing regions in the West.

The Atlantic coastline, stretching from the Straits to the Channel, may be considered a fourth European trading area. Port-to-port trade was overwhelmingly of bulk character, consisting of everyday commodities like wool, wine and salt. As with the northern European trade in general, Dutch and *Hanse* merchants had dominated until the end of the seventeenth century. France and Portugal were the two competing suppliers of sea salt to the Baltic and the lands bordering the North Sea, while grain moved in the opposite direction, all the way to Portugal and Spain. The Atlantic coastal area was also the point of departure for the most dramatic change in early modern trade – that with Asia and the Americas. In both of these trades the Iberian nations made pioneering contributions. The Portuguese monopoly of oceanic traffic to the East lasted for about a hundred years before various countries of northern Europe (the Netherlands, England and France) appeared as rivals. A common feature of all the European trade with Asia is its concentration on imports. The purpose of this trade was not to find new markets for European products but to supply Europe with spices and luxury goods. With the notable exception of weapons and ammunition, the only commodity that could be disposed of regularly in the East was specie, and large quantities of it flowed in that direction (see Attman, 1986). In the sixteenth century trade was dominated by spices, especially pepper, but during the course of the seventeenth century spices were supplemented by Indian textiles. Around 1700, these accounted for over 40 per cent of the Dutch East India Company's imports. Later on, during the early eighteenth century coffee and tea emerge as important commodities in this trade, accounting for about a quarter of the Company's imports.

The Atlantic Ocean trade differs from the Asian trade primarily by virtue of the greater colonization that took place in the New World. The primary commodities imported from the New World were precious metals from the Spanish-owned mines of Central America and later on from Peru. Other commodities shipped to Europe included sugar, tobacco and cotton. In the reverse direction, exports from Europe were quite varied and reflected the needs of the colonial communities. These included cloth, household furniture and implements, as well as wine and other consumer goods. Towards the end of the period in particular, the demand for manufactured goods of all kinds was of great importance to England, whose foreign trade, concerned for centuries chiefly with the export of wool and cloth, had lost its one-sidedness by about 1700 and became a more diversified business of supplying the wants and re-exporting the products of the colonies.

During this period the earlier dominance of the Italian regions eroded, shifting to the North Atlantic in general and the cities of Antwerp, Amsterdam and London in particular. The traditional explanation for the Dutch and English success was their creative exploitation of newly favorable maritime routes and by efficiencies in transportation services. An alternative explanation offered by Rapp (1979, p. 501) is the pursuit of competitive advantages in industrial production against Venice and other Mediterranean commercial and manufacturing centers.[14] Whatever the explanation, the Netherlands and England expanded trade with the Mediterranean region as well as with the New World.

British trade in the hundred years between 1550 and 1650 expanded dramatically – and diversified considerably. The main product of the early sixteenth century (and earlier) was wool in both its raw and processed states but significant changes occurred in the pattern of trade thereafter. A common argument is that a crisis in the wool export trade in the 1550s prompted a search for new avenues and these were found, in the form of an increasing variety of product and increasing penetration into new markets – notably into the Mediterranean.[15] We could tag this view the 'necessity breeds trade' hypothesis. In contrast to this, Brenner (1972) argues that it actually was not the traditional cloth traders, but a new set of merchants, dealing in new products and operating in different markets, that provided the source of the new developments in this century. In this the merchants had the assistance of 'exclusive rights to valuable markets' as was, indeed, the common practice in this period. While specific companies flourished and declined (the Merchant Adventurers, for example), overall British trade flourished, and new companies (such as the Levant Company) came to dominate older ones, only to perish eventually themselves. Thus it seems that aggressive entrepreneurship and not a 'crisis psychology' is what led Britain to expand and diversify as the revolution in early modern trade progressed. Furthermore, an important aspect of this trade is its emphasis on imports, a fact that attests to the strength (and stimulus) of the British home market.

Although it is hard to come by any firm data because of the diversity (and changing patterns) of trade during this period, by all accounts European trade expanded dramatically by historical comparison. For example, during the first half of the so-called 'long seventeenth century' overall British exports roughly doubled and Hill (1968) suggests that in the period from 1600 to 1640, the value of exports from London tripled. Overall, English exports were[16]

1601   £0.96 – £1.08 million
1640   £1.69 – £1.80 million

which is a gain of between 48 per cent and 87 per cent, depending on the figures one uses at the limits. Using the midpoints of the two ranges yields an average annual compounded rate of growth of 1.35 per cent, which was possibly two or three times the rate of overall economic growth during that period. This certainly creates the impression that overall growth was between ½ to 1 per cent per year in this period, based, of course, on just this evidence.

In terms of leading industries, in 1640, woolens possibly constituted 80–90 per cent of London's exports, whereas 60 years later they were only 47 per cent of England's total (Davis, 1954). In place of the old almost single-product line, England was now a diversified trader in the re-export market (up from 6 per cent to 30 per cent of the total) in American and Eastern products. By 1700 total English exports and re-exports were now £6.419 million, a more than six-fold increase from £.96 million in 1640; much of this increase came after 1650. This expansion did not necessarily follow from the mercantilist policies of the day, as some writers have asserted (see for example, Hill (1968)) but those policies were probably a contributing factor. Davis (1954), in turn, argues that sharply lower prices stimulated demand from classes that previously had not participated in mass consumption; in fact he refers to a 'collapse' of prices. We rather favor the idea that trade expanded for the usual reasons: new markets were being opened and incomes were rising. In our view this expansion 'penetrated' (to use Hicks's term) lower levels of the income distribution. This period, in a nutshell, is not unlike any other before or after, in the long period between 1500 and 1914, at least in the general characteristics of trade.

Many historians concentrate on export figures as economic indicators, and rightly so. But import figures may serve as well and there is an added bonus: the growth of imports reflects the growth of incomes in the importing country! The data for London, as an example, provide us with information at two points in time:

London Imports – £ million		
Manufacturers	Food	Raw Materials
c. 1666 1.292 (37%)	0.945 (27%)	1.258 (36%)
c. 1700 1.617 (35%)	1.583 (34%)	1.467 (31%)

Total imports passing through London averaged £3.495 million for the period 1663–1669 and £4.667 million for 1699–1701. If one were to assume that the income elasticity of the demand for imports was unitary, then this would suggest that the average annual compounded rate of growth of income was roughly 1 per cent; this actually might understate the growth rate of income,[17] but at the least, the trade figures themselves indicate that this period was not one of domestic economic stagnation.

The combination of maritime expansion and the shifting trends in continental and transcontinental trade characterizes the growth of seventeenth-century commercial capitalism. This economic expansion did not occur in a political vacuum. Indeed the expansion and how it was managed was an integral part of the emergence of the modern nation-state. Broadly speaking, the political economy of the West during the early modern era has come to be characterized as a coherent collection of policies and objectives and we now turn to an evaluation of that collection.

3. MERCANTILISM: AN EARLY MACROECONOMIC POLICY?

The English trade figures that we reviewed in the previous section suggest that the value of international trade probably grew faster (on average) than the national products of the major countries participating in this trade. This conclusion is probably not particularly surprising to most readers. The engines that produce these gains are comparative advantage, specialization and technological change in shipping. Furthermore, the time and risk components of this trade also create markets for financial intermediation. Together these influences led the overall economy in its upward direction.

Recalling from our discussion in Chapters 2 and 4 that these developments were closely linked with the rise of the modern nation state, one should not find it surprising that there is also a political dimension to the progress that we have been discussing. Specifically, in this section we consider the role of the so-called 'mercantile system' in the growth of pre-industrial trade. In particular, we explore whether or not the mercantile system was an effective force in promoting early modern growth. It follows that if, as is generally claimed, mercantilism was predicated on the proposition that a favorable trade balance is the way to increase national wealth, then one can tie up at least three loose ends in the historiography of this era: (1) the causes of the rapid growth of trade; (2) the energetic search for specie and new markets; and (3) the apparently increasing role of government in macroeconomic activity.[18]

Curiously, the clearest picture of mercantilism can be gained from its critics, both historically and in modern discussions. Adam Smith's *Wealth of Nations* (1776) was first and foremost an attack on the logic of the mercantile system and, while it is no longer fashionable to treat mercantilism as a school of thought, it is still permissible to treat it as possessing a core intellectual consensus, the focus of which was on the employment of the coercive powers of the state to manipulate the economy. This consensus, then, has six major propositions behind it (Blaug, 1985). First, there are two general ones:

1. A nation is enriched to the extent that it accumulates precious metals.
2. The regulation of international trade can produce a balance of trade surplus, which in turn will produce an inflow of precious metals into a country.

There are also four subsidiary proposals which argue that proposition 2 (and therefore proposition 1) can be achieved by:

3. Aiding domestic industry by promoting the acquisition of inexpensive raw material inputs;
4. Levying protective (import) duties on manufactured products;
5. Encouraging the export of manufactured goods (by subsidy, especially);
6. Emphasizing population growth to keep wages low so that domestic industry would tend to remain competitive.

These, taken together, define 'mercantilism' and it is easy to document their existence in the literature (mostly pamphlet) of the time.[19]

Although the quest for specie (itself identified as wealth) is the activity that motivates the system, the resulting policies were also thought to be directly productive in the development of domestic commercial and manufacturing sectors. This dimension to the policy is by no means peripheral and French mercantilists, in particular, emphasized it. More generally, it was believed that using the protection and privilege of the state to raise output prices and lower input prices would establish and expand sectors that would produce the largest and most consistent surplus on the balance of trade; some mercantilists, indeed, noticed the domestic employment aspects of this policy, as we shall discuss below. But the main event at this time was the protective policy for domestic economic enterprises. Even in the 1660s this was nothing new, but whether it was designed to shield infant industries or merely to yield economic rents to those industries able to gain protection, the former rationalization has survived to this day in both practical and academic discussions of protective policies.

The general attack on mercantilism (from Adam Smith and others) involves three major aspects of the system. The first of these concerns its tendency to concentrate on the (public) stocks of gold and silver as a measure of wealth, rather than on (say) per capita real output or consumption. It is perhaps this first point that resonates most firmly today from Smith's original attack. Indeed the entire system of national income and product accounts as the benchmark for the 'wealth of a nation' gives support to the power of Smith's refutation. The second aspect of the opposition to mercantilism is the technical point that a favorable balance of trade is neither necessary nor sufficient to induce a specie inflow, since its effect on the balance of payments could be offset by invisibles, by capital flows or by transfer payments. Indeed, comparative advantage might well lead one country to specialize in the provision of invisibles and another in goods, thereby enriching both. The third point is that a specie inflow would increase the monetary base, *ceteris paribus*, and thus tend to raise the domestic price level. This would undermine the price-competitiveness of the specie-acquiring country in world markets. This, at least, is what one deduces from the existence of a 'specie-flow mechanism' at the time and it implies that the pursuit of specie would be unproductive in the long run.[20]

Before one concludes that Smith and his Classical allies destroyed mercantilism by this powerful attack it should be firmly stated that the theory (at least its protectionist and trade balance components) gained so much force in the two centuries after Smith that it still has a considerable following among the public, governments and even the academic community. We may appreciate some of the enthusiasm for the balance of trade doctrine in the following terms. For one thing, whether or not it can be shown to enrich a country, commercial policy is a weapon that can be wielded by an aggressive state if only to attempt to impoverish one's rivals or to wrest away resources considered vital for military (or geopolitical) reasons.[21] This notion is one of the main props of the German Historical School and even Smith said that 'defense is more important than opulence'. Defense, of course, can be expanded to include 'self-sufficiency' which is the way one hears it most often in modern times.

The actual policies adopted during the early modern period – mainly by Portugal, Spain, the United Provinces, England and France – were numerous and potentially far-reaching, though to be sure they are dispersed across time and space (and some even predate the mercantilist literature of the seventeenth century). Following the voyages of Columbus, colonization of the New World was an objective of all of these governments, and immense effort was made to found this objective on a self-sustaining economic basis. The Portuguese and Spanish were the first to establish settlements in the western hemisphere.[22] While the quest for specie characterizes much of the historiography of the era, their activities were not limited to silver mining, although this was no doubt their most spectacular adventure. Soon the Dutch, English and French were involved in the Caribbean and on the North American mainland and the network of trade spread, literally, around the world.[23] The English were the first to form an East India Company (1600); the Dutch (1602) followed shortly thereafter and the French (1664) eventually followed suit. It was the practice to license trade of all sorts during the period – partly for military reasons (to establish occupation forces) and partly in order to induce private agents to put up their own capital (and military forces for that matter!) – and much of Europe's long-distance trade was tied up in this way.

Considering the risks in these activities, it is hard to see how governments could have acted otherwise, in view of their geopolitical (or simply military) objectives. Even so this trade was small relative to European trade in general and the international grain and wool trades in particular.

In *England* the prototypes of the legislation associated with mercantilism were (initially) the Navigation Acts and (later) the Corn Laws. The Navigation Act of 1651 was drafted partly in response to the high freight rates at the time and required imports to be carried in English ships or in ships of the country of origin. Ownership and origin proved to be difficult to define, so the Acts of 1660 and 1661 sought to provide for the registration of foreign-built ships in England. Eventually, all colonial trade had to be conducted on English-built and English-owned ships, commanded by a English subject and manned by a crew, at least three-quarters of whom had to be English subjects. In addition, all colonial trade with other countries had to be conducted through England. No doubt such devices redirected the flow of trade a little, especially between the United Provinces (an entrepôt) and England and particularly in certain 'enumerated' commodities, such as tobacco and sugar, which could only be exported to England from the colonies. However, in recent decades, much of the quantitative research on the Navigation Acts suggests that their net effect was economically small.[24]

While it is not immediately obvious that the Acts had much of an economic effect other than to stimulate the explicit (or, more accurately, apparent) British ownership of foreign-built ships, and while it is true that large areas of Europe and many commodities were simply unaffected by them, we nevertheless would argue that a geopolitical perspective suggests an important role for these Acts. It is difficult to imagine what the Atlantic trade might have been like in the absence of the Navigation Acts. In particular, small price or cost differentials between firms in various countries may have had tremendous effects on the resulting quantities of trade they controlled. Given that shifting combinations of the Great Powers were engaged in war with one another throughout the period, the failure to militarize trade might have threatened the perpetuation of the political regimes that passed the Acts. Indeed, the ease with which the American colonists aligned with enemies of the British Crown after the onset of the Revolution suggests Parliament's efforts to bind the Empire with economic ties were well founded on mercantile grounds. In a Smithian world, in which the nation's wealth depends on the economic prosperity of its citizens, comparative advantage and the gains from trade trump the *realpolitik* of the mercantilists, but such views did not dominate at the time and, given what the rulers considered to be a life and death struggle among themselves, it is not all that difficult to see the logic of the policies.

The Corn Laws, also, are not to be lightly dismissed as instruments of the mercantile state. The original Corn Law provided for subsidies to the export of grain when prices had fallen below a certain point and, while this feature seems to fit the mercantile system nicely, it also seems clear that it was legislation designed to protect the incomes of farmers. This is especially clear as the original Act came to be modified to regulate both imports and exports. Given the relatively low price elasticities of basic foodstuffs, the farmer (and the exchequer) clearly gained from such legislation. By the early nineteenth century the act was phrased in terms of a schedule of prices and during the inflation associated with the French wars from 1790–1815 it became necessary to raise this schedule and make it more flexible. In 1815, responding to agriculturalists demands, Parliament again revised the Corn Laws so as to prohibit importation unless domestic prices were above a certain level. In fact, England was not feeding itself at the time (and had not been for some time) and both domestic and foreign grain prices were falling, so that British farmers did not gain what they had hoped for, while British consumers were denied the even lower prices from abroad. As it turned out, the Corn Laws, like the agrarian society they served, were overcome by industrialization (and popular protest), but we think that the Corn Laws are not really part of a mercantile 'system' to enrich the nation but rather the result of special interest legislation; to some, this characterizes the mercantile system itself, but we disagree, on the grounds that such rent-seeking behavior is a natural consequence of the foundation of nation-states and arises because of a principal-agent problem that is inherent in any form of government at any time, rather than as a *defining* characteristic of one of the manifestations of this principal-agent problem (i.e. mercantilism).

The *Dutch*, as one might expect, were the proto-typically successful mercantile nation, though coming before formal mercantilism was born, this was without benefit of 'theory'. In 1602, the Dutch East India Company was formed after a series of successful voyages to the East Indies, and a combination of trading acumen, government assistance and aggressive colonization led to virtual control of the spice trade by 1680. In this the Dutch beat off the advances of the French and the English (in a series of wars). A West India Company was formed in 1621, at the time of the Dutch war with Spain, and it was especially profitable while the Thirty Years War was raging in Europe. In the pre-industrial development of the Netherlands, labor immigration was also encouraged, especially in the textile trades, and since the Dutch relied on imported goods for their re-exporting and manufacturing industries, there was little scope for aggressive protective tariff legislation, although, of course, the Dutch were able practitioners of the art of tariff warfare. Indeed, Heckscher (1935) credits the Dutch with being the first users of such devices in northern Europe (in 1359–60), in the form of a ban on English cloth.

In *France*, attempts to promote industry and to tax foreign goods in the national interest date from the mid-fifteenth century. Virtually anything one could think of as a mercantilist policy was tried, again without benefit of theory, of course. Colbert, Louis XIV's finance minister after 1661, is credited with bringing the modern form of mercantilism to France, originally, at least, because of fiscal needs. To encourage industry he sought Dutch shipbuilders, Swedish miners and German tin workers (among others). In addition, he granted monopolies, made contributions of capital and interest free loans and provided tariff protection. Regulations were also imposed to ensure quality, and the guild movement, not particularly strong in France at this time (outside Paris), was promoted as a means to ensure quality (he even had a code of commerce to be administered by the guilds). Colbert raised import duties in 1664 and then doubled them in 1667, mainly to hurt the Dutch, who retaliated.[25] A war broke out – perhaps the most obvious of the mercantilistic wars – that proved unsuccessful for the French (and the 1664 tariff levels were restored).

In the area of industrial support, it seems that in France the military and luxury industries did well, aided no doubt by the fact that the government and the wealthy provided the demand, but most of Colbert's other industrial schemes were failures, and his transportation projects – on roads, rivers and canals – were disastrous. The best example, the Canal du Midi connecting the Garonne to the Mediterranean, cost 17 million francs and returned virtually nothing. The French also formed trading companies in this period; indeed, the Company of the North (1669), the Levant Company (1670), The East India Company (1664), the West India Company (1664) and the Senegal Company (1673) were modeled on companies in existence in other countries. These efforts generally failed quickly, although government-sponsored forays into the North American fur trade and the West Indies trade were successful for a time. The East India Company, too, was revived later and made significant gains in India, especially in the first half of the eighteenth century. In all of this, one can be sure that rent-seekers swarmed around the French crown during this period.

In *Germany*, whose export trade was not vigorous in the mercantilist period, the more powerful states resorted mainly to protectionism (largely after 1670)). Notable here were the 'admonitory patents' of 1673 (of Leopold I of Bohemia and Hungary), which started a strong movement toward protection. The Prussians were included in this movement, of course (Bog, 1961). Other projects that were tried were a commercial college that was proposed for Bavaria in 1663 and actually founded in Vienna in 1666 (it failed in 1673). Johann Becher, the originator of this idea in Germany, also proposed five trading companies. The 'college' movement was vigorous in the eighteenth century, with numerous commissions, colleges and councils all over what is modern Germany and Austria. Bog (1961) seems inclined to treat these efforts, which are more along the lines of business education and promotion, as successes of mercantilism that had some positive bearing on Germany's subsequent economic achievements. However, even if promoted by mercantilists, these information-providing activities seem to fall outside the more traditional definition of mercantilism.

In *Sweden*, mercantilism, at least as an intellectual movement, probably dates from the period after 1721, that is after Sweden had lost its empire in the Great Northern War (of 1700–1721). Of course, the Sweden of the preceding hundred years offered a classic example of a country whose leaders were driven to conquer, colonize and dominate trade in the Baltic, but this activity is not, of course, necessarily mercantilist. Even so, the Swedish government promoted manufacturing as early as the beginning of the seventeenth century and, from the 1660s, protectionism was especially strong in Sweden. This stance was maintained, for the most part, until the commercial program was broadened after 1721 to include commercial education and the general support of manufacturing. Magnussen (1987), incidentally, in drawing parallels with German mercantilism at the time, explicitly rejects the rent-seeking explanation in favor of the broad view that this was the largely beneficial effect of the early rise of the industrial state.

Overall, then, when evaluating mercantilism one is struck with certain paradoxes in the literature. Adam Smith thought it a dominant system in an economic sense and many writers have mentioned its political prowess as well. Marxist economists give it credit as an early capitalist form of exploitation of the workers. The accompanying regulations on apprenticeship and the calls by mercantilist writers for a growing population in order to keep wages low were viewed as instruments of the state that emerged because of the demise of feudalism, only to be themselves replaced by a superior system of expropriation – the factory system – during the industrial revolution. Other writers have mentioned the consistency of mercantilism with the general integration of government and business as the latter turned into a flood-tide, and are especially fond of emphasizing its role in shaping the role of the corporate form of business (without which we could have no large-scale capitalism).

There are some controversial elements to this story, however. Recently it has been claimed that mercantilism was little more than a rent-seeking society whose purpose was individual gain – using the patronage and protection of the state – without the benefit to society that comes from (say) competitive market activity. Resources are created by this activity, of course, but many of them have been shown to be patently useless in the modern world – for example, the acquisition of specie reserves – and in any case purely rent-seeking behavior uses up resources (generally without any equivalent gain in overall output) while simultaneously undermining the role of the market in resource allocation. This scenario is, indeed, a likely enough one, and it certainly explains the special interests represented in the legislation of this period, but it is also argued that the wastes here are significant and the society's tendency toward stagnation has been emphasized in this literature. Here we must part company with the literature on at least three grounds. First, the figures already given suggest that all trade grew more rapidly than did real output in this period. Second, as we will see below in this chapter, real output probably grew more rapidly in the countries and regions affected by these policies than is implied in this literature. Third, the mercantile policies were piecemeal, easily recognized and easily evaded by rational economic agents. They were also a consequence of rent-seeking, not a cause.

We believe that, in terms of overall economic growth, there is little that mercantilism could have done to promote it (at least as it is conceived today) in theory, and in practice mercantilism probably did not hinder early modern growth much, if at all. In a nutshell, we think of mercantilism, at least as a coherent economic system, as something of a chimera, which existed mainly in the writings of a minor group of English writers and was legitimized mostly by Colbert, whose aggressive policies were often ill-conceived, and by Adam Smith (an opponent). The Acts that were constructed were widely scattered and served local interests/problems only temporarily. Mercantilism did not generate capitalism, because as we note below, that system had deep roots in the West, and it did not represent an engine for exploitation of the working class because the working class did not exist as such and because workers were largely unaffected by the specific devices employed. Of course for some contemporaneous policies (for example, the Statute of Artificers or the Old Poor Law) other arguments might be made, but these are not mercantilist policies, *per se*.

Keynes, in a note to the *General Theory* (1936), thought that he saw an early recognition of his emphasis on the principle of 'effective demand' in the mercantilistic system. The idea was that if a nation has chronic unemployment, then a policy that successfully restricts the foreign competition for domestic goods could easily provide assistance to the unemployment rate. This proposition, that demand is insufficient to generate full employment, implies that there are excess savings (in the system) and, of course, it also implies that other countries will not take measures to protect their own labor force. Blaug (1985) suggests that it is ridiculous to argue that there were excess savings during the period of mercantilism (1660–1776, let us say) when, he asserts, the problem was overpopulation and too *little* saving. He is probably right to criticize Keynes on his 'ineffective' demand hypothesis, and it certainly would not be particularly consistent of the mercantilists to foster growth of population in order to hold down real wages and at the same time worry about keeping their 'army of unemployed' busy. Unfortunately, the available data do not permit the formal testing of these hypotheses. In any case, this is an important debate and it does involve macroeconomic policy, which is why we have brought it up.[26]

Another macro-sounding rationale for mercantilism concerns the money supply. From 1500 to 1650 or so, Europe had a steady inflow of specie and along with this a steady rise in its monetary base (and its money supply). After 1660 there is a notable decline in the flow of specie imports and, if anything, prices either fell or were stable over the last 40 years of the century. Thus, the proposition is that countries in general were short of the medium of exchange, especially for international dealings, and, lacking any appreciation that chasing gold and silver through the balance of trade was at best a zero-sum game, sought to keep the flow going through export/import policies that they thought would bring a (net) precious metal inflow. This argument is, strictly speaking, a rationale, for no contemporary writer put it that way precisely. Indeed, if money were 'short' in some sense internationally or domestically, then one might expect a more rapid institutional development in the financial markets and that is exactly what one finds in the period, with England's modern banking system and central bank dating from that time. It is arguable, especially on the evidence of the accelerating international trade, that financial impediments were not actually a factor in this period.

The monetary aspects of mercantilism had another component. In the early modern era specie served as a strategic reserve. You may recall from Chapter 2 that this era witnessed the emergence of the modern nation state and much of the political activity at that time was aimed at nation-building. Furthermore, as we saw in the previous chapter, modern financial markets were also evolving at this time. The combination of nations and political institutions without long-run credit histories and nascent financial institutions meant that specie was literally the coin of the realm. Furthermore, specie served as more than a medium of exchange because it was also a strategic military reserve. Viewed in this light, it was easy for Adam Smith to criticize the doctrine roughly a century after the policies were put in place. It was easy because by 1776 the resulting constitutional monarchy was secure enough to put faith in its farmers, merchants, manufacturers and bankers as generators of the wealth that might be required to defend and perpetuate its reign.

4. INDUSTRIALIZATION PRIOR TO THE INDUSTRIAL REVOLUTION

During the Middle Ages, when most trade was local and most manufacturing was consumed in the local community, the town was the major location for both activities. There were established shopkeepers in some areas, but quite often agricultural and handcrafted products were brought to town on market day. As trade expanded and diversified, well before modern times, some regions began to specialize in commercial agriculture, while the same or other regions experienced rapid growth in rural handicrafts destined for local, national and even international markets. From 1500, many parts of Europe were already in this advanced stage, with substantial development often noted in southern England, the northern Low Countries, Saxony and Northern Bohemia; by 1750, as we shall see, many other areas joined this group.

In order to place the industrial revolution in a broader historical setting, de Vries (1994) proposes a concept that focuses on the economic history of the household. This concept, the 'industrious revolution', is a combination of commercial incentives and changes in tastes that preceded and prepared the way for the industrial revolution itself. In England and throughout much of northwestern Europe, a broad range of decisions made by the household increased the supply of marketed commodities and labor as well as the demand for goods offered in the marketplace. This transformation was seen in rural households using underemployed labor in proto-industrial production and in the more extensive market-oriented labor of women and children.

This major expansion of rural industry – primarily in textiles – formed a phase which many believe to be the precursor to modern industrialization in these regions. This phase is termed 'proto-industrialization'. Its primary characteristics are rural handicrafts, the 'putting-out' system and the decentralization of manufacturing. The central feature of proto-industrialization is the growth of rural industry within a specific region involving peasant participation in handicraft production for the market. Industrialization, then, evolved naturally from this as new inventions and technological innovations facilitated a larger scale in operations; the drive for greater efficiency drove these activities, and their (industrially trained and literate) workers, into the cities. The initiator of the modern version of this theory is Mendels (1972).

This activity provided important incomes either by employing women and children or by utilizing male workers in the off-season – that is, the off-season in agricultural production. Urban merchants often provided the capital for these activities, much of which was 'in kind', and the towns provided the marketing facilities. A region with farms that produced for the broad market, with good transportation facilities and established urban populations, provided the best environment for such activity. It was also useful to have an abundant supply of agricultural workers (some made available by the productivity gains described in Chapter 3, although this was not a major source of new industrial employment in most regions in view of the expansion of the agricultural sector); adequate water power and appropriate natural resources (such as minerals, timber and coal) were important as well.

Much of the recent research on the industrial revolution has focused on the extent to which it represented a discontinuity in the long-run economic progress of the West.[27] We will explore that debate in subsequent chapters, but here we offer a summary of research on the industrial foundation upon which the industrial revolution rested. There are many topics and issues to be reviewed and it is worth noting that to the extent that industrialization occurred before the industrial revolution, the latter would probably look, well, less revolutionary.[28] Broadly speaking, we might classify research on western industrialization before the mid- to late eighteenth century into four categories or schools, which include: (1) the social control school, (2) the technological change school, (3) the organization school and (4) the resource base school.[29] While we hasten to point out that these are not mutually exclusive points of view, we find that reference to one or the other does explain most of the specific differences among European nations, at least broadly, before 1750.

The *social control* school is largely associated with Marx and his intellectual descendants.[30] As we noted above, Marx viewed the early modern era as a transitional period from feudalism to capitalism. In this context the so-called 'putting out' system was the foundation for the relationships between capital and labor in a capitalistic system. Specifically, once the merchant or small-scale capitalist who organized proto-industrial production controlled, through formal ownership, both the means of production – that is the physical capital – and the materials being processed, then the relationship between capital and labor was essentially the same as that under capitalism proper. The only differences from modern capitalism would then be the lack of a centralized location for production – that is the factory – and the coordination of daily work by the clock. In a nutshell, according to this view the dominant characteristics of the proto-industrial putting-out system was its role in originating the exploitation of labor.

The second school, the *technology* school, emphasizes the technological changes of the early modern era.[31] These may be found in finance, shipping, and perhaps most importantly, mining. Here the keys to growth are in the largely organizational changes in the shipping industry, which exploited the technological changes of the previous century and which if nothing else at least provided access to new markets around the world.[32] In addition, the financial gains, such as the rise of the joint-stock company, lowered the transactions costs associated with early modern trade and industry. Finally, the technological improvements, such as improved pumps, were particularly important because they eventually contributed to the industrial revolution.

The third view, the *organizational* school, comes closest to that of Mendel's original discourse on proto-industrialization. The key here is that the human capital acquired in both the organization of the putting-out system and the primitive regimentation of the workers were precursors to the factory system. In other words, it is the converse of the social control school. While both stress the changes in the organization of economic activity, the organizational school sees those changes as the source of the efficiency rents ultimately shared between capital and labor.[33] In particular, it emphasizes the fact that industrialization often proceeded most rapidly where there had been pre-industrial activity in the rural sector. Mendels argues that the Industrial Revolution was importantly facilitated by prior proto-industrialization in those areas that prospered. This process facilitated capital accumulation, the development of market connections, the development of entrepreneurial and technical skills and agricultural progress. In the important industrial areas of Alsace, the Rhineland and Lille, a clear connection of this sort can be shown; that is, in these areas there were important handicraft industries, many market towns and a network of transportation facilities.

The fourth view of early modern industry is that of the *resource base* school. The traditional view is that industrialization was built on particular resource bases.[34] Most typically, these were specific mineral deposits (iron and copper), timber (fuel for blast furnaces and smelting), and (later) coal deposits as the most important, although potential (or existing) water transportation was probably not far behind. Here the key is matching *current* technologies with the resources they would come to exploit.[35] Because the resources were typically less expensive in the area in which they were naturally found, and because those same resources typically have relatively low value-to-weight or volume ratios, processing typically took place near the resources. The economic development of the area around Liege represents perhaps the best example of early industry based on the locational rents associated with access to resources (coal) and output markets; thus the resource base school argues that the regional character of the industrial revolution was the result of the regional character and earlier development of particular resource bases.

In all this, it seems, the resource base hypothesis makes too much of the specific location of pre-industrial activity and does not give enough weight to the mobility of both capital and labor in the face of economic opportunity. This statement is not so much a criticism as an observation, since early proto-industrial activities clearly paved the way for later developments. It is necessary, however, to emphasize that physical resources are also important, and access to coal, bulky and expensive to ship, was particularly important in promoting subsequent growth. But it took capital, labor and other inputs to get the job done!

To see the usefulness of these views of proto-industrialization, consider the record of European countries that did not prosper in the first round of industrialization (to 1800 or even later). Foremost among these was Spain, which enjoyed a relatively high standard of living around 1600 and had good transportation facilities along its southern and eastern shores. Spain had no enclosures, no substantial proto-industrial workforce and not much of a middle class either. Furthermore, the coal resources were unapproachable – and foreign coal was unavailable at a reasonable price – that is, given shipping costs. Much of Italy was in the same position, as was Hungary, southern France and Prussia, although the last named eventually prospered by the absorption of better-situated neighbors. Perhaps the best case for the hypothesis has been made by Mokyr (1976) who compares the development of the United Provinces and Belgium in these terms. In his view, Belgium jumped into the stream of industrialization pretty much at its inception, while the United Provinces, richer and well-developed in its urban centers, lacked both coal and a sizeable proto-industrial workforce.

5. CONCLUSIONS

What then can we say in concluding this discussion of the role of trade in early modern economic growth? Certainly, it is true that by most accounts trade was a 'leading sector' in this era. The relative importance of trade is illustrated in two ways. First, the narrative accounts (social and political as well as economic) of the day are filled with discussions of the importance of empire, a major component of which was the economic growth associated with imperial trade. Second, back-of-the-envelope estimates suggest that international trade expanded at rates substantially greater than those for the overall economy, which itself was expanding relatively rapidly by historical comparison.

Furthermore, the importance of trade was manifest in the moral philosophy of the era, which was dominated by the doctrine we came to know as mercantilism. The system, such as it was, was both a guiding doctrine for contemporary rulers and, retrospectively, a collection of policies and objectives that subsequently characterized the political economy of the era. At one level – that of a doctrine for long-run economic growth – mercantilism was a failed system. Its beggar-thy-neighbor protectionist properties worked against any long-run gains from trade; the specie flow mechanism undermined any gains from specie accumulation; and the unavoidable choices of winners and losers among domestic firms and industries created a rent-seeking behavior that consumed resources in the quest for what were ultimately mostly distributional favors. The net result is that we doubt that our observations on growth (via trade) would be much altered by a doctrine that actually had so little an effect in its own time.

Elsewhere in this volume we have been careful to attempt to judge economic decisions and performance relative to the prices and constraints faced by economic agents at the time.[36] In this context mercantilism – and here we mean the set of policies rather than the guiding philosophy – may yet have served a valuable function. Under the fundamental doctrine that mutually agreed-upon exchange benefits both parties, a Virginia tobacco planter might not care how much a Dutch merchant gained from the free exchange of tobacco. However, if the rulers of the United Provinces were able to parlay their cut of the Dutch merchant's gain into a military force that could defeat the forces the British Crown could muster, then mercantilism stands Clauswitz's dictum on its head: trade, and hence politics, becomes war by other means. Of course, the Virginia planter might have something to say about the matter, as indeed he eventually did; just as urban grain consumers ultimately had something to say about the Corn Laws. Nevertheless, in the end the nation states of Britain, France, the United Provinces and Spain were all able to survive and prosper, by historical standards, in this era, and so we must remember this political dimension before we set mercantilism entirely to one side.

In any event, what our survey does is establish that a good index for industrial (and commercial agricultural) growth rates can be established from figures on urbanization, exports, coal production and, for that matter, from iron production when such figures are available. In Chapter 6 we will attempt to tie all this together to produce estimates of actual real growth rates for European countries from 1500 to 1750.

NOTES

1. By 'trade' we mean roughly what today is referred to as the services sector. Since much of the early modern services sector was dedicated to mercantile pursuits, trade seems like the more appropriate term.
2. The reader should note that, following convention, we often refer to trade as taking place between countries or regions. Obviously, in practice trade typically occurs between firms or individuals who reside in, or at least transact from, a particular geographic location.
3. Here the term 'commercial revolution' refers to the collection of changes in finance that antedated the early modern era (see above, Chapter 2); there are other usages of the term.
4. The life and death of Lope Aguirre, the Wanderer, serves as a metaphor for the fate of numerous such wanderers.
5. A papal bull of 1493 granted all land 100 leagues west of the Azores (the 'line of demarcation') not claimed by a Christian prince on Christmas Day 1492 to the King (and Queen) of Spain. In the absence of subsequent secular developments, the authors, both U.S. citizens by birth, would be technically subjects of the King of Spain.
6. These developments are described in Mokyr (1990, pp. 46–47).
7. The specialization in commercial shipping coincided with the specialization in military ships – specifically, the man-of-war. To the extent this latter development represented a public good that was financed by the state, it both required the rise of and contributed to the expansion of the modern nation state (see above Chapter 2).
8. The Dutch *fluyt* did not mark any great technological breakthrough; rather it represented applications, presumably guided by experimentation, of known technologies.
9. It is worth noting that of the intra-European trade the majority, largely perishable agricultural products, was local in nature.
10. The overland trade with the East, broadly speaking, followed three paths: a northern route

led from the mouth of the Danube, along the northern coast of the Black Sea, across the Crimea to Azov on the Don, and on to Astrakhan at the mouth of the Volga on the Caspian Sea; a central route led from Byzantium across Anatolia to Trebizond on the southeast corner of the Black Sea, and on to Samarkand; a southern route led from Damascus to Baghdad and on to Samarkand. Both Damascus and Baghdad were connected to the Red Sea (as was Alexandria), which served as an artery for the trade in south sea spices. It is worth noting that all of these routes had spurs and the flow of trade through them varied considerably over time depending on the political and military fortunes of those along the routes.

11. Copper, tin and lead had been in use since antiquity. By the dawn of the early modern era, they all had particular day-to-day uses in Europe. Copper was used in subsidiary coinage, construction and marine construction. Also copper (and lead) were used in the smelting of silver. Tin alloyed with lead made solder, which was used in construction, and tin alloyed with copper made bronze. Lead, in addition to its use in solder, was, like copper, used in general construction for piping, guttering and roofing. In addition, lead served as a component of paint and as a projectile for weaponry. Finally, lead was often used to debase the coinage or in outright counterfeiting.

12. For the history of wheat specifically and other grains generally, see Collins (1993).

13. Collins (1993) argues that this fact results largely from wheat's biological characteristics, which in terms of palatability and digestibility make it generally superior to other grains typically consumed by *homo sapiens*.

14. Reed (1973, p. 177) relates this competitive advantage to the lack of market restrictions imposed by governments in order to maximize the collection of tariff revenues.

15. It was once common to link British trade figures almost entirely with exogenous events at home or, especially, abroad, and this tendency has not entirely died out. Thus, for this period, one reads that the Mediterranean had a growing population and a static food supply, the Portuguese were increasingly weak in the Indian Ocean, the gold and silver stream was deflected from Antwerp to Genoa and there was less piracy after the Turks lost at Lepanto in 1571, to use the list compiled by Ramsey (1957, pp. 38–9). These reasons are in addition to the 'cloth crisis' argument (in this case an exogenously lost market) of, for example, Fisher (1950) or Davis (1954).

16. These figures are based on those found in Minchinton (1969).

17. The assumption of a constant and unitary income elasticity might be untenable. Given the growth of the food component of imports, the overall income elasticity of the demand for imports may well have fallen during this period. Also, Davis notes that the value of import figures in 1663–1669 are overstated relative to those of 1699–1701. This, too, leads to an understated rate of growth compared to our calculation. Of course, the London market was expanding more rapidly than the country as whole during this period, a consideration that tips the scale in the other direction.

18. We say 'macroeconomic' because governments had been involved in local markets since time immemorial. What marks the (modern) period we are discussing is the attempt to control the direction of a *national* economy.

19. Thomas Mun's *England's Treasure by Forraign Trade* (1666, but written in the 1620s) is the representative mercantilist document.

20. Or, more accurately, the pursuit of specie could provide at most a short-run benefit for the successful nation.

21. In this context the criticism that mercantilism amounts to 'beggar thy neighborism' would seem like praise.

22. And importantly, they were the first to have their claims legitimized by the Pope (see above).

23. The best example of this international system was the direct flow of New World specie (largely silver) to the Far East to pay for the goods which largely went to Europe and to the Atlantic coast of North America.

24. See, for example, Clarkson (1971), who argues that the laws, at most, merely re-labeled a flow that continued to follow the same channels as before the laws took effect.

25. So did the Spanish, the German and Italian states and the English.

26. There are no hard data on savings rates, but if our conjectures about growth rates are at all accurate, savings may well not have been inadequate in this period.
27. For a summary of the issues involved, the interested reader should consult the debate between Cameron (1990) and Hartwell (1990).
28. This is in fact Cameron's (1990) point.
29. This taxonomy is derived solely for the purpose of exposition and should not be interpreted as a classification created or necessarily accepted by the authors of the pieces cited below.
30. The articles in Kriedte et al. (1981) offer a good summary of this approach.
31. Mokyr's (1990) history of technological change offers a good starting point for understanding the importance of technology in the economic development of the period. Interestingly, Mokyr's emphasis on technological change as the primary factor in the collection of events we call the industrial revolution makes the quest for precursors all the more important and leads us to a set of earlier, though clearly different, technological innovations. Perhaps it is such observations that so soured Cameron about the term 'Industrial Revolution'.
32. Here we mean, for example, the Columbian exchange, the slave trade, and the expanding trade with the Far East. The cost per ton mile between Seville and Cuba in 1575 may have been the same as was in 1475, the key technologies having been unchanged, but knowing that Cuba existed and that one could grow sugar cane there made a bit of difference.
33. 'Organizational' rents in Aoki's words (1984), 'enforcement' rents according to Bowles and Gintis (1993).
34. Nef (1964) provides perhaps the best summary of the importance of exploiting natural resources in early industrial activities.
35. Here we have to acknowledge that there is no good reason not to think of human capital (arbitrarily placed in the 'organizational' box) as just another resource. We could, then, really combine the organizational and resource base schools in order to streamline the discussion a little.
36. See for example, our discussion of early modern Spain in Chapter 2 above.

6.   Trends and cycles in the pre-industrial European economy

1.   INTRODUCTION

Let us begin with a recapitulation. What we have established in earlier chapters is that over the 250 years after 1500 there was economic growth in all of the countries that we are studying. Most obviously, as explained in Chapter 3, there was population growth. In addition, trade generally expanded as, no doubt, did the gross domestic products of every one of the countries we are considering. The agricultural sectors of these countries also expanded; this is arguable simply with reference to the growing populations, but there is a lot of direct evidence as well. In addition, there was technological change in all sectors of these modern economies, although in this period the importance of the invention and innovation in the agricultural sector is probably the greatest. Shipping and early 'industry' also experienced technological change, particularly the former. These sectors were small by modern standards for most countries but, as we know, the future lay in this direction, so we need to be firm about the identification of these seeds of modern growth. Finally, and by no means peripherally, there was growth and change in the financial sectors of these countries, and there was a trend toward more egalitarian governments aided by and even provoked by some of the economic forces that we have just identified.

Throughout our discussion, however, two topics have not been treated. One, quite simply, is the actual extent to which there was per capita growth in these countries, and the other has to do with the nature of the pre-industrial business cycle. Those tasks, but primarily the latter, are the topics of this chapter. With regard to growth, the issue is, in our minds, not whether these countries grew, but how fast they grew relative to the growth rates of their populations. That is, to what extent, and when and where, did aggregate living standards rise? We have neither the space nor the data to explore this topic as much as we would like, but in this chapter we do consider a metric, the difference between the population growth rate and the rate of urbanization, as a rough indicator of per capita growth. We will begin with that discussion in Section 6.2. Note that we are not going to say this is the only metric or, indeed, that it should be relied upon heavily, but in the final analysis we are encouraged in this line of thinking by the many instances when our metric appears to be echoed in the narrative literature about the individual countries, at least broadly speaking.

The second topic – that of the business cycle – gets us involved in one of the more perplexing debates in the literature. The problem is that much of the discussion is in terms of what are often called *cyclical* 'long waves' in economic activity. Thus, typically, the sixteenth century has an upward wave, much of the seventeenth century has a downward wave, and so on, for all of the countries we have been studying or, for that matter, for Europe as a whole. In this approach, discussions of growth and cycles are typically merged: the causes of the sixteenth century expansion are, in effect, the causes of the cyclical upturn of that century. Furthermore, again typically, any reference to short, *modern* cycles is simply suppressed in these narratives, with the cycle-initiating shocks appearing in the discussion mainly as at most random deviations from the dominant trend, unadorned with any cyclical connotation. To these writers, apparently, the 'birth of the business' cycle as we now know it occurs later than in the 1500–1750 period.

We believe, in contrast, that it is a fruitful research strategy, even for this period, to distinguish between growth and cycles. Again repeating our earlier discussion briefly, we would look for trends to be generated by factors that push an economy in one direction for some considerable period of time. In practice, the time-span involved would probably encompass a number of short cycles. In a sense our designation is little more than the division of the subject into two distinct sets of causes. For the trend, the causes are structural or, at least, enduring. For the cycle they are temporary (meaning that once the cause is removed, the economy reverts to the trend fairly rapidly). What we have in mind as trend factors *for this period* are technological change (especially in the agricultural sector), the presence or absence of *long* wars, recurring pestilence, changes in savings habits, changes in the investment environment that led to either more or less investment over long periods of time, and, possibly, enduring population change. What we have in mind for the causes of the cyclical downturns are 'shocks'.

In Chapter 1 we discussed the general nature of business cycles. There we argued that for various reasons occasionally an unanticipated 'shock' (or shocks) to either the demand or the supply side of the economy temporarily drives the economy from its long-run trend rate of growth. This phenomenon is so familiar and the literature analysing it in capitalist economies so vast that we will not pursue the topic in a modern context here, but we do want to alert the reader to our belief that this fundamental characteristic of the modern cycle was present at the dawn of the early modern era. Of course as the structure of the economy changed over time, the nature and sources of the shocks themselves changed. For example, today unanticipated monetary policies – initiated by central banks – sometimes contribute to the cyclical behavior of economic activity; the equivalent in the 1500–1750 period would be unexpected debasements or, after 1700, financial panics. Furthermore, modern cycles have largely been dominated by changes in industrial production, whether as a cause of or a reaction to events going on elsewhere. In 1500 to 1750, however, industrial production was a small fraction of total economic output and we will certainly have to look elsewhere for much of our explanation. In the modern literature also, technology shocks are often featured, especially in the 'real business cycle' approach. These, too, come from the industrial sector (or from the supply of raw inputs such as oil); in the 1500–1750 period, however, the only realistic source of such shocks is the agricultural sector where, we believe, there are no important cyclically-related technological shocks, although there certainly are 'weather shocks'.

In spite of what we have just said, we are going to present our discussion of trends and cycles in an integrated fashion. Mainly, we are guided by the literature, but in any case it is appropriate to move through our material century-by-century and country-by-country and an integrated discussion proves to be useful. However, we will begin with some general issues, starting with a discussion of our metric for per capita growth in Section 2, and then featuring a general discussion of what to look for in terms of business cycles, in Section 3. Later sections will run through the historical record, employing the perspective we will have built up through Section 3.

2. URBANIZATION BEFORE THE INDUSTRIAL REVOLUTION

While the population growth of a country provides a basis for the estimation of overall growth, it is unable, by definition, to help us at all on the more interesting question of the extent of *per capita* growth. We believe that there was per capita growth in this period, but, of course, we lack direct figures on national product. The general idea is that improvements in the technology of trade, agriculture, 'industry' and finance, and the increasing movement of goods and factors of production toward the best opportunities, spurred the growth of the urban areas that had advantages in one or more of the above activities. For example, improvements in farming, such as the enclosures that were widespread in the sixteenth century, released resources, relatively speaking, some of which, both laborers and capital, ended up in the cities where they found other employment. For another example, as trade expanded, the number of jobs in trade, and in the construction of warehouses, docks and ships, also expanded. These jobs were in the cities for the most part. Early industrialization also had this characteristic. The expansion of trade and manufacturing in the cities brought the financiers, who not only created jobs but helped improve the flow of funds and the production of useful information about profitable opportunities. The growth of urban population relative to the growth of the overall population is an index to all of this activity.

While a decline in overall mortality rates had some effect on urban growth, the primary 'proximate' cause of growth in pre-industrial European cities is immigration from the countryside; of course, some population migrated from one urban area to another. (It is worth noting that urban mortality rates generally were higher than rural rates throughout this period.) Of course, some cities experienced a decline in the level of population. Between 1300 and 1700 at least one town in five experienced such a decline. In the sixteenth century, for example, 26–30 per cent of Spanish towns and 15-21 per cent of French towns experienced declining populations. Even in England where the urban population more than doubled in the sixteenth century, about a quarter of the towns for which documentation exists were in decline in that century. The reasons for the declines are varied and generally very specifically related to the local environment, whether geographic, political or economic. One such case was the important financial capital, Bruges, which declined in the fifteenth century because of the silting-up of its port; at this time its population fell from 125,000 to 35,000. It was not until the industrial revolution that examples of decline became much rarer and European towns began to experience the explosive growth that we associate with industrialization.

Table 6.1 contains overall figures on urbanization for a set of European countries as put together by Bairoch et al. (1988). The numbers provided are for urban population and the urban percentage of the total population. These two numbers appear in the second and third columns of each set. The population figure in the first column is deduced from the other two numbers (thus it differs from the population figures given for (approximately) the same dates in Table 2. 1). We do this here for consistency within this table. In the 250 years covered in the table, the urban populations of these countries, which are the ones we are featuring in this survey, grew by 57.6 per cent. The annual growth rate of the urban population over the entire period in Table 6.1 is 0.27, while that of the total population is 0.18. If our interpretation of these numbers is at all correct, an estimate of the per capita growth rate of these economies, taken together, is the difference between these figures, which is 0.09 per cent per year. The overall growth rate of the economy, that is to say, is 0.27 per cent, while per capita growth is 0.09 per cent. This interpretation depends on how trustworthy the index of urbanization is as a guide to the extent of economic progress beyond population growth.

We should pause to note some of the interesting economy-wide figures in the table. Over the 250 years, the United Kingdom shows a very large rise in

Table 6.1 European urban population 1500–1750

	1500			1600			1700			1750		
	Population	Urban	% Urban	Population	Urban	% Urban	Population	Urban	% Urban	Population	Urban	% Urban
Aust.-Hung./ Czech.	6.67	0.32	4.8	7.96	0.39	4.9	8.98	0.44	4.9	10.68	0.78	7.3
Belgium	1.25	0.32	28.0	1.50	0.44	29.3	2.34	0.52	22.2	2.30	0.51	22.2
France	16.93	1.49	8.8	18.98	2.05	10.8	21.95	2.70	12.3	24.49	3.11	12.7
Germany	10.49	0.86	8.2	12.47	1.06	8.5	12.99	1.00	:7.7	15.91	1.40	8.8
Italy	10.00	2.21	22.1	13.27	3.00	22.6	13.41	3.03	22.6	15.51	3.49	22.5
Netherl.	0.95	0.28	29.5	1.50	0.52	34.7	1.90	0.74	38.9	1.90	0.69	36.3
Portugal	1.20	0.18	15.0	1.80	0.30	16.7	2.00	0.37	18.5	2.46	0.43	17.5
Scandin.	1.82	0.04	2.2	2.37	0.09	3.8	3.12	0.15	4.8	3.71	0.23	6.2
Spain	7.50	1.38	18.4	8.68	1.85	21.3	8.62	1.75	20.3	9.58	2.05	21.4
Switzerl.	0.59	0.04	6.8	0.91	0.05	5.5	1.19	0.07	5.9	1.30	0.10	7.7
U.K.	5.00	0.23	4.6	6.33	0.50	7.9	8.90	1.05	11.8	10.52	1.82	17.3
Total	62.40	7.38	11.83	75.77	9.95	13.13	85.40	11.82	13.84	98.36	14.61	14.85
(Less U.K.)	57.40	7.15		69.44	9.45		76.50	10.77		87.84	12.79	

Note: Total population is derived from columns 2 and 3 in each year and thus will not agree exactly with the figures in Table 2.1.

Source: Bairoch, et al. (1988).

its population (which more than doubled) and in the percentage of its population that resided in urban areas (from 4.6 per cent to 17.3 per cent). Italy, a country that had passed its early zenith, saw essentially no change in its rate of urbanization, while Spain, which had considerable urbanization in the sixteenth century, stagnated after that. Germany, whose heyday was yet to come, also showed no gain in relative urbanization in this period. We think that these numbers provide results that are consistent with those of the scholarly literature on economic growth.

Another way of looking at the data is provided by Table 6.2. Here we have calculated the compound annual growth rates for the total population and for the urban population given in Table 6. 1. These are in the first two columns for each of the four periods. The column labeled 'difference', then, is the difference between the first two columns. When it is positive, this measure indicates per capita growth of that amount for the entire economy. When negative, which is rare, the suggestion is that per capita income and product were declining. In Table 6.2, most of these countries, most of the time, had increases in per capita income. However, the increases are quite small (by modern standards) in many cases. For example, in the 'overall' set of figures, Germany, Italy, the Netherlands, Portugal, Spain and Switzerland all had per capita growth rates of less than one-tenth of one per cent per year. In these cases, the general progress would not be readily noticed at the time (or by later scholars). Furthermore, it is also quite possible that classes below the small middle class in most of these countries saw none of this gain, as is often claimed. At the other end of the spectrum, the countries making up what eventually became the United Kingdom did very well in every period and per capita growth rates were up to one half of 1 per cent per year for the sixteenth century and from 1700 to 1750. Only the Scandinavian countries consistently approached the United Kingdom in these calculations.

What the data in Table 6.2 indicate is the following. In the sixteenth century the countries of the (later) United Kingdom and the Scandinavian countries led the way, with growth rates near one half of 1 per cent per year, while the Netherlands, France and Spain were the next three countries in per capita growth. We believe that most scholars would agree with this ranking. In the seventeenth century, per capita growth rates were generally substantially lower than in the sixteenth century across Europe. Again, we believe that the historical record says exactly that, with the Thirty Years War, agricultural disasters and episodes of cholera and the plague coming in for a lot of attention in this connection. In the next half century, as industrialization picked up steam, many countries saw their urbanization rates increase. Many of those countries that did not progress in this sense were those that had no industrial presence to speak of by 1750 (Portugal, Italy and the Netherlands,

Table 6.2 Annual growth rates of European urban population 1500–1750

	1500–1600			1600–1700			1700–1750			Overall		
	Population	Urban	Difference	Population	Urban	Difference	Population	Urban	Difference	Population	Urban	Difference
Aust.-Hung/ Czech.	0.177	0.198	0.021	0.121	0.121	—	0.347	1.145	0.798	0.188	0.356	0.168
Belgium	0.182	0.229	0.047	0.445	0.167	-0.278	-0.034	0.039	0.073	0.244	0.151	-0.093
France	0.114	0.319	0.205	0.145	0.275	0.130	0.219	0.283	0.064	0.148	0.294	0.146
Germany	0.173	0.209	0.036	0.041	-0.058	-0.099	0.406	0.673	0.267	0.167	0.195	0.028
Italy	0.283	0.306	0.023	0.010	0.010	—	0.291	0.283	-0.008	0.176	0.183	0.007
Netherlands	0.457	0.691	0.234	0.236	0.353	0.117	0.000	-0.140	-0.140	0.277	0.361	0.084
Portugal	0.406	0.510	0.104	0.105	0.210	0.105	0.414	0.301	-0.113	0.287	0.348	0.061
Scandinavia	0.264	0.811	0.547	0.275	0.511	0.236	0.346	0.855	0.509	0.285	0.700	0.415
Spain	0.146	0.293	0.147	-0.007	-0.056	-0.049	0.211	0.316	0.105	0.095	0.158	0.060
Switzerland	0.433	0.223	-0.210	0.268	0.336	0.068	0.177	0.713	0.536	0.316	0.366	0.050
U.K.	0.236	0.776	0.540	0.341	0.742	0.401	0.344	1.100	0.766	0.298	0.827	0.529
Total	0.194	0.299	0.105	0.120	0.172	0.052	0.283	0.424	0.141	0.182	0.273	0.091
(Less U.K.)	0.190	0.279	0.089	0.097	0.131	0.034	0.276	0.343	0.067	0.170	0.233	0.063

Source: See Table 6.1.

in particular). In terms of simple rankings, the top five achievers in each period were as follows.

	1500–1600	1600–1700	1700–1750
1	Scandinavia	United Kingdom	Austria-Hungary/Czech
2	United Kingdom	Scandinavia	United Kingdom
3	Netherlands	France	Switzerland
4	France	Netherlands	Scandinavia
5	Spain	Portugal	Germany

The bottom three countries in these periods were the following.

	1500–1600	1600–1700	1700–1750
9	Italy	Spain	Italy
10	Austria-Hung./Czech.	Germany	Portugal
11	Switzerland	Belgium	Netherlands

In our view, these observations accord well with the narrative record for these countries.

Whether or not these figures are significant in an absolute sense, they surely have some credibility in a relative one. We expect to see the United Kingdom at the head of the table and we also expect to see lower figures for that country – and most others – in the seventeenth century. Indeed, the negative German per capita growth rate (of –0.099 per cent) in the seventeenth century, influenced as it was by the ravages of the Thirty Years War and plague, also seems plausible. Rather than continue with this discussion, however, we will move on to some general issues associated with cyclical deviations from these trends before returning to the historical record for individual countries.

3.   THE NATURE OF EARLY MODERN CYCLES

Let us begin by undertaking a general discussion of the events or shocks that were potential sources of early modern cycles or, for that matter, of changes in long-run trends. In the early modern era there were at least four not entirely unrelated elements that have typically been identified as the causes of driving the economy from its long-run trend: climatic disaster, war, specie flows and institutional change.[1] We wish to distinguish between the effects such changes might have had on the long-run trends in economic activity and the cyclical components of those trends.

Agriculture

Beginning with agriculture, one must recall that at the dawn of the modern era, the typical national economy, to the extent that such a term was meaningful, was largely agricultural. In an accounting sense, agriculture tended to dominate the economy because the agricultural sector did not generate the output necessary to support large non-agricultural sectors. By the seventeenth century, however, the typical European agricultural household generated enough of an output to feed one to two people outside the rural extended family. Clearly, trends in agricultural productivity affected urbanization, industrialization and commerce, and shocks to the agricultural sector also affected all of these other sectors.

Perhaps the most prominent events that shocked agricultural production were significant deviations from climatic norms. Given that transportation costs were relatively high and that there was a dearth of financial instruments to insure against such disasters,[2] a cold wet summer followed by a wet autumn could severely damage the yields of winter grains – wheat and rye – and two consecutive such events could produce a local or regional crisis depending upon the extent of the disaster. Even if the resulting crop failures did not lead to outright famine, they would have yielded lower nutritional consumption and, in any case, would have made the human population more susceptible to disease (and hence to further reductions in economic activity). With the exception of the epochal climatic changes that demarcate geological time, such climatic events as described above are typically cyclical, almost by definition, since human populations would necessarily adjust their economic activities in response to any noticeable effects of changes in long-run climatic trends. On the other hand, to the extent that climatic events are random, a succession of poor crop years associated with bad weather is certainly possible and to the population experiencing them such a succession might well look like a trend. Even so, poor yields in one region would increase the demand for grain from other regions and might well be associated with a cyclical upturn in that other region. We conclude that the weather probably played an important role in local and perhaps even regional cyclical behavior but could not have served as a cause of anything like a century-long economic crisis.

The discussions of agricultural shocks in the literature often confuse the effects of good and poor harvests. For example, one early modern farmer, lamenting the result of a harvest failure, asked 'Who could forget the terrible years of soaring prices ... that so harshly oppressed almost the whole of Europe?' While Abel, citing a contemporary observer, notes that 'If the price of corn became too low, the tenant farmer tended to leave his fields untilled ... A crisis arose and soon spread to the towns simply because corn was sold too cheaply' (1980, pp. 11–12). What these statements seem to mean, taken together, is that if prices were high that was bad, but if prices were low that was bad, too. Partly, this confusion results from reliance on prices as the sole indicator of economic activity. This reliance seems to be the result of the relatively plentiful data on prices and the absence of output figures. In addition what such discussions often fail to recognize is the simple distributional effects of such deviations from long-run trends. Because the demand for basic foodstuffs is inelastic, a harvest failure will result in higher incomes for farmers who generate a disproportional share of the marketable surplus – that is, those who own or manage large farms. In this case the redistribution is from the customer to the producer. The shock, clearly, would be first felt in the city, but there is no obvious reason why it would spread to the farm, at least if our observation about the elasticity of demand is correct. Conversely, an abundant harvest (a 'shock' after all), under the same assumptions, would reduce farm incomes and confer a bonus on urban dwellers in the form of lower prices. This redistribution in favor of the urban dweller could hardly be described as the negatively-used 'spreading to the town'. Nor, in either case, would the farmer abandon his enterprise, since he would certainly know that weather shocks (of short duration) are part of his economic environment. In either case, the loss of agricultural output in the wake of the bad weather was the more likely of the two shocks to produce a significant decline in real GDP.

War

From some of the literature it appears the economic effects of war are sometimes misunderstood. Although in modern times it is not uncommon for standard measures of economic output, such as gross domestic product, to increase during wars, it does not follow that such increases necessarily result in increased economic well-being for the citizens of the warring states. This, of course, is due to the greatly increased government consumption of scarce resources. Furthermore, almost inevitably, wars produce a negative effect on investment spending by means of the phenomenon known as 'crowding out'. This effect is not a shock as such, and is likely to be spread over a period longer than the war, insofar as the private capital stock is smaller than it otherwise would have been. The geographical area in which the war is fought may face economic disruption and the destruction of local infrastructure, circumstances that typically lead to a reduction in economic output. A war that disrupted agricultural production over a region of some size for a notable period of time would have had a potentially devastating effect on the economy; indeed, a short war would produce a shock and a long war a significant and enduring deviation from trend. In practice, disruptions took several forms.

The confiscation of output by military authorities reduced current civilian consumption and, if the army remained in the vicinity, reduced the incentive for future production. Also fields, fences, and structures were damaged by military activity. Diseases were introduced and/or spread as a result of mixing different populations. Finally, farm labor was often conscripted, both at home and in a conquered nation. Taken together, these negative effects on food production coupled with the exposure to new disease pools led to famine and/or a reduced capacity for work, both of which lowered output as well. Finally, it is also not necessarily the case that the economic growth that sometimes follows war is 'caused' in an economic sense by the war that preceded it, nor is it the case that the growth would not have occurred in the absence of war.

Specie Flows

In addition to climate and war, much of the traditional narrative of early modern European growth emphasizes the effects of the flows of New World specie, since this was after all the signature event of the 'price revolution'.[3] However, one must be careful to disentangle the price effects of specie flows from the effects of specie flows on *real* economic activity. In its simplest form disentangling these influences involves differentiating between expected and unexpected flows. To the extent that the flows were expected, both sides of the market would have adjusted their actions so as to offset the effects of any resulting economic changes – the most conspicuous of which would have been, according to the quantity theory of money, inflation. Based on these observations, we tend to take a rather skeptical view of the association of specie flows and the resulting inflation as indicative, in and of themselves, of either economic growth or even of real activity of a cyclical nature. Of course, discoveries of precious metals represented an increase in the purchasing power of the discoverer and provided one of the primary motives for the establishment of worldwide trading empires; the resulting expansion of trade may well have contributed both to economic growth – that is to an increase in the long-run trend rate of growth – and to deviations from that trend – that is to cycles.[4] In a nutshell, the specie flows, at least for a time, serve as a metric for expanding trade. It is expanding trade, then, that is associated with real economic growth and it is increasing international integration that provides a vehicle for cross-country influences on growth rates, business cycles *and inflation*.

Institutional Change

Finally, then, the last dramatic set of events that marked the early modern economic scene was institutional change. Among the many social, economic and political changes that separate the so-called 'modern' era from the 'middle ages' is the replacement of feudalism and manorialism with constitutional political rule and capitalism. While these concepts are too vague to be of practical use to us here, a considerable part of the conversion did take place during the early modern era, and it is exactly this process that differentiates the era from those that preceded and followed it. Unlike earlier studies, such as Hobsbawm (1954) and de Vries (1976), which emphasize the effect of these changes on the demand side of the market, we follow the contemporary economic literature on cycles and focus on the supply side.

As we noted above, if one is looking for shocks or structural changes large enough to affect substantially the pace of overall economic activity during this period, then one must look at either agriculture or trade. We have reviewed both of these subjects in earlier chapters. Here we want to emphasize that the underlying institutional changes in these sectors could have substantially altered the trends in economic growth, though by its nature, institutional change does not tend to generate year-to-year fluctuations in economic activity. In agriculture, for example, we noted the effects of enclosure, new crops and rotations, and improvements in animal husbandry, all of which proceeded over several centuries and none of which was of the type to create a temporary deviation from the trend rate of economic growth. Similarly, the creation and expansion of New World (and East Indies) trading empires was largely a private, though publicly sanctioned, enterprise that continued for roughly four centuries; thus, international trade can reasonably be said to have altered the trends in the economic growth rates of Western nations. Associated with this positive trend, however, were occasional temporary deviations in the rate at which trade expanded, sometimes related to specific military or climatic events, and these may have caused short-term deviations from the long-run trend.

We have gone to some length to lay out the types of events that are typically identified as the causes of the great cycles that supposedly characterized the early modern European economies. It might be worth noting at this point that of the four factors, three – climatic aberrations, war, and specie flows – represent potential shocks and thus should also be considered sources of cyclical behavior; whereas the structural transformation embodied in the institutional changes more likely caused a change in the long-run trend in economic growth. Having said that, we do recognize that long-term climatic change, wars that lasted decades, and specie flows that represented new international trading patterns could all legitimately have affected the long-run trend rate of growth as well. Perhaps what this discussion indicates more than anything else is that to disentangle these issues requires a close look at particular historical episodes.

4. THE 'GREAT EXPANSION' OF THE SIXTEENTH CENTURY

The sixteenth century is often characterized as one of extraordinary economic growth in Western Europe.[5] Obviously, questions concerning the rate of economic growth, at least as measured by, say, the growth of real output or output per capita, are empirical in nature; however, it is in fact not possible to construct national product figures for the sixteenth century. For one thing the necessary data are too scarce to support such calculations, and for another the notion of the nation state was in its infancy during the century; so the whole exercise of constructing gross national product figures for the sixteenth century is somewhat suspect for many countries. Having said that, it is important to keep in mind that the underlying economic activities that in the aggregate constitute national product still took place, even if the *ex post* aggregation of those figures is not possible. Of the factors that might have contributed to deviations from the long-run trend in early modern economic growth, two are typically cited as being responsible for the 'boom' of the sixteenth century: population growth and specie flows.

To give the reader some evidence of the discontinuity in population growth that marked the sixteenth century, consider that the compounded annual rate of growth of European peoples was in the neighborhood of 0.18 per cent between *c.* 1000 AD and 1450,[6] and this rate was itself almost certainly higher than that dating back to the fall of Rome.[7] Contrast that with the growth rate of 0.54 per cent between 1450 and 1600.[8] To further highlight the sixteenth century, we should also point out that population growth in the *seventeenth* century was comparable to pre-1450 rates and in some parts of Europe it was negative in the later period. It is small wonder that traditional narratives of the sixteenth century emphasize population growth as the leading economic indicator of the age.

Our discussion of population's role in economic growth (see Chapter 3), argues that it does not follow *ipso facto* that population growth *causes* economic growth and it is probably safer to say that sixteenth-century population growth reflected the relative absence of a general European war, some relief from famine and disease and the accompanying increase in per capita income, at least relative to the centuries immediately before and after, rather than being an independent cause of growth. Of course, a Malthusian on population growth would want to go further than this, but the facts appear to contradict such an interpretation rather decisively. So, to the extent that the sixteenth century as a whole was one of extraordinary economic growth and that the expansion of European population played some role in that growth, we interpret that role as *reflective* of the other factors, some of which ordinarily might have spawned a considerably lower rate of growth of population.

Turning to the details, we note that among the factors that might have contributed to higher population growth in the sixteenth century relative to the centuries immediately before or after was the absence of general European wars that marked those other centuries. The Hundred Years War ended in the first half of the fifteenth century and the Thirty Years War began in 1618. Between those two conflagrations there was no comparable military conflict of breadth, length and severity. The absence of such conflicts lowered the mortality that resulted directly from battle and indirectly from disease. Furthermore, the reduction of disease and the economic destruction associated with war surely contributed to an increase in economic output. Aside from that, it is also likely that epidemics, while far from nonexistent, were less influential in the sixteenth century. Furthermore, agricultural disasters were probably less influential, especially in the last third of the century. Put all this together and you have a more rapid rate of growth that itself would have produced the rising incomes that also directly increased the rate of growth of population (through higher living standards). Take away the three positive influences, then, and you have the seventeenth century!

The other factor that often shows up in traditional narratives of how the sixteenth century came to be so prosperous is related to the flow of specie from the New World. Before going any further with this topic, the reader should recall our discussion of the price revolution in Chapter 4. In particular, one should not confuse an increase in the money supply and the resulting increase in the price level, which was after all the end result of New World mining activities, with *real* economic growth. Employing the quantity theory of money, we note that a doubling of the money supply as a result of New World silver discoveries would ultimately lead to a doubling of prices in the long run. Even so, as with all inflationary periods, there were short-run and distributional effects from the price revolution, and those who mined the 'money', along with the Crown that sanctioned the enterprise in return for a share of the lucre, saw their share of the Empire's output increase. Although inflation was the most conspicuous consequence of these discoveries, the discoveries also contributed to an increase in world trade, to the introduction of new crops (including the potato and tobacco) into European agriculture and households, and the increased exportation of Old World crops, most notably sugar cane, to the New World. Associated with these developments, as Adam Smith emphasized, were the resulting gains from the expansion of the market. The specie flows, accordingly, might have provided a lure, but the fundamental economic activity that transformed the Western economy was not financial but increased trade – and the innovations that went with it.

Our discussion surely suggests that, aside from a few conclusions of the most general type, little is to be learned about the trends and cycles of the early modern European economy without looking at specific countries and episodes. Of course, the effect of the changing political economy of early modern Europe varied by region and across nation states, but economic patterns emerged, and so we next consider the 100-year period on a country-by-country basis. Space and the relative scarcity of data prohibit a comprehensive review of every country, but we focus on four whose varying fortunes characterize some of the more interesting and important aspects of the growth of the early modern European economy.

Spain

As we have argued elsewhere (Craig and Fisher, 1997), Spain was the archetypal great power. The consolidation of the Houses of Castile and Aragon in 1469, the reconquest of Iberia and the creation of the first worldwide empire coincided with the onset of Europe's modern era. These events probably contributed to what appears, by the economic indicators noted above, to have been a period of subsequent economic growth in Spain – a 'golden age' according to Hamilton (1934, p. 73). In Castile, for example, population growth between 1530 and 1600 was in the neighborhood of 0.25–0.50 per cent per year.[9] Furthermore, Spain's most conspicuous agricultural product was wool produced from its flocks of Merino sheep, which peaked at 3.4 million head just before 1530.[10] Although there was considerable year-to-year fluctuation in the number of sheep, after the mid-1520s the long-run trend was downward – though there were still 2.6 million head as late as 1556. Perhaps not coincidentally, the 1550s saw the beginning of a dramatic and general increase in the price of wheat relative to wool: 'The heyday of sheep depopulation was over by 1550, checked by ... the recovery of the relative profit of corn against wool' (cited in Abel, 1980, p. 114).

Although aggregate data on agricultural production before 1600 are unavailable, petitions to clear new lands for agricultural production extended back to 1514 and continued throughout the century. While some of these petitions seem to have resulted from the diminished yields on older arable, the narrative suggests that the inputs of land and labor generally rose throughout the century, which would in turn imply an increase in output, *ceteris paribus*. Wheat harvests in Castile peaked in the first decade of the seventeenth century before the onset of a long-run decline (see below), though other regions saw grain shortfalls in the late sixteenth century. To cover these shortfalls, which may have been associated with its price control policies, the Crown was importing grain – paid for with New World specie – '[a]s early as the 1570's' (Weisser, 1987, p. 311).

As we noted above, the trade in commodities and the gains to the real economy from such activities are, in the context of early modern Europe, often confused with New World specie flows. Still, given our earlier discussion of the price revolution, it is probably safe to say that the shipments of specie to Spain in the sixteenth and seventeenth centuries reflected Imperial economic activity in general and the volume of trade in particular. Indeed, trade, as measured by tonnage shipped through Seville – and specie imports, measured by value – rose steadily from early in the century, peaked in the last decade of the sixteenth century, and subsequently experienced a long-run decline. Between 1500 and 1580 tonnage through Seville grew at more than 2.7 per cent per year. Tonnage leveled off in the last decade or so of the century and over the sixteenth century as a whole the growth rate was roughly 2.2 per cent per year. Over the same period the value of specie imported into Spain grew at roughly 4.5 per cent per year. Given the overall trend in early modern Spanish economic growth, these figures would seem to be indicative of a fairly robust expansion of real economic activity.

A little arithmetic might shed some light on economic growth in Spain. Molinas and Prados de la Escosura (1989, p. 387) estimate that Spanish per capita income was 68 per cent that of the United Kingdom in 1800 and Maddison (1982, p. 9) estimates that the average annual compounded rate of growth in the United Kingdom between 1700 and 1820 was 0.83 per cent. Now, if British growth after 1700 was roughly twice as rapid as before that date, and if Spanish growth was roughly twice as rapid before 1600 as after (which seems plausible, given our discussion of the post-1600 era below) and if the Spanish and the British had comparable living standards at the end of the middle ages (which is consistent with narrative evidence), then it follows that per capita growth in sixteenth century Spain must have been in the neighborhood of 0.50–0.60 per cent per year. Such a figure would have marked a tremendous discontinuity from the growth rates of the Middle Ages.

To this point we have emphasized long-run trends; however, agricultural production, specie flows, and international trade all showed tremendous variability around those trends. For example, there were 19 cycles (peak to peak) in tonnage shipped through Seville between 1500 and 1580 or roughly one every four years. Similarly, the trough to peak change in Castilian wheat production between 1600 and 1610 averaged 38 per cent over four such cycles! These figures suggests considerable volatility.

In addition to this evidence of cycles in real activity, there were a number of financial crises during the century. The Spanish Crown either defaulted outright or at least went to the brink of bankruptcy on several occasions (most notably, 1557, 1575 and 1596) and associated with each event was the early modern equivalent of a financial panic. Interestingly, each of these crises coincides with a downturn in imports of specie. Furthermore, the late 1550s, which coincide with the war with France, was the worst period of the century for trade as measured by tonnage through Seville. The years 1575 and 1596 also coincided with substantial downturns in tonnage imported. Because the Crown's domestic and imperial activities were largely financed by New World treasure, the causality probably ran from real events to financial ones. We explore this possibility in more detail below, but in any case these observations lead us to conclude that, not unlike modern developed economies, the economy of sixteenth century Spain had a long-run positive rate of growth, perhaps even in per capita terms, around which there were numerous real and financially induced downturns.

Italy

At the end of the Middle Ages, several of the polities that in the nineteenth century consolidated to form Italy could arguably be described as the major economic powers of Europe. These were the city-states of Venice, Genoa, Milan and Florence. These entities oversaw both the physical trade in goods and the financial markets that facilitated that trade from the plains of Anatolia to the North Sea.[11] Spain's expansion to the West via the Atlantic marked its rise as a great power – a rise that coincided with the emergence of the Ottoman Turks in Europe. These events marked the beginning of the end of Italian economic prominence, but that end was not immediate. Indeed, according to Kindleberger (1993, p. 46) until the crisis of the 1620s the Genoese, at least, remained at or near the top of European financial and commercial activity.

In fact, by at least some real indicators, the sixteenth century was one of prosperity for northern Italy.[12] For example, population grew by 0.24 per cent per year over the century (Table 3.1) and the rate of growth was probably accelerating towards the end of the century. Although data on agricultural production are quite scarce, there seems to have been a similar expansion of land employed in agricultural production. Although the decline in the Venetian shipping fleet (43 per cent between 1567 and 1605) is emblematic of the onset of Venice's declining role in European trade and finance, as noted above, the close ties between Genoa's bankers and the Spanish Crown allowed the former to prosper at least until the latter's seventeenth-century defaults (see below). Similarly, although the Italian manufacturers were buffeted by the same trends in European textile markets as the Spanish wool producers, at least some of the city-states managed to specialize successfully in the production of high-end textiles. For example, between 1516 and 1604 Venetian textile production expanded at a rate of roughly 1.6 per cent per year, though with tremendous cyclical variation, to be sure; indeed, there were 25 cycles, or one every 3.5 years, and in five cases the peak-to-trough decline was 30 per cent or more! Overall, then, the available indicators of real economic activity in sixteenth-century northern Italy suggest a positive long-run trend with considerable cyclical variation.

The Netherlands

While the absence of time-series data makes discussion of cycles in the Low
Countries (at this time, formally, the Spanish Netherlands) difficult, the first
two-thirds of the sixteenth century seem to have been marked by peace and
growing prosperity; from 1568, however, the Dutch were in open revolt
against their Habsburg rulers. Although the fighting was sporadic and generally inconclusive, it lasted until the Twelve Years Truce of 1609 and by most
accounts disrupted local economic activity. Even so, the last third of the
century marks the onset of the Dutch 'golden age' and a little arithmetic
suggests that the Dutch economy must have been performing quite well at
this time. Maddison (1982, p. 9) estimates that by 1700 the per capita GDP of
the Netherlands was more than 50 per cent greater than that of the territories
that eventually composed the United Kingdom. If we again assume that
British growth in the century or so after 1700 was roughly twice what it had
been before that date, and if we assume that the British and Dutch had
comparable living standards in 1500, then the average annual compounded
rate of growth in the Netherlands between 1500 and 1700 would have been in
the neighborhood of 0.60–0.70 per cent per year. As with Spain, a growth rate
in that neighborhood must have represented a substantial discontinuity from
that obtained in previous centuries.

This growth is explained by the expansion of trade and agriculture. During
the sixteenth century the Dutch continued developing what was arguably the
most sophisticated agricultural economy in Europe and this development
may well have sustained them during the troubles of the seventeenth century
(see below). Dutch agriculture was distinguished by four characteristics:
intensive husbandry based on sophisticated rotations; a growing specialization in livestock and related products; proto-industrial production based on
agricultural products; and a liberal political economy that included well-
defined property rights and relatively efficient markets in land.

The expansion of regional and transregional trade was increasingly mani-
fested in the growing imports of grain – at this time largely from the Baltic.
This growth was accompanied by Dutch specialization in livestock production. Although the terms of trade for cheese and butter fared poorly relative to
grain during most of the sixteenth century, they did well relative to industrial
products and urban wages; in any case the relative shift from grain to livestock may have been a case of the principle of comparative advantage at
work.[13] In general, the diversification seems to have allowed the Dutch to
better weather fluctuating agricultural markets. In addition, Dutch agriculture
supplied a number of industrial products, such as madder, hemp and hops,
and also tobacco. These supported local industry and further diversified the
rural economy. Finally, the liberal property rights in land created relatively

flexible contracts and thus led to a more efficient allocation of resources than one would find elsewhere in Europe at that time. In short, although evidence on specific cycles is unavailable, by all accounts the economy was expanding rapidly during the century.

England

In England the dynastic wars that followed the Hundred Years War ended with the accession of Henry Tudor to the throne (1485), which in turn was followed by nearly a century and a half of relative domestic peace.[14] As noted above, the early part of the century saw an increase in the relative price of wool. This increase provided an incentive for the substitution of pasture for arable in British agriculture and was accompanied by a dramatic increase in enclosures. Together, these changes yielded an increase in the production of both raw wool and textile products. For example, between 1500–01 and 1553–54 the production of 'cloths' (a standardized unit for customs purposes), doubled from 70,000 to 140,000 units or at a rate of growth of 1.4 per cent per year (Coleman, 1977, p. 50 and p. 63). There were severe downturns in the period 1553–54 to 1562, a spike in 1564 and then further downturns in 1566 and 1572. After the downturn of the early 1570s, a production plateau was reached of between 100,000 and 120,000 units between *c*.1580 and *c*.1610.

Narrative evidence also suggests that the long-run trend in agricultural production was positive and back-of-the-envelope calculations indicate that the growth rate of agricultural output was in the neighborhood of 0.40–0.50 per cent per year (calculated from figures in Clay, 1984, p. 138). This trend masks major harvest failures in 1520, 1527, 1535, 1545, 1551, 1556, 1560, 1562, 1565, 1573, 1586, and 1596 or roughly one every seven or eight years. The evidence for these agricultural recessions comes mainly from the behavior of agricultural prices. Interestingly, in absolute value, as measured by shillings per quarter, these fluctuations in prices were in general not as large as those of the following century and this fact may have something to do with the characterization of the sixteenth century as one of prosperity as opposed to crisis (see below). However, as measured by deviations about the mean and convergence to the mean, the fluctuations in sixteenth-century grain prices were substantially larger than those in the seventeenth century. The coefficient of variation (the ratio of the standard deviation to the mean) for grain prices was more than five times greater for the sixteenth century than for the seventeenth. In other words, because on average prices were much lower in the sixteenth century, a fluctuation of, say, 10 shillings per quarter would have been much larger relative to the 'typical' price than similar fluctuation in the seventeenth century.

This summary of trends and cycles before 1600 has focused on an admittedly small segment of the early modern economy and the data are not well suited for the task. It follows that any true accounting of cycles during this period would include a detailed investigation of the agricultural sector. Still, our review to this point demonstrates two important facts. First, the long-run trends in real output for these economies were generally positive and above those of the previous millennium or so and second, the growing industrial sectors displayed the cyclical patterns that mark them to this day.

5. THE CRISIS (OR CRISES?) OF THE SEVENTEENTH CENTURY

In the broad generalizations that are so common in this literature, the seventeenth century in Europe is often characterized as one of 'crisis'.[15] In terms of the events which might typically have triggered economic downturns in the early modern era, the seventeenth century seems to have had each in abundance. The Thirty Years War, waged off and on between 1618 and 1648, devastated large tracts of central Europe. The migration and disruption of economic activity associated with the war probably increased the exposure to disease and contributed to lower agricultural output, and local famine. It is also likely that instances of the plague were more frequent and more severe than in the sixteenth century, particularly in the last third of the seventeenth century. Furthermore there is evidence suggesting a series of bad harvest years seriously affected Europe later in the century. As with the previous period, it is probably best to review the experiences of particular countries and regions, keeping in mind that our primary quests are for long-run trends and for short cycles.

Spain

Compared to the sixteenth century, the economic indicators in Spain suggest that at least during the first half of the seventeenth century Spain's real growth was negative.[16] Furthermore, whereas Spain's population had grown at a fairly robust rate during the previous century, its population actually fell during the seventeenth century.[17] In addition, both the trade and agricultural sectors displayed long-run negative trends during substantial portions of the century. Between 1615 and 1650 tonnage of New World shipping through Seville fell by 50 per cent; between 1610–20 and 1640 wheat harvests in central Spain fell by 40 per cent; and in some rural areas population fell by almost as much as grain production.

There were numerous cycles around these negative trends with harvest failures occurring in 1622, 1624, 1627, 1631–32 and 1637. Furthermore, as measured by population, shipping and grain production, 1627, 1631–32 and 1637 seem to have been particularly bad years.[18] To see this point, consider that, following each of these years, the previous peaks in wheat production and New World shipping were not reached again for a decade or more.

As with the crises of the late sixteenth century, there seems to have been some correlation between real and financial crises in seventeenth-century Spain. The crisis of 1627 coincided with the default and bankruptcy of the Crown. Burdened with grain imports that had to be purchased with silver, a declining tax base and (hard money) commitments to mercenary troops fighting for the Counter-Reformation, the Crown had followed a policy of currency depreciation since 1599. By the 1620s local transactions were conducted in either copper or, increasingly, credit. The wheat crops of 1622, 1624 and 1627 were the worst of the century to that point. When the Crown defaulted following the last of these, creditors called in their loans from other borrowers, and they found that the agricultural economy, which ultimately underwrote Spanish expansion, had collapsed.

Weisser's (1987) discussion of credit in the early modern Spanish economy suggests that the direction of causality probably ran from the real economic activity both to local lenders and to the Crown. Specifically, rural credit was typically advanced in the form of either cash, draft animals, implements or raw materials for proto-industrial processing. The 'collateral' for these loans, whether the loans were to be retired by cash or in kind payments, was the harvest. When the harvest failed a local crisis – real and then financial – ensued. Given both the long-run trends and the severe cyclical swings during major downturns of the 1620s and 1630s, a pessimistic view of Spain's economy during this period would seem warranted.

The cause of the stagnation of real economic activity in Spain, beginning in the seventeenth century and continuing in the eighteenth century, and which it must be concluded removed Spain from the front ranks of the great powers, must at least partly be attributed to the economic policies of the Crown. Among these were the price controls on grain, subsidies through favorable property rights to the Mesta (see Chapter 2, above) and an expansionist military policy that was costly and ultimately unsuccessful. The subsidies to the Mesta encouraged production of high-quality wool at a time when its terms of trade were becoming less favorable. The price controls on grain simultaneously led to a reduction in grain production and an increase in Crown-subsidized grain imports. As we saw, these imports had to be financed with specie. Such might have been maintained indefinitely, as long as there were no domestic harvest failures; New World shipments continued at extraordinary levels and Crown military adventures offered no competition for specie; however, these conditions did not materialize and the results were the periodic financial crises associated with the Crown's failure to service its debt.

Since these policies were typically funded with credit, one must also consider the possibility that Crown borrowing crowded out other investment. By 1673, the Crown was borrowing (short-term floating debt) at an annual interest rate of 40 per cent, which, even by the standards of the day, was an extraordinarily high rate. Furthermore, the Crown had to service its debt in specie, whereas since early in the century local transactions were conducted in depreciated (largely copper-based) currency. In fact, the Spanish Habsburgs pursued objectives that required an expanding tax base, but attempted to finance those objectives by means of policies that slowed if not impeded such expansion. In a way, the Spanish economy faced an early-modern version of stagflation.

Italy

Like Spain, much of Italy seems to have experienced economic stagnation during a substantial part of the seventeenth century.[19] Between 1600 and 1650 the population of Italy, including the Kingdom of Naples and the islands, fell by 13 per cent (0.28 per cent per year), only to recover and show a fairly robust 3 per cent annual growth rate for the rest of the century.[20] In terms of real output, narratives suggests that the textiles sector was particularly hard hit, with the brunt of decline coming in 'the poorer textiles; [whereas] richer fabrics … fared rather better' (Romano, 1974, p. 186). Still, Venetian production of 'high cloth' declined at a rate of roughly 2.5 per cent per year over the entire century. As was the case in the previous century, there was tremendous cyclical variation around that trend. There were 21 cycles, or one every 4.8 years, and, incredibly, in two-thirds of the cycles the peak-to-trough decline was 30 per cent or more! Venice saw similar long-run declines in its wool, soap and glass industries.

Both Romano (1974) and de Vries (1976) argue that the agricultural sector experienced a similar stagnation with the relatively low price of land and rents as the primary empirical evidence to support such a claim. The explanation for this decline, at least according to de Vries, is the unwise expansion of agricultural production during the previous century. Specifically, the tendency was for farmers to borrow money during the earlier period of rising prices only to see the real value of their debts rise with the (unanticipated) deflation of the seventeenth century. The alleged result was a structural shift in Italian agriculture. The simultaneous decline of urban industry and commerce and the indebtedness of the rural smallholder led many urban magnates to invest in rural estates while the former owners became lessees, marking a form of 'infeudation', which in turn led to a decline in the productivity of Italian agriculture.

Although annual data on trade figures are unavailable, the evidence from harbor and alpine tolls suggests a general stagnation. Furthermore, both the urban construction and financial services sectors seem to have suffered a general decline, with the latter also experiencing periodic crises, the worst of which occurred in 1619–1622, 1627 and 1647. These crises, like those in Spain, can be linked to Crown finance. It should be noted that since the Treaty of Cateau-Cabrésis (1559) most of Italy, with the notable exception of the Papal States and Venice, was under the control of the Spanish House of Habsburg; thus the episodes of financial crisis coincided with those of the Spanish Crown, whose primary bankers were the Genoese until the crises of the 1620s. According to Homer and Sylla (1991, pp. 130–132), the rate of discount on declared dividends at the Bank of St. George in Genoa more than doubled between 1607–1621 and 1622–1625. This increase in the discount rate was caused by a decline in the demand for the bank's liabilities, which was no doubt related to the decline in the value of the bank's assets, which were largely claims against the Spanish Crown. This discussion suggests that for Italy, like Spain, the long-run trend in several economic indicators was negative; there was tremendous variation in them; and they were accompanied by and perhaps caused several financial crises.

The Netherlands

The century following the Netherlands' declaration of independence from Spain (1568) is often characterized as the 'Dutch Golden Age'. Certainly, the population of the United Provinces expanded rapidly by historical comparison and relative to its neighbors, growing at a 0.24 per cent annual rate (Table 3. 1). Furthermore, the narrative accounts of Dutch agriculture suggest that the long-run trend in that important sector remained positive. The trend in the Dutch industrial sector, at least as indicated by textile production, seems to have followed that of agriculture. Leiden became a textile center and the production of Leiden cloth grew from 55,000 units in 1600 to a peak of 120,000 by 1660, or at an annual compounded rate of 1.30 per cent (Braudel and Spooner, 1967, p. 484). After 1660, however, production declined and by the end of the century was back at 50,000 units. There were several cycles in cloth production around these trends. In particular, the years around 1620, 1630 and 1670 witnessed severe downturns.

Dutch prosperity was tied closely to trade and perhaps no series demonstrates the potential effects of war and political instability than the Dutch trade with Iberia. Annual data on the number of Dutch ships conducting trade between Iberia and the Baltic show that prior to the Spanish prohibition of such trade in 1598 the number peaked at 194 in 1595, but fell to zero in 1607 (Israel 1989, *passim*). After the imposition of the Twelve Years Truce (1609–1621) the number rebounded to 135 in 1611 and, although there were recessions in 1612 and 1615, the number of ships peaked at 225 in 1617.

This peak was followed by a slow decline until the reimposition of the embargo in 1621 led to a low of 2 ships in 1622. The trade recovered very slowly thereafter.

Of course, the Dutch had other economic ventures to make up for the declines in the Iberian trade. For example, trade with the New World expanded rapidly during the 1610s and 1620s (de Vries, 1976, pp. 130–31) and Amsterdam became a financial center at that time. Indeed, deposits at the Bank of Amsterdam (or *Wisselbank*) increased by a factor of 10 – from 1 million to 10 million florins – between its founding in 1609 and 1650 (Spooner, 1972, p. 68). That growth represents an astounding 4.71 per cent annual rate. There were two major downturns, one *c*.1615–16 and another *c*.1645. The former seems to have been a temporary downturn, perhaps related to the recession in shipping; whereas the latter marked the onset of a general decline and deposits did not again exceed the 10 million florin mark until late in the century. Clearly, the century was not one of crisis, at least not until after 1660 or so.

England

As we saw in Chapter 2, the seventeenth century was one of political upheaval in England; however, relative to much of Europe, the English economy seems to have progressed well during much of the century. The figures in Table 3.1 show that, whereas the territories that eventually became the United Kingdom had less than 10 per cent of the population of Western and Central Europe in 1600, they accounted for nearly one-third of the population growth during the seventeenth century. De Vries (1976, pp. 75–82) argues that much of this progress resulted from structural changes in English agriculture. Although the rate of enclosure slowed somewhat from the previous century, the combination of the expansion of 'convertible' farming, including livestock production, and more attentive estate management on the part of large tenant farmers increased the marketable surplus. This qualitative description of advance in seventeenth-century English agriculture is consistent with quantitative evidence suggesting the productivity of British agriculture may have been growing steadily well before 1750 (Clark, 1993).

Other evidence suggests a positive long-run trend rate of growth as well. The value of manufactured goods imported to London grew at an average annual compounded rate of 1.5 per cent from 1622 to 1699–1701 (Clay, 1984, p. 155). This trend may mask several cycles, because it begins in 1622, which marked the beginning of a recovery from a severe downturn around 1620. Also, between 1622 and 1634–40 imports fell by 0.6 per cent per annum. Furthermore, although we do not have annual data, the wars with the Dutch (1665–67 and 1672–74) were particularly disruptive to trade. These trends and shorter cycles are reflected in the capital markets as well. Whereas the long-run rate of interest, as measured by the legal ceiling on private loans, fell from 10 to 8 per cent in 1624 and to 6 per cent in 1651 (Homer and Sylla, 1991, p. 126), the interest rate on Crown loans more than doubled after 1665 and the creation of the national debt to finance war with France in the 1690s may have resulted in some private 'crowding out'.

In addition to the cycles suggested by the trade and interest rate figures, the agricultural sector and the textile industry displayed cyclical behavior. There were major harvest failures, as measured by Winchester prices and reported by Appleby (1979, p. 881), in 1630, 1647, 1661, 1673, 1677, 1693 and 1697.[21] As noted above, although in absolute value these fluctuations were typically larger than those of the previous century, relative to the mean or typical price they were substantially lower. Although one often finds that the absolute value of the fluctuation is used as an indicator of a general crisis, we argue that it is the relative fluctuation that better indicates the shock and the potential economic problems associated with it.

In the textile industry, the years around 1620 and 1630 witnessed major declines in the export of cloths. Note that the downturn in 1630 coincided with the decline in London imports, a harvest failure, and England joining the Thirty Years War against France. Still, despite the occasional supply-side shock, both agricultural output and industrial production tended to recover relatively rapidly – relative, that is, to the experiences of Spain and Italy – and the long-run trends in England were positive.

France

There are few annual data indicating the pace of economic activity in France before 1700. Evidence on grain prices suggest major harvest crises in 1630, 1649–50, 1661, 1693 and 1697. Appleby (1979) argues that such crises tended to hit France much harder than England because of the more diversified and commercial nature of English agriculture. As our discussion in Chapter 2 indicates, the political economy of France during the seventeenth century is often contrasted somewhat unfavorably with that of the Netherlands and England. In particular, property rights and public finance are typically singled out as French 'failures' (North, 1981), but agriculture is sometimes mentioned as well (de Vries, 1976). This tradition in the literature follows naturally from the question on industrialization a century or so later: why was Britain first? Of course the work of O'Brien and Keyder (1978) raised the question: was Britain first? These issues are important to keep in mind, because Maddison's (1982) figures on per capita income suggest that at the beginning of the eighteenth century the figures for Britain and France were comparable. If that were in fact the case, and if the early modern British economy in some sense outperformed that of France, as the narrative accounts above suggest, then it follows that per capita output in France must have been greater than that of Britain sometime before, say, 1600. Yet, French population growth was a fairly robust 0.15 per cent per year during the seventeenth century (Table 3.1). Given the current state of the data, the performance of the French economy will remain something of an enigma. But it is unlikely to be as bad as much of the narrative literature implies.

6.   BUSINESS CYCLES IN ENGLAND, 1700–1750

Thanks to the work of Ashton (1959) and Mirowski (1981, 1985) it is possible to say a great deal about English business cycles in the 1700–1750 period. Indeed, this is the time-period (along with the next 80 years) in which Mirowski believes the 'birth of the business cycle' occurred. We have stated our case for disagreeing with this particular proposition, but we are in agreement with both authors that there are modern cycles in this period, at least in England. We have argued that English cycles are sometimes echoed abroad even before 1700, but we certainly had no firm proof of this to offer in Chapter 6. This continues to be the case for the short period we are now considering. The problem is that there is essentially little or no literature on cycles in 1700–1750 aside from that on those in England, and there are no data except the English. Consequently, this section concerns only England.

Let us begin with a table and a discussion of the most important series in it. Table 6.3 contains the data, all of it spanning the entire period. Of most interest is the growth rate of the Crafts–Harley (1992) index of output, a

Table 6.3   English cyclical data 1700–1750

Year	CH-Growth	Crude Death Rate	Inflation	Real Wage Index	Shares Index
1700		27.9		0.529	0.742
1701	9.44	26.7	−12.67	0.609	0.673
1702	−13.15	25.2	−0.68	0.619	0.716
1703	15.49	24.0	−5.33	0.661	0.832
1704	10.54	27.0	6.53	0.628	0.832
1705	−2.11	31.5	−6.64	0.679	0.717
1706	−15.13	26.6	6.39	0.645	0.652
1707	2.93	25.2	−8.92	0.717	0.712
1708	5.15	27.0	7.53	0.673	0.784
1709	−1.84	25.7	22.07	0.557	0.778
1710	−19.45	26.4	14.49	0.491	0.716

Table 6.3   (continued)

Year	CH-Growth	Crude Death Rate	Inflation	Real Wage Index	Shares Index
1711	17.10	28.5	11.40	0.441	0.648
1712	0.95	30.1	−28.23	0.617	0.674
1713	6.39	25.8	−6.90	0.665	0.758
1714	−3.60	28.4	6.90	0.625	0.783
1715	1.82	26.2	1.73	0.616	0.836
1716	6.54	26.5	−0.15	0.619	0.884
1717	8.49	24.9	−6.67	0.665	0.995
1718	−2.35	25.6	−4.49	0.699	1.062
1719	3.89	31.8	5.91	0.663	1.053
1720	−3.89	32.4	4.27	0.637	2.139
1721	−3.23	31.4	−4.88	0.673	0.908
1722	9.38	29.7	−8.28	0.736	0.733
1723	0.37	31.3	−5.23	0.780	0.761
1724	−4.18	30.1	12.19	0.697	0.827
1725	1.92	25.4	3.57	0.676	0.976
1726	2.63	27.7	4.43	0.649	0.907
1727	−1.49	35.5	−6.44	0.696	0.945
1728	−5.80	39.8	8.89	0.642	0.987
1729	−4.07	44.7	4.93	0.614	0.968
1730	5.25	36.2	−12.04	0.699	1.010
1731	−1.59	34.1	−7.68	0.760	1.040
1732	1.19	29.8	0.72	0.757	1.046
1733	4.63	29.0	−2.33	0.779	1.016
1734	−0.38	26.0	−4.78	0.820	0.928
1735	0.38	26.9	2.12	0.805	0.966
1736	1.50	28.1	1.89	0.794	1.078
1737	−2.26	30.6	7.79	0.736	1.099
1738	1.51	27.4	−3.10	0.759	1.086
1739	1.12	27.5	−2.84	0.782	0.999
1740	−4.93	31.1	17.73	0.664	0.969
1741	2.69	34.7	10.56	0.601	0.976
1742	−2.30	36.7	−11.38	0.678	0.985
1743	1.92	29.0	−8.24	0.739	1.018
1744	2.26	25.0	−10.54	0.826	0.992
1745	−1.88	25.2	1.93	0.811	0.983
1746	1.88	27.9	12.50	0.720	0.911
1747	2.57	28.6	−3.37	0.745	0.898
1748	2.15	28.6	4.36	0.714	0.898
1749	1.76	26.8	1.67	0.703	0.960
1750	3.42	27.5	−3.12	0.725	1.000

Sources: (1) Crafts and Harley (1992); (2)-(4) Wrigley and Schofield (1981); (5) Mirowski (1981).

series that we will also employ in Chapter 8. The Crafts–Harley series exhibits considerable volatility in the early going, with recessions suggested in 1702, 1705–6 and 1709–10. Other significant declines occur in 1714, 1718, 1720–1, 1724, 1727–9, 1737, 1740, 1742 and, possibly, 1731 and 1745. This provides a good start for our discussion, recognizing, of course, that we do not have anything like GDP in hand.

The other data in Table 6.3 are generally on a narrower basis, although the Crude Death Rate (CDR) published by Wrigley and Schofield (1981) is certainly a strong general indicator at times. This rate would help us identify population shocks in the period. These occur in 1705, possibly 1712, 1719–20, 1727–9, and 1740–2, using the sharp acceleration of the crude death rate as the indicator. The agent in these cases is primarily disease, with the plague occasionally occurring until 1720 and cholera most noticeable thereafter (especially in the early 1740s). Note that 1705, 1720–1, 1727–9 and 1740–2 also appear in the list of output recessions identified by the Crafts–Harley index in Column 1.

Another index that provides macroeconomic information is the inflation rate, in Column 3, although this variable is not without its ambiguities. Since the index is a base-weight one, with the weights never changed during the period, it would tend to overstate price-level movements. Indeed, given its narrow base (it is mostly based on foodstuffs), about all we can do is use the inflation rate to corroborate changes going on elsewhere. Rapid inflation, though, could certainly pick up significant agricultural crisis; if so, these occurred in 1709–12, 1724, 1740–1 and 1746. Rapid declines, on the other hand, usually appear to follow periods of rapid increase, but not the converse, reminding us that the inflation rate is a mean-reverting variable in this period. The reason usually given for this is the gold and silver base of the currency at the time.

There are two other variables in Table 6.3, and at this point we will join the literature on these early business cycles. Much of this is discussed in Fisher (1992), and there are more data for parts of the period discussed there. The one series we do include is Mirowski's (1981) share index. Mirowski identifies a cyclical peak in 1700–1; his share index confirms this and the Crafts–Harley index in Column 1 of the table puts the recession in 1702. Mirowski also identifies 1704 as a peak, on the same basis, and the Crafts–Harley index confirms this, with 1705–6 being recession years. The sharp rise in the death rate in 1705 supplies one factor, although there is, to be sure, no real literature on this event. Similarly 1708 provides a peak in the share index in Column 5, while 1709–10 are evidently recession years, in view of the sharp decline of real wages, a very sharp decline in the Crafts–Harley index (in 1710) and very rapid inflation in 1709–11. The crude death rate, in this case, rose in 1711–12, suggesting this might have been a result rather than a cause of the event. 1714 is a possible recession year, although we have only the Crafts–Harley index on which to base this and 1718 is another such year.

The literature on business cycles in this period begins with the infamous collapse of the South Sea Bubble in August 1720. This was a classic speculative bubble that, when it burst, took all share prices with those of the South Sea Company. This is evident in Column 5 of Table 6.3. By January 1721, shares of the South Sea Company were 15 per cent of the peak value and even the solvent East India Company was down to 38 per cent of its peak value. This was clearly a financial crisis of some magnitude. Hoppit (1986) claims that there was no general recession associated with this event and Mirowski, apparently, agrees with him. Since others do not agree (see, for example, Deane (1979) and Ashton (1959)), we need to bring some other numbers to bear on the issue. Most noticeably, the Crafts–Harley index fell in 1720 and 1721, the crude death rate was much higher in 1719–21, and real wages fell somewhat in 1720. Surely there was a recession in 1720–1 on the basis of this evidence, although the real wage decline is mostly predicated on the rise in the price level, by construction, as discussed in Chapter 3.

Mirowski advances another hypothesis about this period that is worth investigating: This is that the 1720s were like the 1930s in featuring a Great Depression. If he had called it a Great Stagnation, we could agree with him, since output figures are about the same in 1730 as they are in 1720 (by the Crafts–Harley index, but noticed, also, by Ashton (1959)), but this is, in any case, a period of little aggregate advance in the British economy, on our somewhat limited information. Looking at the details, there was a crop failure late in the decade, although the sharpest rising prices occur in 1724. There was also a collapse of an export boom in 1725 and a financial collapse in 1726 that seems to have been associated with a significant increase in bankruptcies in 1727 and 1728. The years 1723–4 show a rise in the crude death rate, but the real shock came in 1729 when the death rate reached its highest value for the entire period. This underscores the claim of an agricultural failure in those later years. We would tend to list 1724 and 1728–9 as recession years in this period, noting that Ashton puts the *peak* in the middle of the decade in 1725–6, perhaps because he weighs financial failure more heavily than we do. Ashton, incidentally, sees no recession in 1728–9.

The crude death rate was still high in 1730 and 1731, with cholera also an agent, but there appears to be no other sign of trouble in that period. In 1733 there was a financial collapse that Mirowski says was also apparent in Scotland and Amsterdam. This involved business failures and, we see in Table 6.3, a marked decline in his share index. Output, by the Crafts–Harley index, declined only mildly in 1734 and real wages were high and rising in that period, so it is hard to agree that this constituted a recession just on the strength of the financial events. We should note, though, that the much-maligned Hoffmann (1955) index shows a sharp decline in 1734; Ashton concurs in marking 1732–3 as the peak years in this period and 1737 shows a significant decline in the Crafts–Harley index and another rise in the crude death rate, but the profit index remains strong. Real wages fell in 1737 and the inflation index (not surprisingly!) rose in that year, so there is certainly the possibility of a slight recession that year.

In 1739–40 there was a run of bad weather that produced two successive bad harvests (Ashton, 1959); there was also a fuel shortage in London in 1740 and high wheat prices in 1740 and 1741. Furthermore, the building trades were depressed. There is a long (slight) dip in the Mirowski share index covering the four years 1739 to 1742 and, not surprisingly, a lot of inflation in 1740 and 1741. Real output only fell in 1740 and 1742, but the crude death rate rose sharply in 1740, 1741 and 1742. Real wages also fell sharply in 1740 and 1741. It is hard not to see a three-year recession (we would call it a depression if it weren't mainly an agricultural event) in these data. We would put the years down, incidentally, as 1740, 1741 and 1742. We note that Deane, Ashton and Mirowski would disagree, apparently.

In September 1745 there was a run on the Bank of England and a slight decline in the Crafts–Harley index. There was also a sharp decline in the Mirowski share index in 1746. Most of this event, accordingly, seems financial, although there was rapid inflation in 1746 and (by the arithmetic) a fall in real wages that year. Possibly 1745–6 was one of those rolling adjustments contained mostly in one year that modern economies sometimes make. There may have been another peak in 1748, although this does not show up in any of the series in Table 6.3. The Hoffmann index is the source of this possibility, although Mirowski also mentions a significant increase in the number of bankruptcies in 1749 and 1750. This was often a sign of trouble during this era. We are reluctant to locate a recession here, in view of the weakness of the support among the other data for such an event.

The following, then, represents the chronology of recession in this period. With confirmation from several sources, we locate recessions in the following years: 1702, 1705–6, 1709–10, 1720–1, 1724–5, 1728–9, 1734, 1740–2 and 1745. Furthermore, there is some evidence that there might have been recessions in 1714, 1718, 1737 and 1748. Ignoring the last four years mentioned, this is 16 years out of 50, which is roughly a year of recession followed by two years of expansion, on average. This reasonable result (recessions occurring in 32 per cent of the years) is typical of later periods, and not unusual or uncommon of the frequency in economies dominated by their agricultural sectors. Of course, the specific years chosen are very tentative, since a monthly dating has never been attempted, but we would be surprised if the frequencies noted here were not close to the truth. We should note, too, that we are unaware of any long cycles in this period, with the only such conjecture in the period involving merely a statistical point about the 1720s. While this material provides little help on the international cycle, we note that declines in 1705–6 during the War of the Spanish Succession, in 1720–1 at the collapse of the South Sea Bubble, in the mid-1720s when there was a collapse of exports, in 1733–4 when other capital markets appeared to have been affected and possibly in the early 1740s when there was a significant failure of the agricultural sector, might well turn up as recession years in other European countries.

7. CONCLUSION

How then can we summarize the information presented in this chapter? First, we tend to think that the characterization of the sixteenth century as a golden age followed by a century of general crisis overstates the case. Second, such characterizations either ignore the cycles running through those trends or simply confuse the two processes.

It is safe to say that most of the available economic indicators displayed long-run positive trends in Spain, Italy, the Low Countries, and England during the sixteenth century. Population, specie flows, trade, industrial and agricultural production all showed not only positive trends but probably substantial deviations from earlier trends as well. Accompanying these trends were changes in the distribution of income and in many cases sizable cyclical fluctuation. The distributional effects were largely the result of structural shifts associated with the expansion of world and regional trade and both structural and institutional changes in the agricultural sector. The scarcity of time-series data on real economic activity leads us to be cautious in identifying an international business cycle at this time, but the cycles we could identify typically resulted from local agricultural crises, which, at least in the case of Spain, were also tied to international financial markets.

For the seventeenth century, perhaps the most striking thing about the long-run trends in the economic indicators we reviewed is the divergence they show across countries. In the Italian states and Spain the trends in every series were negative for substantial portions of the century and although, given the relatively scarce nature of the data, one must be careful in interpreting the cyclical behavior of the series, the severe downturns in grain and textile production as well as trade figures accompanying the negative trends bring to mind a downward economic spiral. In England and the Netherlands, on the other hand, despite the political crises accompanying the English Civil War and the Anglo-Dutch wars, much of the century was marked by positive trends in trade, agricultural output, and population – though the Dutch decline begins after 1660. The English and Dutch economies experienced cycles in the output and trade series to be sure, but recovery from the downturns was considerably more rapid than that in either Spain or Italy, with the result that one sees much of the century as one of growth, albeit at perhaps slightly slower rates than in the centuries preceding or following it.

Much of the discussion of trends and cycles involves the role of the state in such matters. By the end of the seventeenth century the institution of the nation-state and the competition among those states we call the 'Great Powers' was well established. France and England (soon-to-be Great Britain) had established themselves as the dominant powers in terms of military and economic influence. Spain and the Netherlands had fallen to the next rung and the largely land-based powers of Sweden and Austria, the former on the rise and the latter on the decline, were arguably a little further down the ladder. Although the winds of war would blow hot and cold, the global struggle between Great Britain and France lasted until 1815. Much of the economic account of that struggle is tied up with the issue of public finance in general and 'crowding out', in particular. In a narrow sense crowding out means that state borrowing competes with private borrowing, thus driving up the interest rate and reducing private investment. In a broader sense, the notion is related to the state's employment of economic resources to achieve its objectives. In the case of the early modern Great Powers these objectives were often territorial – typically involving colonies – were pursued by military means, and, through mercantilism, ultimately displayed an economic character.

Although we have tended to play down the view of the seventeenth century as one of general crisis, we should note that the more credible proponents of such a view never relied exclusively on the time-series data on which we have placed so much emphasis. Indeed, a close reading of such accounts suggests that the crisis of the seventeenth century was not one of economic recession in the modern sense but rather a crisis of the combined economic, political and social systems. Enclosure, the putting-out system, international trade, representative government, each of which we have discussed in this and earlier chapters, represented, by historical standards, dramatic changes. These changes offered tremendous opportunity to those who took advantage of them, but at the same time they altered the distribution of economic output and in this sense created a crisis for those leaning on the existing structures. The guilds, smallholding peasants, holders of ancient feudal rights – both secular and ecclesiastical – and economic agents located in areas no longer on the primary trade routes (principally the Mediterranean), all witnessed a decline in their relative economic standing; while the merchants, larger tenant farmers, proto-industrial laborers, and those geographically positioned to capture rents from the, now more important, Atlantic trade all saw their position advance. Was the seventeenth century one of *general* crisis? We think not, since there was population growth, economic growth (even per capita) and promising technological advances in virtually every area of human activity. That some of the numbers showed up lower than in the sixteenth century is certainly true, and it is also true that countries moved up and down the economic ladder, but those living at that time must have marveled at the progress they saw; it was Samuel Pepys, after all, who pitied the Elizabethans for their living standard!

With respect to business cycles, we hesitate to push the point too much, but by the seventeenth century, the nation-states are generally well defined and the data plentiful enough to suggest something like a pan-European cycle. Using the series that we have uncovered, it looks as if there may have been downturns and/or financial crises in two or more series in two or more countries in the following years: 1615, 1619–22, 1627, c.1630, 1637, c.1647, 1661, 1693, and 1697. The common themes linking these years would seem to be harvest failures, general industrial fluctuations, and war-related trade and financial difficulties. For the next fifty years, while it is virtually certain that an early international cycle existed, we have made no attempt to locate it. What we have done, instead, is to establish a benchmark cycle for the very good English data of the time. Here we found downturns in approximately one out of every three years, from 1700–1750. To be sure, we do suggest that certain events may have been international in scope, and we identified 1705–6, 1720–1, 1725–6 and 1740–2 as the most likely candidates. We leave the further development of this topic to later research.

NOTES

1. De Vries gives a similar list as possible explanations of the 'crisis of the seventeenth century' (1976, pp. 21–25). These include 'Malthusian crises', war, the money supply, and institutional and social changes, with the last of these playing the primary role in his account. Keynes gave essentially the same list: 'harvest, plague, commercial crises and chances of war' (1930, Vol. II, p. 154).
2. The absence of modern financial instruments and crop insurance does not mean that peasants could not hedge against disaster. For example, McCloskey (1976) argues that the open field system was itself a means of insuring against the output fluctuations associated with soil and climatic variation. This view is that the diversification that came with this system could and did lower risk to the agricultural entrepreneur.
3. See above Chapter 4, *passim.*
4. Trade can be a mixed blessing to an economy in a cyclical sense. On the one hand, access to trade ameliorates the cyclical forces inherent in agrarian economies – for example, seasonal production and bad weather. On the other hand, it exposes the economy to the effects of financial crises and (other) international shocks.
5. Hamilton characterizes the sixteenth century as Spain's 'golden age' (1934, p. 73). Romano calls the century after 1480 'a hundred years ... of splendour and full maturity' in Italy (1974, p. 195). Similarly, Keynes refers to the Elizabethan era as 'the date of dates, when any level-headed person in England disposed to make money could hardly help doing so' (1930, Vol. II, p. 154). No more soberly, Guy claims that 'there is much to be said for the

view that England was economically healthier ... under the Tudors than at any time since the Roman occupation of Britain' (1984, p. 258) and Hamilton argues that economic progress in France and the Low Countries mirrored that of England (1929, p. 338).

6. These figures and calculations are for 'Christian' Europe, excluding Muscovy and Byzantium, and come from those reported in Cameron (1989, pp. 59 and 97).

7. Obviously, these measures of long-run trends obscure particular demographic events, such as the Black Death, a discontinuity in any case.

8. This rate of growth would seem to be above that reported for Europe in Table 3. 1. We have been unable to determine the exact source of the discrepancy but the period after 1450 represents a discontinuity in any case.

9. The data on the early modern Spanish economy come from Chaunu and Chaunu (1955–59), Hamilton (1934) and Weisser (1982 and 1987).

10. This peak is in the moving average of trade; the single largest volume, 45,078 tons, occurred in 1608, though the long-run trend was clearly downward by then. This statement is based on figures reported in Klein (1920).

11. It is not a coincidence that what became the financial center of the world revolved around London's Lombard Street.

12. Much of the empirical evidence in the section comes from Romani (1994) and Romano (1974).

13. The figures are from Abel (1980, p. 121).

14. The brief succession crisis on the death of Edward VI notwithstanding.

15. The classic work here is de Vries (1976).

16. The figures are from Chaunu and Chaunu (1955–59), Hamilton (1934) and Weisser (1982 and 1987).

17. Exact population figures for early modern Spain are unavailable. According to Harrison (1978, p. 1) Spain's population declined by roughly 20 per cent during the seventeenth century. Other estimates put the decline from 8.5 to 7.5 million (0. 13 per cent per year). The figures in Table 3.1, however, show a slower rate of decline.

18. The annual data for population are derived from baptisms in Castile (Weisser 1987, p. 303).

19. The discussion and figures in this section come largely from Romani (1994) and Romano (1974).

20. The figures in Table 3.1 show zero growth for Italy during the century.

21. Appleby argues that England experienced fewer and more mild subsistence crises than France because English crop and livestock portfolios were more diversified than those in France. This argument is consistent with de Vries' characterization of English agriculture.

PART III

The First Industrial Revolution in Europe
1750–1850

7. The British economy 1750–1850

1. INTRODUCTION

This chapter provides a macroeconomic perspective on the development of the British economy during the period typically referred to as that of the industrial revolution. In this period, Britain emerged as the leader of the industrial world, in terms of its early growth and subsequent dominance of the volume of industrial output and foreign trade both in finance and shipping. British agriculture, too, was at the forefront of the relatively rapid technological change that generally characterizes the age. Although we document these developments in this chapter, our main purpose is to develop certain macroeconomic themes and so we must be brief in the discussion of the more disaggregated aspects of the British economy. Of course, aggregated data are somewhat limited for the early part of the period, but for the nineteenth century there are actually quite a few data series available and so it is possible to investigate a wide range of macroeconomic questions.

The chapter begins with a discussion of population and agriculture in Sections 2 and 3, respectively. The discussion of these topics is mostly limited to presenting data characterizing these two important areas, as background, but also partly because in 1750, at least, agriculture was still a large part of the British economy. In Section 4 we discuss other key sectors in the British economy – manufacturing and finance. There is, in this early material, no really surprising information, although we do need to emphasize that many sectors of the British economy grew relatively rapidly before a traditional starting point (c.1780) for the industrial revolution. We continue by analysing industrial production indices from 1750 to 1850. These indices have been revised a number of times over the years, partly as a result of dissatisfaction with the original Hoffmann (1955) estimates and partly as a result of academic jousting on other issues. In any case the figures we report are arguably the best one can use to provide a general picture of growth and cycles over much of the period. Section 4 also features a brief discussion of the English banking sector as it evolved over the period. This material is also designed to shed light on our main topics of growth and cycles.

In Section 5 we consider the various overall measures of the British economy's performance. We look at aggregate figures as well as some disaggregated numbers (investment, consumption, and so forth) because this approach gives us some leverage on factors influencing the growth rate of the British economy. Also, in this section, we consider the evidence on the crowding out of British investment in this period. This issue merits discussion partly because growth rates up to 1815 are described as 'disappointing' by some scholars and the increased demands on the real resource base during wartime may well be the cause of this disappointment.

In Section 6 we review the record for British business cycles. This material is quite extensive and contains a surprisingly large quantity of statistical information, although this is not to say that the review yields much more than a convergence toward an acceptable set of amplitudes and dates for these events. In the course of our discussion, we discuss the relative merits of the data and review the literature. After presenting this material, we offer our best guesses as to the timing of the cyclical events in this period; we also offer some conjectures as to amplitudes. Taken together, this material provides both an economic picture of Britain and a useful starting point for the discussion of cycles in other European countries (in Chapters 8 and 9). Indeed, and this is an important theme of our subsequent chapters, cyclical events in Britain influenced other countries in this period and thus can provide a starting benchmark for *European* business cycles.

Finally, in Section 7 we briefly consider the standard of living debate as it applies to the patterns of British growth and cyclical activity in this period. While we offer a few brief conclusions in Section 8, the reader should note that our complete set of conclusions will appear in Chapter 13, when we pursue our pan-European themes for the entire 1500–1913 period.

2.   POPULATION GROWTH

Table 7.1 contains the basic figures for U.K. population growth from 1751 to 1851. Here one gets the distinct impression of a population spurt in the United Kingdom beginning after the middle of the eighteenth century. Recall from Chapter 3 that in the two centuries before 1750 the British population was growing at less than 0.30 per cent per year. Furthermore, note that the higher rates that begin around 1750 continue into the nineteenth century (actually, into the twentieth century). The table contains three different sets of figures. The broadest of these (for the United Kingdom) are from Deane and Cole (1962), but they are also the least accurate, especially before 1801. The Wrigley and Schofield (1981) calculations, on the other hand, while on a narrower basis (England alone) are arguably the best population figures for any country in this period.

Table 7.1   British population 1751–1851 (millions)

Date	English Population	Growth Rate (%)	British Population	Growth Rate (%)	U.K. Population	Growth Rate (%)
1751	5.772	0.34			10.515	0.23
1761	6.147	0.63				
1771	6.448	0.48				
1781	7.042	0.88	8.900		13.000	0.71
1791	7.740	0.94	9.700	0.86	14.500	1.09
1801	8.664	1.13	10.686	0.97	15.902	0.92
1811	9.886	1.32	12.147	1.28	18.103	1.30
1821	11.492	1.50	14.206	1.56	21.007	1.49
1831	13.284	1.45	16.368	1.42	24.135	1.39
1841	14.970	1.19	18.551	1.25	26.751	1.03
1851	16.736	1.12	20.879	1.18	27.393	0.24

Sources: English: Wrigley and Schofield (1981); United Kingdom and British: Deane and Cole (1962).

Whatever set of numbers one prefers, it is clear that population growth rates increased sharply from the 1750s to around 1830 and then trailed off somewhat after that. The extremely slow growth in the U.K. population in the 1840s is mainly the result of the mortality and migration associated with the Irish 'potato famine'. As we shall see in Chapter 10, the subsequent downward drift in the population growth rate continued, unevenly, until 1913.

Looking briefly at proximate causes, in Figure 7.1 we take advantage of the breakdown in the Wrigley and Schofield annual data on English population to exhibit both crude birth rates (CBR) and crude death rates (CDR); these are births and deaths per 1000 people. Interestingly, there is only one year (1763) in which the rate of natural increase (CBR–CDR) approached zero; indeed, the population growth rate also included in Figure 7.1 is remarkably stable over this 100-year period.

Looking more closely at the CBR and CDR figures, we see that the crude death rate declined from the 1760s, when it averaged 28.4 deaths per 1000 of the population to the 1840s (and beyond) when it averaged 23.0. The birthrate, on the other hand, rose until the second decade of the nineteenth century and then it, too, started to decline. This phenomenon, whereby *both* rates display long-run declines is known in the literature as a 'demographic transition'. This phenomenon occurs throughout the West during the nineteenth

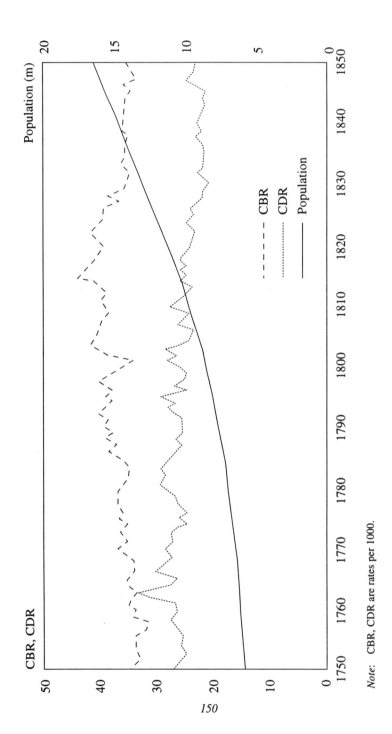

Note: CBR, CDR are rates per 1000.

Figure 7.1   English population statistics 1750–1850

century, and the United Kingdom is one of the earliest nations to experience it; in England this transition clearly started after 1815 (the peak year in the CBR). (France, as we shall see in Chapter 8, appears to have had an even earlier start). Also note that most of the long-run behavior of population growth in this period (speeding up and then slowing down) is attributable to what happened to the birthrate.

One reason for being interested in population growth is the desire to exploit the prediction of the standard economic growth model that economic growth (in the West) is generally in excess of population growth in this period. We have already explained this relationship in Chapter 1 and used it in Chapter 6. Thus one way to use Table 7.1 is to assert that it shows *minimum* estimates of the growth rates of the GDP of the United Kingdom and its constituents over this period. However, later in this chapter we will be able to demonstrate that actual growth rates are often greater than population growth rates.

Another important component of British demography during this period was the rate of urbanization. Here again we are motivated by the thought that, given the structure of the economy at that time, the growth of urban population contributed to (and possibly measured) overall economic growth and the following figures surely suggest the main developments of U.K. urbanization for the 100-year period we are considering.

In Table 7.2, then, we find that many of the larger U.K. cities grew very rapidly in both of the (admittedly arbitrary) 50-year periods, with 1800–1850 showing an acceleration (in seven of eleven cases) compared with the 1750 to 1800 period as well as in comparison with the overall figures at the bottom of the table. The cities with an accelerated growth are marked with an asterisk in the table; these are, typically, the industrial and commercial centers of Britain. Indeed, these comparisons would be even more remarkable were we to use British rather than U.K. figures (seven of nine cases).

The bottom of the table also indicates clearly that (overall) urbanization proceeded faster than population growth, since the urban percentage increased (17.3 to 22 per cent). From the source (Bairoch et al., 1988), the growth rate of urban population was 1.23 per cent from 1750 to 1850. This rate is close to the 1.17 per cent reported for 11 cities in the table and close to, at least, some of the estimates of the overall growth rate for the British economy for this period, as we shall see below.

As our discussion in the previous chapters suggests, we are using demographic developments as indicators of economic activity rather than as causal factors. In other words, population growth and the trends in urbanization were responses to the broad structural changes taking place in the British economy after 1750 and we now turn to the discussion of those changes.

Table 7.2   Population of major U.K. cities 1750–1850 (thousands)

City	Circa 1750	1800–1	1850–1	Growth Rates (%) 1750–1800	1800–1850
Belfast	9	37	103	2.83	2.05
Birmingham	24	74	233	2.25	2.29*
Bradford	–	13	104	–	4.16
Bristol	45	64	137	0.70	1.52*
Dublin	90	165	272	1.21	1.00
Edinburgh	57	83	202	0.75	1.78*
Glasgow	24	77	357	2.33	3.07*
Leeds	16	53	72	2.40	0.61
Liverpool	22	80	376	2.58	3.10*
London	675	1117	2685	1.01	1.75*
Manchester	18	90	303	3.22	2.43
Sheffield	12	31	135	1.90	2.94*
Total	992	1784	4979	1.17	2.05*
Urban (%)	17.3	20.8	22.0e	1.20e	1.26e
U.K. Pop. (m)	10.515	15.902	27.393	0.83	1.11e

Notes: Asterisk indicates higher growth rate in second period.

Sources: Population: Mitchell (1992); Urbanization: Bairoch et al. (1988). The figures marked by 'e' were deduced from the growth rates and percentages given in Bairoch.

3.   AGRICULTURAL GROWTH

The steady progress of the British agricultural sector over the eighteenth century contributed to population growth, urbanization and growth in other sectors. In our view agriculture both stimulated and responded to real growth and human capital development as well as generating raw materials for industry and commerce. This view is not really controversial. By the early eighteenth century, there were strong signs of vigorous agricultural growth and by the mid-eighteenth century, the effect of rising demand, as reflected in rising real land rents, was so great that dramatic changes – most notably the final erosion of the 'open field system' in England – were well under way. Not every observer sees the situation in this light, of course, and some generally pessimistic conclusions are easy to find in this literature. Our argument, at any rate, does not require an especially rapid pace of technological progress in agriculture, but could be sustained if the pace of the application of existing knowledge proves to be adequate in some economic sense. In other words, given the protective trade legislation in place at the time, if the development of British agriculture lagged substantially behind that of the rest of the economy, then it is a distinct possibility that it would have been a drag on overall economic growth. This does not appear to be the case, however.

Table 7.3   *English and Welsh agricultural output and productivity growth 1750–1850 (£m)*

		1750	1800	1850	Annual Growth Rates 1750–1800	1800–1850
1.	Volume (a)	59	88	135	0.8	0.9
2.	Real Output	28.1	36.2		0.5	
3.	Employment Index (b)	97.5	95	116	–0.0	0.4
4.	Capital (c)	195	242	353	0.4	0.8
5.	Total Factor Productivity (d)				0.6	0.5

Notes: (a) volume of output of principal commodities (in 1815 prices); (b) first figure interpolated; (c) 1851–60 prices; (d) first percentage change is 1700–1800.

Sources: Lines 1, 3, 4, 5 (Allen, 1994); Line 2 (Cole, 1981).

The figures in Table 7.3 suggest that the English (and Welsh) agricultural sectors expanded steadily between 1750 and 1850, but that agricultural output (Lines 1 and 2) probably grew more slowly than population. Looking at input growth, we see that the growth of the agricultural labor force (Line 3) was slower than the growth of the capital stock (Line 4) in both sub-periods; indeed, between 1750 and 1800 neither of these contributed much to the total output growth in Line 1. Rather, much of that growth can be attributed to a change in total factor productivity (TFP) (Line 5). Recall from our discussion in Chapter 3 that TFP is the 'residual' of growth accounting after the effect of inputs has been accounted for; it is often used as a general measure of technological change. Before 1800, 75 per cent of output growth was attributable to TFP (0.6/0.8); after 1800 the figure was still greater than 50 per cent (0.5/0.9). By the standards of the day, as we will see in subsequent chapters, this was a tremendous technical achievement.

Of course, one of the most important aspects of the information in Table 7.3 is that agricultural output did not keep up with population growth. This observation does not necessarily imply a decrease in living standards in the United Kingdom, because food imports increased considerably (Deane and Cole, 1962). In fact, what we may be observing about British agriculture is simply an outcome predicted by the theory of comparative advantage: Britain, while more productive in both agriculture and industry, specialized in the latter. Even so, while total imports increased by a factor of five during the eighteenth century, the share of total imports attributed to foodstuffs increased by 50 per cent (Engerman, 1994, p. 190).

As we can see from the employment index in Table 7.3, employment in the agricultural sector grew over the entire period (16 per cent from 1700 to 1850), mostly in the period 1800 to 1850, but it grew by much less than population. Indeed, between 1750 and 1800, a period marked by substantial enclosure, agricultural employment may not have increased at all.[1] We can certainly say that *relatively* the agricultural sector did release human resources in both periods, but we should note that the oft-told story of farmers, displaced by the enclosure movement, trudging to the cities to slave away in the factories seems to be an exaggeration. According to a substantial body of recent literature on the subject the main effect of enclosures (and other similar productivity changes) on labor was to create a kind of structural unemployment in the affected regions, rather than to generate a stream of laborers for the factories.[2] Indeed, as we discussed in Chapter 3, enclosure *per se* may not have raised productivity as much as earlier writers have suggested. This is partly because improvements had been ongoing in the displaced open-field system and partly a matter of a shift in the types of agricultural product on which British farmers focused. In particular grain and potatoes became less important and livestock products more so and the latter were particularly labor-intensive – at least in the sense that they required attention all year around.

This issue of agriculture's role in industrialization has been one of contention since the notion of an 'Industrial Revolution' was first introduced. It appears that the agricultural sector produced substantially more output (but as a rapidly diminishing percentage of GDP and at a slower rate of growth than population) and that technological change was more important than increasing inputs as a source of this growth. Furthermore, the agricultural sector generally did not absorb much of the output of the manufacturing sector (Crafts, 1985); it did not provide much capital to the industrial sector from agricultural savings;[3] agriculture did not even release capital relatively (see Table 7.3); and it did not release labor directly to manufacturing (though, again, it did so *relatively*). On the whole, then, it seems important to keep in mind agriculture's contribution to output growth and to overall productivity growth and to at least consider the difficulties British industrialization might have encountered in the absence of the robust technical change that occurred in the agricultural sector. Still, it seems one should make less of agriculture's other possible effects on overall growth compared to the influence of developments in manufacturing and commerce.[4]

4.　BRITISH INDUSTRY AND FINANCE

During the period often referred to as the 'first' industrial revolution, Britain became the acknowledged world leader in both manufacturing and finance, though its industrial leadership is easier to document than its financial leadership. In this section we are not so much interested in the causes of industrialization as we are in generating a macroeconomic perspective of the process. Obviously, such an approach is controversial, since the activities typically associated with industrialization – for example, technological change in specific industries – are usually considered to be microeconomic topics; however, our interest is in the macro impact of those events.[5]

The figures in Table 7.4 show the growth of several important industries between 1750 and 1850. These illustrate the traditional – and oft-discussed – acceleration of the cotton, iron and coal industries, as well as some detail on other important industries. The cotton and iron industries seem most important in the story of British industrialization because they experienced some of the most dramatic technological innovations and they were relatively large industries in terms of employment and their contribution to British GNP. Because it was an important input in the production of both consumer and producer goods, iron is often portrayed as the quintessential early industrial product and Britain quickly moved into a dominant world position in the production of pig iron and finished iron products in this period. In addition the expansion of the iron industry (and the general application of steam power) contributed to the growth of the coal industry. There are several other aspects of the iron industry that make it of macroeconomic concern. For example, the iron series provides a good grip on real output since it is such a basic industry. While the rapid growth of the industry is especially important, an additional aspect is the tendency for iron output to fluctuate over the cycle. This provides a possible indicator of general business conditions. It also provides occasional excess capacity that looms larger later in the nineteenth century. In any case, all of these industries – and quite a few more as Table 7.4 indicates – had strong growth records at approximately the same time, making a general story easier, while at the same time leaving one in doubt as to which might be termed the 'most important industry', if that matters.

Before 1780, the copper and cotton industries grew the fastest, while after 1780, the growth rates of cotton and iron production dominate the story.

Table 7.4   Growth rates of real industrial production

| | Growth Rate in Decade Ending in | | | | | | | | | |
	1760	1770	1780	1790	1800	1810	1820	1830	1840	1850
Cotton	−2.65	4.92	6.16	14.33	4.93	5.42	4.12	6.92	6.19	2.50
Linen	2.51	4.54	1.62	−0.62	1.66	1.02	2.88	3.12	2.56	3.62
Silk	2.46	3.44	−0.95	2.15	−0.58	0.58	6.18	5.90	−0.49	1.95
Wool	1.30	1.26	0.72	0.49	0.56	1.19	1.69	1.84	4.21	0.95
Coal	1.47	2.05	2.11	2.39	2.74	2.71	2.38	3.12	3.34	3.83
Copper	5.72	5.56	3.86	3.78	−0.93	0.79	1.30	3.34	0.19	0.52
Iron	−0.14	1.04	2.11	3.58	4.75	4.99	−0.40	8.11	7.22	4.74
Beer	0.10	−0.65	1.16	0.58	0.99	0.25	−0.51	1.08	2.53	−0.22
Candles	1.04	0.60	1.51	0.68	1.79	1.18	1.66	2.76	3.15	1.37
Leather	0.67	0.10	0.62	0.86	0.71	2.21	−0.78	0.71	−0.06	2.02
Paper	2.67	2.21	−0.10	2.31	1.26	3.15	1.86	2.73	3.31	3.79
Soap	0.13	0.61	1.74	0.95	2.05	2.71	2.04	2.90	3.15	1.37
Average	1.27	2.14	1.71	2.62	1.66	2.18	1.87	3.54	2.94	2.20

Sources: 1750–1830: derived from Jackson (1992). 1840s, 1850s: cotton, coal, iron, linen, wool from Mitchell (1992); remainder from Hoffmann (1955). Soap and candles are combined as one in the Hoffmann data.

Throughout the period, coal production increased at a substantial rate and could also serve as a useful indicator of the decadal rates of progress since coal represents the main energy source, at least in urban and industrial areas. The average at the bottom of the table is nothing more than a simple average of the figures. Even so, it seems that according to these figures growth was roughly as rapid before 1780 as it was immediately after. Furthermore, it is evident that the 1780s stand out mainly because of the phenomenal growth rate of the cotton industry.

From a macroeconomic perspective the figures in Table 7.4 are important for two reasons. First, the growth of output per capita varies *directly* with the growth of output per worker; the latter, of course, is labor productivity – which, for the economy as a whole is a weighted average of productivity across industries and sectors. Industries typically expand when falling costs (rising productivity) create profit opportunities. So, expanding industries are typically the relatively more productive ones and as resources are attracted from less productive industries to more productive ones the result is economic growth. Second, many industries produce goods that are inputs into other industries and increases in productivity in those industries resulting in lower output prices that are then passed on to other industries.

We mention both of these points because the 1780s are often identified as the decade of the British 'take-off' into the industrial revolution (Rostow, 1962) and the 'backward and forward linkages' between industries was once thought to be a key element of the move to modern economic growth.[6] Even when reduced to these simple terms, the data in Table 7.4 do not appear to support the case for a strong take-off, and much of the recent literature discussed below concurs.

Taken altogether, the industry-level data can be used to illustrate overall industrial production; however, the industrial production indices for Britain have generated considerable controversy over the years. Since these series are the basis of the GNP estimates discussed below, the controversy to which we refer continues into Section 7.5.[7] Three such indices – those produced by Hoffmann (1955), Gayer, Rostow and Schwartz (1953) and Crafts and Harley (1992) – provide annual data for growth rates over periods of time other than for the much longer frequencies usually featured in the literature. They are also of use in our discussions of business cycles later in this chapter. In an entirely arbitrary way, we have divided the 1750–1850 period at 1791. Our main motive for doing this is the fact that the Gayer, Rostow and Schwartz (GRS) business activity index begins in 1791; even so, this, division turns out to be interesting.

The controversy surrounding these series covers a number of areas, although the biggest differences seem to come from different statistical procedures employed in their construction, rather than from substantially different data, *per se*. In fact, by far the most striking difference occurs between the indices constructed by Crafts–Harley (1992) and Hoffmann (1955). Specifically, Crafts and Harley (CH) place less weight on the cotton textile industry, which tends to put downward pressure on the resulting series. We think it unnecessary to take the reader through the details of these calculations, but we feel it is important enough for our general themes to present what are arguably the boundaries of Britain's early industrial growth.

Each of the indices presents a unique view of the path of British industrialization, with the dominant visible characteristics being the smoothness of the Hoffmann series compared to the other two and the relative volatility of the GRS index. The CH index is constructed from the Hoffmann data, with many adjustments in addition to the one involving cotton noted above; so it has much the same flavor as the Hoffmann series (without the smoothing). The GRS index, on the other hand, is not a production index, but a business activity index with industrial production as one of its components, and so it has a different character. Indeed, it has its own critical literature, a topic that we will refer to briefly later in this chapter when we look at British cycles in this period.

Figure 7.2 shows the Hoffmann and CH indices from 1750 to 1790. Note that we have rescaled the original indices at 1800=1 for this presentation.

Here the differences are extreme. In addition to the relative smoothness of the Hoffmann index, its acceleration around 1780 compared to the slower rate of growth of the CH index stands out.[8] Estimating these growth rates using the regression of the logarithm of the variables on a time trend yields a growth rate of 1.56 per cent per year for the Hoffmann index and 0.90 per cent for the CH index. This is a sizeable difference.

If we were to accept the general drift of the CH index, as much of the profession is currently disposed to do, then there are two important findings that contradict the older literature on the industrial revolution in Britain. First, a growth rate of less than one per cent per year in production may not be enough to generate enthusiasm for the idea of an industrial *revolution* in Britain in this period.[9] This is partly a semantic dispute, of course, and we would be remiss if we did not point out (as CH do) that the growth and structural change in this period are not only profound by comparison with earlier periods, but adequate to establish the base for a very rapid – albeit subsequent – expansion, particularly once the Napoleonic Wars ended. The second point is that the idea of a spurt of some sort in 1780 seems unlikely. Of course we also saw this in the individual industry series, discussed above.

When we consider the period 1790 to 1850, much of the foregoing dispute disappears. Figure 7.3 shows the three annual indices we have for that period, again based on 1800=1. Here the Hoffmann and CH indices clearly have almost identical growth rates (they are 2.90 and 2.88 per cent respectively) while the GRS business activity index grows considerably slower (at 1.94 per cent).

In this case there are no prominent disputes in the literature and we can readily accept an industrial rate of growth of 2.5–3.0 per cent per year as reasonably representative. A rate in this neighborhood is quite rapid by most standards and one that would have been sufficient to give Britain (and hence the United Kingdom) a sizeable world lead in the production of the main industrial staples of the day (for example coal, iron and cotton textiles) by the 1840s. Note that although we are not going to look into cycles until later in this chapter, the cycles in the GRS index, which was designed to reveal the business cycle pattern of the period, look to be fairly closely related to those in the CH index. This finding is encouraging for our subsequent use of the CH index to help in identifying cycles in the 1750–1790 period. The smoothed Hoffmann index, which rarely declines, is of no real use for this purpose, although the Hoffmann worksheets, which contain individual industry data, would be.

Let us finish this discussion of industrialization during the first Industrial Revolution in Britain with a summary of three major indices in the literature grouped into ten-year averages of some sort. We have added some calculations by Jackson (1992) to our basic collection, though they are not annual figures.

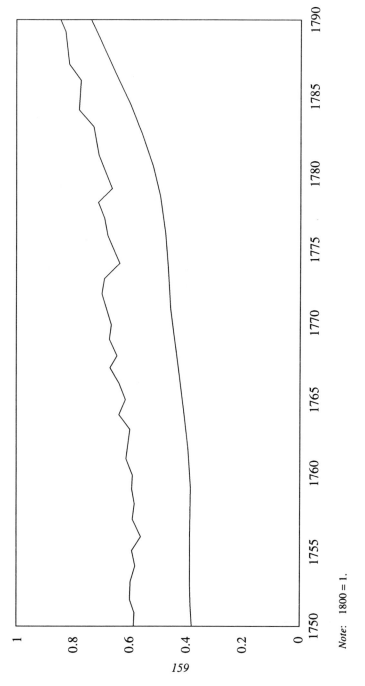

Note: 1800 = 1.

Figure 7.2   Hoffmann and Crafts–Harley indices 1750–1790

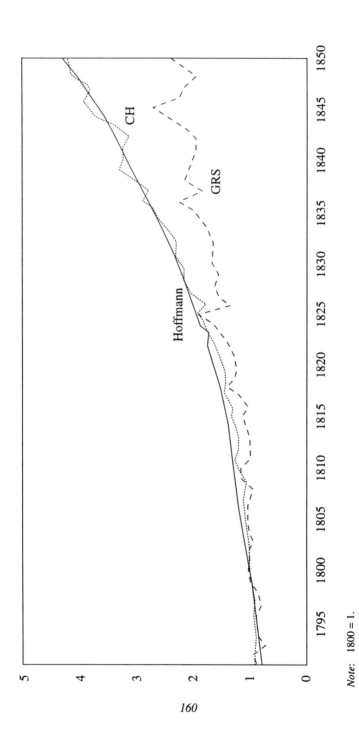

Note: 1800 = 1.

Figure 7.3 Three production indices compared 1791–1850

Table 7.5   A comparison of British production growth rates 1750–1850

	Growth Rate in Decade Ending in									
	1760	1770	1780	1790	1800	1810	1820	1830	1840	1850
Hoffmann	0.28	1.48	1.29	3.72	2.98	2.43	2.41	3.33	3.34	3.10
Jackson	0.94	1.32	1.16	2.31	1.94	2.68	1.91	4.00	–	–
CH	0.67	1.26	2.91	2.09	1.24	1.83	1.95	4.41	3.42	2.69

Notes: The Jackson index is computed using the log-change form on the end of period dates; the other two indices are annual averages for each decade.

Interestingly, the Hoffmann index, as noted earlier, shows the oft-cited spurt in the 1780s, and this finding is echoed by Jackson's calculations. The CH index shows a spurt in the 1770s, but their figures for the next three decades are well below those of the other two indices. This particular finding, while not agreed upon in all quarters, is sometimes linked to the crowding-out debate, centering on the Napoleonic War expenditures of the British government, which we shall discuss below after we have looked at some investment and interest rate data. The effect of wars is an important sub-topic of this literature and one that is inextricably linked to the financial sector. After 1820 there are some differences, but they have not generated the controversy that the earlier figures have. If the early spurt disappears from the literature, then the traditional story of the ignition of some sort of industrial and entrepreneurial burst in the 1770–1790 period – an ignition that created a permanent flame, to take the metaphor further – is difficult to support, at least at the macro level. Rather, the industrial story, at least, becomes one of a more gradual process, probably reaching back well before 1750.

In addition to the path of industrialization, the role of the financial sector in the promotion of British industry has generated considerable controversy.[10] Theoretically, financial intermediation plays an important role in economic growth because it permits a wider sharing of risks, improves the allocation of capital and provides credit information to both borrowers and lenders. In short, it lowers transaction costs. Furthermore, with respect to macroeconomic issues, the money stock is a potential policy control variable and typically the quantity of money is a useful indicator of overall economic activity. Indeed, from time to time, banking crises are alleged to be the primary causes of major downturns in the economy.

We discussed money growth earlier (see Chapter 4) and we will review business cycles below. Here we focus exclusively on the role of banking and the promotion of industry. First, it is worth recalling the various types of banks discussed in Chapter 4. Although a plethora of financial intermediaries existed in early modern Britain – including, according to Neal (1994, pp. 165–68), goldsmiths, scriveners (essentially, legal scribes) and attorneys, beginning around the middle of the eighteenth century, and increasingly so after that time, the most important were the so-called 'country' banks and the London merchant banks. By the classification in Chapter 4, the country banks were primarily commercial banks, providing local credit, accepting deposits and connecting the local market with London. The London banks, on the other hand, were the prototypes of the merchant bank, largely discounting bills of exchange.[11]

In considering the role these institutions played in British industrialization, one might simply look at the size of the British banking sector, both absolutely and relative to, say, national income. The period 1750 to 1844 makes for a natural era of analysis, because the former date is near the beginning of the rise of the country banks and the latter marks the dramatic reorganization of the Bank of England and British finance in general (see below). The country banks were exclusively 'private' (i.e. partnerships) until joint-stock banking was generally legalized in 1826. In 1750 there were only about a dozen actual country banks in existence. By 1775 there were about 100 and in 1797, 334 country banks were counted in England and Wales. Including branches, the figure grew to between 600 and 700 from 1810 until the legislation of 1826 (Cameron, 1967, p. 25), which simultaneously established the onset of the Bank of England's note issuing monopoly and joint-stock banking beyond London. After 1826 the number of private banks began to decline, while the number of joint-stock banks grew from zero to roughly 600 over the next 18 years. The private country banks largely filtered money from agricultural households to industry and between London and the countryside, attesting to the potential strength and breadth of the industrial and commercial growth of the period. In terms of the London merchant banks, in 1750–65 there were 20–30 and by 1770 there were 50; there were probably no more than that number by the beginning of the nineteenth century.

Of course, the number of banks is a crude indicator of the size or importance of the financial sector. Since the primary contribution of banks to industry is credit, it makes sense to look at the growth of bank assets. These grew from £20.5 million in 1775 to £139. 0 million by 1844 or at an annual rate of 2.81 per cent, which was faster than the growth of either industrial production or GNP over roughly the same period (Cameron, 1967, p. 35). In terms of the sector's size relative to the overall economy, the ratio of bank assets to national income more than doubled over the same period of time, increasing from 15.2 per cent in 1775 to 34.4 in 1844. While these are also relatively crude measures, since they tell us nothing about the composition of bank assets, the relatively rapid growth of bank assets suggests that the British financial sector surely did not retard economic growth. Curiously, the primary cause of the progressiveness of British financial institutions is often argued to have been the relatively conservative currency policies of the government, which led financial entrepreneurs to seek profits in other financial innovations.

While the growth of the banking sector both absolutely and relative to national income is suggestive, it is possible that the size of the sector is less relevant to economic growth than the responsiveness of the banking sector to the financial needs of industrialists. By 'responsiveness', we mean the elasticity of the supply of credit. For example, Neal (1991, p. 155) argues that the representative firm might have turned to external finance only after exhausting its own retained earnings or other means of self-financing. Once those avenues had been exhausted, the subsequent extension of lending, and therefore investment, depended on the supply of credit emanating from the banking sector. In general the small scale of manufacturing technology at the time – small-scale by subsequent standards – which relied so heavily on working as opposed to fixed capital, was well suited to take advantage of both the local market in credit supplied by the country banks and the international market in discounts centered in London. Although the data required to evaluate these relationships do not exist, taken as a whole the narrative evidence suggests that, at least relative to the rest of the world, British finance was, shall we say, especially accommodative of industrial demands.

5. BRITISH NATIONAL INCOME

Not surprisingly, the dispute concerning the path of British industrialization extends to the broader measures of national income (and real product). Here we focus on the GNP calculations of Feinstein (1978, 1981) in order to illustrate the broad patterns discernible in the data. Feinstein's figures are reproduced in Table 7.6.

The figures in the table show that, although all of the components of real GNP grew substantially over the period in question, most of the growth, at least as a proportion of GNP, came from investment, which, as a share of GNP rose from 8.1 per cent in 1761–70 to 11.8 per cent in 1841–50. The government grew in size up to 1811–20 (12.8 per cent of national product), after which it declined to 3.0 per cent of GNP in the last decade in the period. Although consumption spending as a share of GNP was almost the same at the end of the period as it was at the beginning (83 and 84 per cent, respectively) it declined until 1811–20, reaching a low of 73 per cent, before rebounding thereafter.

Table 7.7 contains the relevant growth rates behind the data in Table 7.6. First, note that for all except the first decade, these figures exhibit growth

Table 7.6   Real GNP and its components 1761–1850

Date	GNP	Government Spending	Investment Spending	Net Foreign Spending	Consumption Spending	I/GNP
1761–70	93	7	7.5	0.5	78	8.1
1771–80	98	7	9.0	1.0	81	9.2
1781–90	111	8	13.0	1.5	88	11.7
1791–1800	134	15	17.5	1.5	100	13.0
1801–10	161	25	17.5	–2.0	120	10.9
1811–20	203	26	22.5	5.0	149	11.1
1821–30	278	14	32.5	7.5	224	11.7
1831–40	372	12	42.0	4.5	313	11.3
1841–50	460	16	54.5	6.5	383	11.8

Note: Annual averages, 1851–60 prices, £m.

Source: Feinstein (1981). These figures are mostly from Deane and Cole, as adjusted by Feinstein.

Table 7.7   British real growth rates 1771–1860

Date	GNP	Consumption	Investment	Government	Population Growth	Technical Change
1771–80	0.52	0.38	1.82	0.00	0.87	–0.35
1781–90	1.24	0.83	3.68	1.34	0.90	0.34
1791–00	1.88	1.28	2.97	6.29	1.17	0.71
1801–10	1.84	1.82	0.00	5.11	1.27	0.57
1811–20	2.32	2.16	2.51	0.39	1.46	0.86
1821–30	3.14	4.08	3.68	–6.19	1.48	1.66
1831–40	2.91	3.34	2.56	–1.54	1.22	1.71
1841–50	2.12	2.02	2.60	2.88	1.10	1.02

Note: Compound rates, per annum, for the decade.

Source: Feinstein (1981).

rates of GNP in excess of population growth. Second, note that in the last column in the table we report a residual measure of technical change derived from the standard neoclassical growth model of, for example, Phelps (1965). The general argument is that growth can be attributed to an increase in population and to technical change, with the capital stock taking the role of an endogenous variable, forced by economic pressures to grow at a rate consistent with overall equilibrium.[12] Very simply, we deduct the population growth rate from the overall growth rate in the first column of the table to arrive at a crude estimate of the contribution of technological change (from this perspective). If these back-of-the-envelope calculations have any merit, they show accelerating technical change as one of the important causes of growth from the beginning of the period until the 1840s. Although Crafts' (1987, p. 251; and 1994, p. 51) estimates of total factor productivity growth (TFP) for the economy as a whole are somewhat lower than those just reported, they do show the same general trend.[13]

Turning to government spending, we note first that governments prior to the industrial revolution did very little spending compared with modern times. To see this more clearly, consider that during the American Revolution the British government accounted for only 7 per cent of GNP; most modern economies run over 25–33 per cent. Of course when states found themselves at war, they tended to employ whatever fiscal machinery they had at their disposal. Normally, governments would attempt to finance their expenditures through taxes, but partly because the (heavily agricultural) tax base at the time was capable only of moderate increases in the generation of extra revenues over the short run, the British government would either run its cash-creating machinery (as it did during the Napoleonic wars) or issue debt, as it did during all of its major wars, to make up the shortfall. Of course these choices (taxes, money creation and/or debt) exhaust the possibilities for governments at any time.

'Crowding out' typically refers to the situation in which a government faces *temporary* expenditures, and the expenditures are known to be temporary by the general public, with the result that the general public alters its current saving plan in a way that frustrates the government's efforts to obtain resources to finance its expenditures. To see how this might occur, consider the following: assume, for simplicity, that the government issues bonds in order to raise the funds for its current (wartime) expenditures.[14] Although the market will determine the price of the bonds, the government can adjust the quantity of bonds in order to raise the capital required to pursue the war effort; thus the current economy releases the required resources. If the expenditure is perceived as temporary, consumers will attempt to smooth the impact of the loss of resources by shifting (planned) expenditures from future periods. They do this, of course, by running down their savings. If consumers are currently saving at a lower rate than originally planned, the government will have to compete for those savings with other (private) investors in the capital market (or borrow abroad – which only transfers the problem to international capital markets). This competition drives up the *real* interest rate. At the higher real interest rate both private investment and consumption decline – i.e. they are 'crowded out' by *temporary* government expenditures. If investment is crowded out, then the capital stock is lower than it otherwise would be and, arguably, the growth rate of the economy is lower.

In a controversial analysis of the crowding-out effect of large temporary government expenditures in Britain, Barro (1987) notes that for the wars of the period up until 1780 there were significant deviations of the ratio of military spending to the trend of national income, for example during the Seven Years War and the American Revolution (of 16 per cent and 10 per cent, respectively). During the first of these wars the national debt rose £52.2 million; it expanded further during the second war to £104.7 million. At all other times during this period, until the Napoleonic wars, the national debt either declined or grew very slowly. This sets the stage for the possibility of the crowding out of private investment.

The way one might judge the extent of crowding out is with reference to the behavior either of the ratio of investment to output or of the real interest rate. In the wars studied by Barro, the empirical work was conducted in terms of the interest rate, which showed some effect, although arguments over the method of calculation of the real rate have tended to obscure the larger argument concerning crowding out. In any case, the effect was probably not that large in many of the early wars he studied. However, a furious debate exists about the Napoleonic period, a debate that even spills over into writings on the French economy of this time.

Williamson (1987a, pp. 287–90) argues that the extraordinary demands placed on British government finance by the Napoleonic wars directly crowded out private investment and thus tended to put downward pressure on the rate of economic growth before, say, 1820. Much of the debate hinges on three factors: the behavior of real interest rates and investment and the role of investment in industrialization. With respect to the last of these, we have already discussed the potentially important role of capital markets in early industrialization. Although Heim and Mirowski (1987) note that any upward pressure on government borrowing was probably felt most acutely in the non-industrial areas of housing, infrastructure and improvements in agricultural land, Williamson argues that such 'social overhead capital' was an important contributor to British industrialization. With respect to interest rates and investment we have to look at the data.

Table 7.8 reproduces a set of figures from Crafts (1987) that tend to corroborate the crowding-out thesis rather dramatically. Here we find the savings ratio actually growing during some of the periods in which government spending increased most sharply (1791–1800 and 1811–1820), but there is still a huge gap between savings and investment (as ratios of GNP) that was drained by the government. It is not so much that investment was retarded by some historical standard, but that the government war effort seems to have stalled the growth of private capital during the period (until around 1815) that some observers have argued contains (or, we suppose, would have contained) an important part of the Industrial Revolution. In the

1820s and 1830s, the savings ratio and the investment ratio are nearly the same, and the latter is higher than in the earlier periods, suggesting one contribution to the faster growth rates of those periods. Of course, the potential role of technological change in this connection was illustrated in Table 7.7.

Looking back to Feinstein's data on real GNP growth rates in Table 7.7, we can again see the possibility of crowding out. In the two decades, 1781–90 and 1800–1810, government expenditures increased dramatically. In the second of these investment growth was zero. In the 1820s and 1830s, government expenditure in real terms declined, while investment growth was robust. If the 1801–1810 period shows crowding out, then the latter two periods mentioned show that if government borrowing declines then private investment increases.

There is one anomaly in this parade of evidence, however, and that is the large rise in savings shown in Table 7.8 in both periods – i.e. 1791–1800 and 1810–1820 – in which government spending rose sharply. It looks as if additional resources were actually created and saved in those periods, a phenomenon that is easiest to explain if there were substantial unemployed resources in the economy. Note, in this connection, that in both of those periods, the investment ratio actually rose relative to the previous decade. We would not go so far as to say that crowding in occurs in these periods, as some have argued, but it certainly looks as if the argument for an adverse effect of increased government spending needs to be stated in a relative sense – that is, relative to what might have been possible without the wars –

Table 7.8   National income and some components in Britain

Date	GNP	Savings	S/GNP	I/GNP
1761–70	78.00	7.80	10.0	5.9
1771–80	92.75	10.76	11.6	6.4
1781–90	112.50	17.17	15.3	7.7
1791–1800	176.00	36.11	20.5	8.3
1801–10	266.55	35.90	13.5	8.0
1811–20	296.05	58.19	19.7	9.7
1821–30	315.50	38.27	12.1	11.0
1831–40	396.15	46.87	11.8	10.7
1841–50	487.80	59.77	12.3	11.0

Note: Nominal Figures, 1761–1850.

Source: Crafts (1987). Crafts computed the nominal, not the real, from his own estimates of real income (not published for these dates) using the Schumpeter–Gilboy price index.

assuming the resources used to wage war would actually have been employed in the private economy.

Unfortunately when we turn to annual data, we gain some information (we have deficit figures, inflation rates, and real rates) and lose some (we do not have investment figures, and we must rely on the production indices of our earlier discussions). In any case, Table 7.9 contains the available annual series, including a new series of our own construction, for the real interest rate.

Table 7.9   Annual data for crowding out 1793–1816

Date	Net Borrowing	Bank Notes	Real Rate	Inflation	CH Growth
1793	3.68	–	–0.48	7.33	–3.72
1794	7.05	–0.87	–2.10	2.64	0.45
1795	19.80	1.93	3.29	16.27	3.73
1796	21.30	–2.45	5.27	3.64	2.97
1797	28.44	0.40	11.04	–13.90	–4.71
1798	22.28	2.25	10.52	–1.38	3.24
1799	14.19	0.53	–3.95	12.87	8.54
1800	20.97	2.78	–5.39	28.53	–1.18
1801	27.01	–0.57	6.79	5.22	–4.02
1802	14.18	0.76	19.45	–30.46	5.40
1803	8.43	–0.49	15.32	–2.58	0.97
1804	13.73	1.47	–11.08	2.14	3.22
1805	17.78	0.01	–12.38	15.31	2.21
1806	11.40	2.25	1.07	–4.49	0.73
1807	10.55	–1.07	9.40	–5.41	3.91
1808	10.36	–0.66	4.82	6.52	–5.00
1809	11.61	1.41	–3.74	12.68	2.53
1810	9.01	3.85	1.64	5.00	8.34
1811	15.70	0.41	9.66	–5.19	4.96
1812	24.45	–0.10	8.86	14.20	–6.12
1813	37.37	0.80	0.66	–2.45	0.83
1814	32.47	2.56	5.88	–12.34	1.63
1815	21.60	0.67	5.28	–10.74	8.39
1816	–1.70	–	–5.72	5.07	–2.41

Sources: Cols. 1, 2: Bordo and White (1990); Col. 3, Craig and Fisher (1997); Col. 4, Lindert and Williamson (1983); Col. 5 Crafts and Harley (1992).

The first column here represents data on the deficit of the British government for each year of the sample. The second reports changes in bank notes issued by the Bank of England during the period, while the fourth column shows the annual inflation rate, using the Lindert–Williamson (1983) data. The last column merely repeats the Crafts–Harley growth rate for industrial production in an attempt to indicate the phase of the cycle in a quantitative sense.

The data on the real rate of interest in Column 3 require some explanation since they are calculated in a manner different from anything in the literature. In the literature, the equation known as the 'Fisher equation' postulates that observed market interest rates consist of a real component and an estimate of inflationary expectations:

$$i = r + \pi_e \qquad (7.1)$$

In this expression, r is the expected real rate and π_e, represents inflationary expectations. While in modern times economists sometimes have data on what are presumed to be inflationary expectations – gathered from market forecasters, for example – in historical studies about all that are available are observations on the past behavior of the inflation rate. Indeed, in the absence of any other information, economic agents could hardly do better than to use past data on inflation rates, supplemented, if possible, with some information concerning the behavior of the monetary authorities.

Typically in the literature, inflationary expectations for any future period are constructed as moving averages of past inflation rates, with declining weights so that the most recent inflation rates get the highest weight. We tried this, to be sure, but what we discovered is that a better model to predict inflation was one in which inflation was forecast as a 'mean-reverting' process, by which we mean that when the inflation rate shoots up, economic agents would have made a better guess as to the next inflation rate if they picked a significantly lower rate. We experimented over the entire period from 1750 to 1850, and found three distinct periods, all of which showed that the assumption of mean-reversion would have produced a better prediction than any moving average.[15] The period covered in Table 7.10 – 1793–1816 – was one such period and the real rate data shown in the table are calculated from Equation 7.1, using the mean-reversion formula to generate expected inflation.[16]

Turning to the annual data, then, the crowding-out hypothesis suggests that, when the government runs a deficit in a full-employment economy, the real rate of interest will rise. In 1797 and 1798, for example, real rates were very high and so were government deficits. The economy declined slightly over those two years, as measured by the CH index, and prices fell. It is hard not to see crowding out in those figures. In 1799 the deficit was a little lower, the real rate fell, and the economy expanded. In 1800, a large deficit was still associated with a low (negative) real rate, and while the economy inched downward, inflation was substantial. Neither 1799 nor 1800 appears to show crowding out on any appreciable scale. The large deficit in 1801 is associated with a rise of the real rate and a decline in the economy, while in 1802 the deficit fell, the economy spurted ahead and the real rate was very high (there was rapid deflation that year).

We forbear to push this analysis any further, but we note that, glancing over the whole table, it looks as if some of the higher real rates are associated with relatively large deficits and, further, that some of the recession years are associated with relatively high real rates either in the same or the preceding year. Broadly, then, though we are especially concerned about the quality of the inflation data for the war period, it looks to us as if crowding out may well have occurred in this period, although there is enough in these crude data to keep the dispute going for some time.

6.   BUSINESS CYCLES

In contrast to Chapter 6, which relied entirely on narrative supported by a few data here and there, we have a substantial set of British data available for pinning down the frequency and (in some cases) the amplitude of British cycles. The most obvious data are those on industrial production, especially the annual indices of Crafts and Harley (CH) and Gayer, Rostow and Schwartz (GRS); the former spans the entire period and is especially useful for our purposes. In addition, we have an 'adjusted profit' index compiled by Mirowski (1985), a share-price index, some inflation figures, figures on Bank of England deposits, figures on the number of bankruptcies, and, from the last section, figures on the real consol (interest) rate. Not all of these series cover the entire period, but as will be readily apparent, this is a rich, if sometimes ambiguous, pool of annual data.

Mirowski's adjusted profit index is calculated from the profits of a small number (six) of publicly-traded companies (e.g. the East India Company). He has also computed a share price index for the same companies, which we have included. In addition we have included liabilities of the Bank of England, which is a component of the money supply and would be expected to be procyclical in its behavior. That is, one would logically expect the liabilities of the Bank of England to increase during expansions and decline during contractions. Finally, the bankruptcies in the table are those reported in London newspapers; they come from several sources, as noted. The other data are obvious or have already been explained in this chapter.

1750–1790

We used the Crafts–Harley growth rate as the basis of our speculations for this period, and supplemented this with the other data and the narrative record, although, as we discussed earlier, the latter is often unreliable. The data for this section appear in Table 7.10. In 1754 the industrial production index declined, as did the share-price index. The real consol rate rose, the money supply dropped, and bankruptcies increased. We judge this a clear recession year. In 1756 and 1757 there were harvest failures leading to high wheat prices (and inflation overall), and Mirowski's adjusted profit index fell. Ashton's (1959) narrative of the era omits this event (there was no general financial panic, although there was a minor crisis in 1755) but bankruptcies were also up and so was the real consol rate.

Ashton identifies a recession in 1762 and a financial crisis in 1763 (late in the year). These events seem related to the end of the Seven Years War and also involve stock prices (Mirowski's quarterly indices show lower prices in early 1762 and late 1763). Bankruptcies, though, were up sharply in 1764. In general it seems that the trouble here was more financial than real, but several shocks to the financial system did produce some real effects. The Crafts–Harley production index puts a recession in 1765 and this downturn is reinforced by rising bankruptcies in the following two years; 1768 is also a bad year in terms of industrial production, and profits were down while the real consol rate was up in the same year. This recession, which appears to have been passed over in the literature, may have been relatively steep, but short.

There were several consecutive years of bad weather in 1771–74 in England; while these years did not witness a famine, they did produce relatively high wheat prices from 1772–1775; the latter shows up in the inflation rate for 1771 and 1772, which was around 20 per cent for the two years. Ashton (1959) says that the export market collapsed in 1773 and the East India Company was particularly affected, and he identifies June 1772 to January 1773 as a period of financial crisis.[17] Bankruptcies shot up in 1772 and 1773, with the building trades in particular witnessing a substantial amount of failure in 1772 and construction was generally slow in 1773–75. The years 1773 and 1774 were also bad years for industrial production. Ashton identifies 1776–78 as a war-related financial crash-cum-recession. Here bankruptcies were up sharply, stock prices tumbled (in 1779) and the building trades entered a decline that may have lasted into the mid-1780s. With the sharp rise in bankruptcies in 1778, the rapid decline of the CH production index in 1779 and the sharp decline of the profit index, it seems that both years could well have been recession years.

One could easily argue that there were no recessions in the 1780s, and narrative accounts generally omit any mention of one. Nevertheless, 1783

Table 7.10 Cyclical data for Britain 1751–1790

Date	CH Growth	Adjusted Profit	Shares Index	Inflation	Real Consol Rate	Bankruptcies	Boe Money
1751	−0.68	4.34	102.2	−2.75	1.57	172	13.55
1752	2.68	27.97	106.4	4.60	1.81	170	−2.86
1753	−0.33	−44.81	107.6	−2.70	1.23	197	−12.32
1754	−2.68	45.13	104.5	5.00	2.58	243	−5.04
1755	1.69	−24.13	97.2	−6.20	0.30	231	24.36
1756	−5.50	−6.63	89.5	4.07	5.36	236	−1.36
1757	5.16	−31.75	90.9	19.69	−0.71	250	11.62
1758	−1.35	81.34	91.9	−0.27	4.98	278	−13.00
1759	1.69	−29.10	83.9	−8.27	7.86	280	−11.78
1760	0.00	−2.33	83.0	−4.56	3.71	216	6.06
1761	3.29	−16.43	79.9	−4.61	5.32	178	4.32
1762	−1.30	−7.32	75.8	3.83	1.47	188	11.93
1763	−0.66	29.23	94.0	2.63	−1.71	214	−14.79
1764	6.08	−4.39	87.1	8.48	2.62	284	10.97
1765	−2.83	−5.92	96.8	3.45	1.97	223	−2.63
1766	3.76	9.79	101.5	1.21	6.42	288	−2.70
1767	5.10	1.88	109.9	5.60	4.25	334	−2.78
1768	−3.88	−3.80	115.4	−1.14	5.02	303	6.80
1769	4.17	−23.06	111.4	−8.55	5.35	309	−1.32
1770	−1.17	28.88	103.2	−0.42	2.46	393	−5.48
1771	2.91	−4.50	105.1	8.20	0.93	345	18.00
1772	2.27	−37.76	107.3	10.17	1.73	484	−12.52
1773	−1.98	20.96	99.3	−0.35	2.94	556	3.92
1774	−8.03	−7.02	101.4	0.93	5.89	338	19.72
1775	2.75	17.18	104.5	−5.72	4.46	332	16.46
1776	4.13	−1.31	104.3	−2.23	5.59	388	−6.45
1777	1.43	−9.67	100.7	−0.38	0.58	489	0.95
1778	3.08	−22.31	87.3	3.95	2.86	662	−7.85
1779	−6.86	−26.21	84.5	−8.86	2.04	575	14.24
1780	3.20	8.24	77.5	−3.50	4.58	454	−2.69
1781	3.38	11.83	75.1	4.03	0.82	381	−9.53
1782	1.10	54.81	73.4	0.42	4.00	411	8.62
1783	2.17	−63.14	79.9	2.16	2.64	540	−12.70
1784	5.73	18.28	70.1	−2.91	3.48	534	−16.99
1785	0.25	−62.80	78.3	−5.29	5.56	383	3.64
1786	−0.76	67.66	90.7	−2.43	2.02	509	19.42
1787	4.96	1.30	93.8	2.61	1.67	487	6.64
1788	0.72	35.95	98.2	2.98	1.26	697	9.61
1789	0.96	−14.60	100.5	5.37	2.28	560	4.08
1790	2.35	−5.95	100.9	2.90	3.19	574	3.15

shows a sharp decline of the profit index (the largest decline in Table 7.10) and a jump in bankruptcies. In 1784 the share-price index reaches its lowest point in the table, while in 1785 and 1786 industrial production declined (taking the two years together). We think that 1785 may well have been a recession year, considering the decline of the profit index, the high real interest rate and the rise in bankruptcies (in 1786). Note that prices also fell from 1784 to 1786.

On the basis of these speculations, we feel that the following represents a possible dating for the recessions of this period.

1754,	1756,	1758?	
1762,	1763?,	1765,	1768
1773–1774,	1778–1779		
1783?,	1785,	1786?	

Thus 14 of the 40 years in the period, or 35 per cent, show signs of recession, which by today's standard is quite frequent, but is probably a reasonable estimate of the frequency of recession years in Britain in this period. Note that we can say little about amplitudes here, other than to point out that by the number of series involved and the severity of their downturns, the recessions in 1756, 1768, 1774 and 1779 might well qualify as major recession years. The timing of these recessions might explain how some earlier studies might have found a (roughly) 10-year cycle in the data for this (and other) periods. We think the truth is closer to our estimate of 14 possible recession years, but we freely acknowledge that there is a lot of room for new data to undermine our conjectures.

1790–1850

We continue with a discussion of the 1790–1850 period. This material has been carefully explored in an important work by Gayer, Rostow and Schwartz (1953) and has recently been updated by Mirowski (1981, 1985). Gayer, Rostow, and Schwartz (GRS) calculate broad price and output indices and construct a set of 'reference cycles' from these data.[18] The work involved is truly prodigious and to us it seems unlikely that the broad patterns discerned are seriously wrong, partly because of the care with which the historical literature was consulted. To begin, the reference cycle data appear in Table 7.11, along with some calculations of our own referring to the number of months of decline.

Table 7.11, then, shows upturns that are significantly longer than down-turns with major peaks (1792, 1802, 1810, 1818, 1825, 1836, 1845) coming (on average) every nine years. In another tabulation, GRS identify the following years as being recessions (1953, I, p. 356):

Table 7.11   British reference cycles 1790–1850

| Annual | | Monthly | | | | Decline |
Peak	Trough	Peak		Trough		in Months
1792	1793	Sept	1792	June	1794	21
1796	1797	May	1796	Sept	1797	16
1800	1801	Sept	1800	Oct	1801	12
1802	1803	Dec	1802	Mar	1804	15
1806	1808	Aug	1806	May	1808	21
1810	1811	Mar	1810	Sept	1811	18
1815	1816	Mar	1815	Sept	1816	18
1818	1819	Sept	1818	Sept	1819	12
1825	1826	May	1825	Nov	1826	18
1828	1829	June	1828	Dec	1829	18
1831	1832	Mar	1831	July	1832	16
1836	1837	Mar	1839	Nov	1842	32
1839	1842	Sept	1845	Sept	1846	12
1845	1848	Apr	1847	Sept	1848	17

Source: Gayer, Rostow and Schwartz (1953).

1793*,	1794,	1797*,	1798	
1803,	1808			
1811*,	1812,	1816*,	1819*	
1820,	1826*,	1829		
1832,	1833,	1837*,	1838	
1841,	1842*,	1843,	1848*,	1849

Here there are recessions in 22 of the 61 possible years, with severe recessions in the nine years indicated by an asterisk. When one calculates the actual length of recessions from the monthly data in Table 7.11, however, we find there are 20.5 years of recession, making up 33.6 per cent of the total. This number is very close to that for the 1750–1790 period.

Concentrating on the recessions, and using the Crafts–Harley numbers for 1791–1830 and the Deane and Cole figures (for changes in Real GNP) for 1831–1850, we find that of the 22 GRS annual cycles just listed, 8 years do not show declines in the CH index or real GNP (1798, 1811, 1820, 1833, 1838, 1843, 1848, and 1849), while 4 years in which the CH or GNP data decline (1800, 1801, 1840, and 1850) are not mentioned in the GRS survey. These differences are too large to ignore. To move the two compilations closer together, we consult both the narrative literature and the other series listed in Table 7.12 to make the call, with the expectation that, except for 1811, we are probably discussing smaller rather than larger recessions. In what follows, we actually discuss all of the recessions, featuring the GRS versus CH index differences as an important subplot.

Until the 1816 recession, our source is GRS; the explanations here run heavily toward the behavior of exports. The expansion from 1790 to 1792/3 is described in terms of the growth of incomes, banking, exports and important improvements in social overhead capital, such as on canals and roads. The crisis in 1793 was brought on by the outbreak of war in an economy alleged to have been softened by credit tightness, bankruptcies and mediocre harvests (in 1792 and 1793). The literature, incidentally, tends to emphasize the 'over-expansion' of credit as an independent causal factor. The collapse of the export boom to the United States is mentioned especially and these factors carry over into 1794. Note that the Crafts–Harley index, adjusted profits and the share index also decline sharply in 1793.

The burgeoning war and the industrial boom brought a prosperity that was export-based, say GRS, but bad harvests in 1795–6 and 1799–1800 and the monetary crisis of 1797 stand out as exogenous shocks in the period. The Crafts–Harley index points to 1797 as the recession year and in that year bankruptcies rose sharply and the share index fell, while the real consol rate was quite high in both 1797 and 1798. On this basis, 1798 seems doubtful as a year of recession, although the recession of 1797 surely extended into early 1798.

In the next decade, the economy turned down in 1800, but 1801 was the recession year; GRS admit this, but exclude 1801 from their list of years for some reason. Both years saw declines in industrial production, particularly the latter and 1801 saw a rise in the real consol rate; the profit index fell in 1800, but rose in 1801. The following year was a good one for the British economy, but the war broke out again in 1803, bringing with it the effective elimination of some Continental markets (and thus another export collapse). In 1803 the share index fell sharply and real consol rates remained quite high; there was also some minor deflation that year. If there was a decline in 1803, it was surely more financial than real. Harvests were generally good during these years, with a bad harvest coming in 1804, a year that is not associated in the literature with a general decline. The recession in 1808, however, seems to have been related to a particularly poor harvest that year, along with the loss of Baltic grain (the Continental System had been in place since 1806, but was really felt to begin in 1807), and thus provide agricultural and trade explanations of the shock behind the recession; clearly 1808 stands out as a recession year in this period.

In 1810 the continental system was tightened again (it had been relaxed in 1809); the South American boom collapsed in 1811, and trade with the United States declined substantially. These factors severely hurt the export markets,

Table 7.12 Cycle data, 1791–1850

Date	CH Growth	Adjusted Profit	Shares (1)	Shares (2)	Inflation	Real Consol	Bankruptcies	Boe Money	Real GNP
1791	2.75	23.85	107.8		-3.80	3.60	603	-0.26	
1792	5.29	-42.59	119.2		-2.42	3.13	609	-0.51	
1793	-3.72	-29.05	103.8		7.33	-0.48	1256	-0.03	
1794	-0.45	33.09	95.3		2.64	-2.10	857	0.42	
1795	3.73	-3.68	93.5		16.27	3.29	731	0.51	
1796	2.97	9.11	94.9		3.64	5.27	720	0.28	
1797	-4.71	0.99	76.3		-13.90	11.04	905	0.87	
1798	3.24	18.03	74.4		-1.38	10.52	767		
1799	8.54	16.75	87.0		12.87	-3.95	512		
1800	-1.18	-11.77	97.8		28.53	-5.39	727		
1801	-4.02	38.12	97.9		5.22	6.79			
1802	5.40	-35.46	107.5		-30.46	19.45			
1803	0.97	25.38	91.3		-2.58	15.32			
1804	3.22	-14.58	89.0		2.14	-11.08			
1805	2.21	9.68	97.2		15.31	-12.38			
1806	0.73	-18.22	104.8		-4.49	1.07			
1807	3.91	3.33	108.9		-5.41	3.40			
1808	-5.00	-10.52	111.7		6.52	4.82			
1809	2.53	7.52	119.5		12.68	-3.74			
1810	8.39	-46.13	120.3		5.00	1.64			
1811	4.96	24.33	113.1	103.07	-5.19	9.66	2112		
1812	-6.12	-5.58	103.5	94.36	14.20	8.86	1813		
1813	0.83	-8.35	97.9	89.24	-2.45	0.66	1583		
1814	1.63	36.79	102.8	93.64	-12.34	5.88	1258		
1815	8.39	-1.23	95.4	86.97	-10.74	5.28	1759		
1816	-2.41	0.91	86.0	78.23	5.07	-5.72	2145		
1817	8.90	0.30	92.2	84.10	2.77	3.54	1578		
1818	4.10	-0.29	112.1	102.12	-2.62	1.87	1012		
1819	-3.41	0.77	111.5	101.57	-5.06	2.47	1582		

1820	2.60	-0.54	106.4	97.05	-7.26	10.07	1385	
1821	4.10	-0.12	111.1	101.28	-8.97	7.83	1268	
1822	5.30	0.05	120.1	109.42	-10.64	4.02	1132	
1823	5.15	-0.07	126.9	115.68	4.34	2.24	988	
1824	5.23	0.22	152.2	150.59	5.72	0.11	999	
1825	8.80	0.79	143.1	293.29	4.86	3.21	1141	
1826	-9.14	-1.10	123.2	142.88	-11.68	2.89	2590	
1827	12.63			133.98	-2.45	10.75	1372	
1828	6.64			138.82	1.62	7.25	1214	
1829	-3.74			122.73	0.49	8.92	1656	
1830	9.10			128.16	-1.82	0.97	1308	
1831	0.86			102.13	0.00	6.05	1433	4.71
1832	0.00			95.94	-5.38	7.53	1365	-0.68
1833	5.04			110.07	-7.12	7.21	1020	0.61
1834	5.58			99.41	-5.86	4.46	1101	4.07
1835	3.80			104.36	-4.17	5.00	1032	5.56
1836	9.26			123.83	11.38	2.41	924	3.73
1837	-4.88			105.57	2.19	1.83	1668	-1.50
1838	8.88			104.91	6.81	6.40	984	5.71
1839	8.15			96.48	2.85	5.05	1296	4.69
1840	-2.44			94.25	-2.78	14.87	1872	-3.10
1841	1.83			84.26	-3.75	8.83	1788	-2.10
1842	-4.97			87.37	-7.72	9.84	1920	-2.06
1843	5.57			94.99	-11.86	7.31	1572	1.54
1844	11.91			111.15	4.37	3.06	1308	6.01
1845	5.21			123.32	-2.21	1.56	1260	5.53
1846	0.00			117.73	3.85	3.50	1728	6.62
1847	-3.09			104.33	17.02	-0.14	2232	0.53
1848	9.00			89.39	-21.86	10.42	2376	1.30
1849	1.42			82.86	-9.15	9.86		1.60
1850	0.00			82.60	-1.19	3.20		-0.96

Sources: Cols. 1, 2, 3, 5, 6, see Table 7.11; Cols. 4, 7, Gayer, Rostow and Schwartz (1953), except for Col. 9, Deane and Cole, 1967.

with a consequent building up of inventories in textiles and, especially, iron, resulting in unemployment, again especially in the iron communities. The reason this recession is a hard one to date is that the drying up of foreign agricultural supplies brought an agricultural boom domestically; this expansion in the agricultural sector tied in with the expanded efforts to increase output (by such means as enclosures), so that, weather-induced events aside, the agricultural sector pulled up national product. The year 1811 does not look like a good candidate for a recession, although the share index is down somewhat and bankruptcies are high; one reason is that profits are up sharply; another is the rise in the production index. After all, if both industrial and agricultural production rose, where is the recession? Both years have high real consol rates, but 1812 has a falling stock market and a decline in the profits index. Possibly this is a two-year event, with 1812 being the worse of the two years, though that is not the story GRS tell.

Following the recovery, a long expansion affected the British economy until 1816. The literature is filled with remarks on the severity of this recession, the first to be discussed as such in the academic literature. GRS note significant labor unrest (due to unemployment) and agricultural problems but base their explanation mostly on export markets. There was a 'collapse', in their words, of both the American and Continental markets.[19] Most notable here, however, are the end of the war, the end of the government deficits (already discussed in this chapter) and a very bad harvest in 1816 brought on by a cold summer that at least one writer has linked to the significant eruption of Tomburo (in Indonesia) in 1815. There were poor harvests on the Continent as well.[20] Note that Table 7.12 also shows a decline of the CH production index, a rise in bankruptcies and a decline of share prices.

In 1817 and 1818 there was a vigorous expansion, but the recession of 1819 is visible in at least some of the numbers in Table 7.13. GRS bring out their foreign-trade-induced inventory collapse theory again, but they also mention monetary stringency related to the resumption of the Gold Standard and comment on an echo from a recession in the United States. There were apparently no important agricultural factors to consider. Whether or not the recession of 1819 lingered on very far into 1820 is debatable. GRS put the turning point in September 1819, which makes one wonder why they classified 1820 as a recession year. There continued to be no interesting input from the agricultural sector and no other factors strong enough to warrant calling this a recession. We note that the CH index shows 1819 as the year of decline, while 1820 shows trouble in purely financial indices (share prices, profits and the real consol rate). Note, however, that bankruptcies were down in 1820 and the year showed a modest growth rate of the CH index; the year also shows declining profits and share indices and a sharp rise in the real rate.

Bankruptcies are on the decline at this time, however, and we do not think 1820 was a year of recession.

There were two distinct and strong recessions in the 1820s, one in 1826 and one in 1829. These are not in dispute and no one appears to have supported the inclusion of any other years of decline. In 1826 there was a recession in the United States (a collapse of exports again), and some signs of credit tightness in the British market. The latter shows up in terms of a slight rise in nominal interest rates (but a sharp drop in real rates!) and a decline of profit and share indices. The latter could have provided a second shock to the system with the American recession being the first. The agricultural sector was in good shape, however, although the government released some stocks of wheat to keep the price down (in view of the unemployment). It appears that the drastic decline of exports was the proximate cause of this recession. Note that in 1826 the decline in the CH index was the largest (percentage change) in the entire 100-year period. The 1829 recession has no such explanation in the opinion of GRS; there is, though, a rise in the real rate of interest and a decline of stock prices suggestive of some monetary disorder. The harvest of 1828 was poor, but what happened in 1829 was an inflow of foreign grain (allowed because of the high price of grain in Britain); this shock is of small magnitude, to be sure. Investment in plant and equipment in the period was not as strong as either earlier or later, but 1829 was one of the period's better years, on the whole. Nevertheless we think 1829 was a year of recession.

For the 1830s, we think there were recessions in 1832 and 1837, ignoring the advice of GRS to include 1833 and 1838. Like 1829, 1830 was a relatively good year, but 1831 showed a poor harvest and the effects of a decline of exports to the United States. We somewhat reluctantly indicate a recession for that year, although it must have been a very mild one; 1833 is excluded simply because we could find no support for anything other than financial difficulties that year. The troubles later in the decade are more decisive, with the collapse of the American cotton market, perhaps initiated by monetary stringency in Britain, as the most obvious causal factors.[21] There was also a financial crisis to kick this event off. Weather, as we noted above, also plays a role here, since 1837 and 1838 featured bad harvests (throughout Europe), possibly fueled by volcanic activity (Post, 1974). We mention the inevitable collapse of some sort of 'speculative boom' noted in GRS. The CH index identifies 1837 as the worst year in this set and industrial production was up sharply in 1838 and 1839. In view of the diminished role of the agricultural sector by this time (in Britain), it is possible to doubt the existence of a decline in either 1838 or 1839. Indeed the Deane–Cole real GDP series, which starts in 1830, corroborates the impression that 1837 is a year of recession while 1838 is not. Note that the worst year for bankruptcies was 1837.

The long recession of 1840–1842 may well have begun in 1839. This event was largely shared by the United States, and, as we shall see in Chapters 8 and 9, has echoes on the Continent. The harvests of 1839–41 were adequate, and that of 1842 was abundant, so there is little in the agricultural sector to look to for evidence. In international markets, prices fell and trade was falling throughout this period. In their tabulations, described above, 1841–3 are described as recession years by GRS, but in their discussion it seems that 1840 and 1842 offer a clearer case. They mention mainly the export market (import markets are soft, too) as affecting the British, with collapses particularly of the American market in 1839 and 1841. The CH index declined in 1840 and 1842, but we now have the Deane–Cole real GNP index to rely on; it shows declines in all three years. Perhaps there was a brief recovery in 1842, but the financial indicators also show trouble for that year, so we think this is the first real 'depression' in the literature, with three years of decline. Table 7.12 also shows this to be the longest decline, by far, on the monthly data (of 32 months).

Finally, the precise dating of the recession in the late 1840s is made difficult because of the specific mix of financial, agricultural and trade factors. There was a long boom in railroad construction in the mid-1840s, so strong that a majority of long-term capital expenditures were in this sector alone and there were many other projects on the planning boards. In April 1847 the Bank of England suddenly pushed up Bank rate, in response to a gold outflow, and by October the rout was on, in terms of falling share prices, slowing business and so forth. While the literature tends to focus on overinvestment, bad harvests also figure into the story. Indeed, according to GRS, the recession of 1848 is a severe one, lasting into 1849. As we can see in Table 7.12, however, this is not obvious in terms of the CH or GNP numbers, with only 1847 showing this event clearly. Of course, a collapse of investment spending is not recorded there. In any event, the real cause of this situation appears to at least some observers (Dornbusch and Frenkel, 1984) to be the agricultural failure (especially the potato famine) and the collapse of the railroad boom. The link between the collapse of the railroad boom and the agricultural crisis is a financial one in this case, since the large importation of food brought an outflow of gold and a rise in domestic interest rates. Two shocks, along with shocks administered by foreign economies in recession, were enough to bring about this event.

The following tabulation represents our attempts to reconcile the different series with both the historical record and the analysis and data of Gayer, Rostow and Schwartz. We believe the following were recession years.

1793–1794, 1797
1801,   1803?, 1808

1811?,	1812,	1816,	1819
1826,	1829		
1832,	1837		
1840,	1841,	1842,	1847?,	1848

This is 19 years out of 60, which is 31.7 per cent, again a number that is similar to that obtained for the preceding 40 years. The most severe downturns were probably in 1793, 1797, 1808, 1816, 1826, 1837, 1842 and 1848. This is 8 years out of 60, a slightly higher frequency than in the previous period. We should note that we will be looking for signs of the international cycle around these dates for severe downturns in Britain, as we present our material in Chapters 8 and 9.

We are able, in view of our data from CH and Deane and Cole, to offer some conjectures on the amplitude of these cycles as well. From the CH data in Table 7.12, the typical recession, based on annual data to be sure, was between 3 and 5 per cent. The recessions in Deane and Cole, drawn on a broader basis, show smaller declines of real GNP. These are recessions very much like those later in the century, as we shall see, but somewhat larger than twentieth-century downturns, at least those after the Great Depression. There is a good chance that these events are sometimes 'too large' and sometimes 'too small', in view of the omission of the agricultural sector, but, as we have argued, agricultural events are absent in about half of these recessions, so perhaps these magnitudes might survive scrutiny.

To attempt to get a stronger grip on the unemployment situation for at least part of the period, and to work further on amplitudes, Lindert and Williamson (1983) use data on unemployment in engineering, metals and shipbuilding for 1851–1892 in order to estimate a structural relation; they use this to 'back-cast' unemployment for 1837–1850. 'Backcasted' unemployment turns out to be

1837–39	2.70%	(0–7.70% range)
1840–50	4.41%	(0–9.41 % range)
1842–43	9.44%	(4.44–14.44% range)

where the figures in parentheses represent two standard deviations around the point estimates. These figures are in line with those described for real activity and, for that matter, with recent experience in such matters. We have little else to go on from this sometimes sparse literature, but this is surely both consistent and suggestive of the magnitudes that further research might uncover.

7.   THE STANDARD OF LIVING AND OTHER DISTRIBUTIONAL ISSUES[22]

The standard of living debate is one of the oldest and most contentious in economic history. Basically, the debate is organized around two competing visions of industrialization. On the one hand is the view that industrialization creates economic wealth that is widely, albeit unequally, distributed, and that it generally liberates societies from the drudgery associated with more primitive forms of economic organization, thus providing the time and income for other pursuits, some of which, such as education, further enhance productivity. The proponents of this view are generally referred to as the 'optimists' and, for ammunition to support their views, they typically turn to the long-run trends in per capita income, consumption and wages. On the other hand there is the view that industrialization leads to the alienation and immiseration of the great majority of the populace and, although overall output grows as a result of industrialization, the increasingly unequal distribution of output actually leads to a lower standard of living for most people. The proponents of this view are generally referred to as the 'pessimists' and for ammunition they typically turn to the decline of the artisan and peasant, measures of the distribution of income and, more recently, demographic or biological indicators of living standards, such as infant mortality and human stature.

From a macroeconomic perspective, the information typically employed as an indicator of the standard of living is income (or output) per capita, which would be obtained from the estimates of real national income and population that we have already discussed. Reference to such data casts no new light on our interest in this section, but it is worth noting that by most recent accounts, the British per capita growth rate was quite slow (below one per cent) until after 1820 (see Table 7.7), suggesting a fairly stagnant standard of living from 1760 to around 1815–20, with a noticeable rise thereafter (see Crafts, 1987; Fisher, 1992; Mokyr, 1987; and Williamson, 1987b). Of course, as Mokyr (1993, p. 120) indicates, the more interesting question is what would British growth have been in the absence of the set of events we call the industrial revolution? Even the most pessimistic views of industrialization must admit that the path of output per capita would have been substantially lower between, say, 1760 and 1850 without an industrial revolution and in the absence of a dramatic redistribution of wealth from the rich to the poor, such an outcome would have left the majority of British citizens worse off, at least in a material sense, than they actually were. It is difficult to consume products that are not produced!

Despite the generally optimistic view of the aggregate production series, there are two potential problems resulting from relying on this exclusively. First, there are other measures, or at least indicators, of 'the standard of living' than per capita output. Second, the per capita measures represent averages, which, without additional information, actually tell us nothing about the *distribution* of income. One piece of information that sheds some light on this issue is the behavior of real wages. If real wage calculations show something dramatically different from the GNP per capita calculations, then, at the least, we could argue that the effects of growth were uneven among the factors of production – i.e. capital, labor and so forth. The problem, though, is that real wage calculations are hampered by the scarcity of both nominal wages and reliable price deflators. This situation is particularly true of the Phelps Brown and Hopkins numbers (1956, 1957, 1959) that have formed the basis of much of this literature.[23]

As Flinn (1974) points out, the real wage controversy (over the 1750 to 1840 period) could hardly have sustained itself if real wages had moved decisively in one direction or the other. More recently, Lindert and Williamson (1983, pp. 1–2), analysing data from 1755 to 1850 note that the evidence

> ... suggests that material gains were even larger after 1820 than optimists had previously claimed, even if the concept of material well-being is expanded to include health and environmental factors. Although the pessimists can still find deplorable trends in the collective environment after 1820, particularly rising inequality and social disorder, this article suggests that their case must be shifted to the period 1750–1820 to retain its central relevance.

Perhaps the most interesting of the data to which Lindert and Williamson refer are estimates of 'service sector pay rates', some of which are derived from the annual estimates of the House of Commons; these are dated 1755, 1781 and from 1797 onward. Data from Gilboy (1932) and Bowley and Wood (see Flinn, 1974) are also employed. The result is a sharper rise in nominal wages (in the building trades) than shown by Phelps Brown and Hopkins (1956), for example. Lindert and Williamson also adjust for differences in hours at work, payments in kind, and of course consumer prices. Table 7.13 contains a summary of the resulting series, converted to index numbers, with a more recent set provided by Huck (1992). These figures generally confirm the statement by Lindert and Williamson to the effect that a clear discontinuity occurs around 1820, while before that date real earnings grew much more slowly than they did after it, but note that they *definitely* were not declining. It is worth noting that Huck's revisions suggest considerably slower growth at least back to the eighteenth century which, although not erasing the positive trend, makes the optimists' case somewhat less optimistic.

Of course, to the pessimists Lindert and Williamson are asking the wrong questions. Trends in wages do not measure the losses incurred by self-employed artisans and peasants who may have become 'structurally unemployed' (Allen,

Table 7.13   Real earnings in Britain 1755–1851

	Farm Workers	All Blue Collar (a)	White Collar	All	All Blue Collar (b)
1755	65.46	56.50	23.93	42.74	–
1781	61.12	50.19	22.24	39.24	–
1797	74.50	53.61	23.45	42.48	60.6
1805	74.51	51.73	20.82	40.64	–
1810	67.21	50.04	19.97	39.41	–
1815	75.51	58.15	25.49	46.71	–
1819	73.52	55.68	27.76	46.13	69.9
1827	75.86	69.25	39.10	58.99	79.5
1835	91.67	83.43	66.52	78.69	88.0
1851	100.0	100.0	100.0	100.0	100.0

Note: 1851=100.

Sources: Lindert and Williamson (1983); and Huck (1992, p. 48).

1994). Furthermore, the higher incomes associated with industrialization may have just reflected the inferior living and working conditions associated with the move from village to city. Indeed, measures of living standards such as human stature and infant mortality were apparently eroded during the period immediately after 1800. So, although we generally – or perhaps we should say 'overall' – find the optimists' case more persuasive than that of the pessimists, such a conclusion does not mean that the dislocation – creative destruction, in Schumpeter's words – associated with industrialization and economic change more generally did not yield economic losers. Rather, it is to say that to us the evidence suggests that on balance the majority of the population experienced gains – some quite substantial gains – that would not have been forthcoming in the absence of the British industrial revolution.

8.   CONCLUSIONS

Summarizing the trends and cycles in the British economy between 1750 and 1850, then, we can say that the entire period was one of rapid growth by the standards of the preceding millennium and a half or so. Furthermore, industry and commerce developed rather rapidly – again by historical comparison – replacing agriculture as the largest component of GNP. While there is an ongoing dispute over the pace of growth at different times during this century, we think the most salient feature is the overall growth rate itself, which was at least partly the result of the historically rapid industrialization. This growth was accompanied by rapid financial development and by business cycles, and it was apparently slowed down – even if only marginally – by expenditures on war. Thus, while the specific details of this history will no doubt be debated for years to come, it seems as if the British economy of the period has much of the appearance of a modern economy. It has, that is to say, many of its institutions (speaking quite generally) and certainly some of its more important macroeconomic characteristics and all, really, of its broad problems. It is also an economy that shows growing economic integration with its neighbors, as we shall discuss in later chapters.

There are also some specific findings in this chapter. For one, while economic activity clearly expanded from 1780 to 1850, certain qualifications need to be considered. Most important, in fact, is the finding in the literature that the overall rate of growth of the British economy, at least up until 1815 or so, was not as rapid as the industrial revolution school once thought. Next in order of importance, but last considered in the chapter, is the finding, if that is the appropriate term, that the real wages of laborers – and possibly their standard of living – cannot be convincingly demonstrated to have changed much from 1760 to around 1815. After that, although the precise point of departure is not certain, there is a strong improvement in the overall position of laborers – and an accompanying acceleration in the overall growth rate.

There are other results in this chapter that also should be underscored in a summary. First, with respect to crowding out, we found only traces of this phenomenon, and that only in wartime. Second, there are continuing disputes over establishing a cyclical dating that simply will not go away. Perhaps the most important of these is in the period from 1800 to 1816 – where the size of the shocks experienced by the economy and the unusual (for this entire period) inflation rate tend to obscure the underlying macro events in the economy. One can readily predict that further work will be done on these issues for this entire period, even if there is no real improvement in the data.

NOTES

1. Table 7.3 shows a small decline but that could easily be the result of our interpolations to get the numbers centered. By some other estimates (Jackson, 1985 and Crafts, 1985), agricultural output itself may not have increased in much of the period immediately before 1800.
2. For a different view see Crafts (1985) who argues that the increasingly productive agricultural sector frees labor for manufacturing.

3. The argument here is that the capital generated in the sector remained in the sector (Crafts, 1985).
4. The interested reader might wish to compare these views with those of an earlier generation, as typified by Deane (1979).
5. Much of the quantitative data relate only to England (or England and Wales), though we will certainly use broader data when we have it.
6. The railroad was once thought to be both the quintessential modern industry and an essential component of modern economic growth (Rostow, 1962, pp. 55–57). Although the railroad was an important industry in many regards, especially its size and its contributions to lower transport costs, its stature as an indispensable component of economic growth was severely diminished by Fogel's (1964) results.
7. In addition to the references in the text, perhaps the place to begin is the debate between Crafts (1987) and Williamson (1987b). Another useful source is the earlier book by Crafts (1985).
8. For the interested reader, the growth rates of the Hoffmann index contains a single unit root, while those of CH and GRS do not. The former is often a characteristic of smoothed data.
9. See the debate in Cameron (1990) and Hartwell (1990).
10. For summaries of the various aspects of these debates, see Cameron (1967), Craig and Fisher (1997) and Neal (1994).
11. Interestingly, the London banks also underwrote government debt (Neal, 1994, pp. 169–70), making them investment banks as well. Of course, at the top of the hierarchy was the Bank of England, which from its inception operated somewhat as a central bank, even though it was privately owned and held private deposits. Changes in its size actually provide a potential indicator of general credit conditions in the British economy; we will use these numbers more extensively in our discussion of British business cycles below.
12. Among the many assumptions of this framework are those of a competitive market, flexible prices, full employment (along the equilibrium growth path) and an unchanged labor-force participation rate.
13. These are 'supply-side' calculations. Calculations have been made for a demand-side model in Fisher (1992), producing roughly the same conclusions as given here.
14. We say 'for simplicity' because under the Ricardian Equivalence Theorem it doesn't matter whether the government finances by issuing debt or by taxation.
15. In other words, the effect of lagged prices on current prices is negative rather than positive, and significantly so. It does not take a great leap of faith to imagine that rational economic agents would have been aware of this.
16. In their paper on the topic, Heim and Mirowski (1987) consider the weighted average approaches and opt for the calculation of real rates simply by deducting the current rate of inflation from the nominal rate.
17. In Mirowski's (1985) quarterly index, East India Company stock in the first quarter of 1774 stood 38 per cent below its peak in the second quarter of 1771.
18. The reference cycle, following procedures established by the National Bureau of Economic Research, provides a set of turning points identified judgmentally by examining (in this case) over 200 time series of economic variates.
19. They argue that British manufacturers overestimated the extent to which these markets would recover and had an inventory build-up that produced failure and unemployment. As we have already suggested, 'over-production' and 'credit booms' are a common theme in their explanations.
20. Supposedly, the culprit is the layer of ash spread around the globe. The ash would lower temperatures and could produce events all over the globe. Post (1974) mentions significant activity through 1818, again in 1835–40 and in 1845–50.
21. One of the initiating factors here, beginning with finance, is the move toward hard money in the United States, a move associated with a movement of gold toward that country. This seems to have been over in 1837, the year of the recession in the United States.
22. The material in this section comes largely from the sources cited in surveys by Mokyr (1993) and Floud and Harris (1997).

23. The problem is that there appear to be very few measurements of nominal wages and that these appear to be 'officially' legally determined rather than market-determined wages. The upshot is that much of the variation in real wages in their calculations is actually variation in the price index, since the price index is in the denominator of the real wage.

8. Growth and cycles in the major continental economies 1750–1850

1. INTRODUCTION

Generally speaking, European industrialization spread from west to east during the nineteenth century – that is, from Great Britain to the Continent, with France, Germany and Belgium being the first continental industrializers. In this chapter we explore the proposition that each of the major European economies faced roughly similar economic forces during the period 1750 to 1850, but that economic endowments, population growth and the political regimes of the individual countries often produced unique responses to those forces, which had been initiated by the industrialization of Britain. In a sense, the parallels are obvious, since not only did Western Europe lead the way, internationally, toward industrialization, but the nations of the group considered here did so in ways that are actually strikingly similar on the whole. This observation, in itself, is sufficient to suggest that broad models – macroeconomic models in this case – might produce broadly similar insights across countries. After all, the countries considered (along with Great Britain of course) comprise most of the developed economies at the time of the first industrial revolution.

Although the group of countries is small, a great deal of material must be examined and some interesting hypotheses tested. In Chapter 9, we continue our discussion of the first industrial revolution with reference to the set of countries that began to industrialize after 1850. These countries are rather misleadingly called the 'periphery' in many studies of European development, but in Chapter 9 we will try to show how they, too, were part of the evolving globalization of the European economy at this time.

In the present chapter, we begin, as usual, with figures on population and urbanization for France, Germany and Belgium. Following our argument of Chapter 6, population growth provides some guidance for our conjectures about overall growth. After considering population in Section 2, we have two sections that try to identify the broad patterns of growth in the agricultural (Section 3) and industrial (Section 4) sectors of these three countries; we also offer some selective comparisons with the United Kingdom. Note, again, that we are presenting material at this level of disaggregation both because of the paucity of GNP data and because of the fact that these two broad sectors made up a substantial proportion of GNP. In addition, key industries such as coal, iron, cotton and transportation – the backbone of industrial production at the time – certainly provide good indices to economic progress in general. We will also include a survey of banking developments, for somewhat the same reasons (in Section 5). Following these surveys, where every attempt will be made to uncover the similarity of the forces affecting these countries, we will develop further the topic of integration with respect to the macro data (in Section 6), including a discussion of the extent, timing and integration of European business cycles across the three countries and the United Kingdom in this period. Finally, in Section 7, we summarize the broad themes that emerge from the material surveyed in the preceding sections.

2.   POPULATION GROWTH, 1750–1850

In earlier chapters, we have stressed how important population growth can be to the pace of overall economic growth, if only because in this period population growth generally appears to establish a floor for estimates of the overall growth rate. For the French case, though, the details of population growth are actually a little distracting, because the rate of growth of population is relatively low in parts of the period so that less impetus to growth and change could have been generated in this fashion than in the other countries we are studying. What this situation makes perfectly clear is that in many cases per capita calculations are necessary when one is comparing countries – and especially so when the French are included. In fact, after the recalibration, the French per capita output performance seems respectable by almost any standard, and this is not always conceded in the literature.

In Table 8.1 we have collected some figures for population for the three countries and Britain; note that we run these numbers out to 1910, just to underscore the trends that we believe were established in the period we are studying.

If the Belgian and German figures represent a standard for industrializing countries, then the French growth rates seem low, especially in the later years, and the British rapid, over the entire period. What we have seen in Chapter 7, in any case, is that in Britain simple demographics – falling death rates and rising birth rates (in the early years) – explain British population growth. For France, though, the relatively low growth rates were the result of a rapid drop in the birthrate accompanied by a slow decline in the death rate. Evidently, the culprit is birth control, largely in the form of later marriages. The result was that from having a population roughly three times the British in 1750, the French ended up, in 1910, with about the same population. It

Table 8.1   Population levels and annual growth rates, four major
            economies, 1750–1910 (millions)

	Belgium	Rate %	France	Rate %	Germany	Rate %	Britain	Rate %
1750	2.30	–	21.0	–	15.91	–	7.40	–
1800	3.00	0.53	27.3	0.52	21.49	0.60	10.69	0.74
1850	4.40	0.77	35.8	0.54	35.31	0.99	20.88	1.34
1910	7.44	0.88	39.6	0.17	64.57	1.01	40.89	1.12

Sources: Mitchell (1978) and Bairoch, et al. (1988).

goes without saying that this difference probably played some role in the differences between overall growth rates, agricultural productivity, patterns of emigration, urbanization and even the adoption of labor-saving technology in the two countries; however, the demographic differences also make it possible to misunderstand the true quality of the French transformation before (and after) 1850 and this observation needs to be emphasized.

Belgian population grew from 1750 to 1800, as indicated in Table 8.1 but, evidently, this growth was mainly in the countryside (as Table 8.2 below indicates, the percentage of the population urbanized actually fell slightly from 1750 to 1800). Supporting this point is the fact that by some estimates the *level* of urban population in 1790 was the same as in 1700 (Mokyr, 1976). Of course, one should keep in mind that the Low Countries had a relatively high level of urbanization by 1700, but this is still an unusual result for a growing economy. It seems that population was retained in the countryside because of increased agricultural productivity due to drainage and enclosures and, most importantly, because of the rapid growth of rural industry. This can be understood to fit the general idea of 'proto-industrialization' as defined by Mendels (1972) and as discussed in Chapter 5 above. A key characteristic of the Belgium economy in 1790 then was a large urban population *and* a large non-urban proto-industrial labor force ready to participate in the region's industrialization.[1] A proto-industrial workforce, coal and iron deposits (particularly in the area around Liège) and adequate transportation facilities, gave Belgium an early edge among the continental countries studied in this chapter.

During the first half of the nineteenth century, Belgian population growth accelerated; while the rural population increased during this period, the urban population grew even more rapidly and the relative decline of the rural population turned into an absolute decline in the 1840s. Apparently, a declining rural linen industry (which had retained some of its proto-industrial characteristics) was accentuated by rural depopulation and a worldwide decline in the position of Belgian linen, possibly because of the relative inefficiency of its domestic producers but mostly due to the growing popularity (and declining price) of cotton textiles (Mokyr, 1976). We should note, though, that we shall argue in Section 8.4 that this was by no means a disaster for the Belgian economy, which grew as rapidly as its major competitors in the staple goods of the industrial revolution (coal, iron and cotton) partly on the strength of its relatively large urban population and its large proto-industrial workforce.

The population in the German states grew more rapidly than that of either France or Belgium. Indeed, by 1850 the German population was roughly the same as that of France, a situation which would have been considered fantastic only a generation or so earlier. The primary cause of this convergence in population was the much higher fertility rates in Germany. After 1820, the crude birthrate in Germany was consistently 25 per cent higher than that in France. While we want to remind the reader again that the relationship between economic growth and population growth is not altogether understood, the German economy was expanding rapidly by historical comparison. It is worth noting that before 1850, German industrialization was concentrated in a few clearly defined regions, specifically Silesia, Saxony, and the Ruhr and Rhineland.

Until 1800, then, the growth rates of population for the four countries were very similar, while from 1800–1850, even granting the problems associated with generating totally consistent numbers, these rates appear to diverge. In any case, following our argument that population growth rates can be viewed as lower-bound estimates of the real output growth, we are prepared to argue that the annual growth rates for the four countries were in excess of the following for the period 1750–1850:

Belgium	0.53%
Britain	0.74
France	0.52
Germany	0.60

In the subsequent fifty years, these rates roughly doubled, except for the French. Of course, we are *not* prepared to argue that declining rates of population growth in France somehow represented a retardation of the French economy, as the following sections should make clear.

We are also interested in the patterns of urbanization in this period, mainly as an indicator of progress since the growing commercial and industrial sectors of these three countries are generally urban activities in this period (except for Belgium from 1750 to 1800). Both Germany and France had relatively large agricultural populations during this period and this means that their urban populations were proportionately smaller (than Belgium or the United Kingdom). In Table 8.2, we look at the levels of urbanization and the urban growth rates for the four countries, a comparison that underscores some truly substantial structural differences.

Table 8.2   Urbanization in four countries 1750–1850 (millions)

	1750	%	1800	%	Growth Rate %	1850	%	Growth Rate %
Belgium	0.51	22.2	0.65	21.7	0.48	1.11	25.2	1.07
France	3.11	12.7	3.65	12.9	0.32	5.91	16.5	0.96
Germany	1.40	8.8	2.02	9.4	0.73	3.82	10.8	1.27
U.K.	1.82	17.3	3.37	20.8	1.23	8.87	32.2	1.94

Note: The population figures used as the base for 1850 are from Mitchell (1978).

Source: Bairoch, et al. (1988).

As the table indicates, the four countries urbanized relatively rapidly in this period, with the period of accelerated economic growth (1800–1850) showing more rapid urbanization, as well. Indeed the growth rate of the urban population accelerated in every country after 1800.

Belgium was the most urbanized country in 1750 and, as we noted above, this may have been an important source of its relatively early industrialization (Mokyr, 1976); however, between 1750 and 1800 Belgium's overall population grew more rapidly than its urban population, an observation which highlights the rural character of much of Belgian's industry at that time. In the United Kingdom, on the other hand, the urban population grew much more rapidly, while the French grew the least; we have already explained the divergent demographics behind these results. In any case, as measured by sheer size, the French had the largest urban population in 1750 and 1800, and all four countries urbanized rapidly by any reasonable standard from 1800 to 1850.

Details are available on the growth of individual cities in Bairoch et al. (1988). For example, from 1750 to 1800, *German* commercial centers such as Hamburg (44%), Berlin (52%) and Frankfurt (50%) grew very rapidly, while from 1800 to 1850, mixed industrial and commercial centers such as Cologne (168%), Leipzig (110%), Munich (150%), Stuttgart (150%) and Aachen (116%) joined Berlin (154%) in an explosion of urbanization. In *France*, from 1750 to 1800, the fastest growth was in Bordeaux (55%) and Marseille (49%), while in the next half century, Marseille (93%) was joined by Brest (135%), Lyon (62%), Paris (91%), Toulon (213%) and Toulouse (86%). In *Belgium*, where urbanization was further along than in the other three countries in 1750, Antwerp (44%) was the fastest-growing city in the 1750–1800 period when urban areas as a whole declined *relatively*, while after 1800, the more industrially-oriented Bruges (61%), Brussels (100%) and Ghent (94%) led the way.[2]

Broadly speaking, the population and urbanization data support our general proposition about the relatively rapid spread of industrialization across the European landscape, beginning with the three countries studied in this chapter. Of course, as we have noted several times, the link between economic growth and development and population growth is difficult to generalize and, while we are confident that urbanization was strongly correlated with industrialization during this period, the urbanization figures are still only suggestive of the industrial transition occurring in these economies. In addition urbanization reflects the other side, at least partly, of the transformation taking place in the countryside and before looking at the data on industrialization we turn to the development of the agricultural sectors in these countries.

3.   AGRICULTURAL DEVELOPMENT

It is really impossible to consider the development of European agriculture after, say, 1750 without confronting its potential role in industrialization; however, this issue has generated a great deal of controversy since the term 'industrial revolution' entered the lexicon. Broadly speaking, one encounters two views in the literature: one is that an increasingly productive agricultural sector 'freed' resources for the industrial sector; whereas the other is that the slow productivity growth in the agricultural sector relative to manufacturing made the latter a more attractive venue for capital and labor. As with so many of these types of dispute, there is an element of truth to both positions. The productivity growth in manufacturing *was* generally superior to that of agriculture; however, faced with growing populations and a declining share of the labor force in agriculture (and later an absolute decline), the resources remaining in agriculture had to increase output per unit of input at some margin, or there would have been a decline in food production per capita (putting aside imports). Although there is some evidence of declining consumption of nutrients per capita in the late eighteenth century and of growing inequality in consumption in the first half of the nineteenth century (Steckel and Floud, 1997), in general agricultural production grew fairly steadily, at least after the late eighteenth century. In examining these developments for the countries we consider in this chapter, we focus on four issues: the actual increase in output and productivity; emancipation and the change in property rights associated with enclosure; changes in practice; and evolving markets.

Perhaps the most interesting aspect of agricultural development during this period – at least in terms of agriculture's role in the macroeconomy – is the acceleration of agricultural output. Apparently, this acceleration was a constant companion of the quickening industrial pace in eighteenth- and nineteenth-century Europe and thus leads to the confusion discussed above.

We note that this topic is important partly because the agricultural sector in both France and Germany was actually the largest sector in the economy throughout the 1750–1850 period.

Turning to the *French* case first, an almost overwhelming volume of literature has described the period before the French Revolution as a stagnant one for French agriculture, with a rigidly structured social system and virtually no technological change.[3] Indeed, some of the literature extends the productivity malaise up until 1850. However, in the light of more recent research, such a position is difficult to defend and we argue that the notion that the period after 1800 continued an earlier 'trend' of total stagnation is surely difficult to maintain.

To be sure, if one is looking for dramatic changes one will be disappointed; even so, cumulatively powerful changes took place in the French marketplace and these involved the agricultural sector in an active role (Roehl, 1976). Agriculture was generally commercial in this period and, although most of the marketable surpluses were marketed locally, there was a strong export market as well. This was possible because of 'substantial reserves of potential productive capacity' (Goldsmith, 1984, p. 185) – which were apparently easy to tap with simple adjustments in agricultural practices – and the increasingly efficient use of that capacity (Grantham 1993). This process is especially obvious from the mid-eighteenth century. There is evidence for inefficiency compared to the British, of course, especially in the contemporary literature, and there are also some uncomplimentary data on yields (per acre or per unit of seed). In fact, French yields per acre were roughly comparable, though perhaps a little below those of England in the late eighteenth century; however, French labor productivity lagged that of the English, with output per worker in grain production roughly 50 per cent that of England *c.* 1800 (Clark, 1989).

These comparisons with England or Great Britain, which are the basis of much of the literature on this topic, should be carefully qualified. For one thing, the most often-mentioned yardsticks are single-input measures of productivity instead of ones based on total factor productivity. Furthermore, economic agents in the French countryside faced constraints, possessed information and responded to opportunities that were often local in nature and apparently employed techniques that were profitable in *their* environment. That this process yielded a rural economy unlike that in Britain can and should largely be attributed to demographic and social factors, to the type of product involved, to climate, market size, transportation infrastructures, the cost of inputs, the availability of capital and, of course, to the quality of the human capital involved. Attributing the 'lower' level of French technical prowess to some sort of *ancien régime* mentality is not a particularly persuasive argument; indeed, no such regime is distinctly visible in the available economic data.

In terms of innovation and agricultural practice, the closer one looks, the less backward the French seem. More than thirty years ago Kindleberger (1964), calling on a variety of French sources, noted that the potato was introduced from 1740 to 1770, clover and other forage crops from 1770 to 1790, corn (in the south) and sugar beets (in the north), all by the end of the century. These developments, he alleges, put the squeeze on the fallow-field system and produces the judgment (p. 211) that 'the greater part of France participated to some degree in the agricultural revolution of the eighteenth century'. This proposition is supported by Morineau (1970) and suggests that output increased as follows:

    1700–1750   0.3% per annum
    1750–1780   1.4% per annum.

which would have placed the former around or a little below population growth and the latter considerably above. Speaking for the critics of the established view, Goldsmith (1984, p. 177) argues that:

> In accepting uncritically the popular notions of static agrarian systems and the eternal order of the field, early modernists misconstrued the findings of the geographers and confused historically distinct aspects of farming. The morphology of agrarian systems was not the same as the economic use of land. There was always a broad range of intensification and factor mixes possible without any change in morphology.

Slicher van Bath's essay for the *Cambridge Economic History of Europe* (1977) takes essentially the same view.[4] The effects of these changes show up in yield data, which show a growth of roughly 0.5 per cent per annum after 1750 (calculated from Chorley, 1981, p. 92), and in labor productivity, which grew at about the same rate (calculated from Grantham, 1993, p. 483).

With respect to the expansion of marketable production, the traditional view is summarized in Price (1981). The claim is that in the first half of the nineteenth century, while no area lay completely outside commercial circuits (p. 43), the French agricultural community by the mid-1850s was fragile, fragmented, semi-closed and had only irregular market links and, although a political revolution had occurred, an economic one had not. It is Newell (1973) who is perhaps most responsible for the alternative view and his (and others') results continue to generate controversy. Newell, focusing on output figures, argues that the data show that the actual acceleration in total and per capita agricultural output began in the 1815–1824 period, in spite of two very bad years in 1815 and 1816, and lasted until 1865–1874.

To see what actually happened after 1815, we have access to an agricultural production index published by Toutain (1987); for comparison we present both the agricultural and production indices in Figure 8.1, although we will refer to the latter in Section 8.4.[5]

Here we see considerable growth in agricultural production, not, to be sure, as rapid as that in industrial production. Indeed agricultural production rose 72.7 per cent over the period from 1815 to 1850 and, more surprisingly, 46.6 per cent from 1815 until the business cycle peak in 1832. Put in terms of annual rates of growth, the growth rate in agricultural production was 2.25 per cent from 1815 to 1832 and 1.56 per cent overall. Thus not only was growth rapid – and well above population growth – but it was rapid *from the start of the period*. By focusing on the comparison of French practice with British practice, these gains are often overlooked or sometimes even disparaged in the literature.

The gains shown in Figure 8.1 resulted mostly from increased productivity that occurred across many crops and regions (especially in the central and southern regions). This transformation was the result of the use of less fallow land, the growth of planted meadows, the increasing use of manure fertilizers, and the more efficient use of seasonal labor, all modest innovations that nonetheless had a profound effect in an agricultural sector that had not yet made extensive use of these technologies (Chorley, 1981; Grantham, 1993; and Newell, 1973). We have already made the point that to an economist there is no reason to regard such improvements as in any major way different from tractors and combines, depending, of course, on the environment in which they occur.[6] Indeed. O'Brien and Keyder (1978) emphasize the quality of land, meteorological environment, crop choice (which is also influenced by demand) and availability of capital as influential determinants of productivity. They reduce the question, in a nutshell to whether there is a measurable difference (between French and British agriculture) for a comparable piece of land, standardized for the above factors. Their answer is that there is not, on the whole.

Obviously, emancipation of the peasantry and enclosure represented important changes in European agriculture though, as with English enclosures, the early effects were probably more qualitative than quantitative; however, in England the agricultural revolution that accompanied enclosure had generated and been led by the gentry and by a yeoman class of prosperous farmers. Farm workers simply did not prosper, although, of course, they had jobs. In France, the Revolution made such an outcome politically unfeasible. First, the distribution of noble and clerical lands, at what were arguably lower than market prices, created a windfall both for the peasantry and the formerly landless laborers. Second, given the role of the peasantry and the dispossessed rural laborers in the Revolution itself, it became politically infeasible to carry through the enclosures and rural reforms that had been started before the Revolution, which resulted in the perpetuation of common rights long

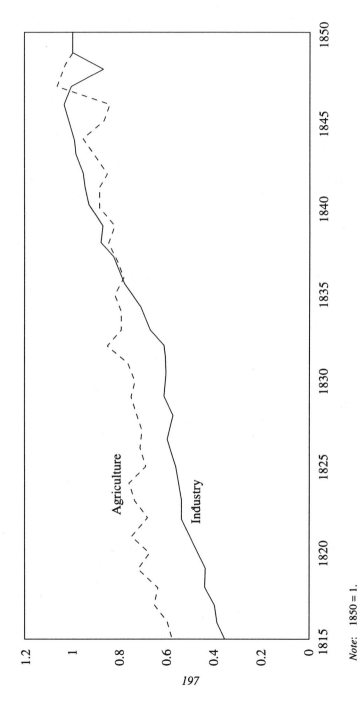

Note: 1850 = 1.

Figure 8.1   French agricultural and industrial production 1815–1850

197

after such rights had been eliminated in the rural sectors of other major economies. This turn of events gave the smallest holders a stake in French agriculture unlike any of their counterparts in England or the German states and, although there was productivity growth throughout the period, it was probably slower than in either Britain or Germany.

In *Germany* the modernization of the contractual arrangements in agriculture began in earnest during the Napoleonic period. Although the nature and timing of emancipation varied from state to state, in general the political reforms are quite consistent with our discussions of the state in Chapter 2. In Prussia, in particular, the leading civil servants realized that a move to freer markets would contribute to the creation of a larger tax base, which was required to compete in the Great Powers game with post-Revolution France. At the same time, there was a concern that in the absence of change directed from above there might well be revolution from below, as had been the case in France. Thus a combination of fear and enlightenment led to the land reforms of 1806–1811; however, with the exception of the western German states, these reforms did not lead to a large yeoman class, as their British equivalent had during the previous century, nor did they generate a nation of smallholders as in France. Instead, these reforms led to the consolidation of great estates, particularly east of the Elbe, and it was on these estates that the modernization of German agriculture took place.

Typically, the transformation from serf to free peasant was achieved through the peasant's payment of compensation to his former lord, but the terms of this compensation varied by region and by the pre-emancipation status of each serf. In Prussia, for example, the narrative record suggests a stratification of the peasantry into roughly three groups. The first group, which became the foundation of the yeomanry, such as it was, contained the more substantial peasants who had hereditary claims to land. These peasants commuted their ancient obligations through redemption dues payable over long periods of time. The second group, the members of which possessed no such claims, essentially forfeited a substantial proportion of their current claims to communal plots in return for ownership of the remaining share. The third group consisted of those with no formal claims to land. The loss of their rights to the commons essentially compelled them to become wage laborers.

What effect did these reforms have on German agriculture? In terms of yields, German agriculture compared favorably with that of France as early as 1800 in the production of rye and oats, though German yields of wheat and barley were substantially below (roughly 66 per cent of) those of France (Chorley, 1981; and Clark, 1987, 1989) both were below the figures for Britain. In terms of labor productivity, pre-emancipation German agriculture compared even less favorably with either France or Britain. Output per worker in Prussian wheat production in 1810 was less than 50 per cent of that in

French agriculture and less than 33 per cent of that in British agriculture in the late eighteenth century (Clark 1989). Although we do not have comparable figures for 1850, by 1870 output per agricultural worker in Germany had risen to more than 50 per cent of that of Britain and to nearly 75 per cent of that of France. More impressively, German yields had risen to more than 80 and 90 per cent of those in Britain and France, respectively. So, clearly, there was a tremendous amount of 'catching up' in German agriculture after 1800, and it should be recalled that this was a period of fairly robust productivity growth in British and French agriculture, though Perkins (1981) puts most of the growth in Germany after 1850 – an argument that we consider in the next chapter.

4. THE GROWTH AND INTEGRATION OF THE INDUSTRIAL SECTOR

This·section contains an overview of the growth of the industrial sectors of Belgium, France and Germany from 1750 to 1850. Our general approach is to compare our findings for the two time-periods (1750–1800 and 1800–1850) and four leading industries of the so-called first industrial revolution (in coal, iron, cotton and later railroads). We frequently present evidence for each country separately, partly for coherence and partly because that is the way the information comes to us from the literature, but we do make a strong effort to stick to our integration and globalization themes by taking as broad a view as possible, geographically speaking. This is made easy by what we discover here, which is that there are remarkable similarities across the three countries considered. Indeed, on occasion, the similarities extend to the United Kingdom as well.

1750–1800

As we noted briefly above, during the years before 1800, *Belgium* had substantial rural and urban industries and, although both saw substantial growth, rural industry was particularly robust. These rural industries included the enormous linen industry (in Flanders), wool in Verviers and the eastern Walloon provinces and metallurgy near Liège, Namur and Hainault (Mokyr, 1976). In addition, lace was manufactured in the urban areas of the Brabant and Flanders (especially in Antwerp and Brussels). The linen industry was very small-scale but produced large exports, especially to Spain; these, of course, exited through urban centers. The wool industry in eastern Belgium was substantial, involving as much as ten per cent of the population and was carried on partly in mills, with weaving and spinning in the mills and spinning in the countryside. Again, most of the wool was exported (to France, Italy and Germany). The metal-working industries were in nails, pins, cutlery and armaments (in Liège); they, too, were largely rural and destined mainly for export. Of course these products required iron and this was produced in blast furnaces in the area. Mokyr notes that in 1795 there were 65 blast furnaces in Belgium, producing some 18,500 tons of cast iron. Furthermore, in the 1750 to 1800 period, calico printing (especially), paper, glass, sugar and earthenware were introduced.

At the very end of the century, following the French conquest in 1795, the modernization of Belgium industry began. For example, in 1798 a Belgian smuggled a 'mule' out of England and in 1801 the first spinning mill was established in Ghent. Wool, too, obtained its first machine-powered production in 1798; in this case a firm in Verviers hired an Englishman to set up the machinery. Metallurgy, as noted above, was well established in Belgium, but it did not experience much fundamental technological change prior to 1800. Even so, the blasts became hotter and the furnaces larger, with the expansion concentrated in the Charleroi region. In fact, coke smelting doesn't appear until 1824 and the Cort process until 1821, with the introduction of the rolling mill coming in 1822–23. The reason for the delay (and for similar delays in the linen industry) appears to be a combination of low rural wages and the relative scarcity of financial capital. The Belgians clearly had access to the technology of the British and in one case (in linen) actually developed the modern process. We should note that coal and iron ore were abundant in Belgium; however, it appears that the gains from the application of British technology to Belgium resources do not seem to have been realized until after 1815.

Traditional explanations of the causes and consequences of the French Revolution contained, either implicitly or explicitly, an indictment of the economic policies of the *ancien régime* in *France*, concentrating on the politics; however, the past two decades have witnessed the rise of a substantial literature rehabilitating the industrial progress of the *ancien régime*. This process began with the early work of Fohlen (1961), who noted that English cloth-making processes appeared in France from 1752, with a mule-jenny put in use in 1782. By 1790 there were a number of spinning mills, several having as many as 10,000 spindles, with Orleans as the center of this activity (Fohlen, 1970). France had its first coke blast furnace in 1785 but charcoal was the standard fuel well into the nineteenth century, though time-series data are hard to come by. While the French employed the current technology of a style similar to the British and while they probably did so as efficiently as the British, evidence suggests that they did not do so as extensively as the British. Still, Fohlen (1970) argues that the industrial revolution did begin in France somewhere between 1760 and 1790, and it produced (p. 68) 'a rapid and brilliant beginning, as a result of new techniques, exploited thanks to the country's prosperity'.

It cannot be said that this view has gone unchallenged. Clough (1972), Milward and Saul (1973), Price (1981) and Trebilcock (1981), for example, provide more skeptical reviews of French industrialization, with perhaps the strongest view in this respect being that of Price, who extends his argument about agriculture (see above) to cover industry as well. This argument, repeated here, is that what growth there was occurred within pre-industrial structures which were characterized by industrial production of mainly consumer goods, mostly by means of handicraft. In other words, France may have been exposed to British technology, but the adoption of that technology was not on a scale that one could call 'revolutionary'.

Trebilcock's overview of the economic policies of the *ancien régime*, the revolutionary period and the First Empire is a bit more subtle. First, the so-called restrictions typically associated with pre-revolution France had been severely weakened by the 1780s. In particular the monopolies, guilds and Colbertist industrial specifications were not the quantitative brakes on the economy that they might appear to have been by simply studying the letter of the law. Furthermore, although the tax system was recondite, overall it cannot be said to have been confiscatory. Second, the policies of the revolutionary governments and the Empire were more likely to restrain growth rather than to promote it. In particular, the emphasis on small peasant holdings noted above was transferred to the industrial sector in the form of a bias against large-scale enterprises, and the continental system, which was very much in line with early modern thought on the promotion of industry, only seems to have further eroded French trade and protected small businesses (many of which did not survive the competition following the restoration). While France's trade policies were designed to give her manufacturers an advantage relative to the British, it was hard to keep continental competitors from taking advantage of the vacuum thus created, and ultimately 'France was clutching a nest of industrial vipers to her bosom' (Trebilcock, 1981, p. 131). Taking this story as a whole, Trebilcock apparently sees no industrial revolution in France, at least to the extent that term describes what happened in Britain. To be fair, though, he argues that to measure the later developments of the continental nations against the British *a generation or two earlier* is to ask the wrong question, since the leading industries, transportation and finance, and the role of the state all changed in the intervening years. This is a view with which we are sympathetic, and thus we tend to speak of industrialization rather than the industrial revolution.

The alternative view of industrialization in France in this period has been promoted by the empirical evidence put together over the past two decades and the authors associated with these data typically agree with Fohlen's earlier assessment. Crafts (1977), Roehl (1976) and O'Brien and Keyder (1978) all seem to agree that France was not as backward as originally thought. For example, O'Brien and Keyder show growth in per capita commodity production from 1781–90 to 1803–12 that is comparable to that in Britain. In fact, in their calculation, British output grew 92.7 per cent while French grew 80.4 per cent over the roughly twenty-year period (see Table 8.8 below). Without going further into the details, we note that it is important to appreciate that the style of French industrialization in this period was unlike that in Britain, being slower in heavy industry, tied up with population dynamics in a different way, probably more labor-intensive and featured a different product mix. Furthermore, comparisons between the two nations – of dubious value in some ways – become confused because industrialization is regionally concentrated in both countries, but with France's considerably larger area burdened with its massive non-industrial heartland.

The early industrialization in *Germany* is typically characterized as 'relatively backward' in the literature (see, for example, the treatment in Gerschenkron, 1962 and Trebilcock, 1981) and there are good reasons for doing so when the British, and perhaps even the Belgians and the French, are the benchmark. Furthermore, for Germany, one has to deal with the legion of writers who see this problem as, at least partly, a manifestation of Germany's early modern political make-up. The efforts of the House of Hohenzollern not withstanding, Germany was not a politically unified country. Centrists see in this period the roots of an apparent retardation in German growth, but it is not entirely clear that Germany (however one might want to define that term geographically) was not moving with the times in this period, at least by Continental standards, with a characteristic emphasis on trading, shipping and, of course, agriculture. In any event, a degree of centralization came with Frederick's attempts to build a northern union to counterbalance the Austrian Habsburgs and, at this time, 'Germany' included a sizeable piece of Poland, as well.

Although we are sympathetic to the interest in the political unification of German and the other European states, as our discussion in Chapter 2 and elsewhere suggests (Craig and Fisher, 1997), we tend to view these matters as resulting from and potentially facilitating subsequent economic growth rather than the other way around. In any case, we do not dispute the claim that German industrialization took place on a limited scale, by the British standard; however, what strikes us the most about early German industrialization is its clear geographical pattern. Early industrialization occurred largely in Saxony, Silesia and the Rhineland and in the state-sponsored factories of Prussia. For example, spinning mills were introduced in Saxony by the mid-1780s and the textile industry there seems to have prospered while the continental system was in effect, growing almost twentyfold between 1806 and 1812 (Kitchen, 1978). Coke blast furnaces were employed in the production of iron in Silesia in the mid-1790s and Silesia remained a center of continental iron production. The Prussian government secured a steam engine for a state-operated factory in Berlin in 1785.

We feel comfortable with Kitchen's view that around 1800 Germany was in a good position to industrialize, but by most accounts she did not, at least not at anything like the pace of the British or the Belgians; however, typical explanations of Germany's continued backwardness until the middle part of the nineteenth century are somewhat less agreeable. As noted above, we do not want to put too much emphasis on political fragmentation, because the states that ultimately composed the Second Reich, e.g. Hanover, Saxony, Brunswick, Bavaria and Prussia, were all large viable states by European standards. Another reason for Germany's alleged failure is that important technical 'backward linkages' (to use Rostow's terminology) ran to the English mainly because that country had a sufficient technological lead to make it appropriate to buy machinery and even finished iron products from it. In addition to the fact that the importance of such linkages has generally been overemphasized, from an international viewpoint this is merely a detail, since the German market was growing quite rapidly and German firms were well represented in certain kinds of manufacturing, as well as in commerce and finance.

In short, we do not see 'failure' in the German economy, at least not by any standard other than that of British 'success'. The problem is that when we look at the frontiers of the leading industries *c.* 1800 the British seem to be the leaders in terms of both volume and productivity and while it seems clear that each of the continental states lagged behind the British somewhat in the application of state-of-the-art technologies and in industrial output, by the late eighteenth century each possessed nascent textile, extractive and metallurgical industries organized more or less along modern lines by the standards of the rest of Europe and, indeed, the world. To be sure, the French and Belgians were better positioned for the early nineteenth century developments than the Germans, but even in Germany, the regions of Silesia, Saxony and the Rhineland were among the most economically advanced on the continent and thus in the world.

1800–1850

Whether one characterizes the industrial revolution in terms of technological change, social changes associated with the rise of the factory system, change in the composition of output and consumption, overall growth or some combination of these factors, the underlying changes occurred in just a few major industries. These included outputs, such as cotton textiles and ferrous metals;

inputs, such as coal and iron ore; and ultimately transportation, such as the railroad, which consumed coal and ferrous metals. Thus, in this section we focus on four industries – coal iron, cotton and railroad construction – with the objective of developing a vision of integration and common development among the continental nations. In other words, we compare Belgium, France and Germany in a way that makes them look quite similar to one another and, risking our hypothesis to some extent, to Britain. We invite this risk, which arises because the British industrial sector is so much larger, and in some sense more technologically advanced than the others, simply because we can see vigorous growth and often convergence in the aggregate data and we believe that is the essential message. In this respect our work contrasts with much of the literature, some of it contemporary, which views the British lead as the result of British capitalists and entrepreneurs having done something fundamentally *right*; while the European lag is evidence of those groups having done something fundamentally *wrong*. The evidence leads us to conclude that this is probably not a fruitful way of looking at the economic history of this period.

The data seem to indicate that in each of these countries there were regions in which industrialization occurred, at roughly the same time as it did in the English Midlands, but that England's advantages, as already discussed in this study, and its sudden and unprecedented success in exploiting those advantages, obscure the fact that the rest of the leaders in European countries were not far behind. Furthermore, by historical standards – that is, those of the premodern age – these countries quickly began to grow more rapidly than the British and in no obvious ways were they impeded in their industrialization by anything other than war and specific resource endowments.

Industrial policy was not central to Britain's development and the arrival of early industrial policy, such as it was, in the other countries is mostly a coincidence rather than an advantage in their rapid growth in the early nineteenth century. In all of this, then, the quick and dramatic start in Britain, based largely on its considerable economic accomplishments prior to industrialization, has created a norm when it probably should be treated as an exception. Industrialization began in Belgium, France and Germany at roughly the same time as it appeared in Britain, and is clearly visible in the post-1815 data. If this seems like an observation that doesn't quite match up with the rest of this paragraph, the reader should recall that no such growth would have been possible without all of the other parts of the economic structure having been in place. The reader could also consult the literature, both contemporary and modern, to see that our hypothesis is still controversial, although it is growing less so as the data are improved.

A common perception of both contemporary and modern scholars is that the French were held back in their industrial development by problems associated with the use of coal as an industrial input; in short, it was more expensive to its users than in Britain, referring, at least, to coal drawn from domestic sources (see the discussion in Kindleberger, 1964). The data indicate otherwise; consider Table 8.3.

Table 8.3   *French coal production and consumption ('000 metric tons and annual growth rates) 1815–1850*

Date	Production	Growth %	Consumption	Growth %
1815	882			
1820	1094	4.31		
1825	1491	6.23		
1830	1863	4.45	2492	
1835	2000	1.42	3256	5.35
1840	3000	8.11	4184	5.02
1845	4207	6.76	6220	7.93
1850	4434	1.05	6985	2.32
Overall		4.61		5.15

Note: The annual growth rate of production, 1830–1850, was 4.34%.

Source: Fohlen (1970).

Here we see a substantial growth of coal production in the French economy at 'industrial revolution' growth rates before 1850 *and before the arrival of the railroad* (in 1835). Of course, importation raised the consumption numbers and, in effect, somewhat smoothed the production figures. Since charcoal was still economically efficient in some areas, these numbers make an especially strong case for rapid French growth in this period. Of course, in 1850 36.5 per cent of French coal used was imported, but we choose to see European economic integration in this fact, rather than to dwell on the potential transaction and shipping costs associated with importation.

Broadening the discussion to include Belgium and Germany, let us look at the coal production of in all three countries from 1815 to 1850. The figures in Table 8.4 are remarkable for showing the similarity in growth rates, the overall *rapid* growth and, more surprisingly, the comparable levels of production throughout the period. It is worth noting that Belgium had a relatively small population and relatively large exports (mostly to France). In 1830, for example, Belgium exported around 20 per cent of its coal production, while in 1850 this had risen to 34.2 per cent. The latter was nearly 2 million metric

Table 8.4   *Coal production in Belgium, France and Germany 1815–1850*
            (million metric tons)

Date	Belgium	France	Germany
1815		0.9	1.3[2]
1820		1.1	1.3
1825		1.5	1.6
1830	2.3[1]	1.9	1.8
1835	2.6	2.5	2.1
1840	3.9	3.0	3.2
1845	4.9	4.2	4.4
1850	5.8	4.4	5.3
% Growth Rate	4.87	4.53	4.13

Notes:
U.K. growth in the same period was 2.94%.
[1]   1831.
[2]   1817.

Source: Mitchell (1992).

tons, and would have been enough to supply 70 per cent of France's imports that year. As the note to the table indicates, U.K. production grew at 2.94 per cent per year over the 1815 to 1850 period; taken together, we view the development of this important industry as emblematic of the convergence and integration of these economies.

Iron ore also moved across the borders of these countries with equal facility as did the finished product. Perhaps the most useful data though are those on pig-iron production in the three countries (see Table 8.5). Again we see substantial rates of growth – much faster than either overall growth or sectoral growth in previous centuries, although, with respect to pig iron production, none of the continental economies kept pace with the U.K. rate of 6.03 per cent from 1820 to 1850. Even in the last decade of the period the U.K. growth rate (down to 4.76 per cent) still exceeded that of these countries, although it was only marginally above the Belgian rate. In this important industry, while the period of 1800–1850 was one of divergence, in view of the large exports from the United Kingdom, these countries were no doubt converging in the *use* of iron in production, and that is an essential ingredient in the globalization of these economies.[7]

A third industrial sector for which comparisons can be made for this period is the cotton textile industry. As noted by the narrative detail above, a domes-

Table 8.5   Pig iron production in Belgium, France and Germany
             1820–1850 ('000 metric tons)

Date	Belgium	France	Germany
1820		113[2]	85[3]
1825		199	95
1830	90[1]	266	110
1835	115	295	155
1840	95	348	190
1845	135	439	190
1850	145	406	210
Growth (%)	2.51	4.12	3.35

Notes:
Note that U.K. growth in the same period was 6.03%.
[1]   1831.
[2]   1819.
[3]   1823.

Source: Mitchell (1978).

tic cotton textile industry emerged in Belgium at virtually the same time as it did in Britain, while the French also quickly established a presence, especially in certain product lines. We have gathered the available annual data in Table 8.6 which compares the three countries over the 1815–1850 period and offers a few points of comparison with the United Kingdom.

These numbers establish the existence of Belgian production before 1815 and hint at the level of production in France. In any case, we see that both Belgian and German growth rates in cotton consumption exceeded that in the United Kingdom, and the growth rate in France is not far behind. (France is ahead in per capita terms.) These numbers attest to the rapid spread of the cotton industry to the three countries being considered and to a pattern of convergence in place well before 1850. Note that it goes without saying that we are speaking of cotton *mills*, since it is hard to imagine such growth rates in the absence of mechanization.

Perhaps the most remarkable comparison, and the last we will attempt here, is that for the development of the railroad. Among the many hypotheses advanced about this important industry, the one of most interest here is the argument that the United Kingdom had a huge lead and that the other nations lagged in ways that actually hurt their development. The data appear in Table 8.7.

Table 8.6   Raw cotton consumption in four countries 1815–1850 ('000 metric tons)

Date	Belgium	France	Germany	U.K.
1815	1.3[1]			37
1820	1.1			
1825	2.4			
1830	3.0	28[2]	2.4[3]	112
1835	4.8	39	4.5	
1840	9.1	53	12.8	
1845	8.7	60	17.0	
1850	10.0	59	17.1	267
Growth (%)*	6.02	3.92	10.91	4.34

Notes:
The overall U.K. growth rate was 5.65% from 1815.
*   The growth rates are from circa 1830 to 1850.
[1]   1816.
[2]   1831.
[3]   1832.

Source: Mitchell (1992).

Table 8.7   Railroad construction in four major countries 1825–1850 (km of track in service)

Date	Belgium	France	Germany	U.K.
1830	0	31	0	157
1835	20	141	6	544
1840	334	410	469	2390
1845	577	875	2143	3931
1850	854	2915	5856	9797

Source: Mitchell (1978).

In these figures one again sees the lead of the United Kingdom, but frankly, it appears to be a rather modest five to ten year lead, if one is willing to compare the 1835 or 1840 figures for Britain with the 1840 or 1845 figures for the other countries. Furthermore, over the remaining years in the table, the growth rates for all but Belgium seem remarkably similar.

	1840–1850	1835–1845
Belgium	9.39%	–
France	19.61%	–
Germany	25.25%	–
Britain	14.11%	19.78%

That is, in the ten years after the establishment of the starter system (arbitrarily 1835 for Britain and 1840 for the other three countries), for all but Belgium the growth rates were very rapid and quite close together (ranging from 19.61 per cent to 25.25 per cent). Furthermore, in the decade of the 1840s, France and Germany were converging on the United Kingdom. Belgium is an exception here but it had a much smaller population and geographical area, and a relatively well-developed and effective canal system. This in no way implies the Belgians were lagging in the development of an appropriate transportation infrastructure in this period. In our view the *rapid*, not slow, adoption of the railroad on the Continent, following its successful start in Britain (the first track appeared in 1828 in France) is further strong evidence of the convergence of these economies.

Industrial Production Indices

To this point we have relied on industry-level data, because they permit cross-country comparisons, at least for the data from 1815. We do have some broader production indices for at least part of this period, and some go back into the eighteenth century, so in this brief sub-section we will see what we can glean from these more general numbers. The well-known comparison of industrial production in *France* and England shows that French industrial output actually grew more rapidly than the English, at least up to 1780 (from Crafts' (1977)). The index numbers for industrial output are:

	1700	1780
France	100	454
England	100	197

Moving beyond the 1780s, we see in Table 8.8 that for the first half of the nineteenth century, there is some comparative data on per capita commodity output in France and Great Britain, as constructed by O'Brien and Keyder (1978).

While commodity output would include things not actually made in 'industries', this comparison would still seem relevant because much commodity output was ultimately processed. In Table 8.8 it looks as if the French misfor-

Table 8.8   British and French commodity output (per capita)

Date	Great Britain	France
1781–90	6.94	9.53
1803–12	13.38	17.20
1815–24	12.27	11.31
1825–34	11.86	12.24
1835–44	13.32	13.28
1845–54	13.80	14.27

Source: O'Brien and Keyder (1978).

tunes on the battlefield might be the only real reason their per capita (commodity) output did not actually stay ahead of the British throughout the period of the first industrial revolution.

In Figure 8.1 we illustrated an industrial production index for France, as compiled by Toutain (1987). In Table 8.9 the annual growth rates are listed, but here we want to point out the broad patterns that are more discernible in the figure. In this period, industrial production almost tripled, according to the index. This growth was characterized by two long periods of expansion with only minor setbacks within these sub-periods, from 1815 to 1829 (growing at a rate of 3.97 per cent per year) and from 1832 to 1846 (growing at a rate of 3.89 per cent per year). The two interruptions to this remarkably consistent and rapid growth were the results of the recessions in 1830–31 and 1847–8. We believe that this rapid growth is consistently underrated in much of the literature on France in this period. We shall comment on questions of convergence in a moment, but it should be apparent that French industrialization was not slow and could probably be termed an 'industrial revolution' in this period, if such a term were in vogue.

Turning to less detailed estimates of production that, at the same time, cover the entire period, consider the estimates produced by Bairoch (1982) for these four countries. The figures given in Table 8.9 are levels of indices of 'total industrial potential' and per capita industrial production. The numbers, which are index numbers, are based on the United Kingdom in 1800 (=100) in each part of the table.

The Figures in Table 8.9 roughly corroborate our earlier discussion as to trends. As noted, Belgium is the best performer next to the United Kingdom in all periods and in both level and per capita terms. Growth in France and Germany prior to 1800 is substantial by historical standards (at the time) but per capita growth was close to zero in the same period.[8] After 1800, the growth of industrial production in all four countries was substantial in both

Table 8.9   *Industrial production indices in four countries 1750–1860*

	Belgium	France	Germany	U.K.
A. Level Index				
1750	6.4	80.6	59.7	38.7
1800	11.2	100.0	83.9	100.0
Growth Rate (%)	1.12	0.43	0.68	1.90
1800	11.2	100.0	83.9	100.0
1830	21.0	153.2	104.8	282.2
1860	50.0	288.7	179.0	725.8
Growth Rate (%)	2.49	1.77	1.26	3.30
B. Per Capita Index				
1750	56.2	56.2	50.0	62.5
1800	62.5	56.2	50.0	100.0
Growth Rate (%)	0.21	0	0	0.94
1800	62.5	56.2	50.0	100.0
1830	87.5	75.0	56.2	156.2
1860	175.0	125.0	93.7	400.0
Growth Rate (%)	1.72	1.33	1.05	2.31

Source: Bairoch (1982).

level and per capita terms. Only Austria–Hungary among the rest of the European countries performed up to the broad standard of these four countries. Of course, the United Kingdom still seems to be pulling away from the pack (looking just at the 1830–60 figures), but if Bairoch had looked at, for example, 1845–60, he would have recorded the beginning of a convergence that was very visible by the end of the century. The main point, however, is that the industrial revolution clearly took hold in this period and produced relatively rapid growth rates in each of the countries studied in this chapter.[9]

Napoleon, curiously, is given some credit for setting *Germany* on the path of its final (nineteenth-century) political cohesion, partly by design, since he literally helped redraw the German political map with a bias towards unity. Furthermore, since his military success was based on the exploitation of the resources of a large, politically integrated nation state, that model became the standard against which other European countries measured the progress of their own states. In fact, the German reformers – such as Stein, Hartenberg and Yorck – used France as a mirror if not a model. Napoleon's decline left Prussia in charge of a virtual empire of the North, stretching from the Polish frontier to Westphalia and the Rhine; since this area contained the regions associated with the first industrial revolution in Germany, the stage was adequately set for further decisive political and economic developments. These came in the form of the elimination of internal tariffs through the creation of the *Zollverein* in 1834 and in the development of a first-rate railroad system (beginning in the mid-1830s).

There is a tendency in much of the older literature to exaggerate the influence of the railroad in provoking industrial revolution rates of growth in Germany; occasionally, the *Zollverein* is similarly overrated. As an antidote, we recommend numbers such as those in Table 8.9, which show growth in Germany before 1800 (not in per capita terms, though) and real economic growth of around 25 per cent from 1800 to 1830. In the latter period there is also a 12 per cent growth in per capita output. In our detailed discussion we documented this on a industry-by-industry basis, but here we feel that it is perhaps useful to think of the *Zollverein* and the railroad as the result of a broad growth that required less obstruction from minor tariff blockages and also a competitive transportation infrastructure. In short, what was driving development in Germany was the same force that was driving her competitors: the increasingly global force of industrialization itself.

5. BANKING

Before 1776, that is before the financial administration of Turgot, banking in *France* was allied with businesses that sought a vehicle for discounting commercial bills (both real and financial). Quite a bit of this was done by foreign firms, but there was a substantial French banking community in the major cities (especially in Paris, Lyon and Bordeaux), and in these places there also existed clearing houses. Among the companies that used these institutions was, of course, the French East India Company. From 1767 there were a number of failed attempts to establish a national bank of discount; this was done, finally, in 1776, although the Caisse d'Escompte that was created quickly came to be dominated by the increasingly desperate financial strategy of the national government, which was in persistent and severe financial difficulties after 1772. Prior to 1789, the French note issue was monopolized by the Caisse d'Escompte, which, of course, held substantial government debt among its assets. In 1789, in the throes of the financial crisis, there was a run on the bank and it suspended, making its banknotes a fiat currency. The government then began the direct issue of the assignats.

French banking took a different turn after the French Revolution, with a brief era of 'free banking' that was followed, after a lag, by the establishment of the Bank of France as an early-modern central bank (see White, 1990). These free banks (*caisses patriotiques*) were established in the first instance to provide small bills (*billets de confiance*) to supplement the fiat currency, which was issued only in large denominations. These banks operated with fractional reserves. The currency was issued recklessly by modern standards, but it did comprise the bulk of the monetary base at the time. The fact that entry into banking was easy and regulation haphazard permitted counterfeiting, fraud and speculation (the extent of which, however, was apparently exaggerated both by contemporaries and by historians), and these aspects were linked in the public eye with the rapid inflation of the time. In view of the fact that banks could not keep their notes in circulation (under what is known as the Law of Reflux) and with the existence of an attractive alternative explanation of inflation (in the form of the rapid growth of the monetary base, with the assignats at the core of this), one must question such a perception. The detractors of the *caisse patriotiques* were persuasive, in any case, and the experiment was terminated on January 1, 1793.

Given the record of banking in late-eighteenth-century France, it is safe to say that modern banking in France starts with the Bank of France, which began operations in February, 1800.[10] It was an invention of the government and primarily operated to discount bills of exchange for, and make advances to, the government. For a time it had a national monopoly of the bank note issue (from 1803 to 1814), which was subsequently restricted to the Paris area until 1848, when it once again obtained the national monopoly of issue. From 1817 to 1838, a small number of private banks were chartered in France, mostly in other economically important cities (e.g. Bordeaux, Lyons), and in 1836, the Bank itself began to spread out, with 13 branches in operation by 1848. In the financial crisis of 1848, when all other banks suspended, it absorbed all of the private commercial banks.

The Bank of France followed a very restrictive discount policy and so there were quite a few private discount operations in place around the country, although very little of this was formally money, in the legal sense. A group of banks – *la haute banque Parisienne* – beginning for the most part after 1815, operated as merchant banks (especially concentrating in international trade), although they also dealt in insurance and (even) operated savings banks.[11] From 1837, a new type of institution, a kind of credit bank, was founded.[12] These were significant in the early days of the industrial revolution, but did not survive the financial crisis of 1848. The deliberate policy of the Bank of France also had something to do with their fragility. Finally, following the financial crisis of 1848, the government permitted the establishment of discount offices – *comptoires d'escompte* – this time with a formal link to the Bank of France.

Following the Congress of Vienna, *Belgium* was unified with the Netherlands. In 1822 the unified states chartered the Société Générale de Belgique. This institution was the world's first joint-stock investment bank. Indeed, its charter gave it the ability to perform every major banking service: it could discount bills of exchange, issue notes, accept deposits, make loans (personal, industrial and real estate), manage royal estates and sell bonds to finance industrial investment. In short the Société was the first great mixed bank, and potentially the most sophisticated financial institution in the world at the time. We say potentially, because it was not until the following decade, after Belgian independence, that the Société really expanded to be a powerful financial intermediary. Between 1835 and 1850 its portfolio of industrial loans grew from 3.8 to 54.8 million francs (Van der Wee and Goosens, 1991, p. 115). By the latter date there were three other joint-stock banks in Belgium: the Banque de Belgique, the Banque de Flandre, and the Banque Liégeoise. In the same year, 1850, the state chartered a central bank, the National Bank of Belgium, to handle state accounts, control the money supply and serve as a lender of last resort. Belgium also had an assortment of other financial institutions that provided financial services to smaller-scale savers and borrowers. Cameron (1967, p. 138) estimates that by 1830 there were at least 80 such institutions in the territory that became Belgium.

Frederick the Great's experiences with debasement and borrowing to finance the Seven Years War, and the loans he floated on the Amsterdam market to re-establish the Prussian coinage after the war, led him to create the Königliche Giro- und Lehnbanco in 1765 and this institution eventually became the Prussian Bank. However, it does not seem to have served the interest of the Crown as effectively as the Bank of England did the House of Hanover (Kindleberger, 1993, p. 119). Its ineffectiveness as an instrument of state was due to a combination of Spartan reserves and conservative lending policies. Modern-style banks of issue first appeared in *Germany* in the 1830s; the first was the Bavarian Mortgage and Discount Bank. The more important Prussian Bank of 1846 took over the assets and liabilities of the Royal Bank of Prussia; it was privately owned but regulated by the government – a style that marked most European central banks of that period. While it never held a monopoly of the note issue, the Prussian Bank's note circulation dominated the total. Other states set up note-issuing banks from 1847. Even so, private banks were the dominant form of banking enterprise, and they were ubiquitous throughout the period from 1815 to 1850. In Prussia alone there were 330 of these institutions in 1820–21 and their number grew to 642 by 1861 (Tilly, 1967, p. 161). These banks did not issue notes but they did considerable business in banker's acceptances and discounts. They also dealt with the government, sometimes on a very large scale (e.g. the Rothschilds of Frankfurt). But their direct contribution to industrial fixed capital was probably quite small. The banks that did lend to industry were the so-called Kreditbanken, the first of which was the Schaaffhausen'schen Bankverein in Cologne, which was founded in 1848. Most of the development of this sort of institution occurred after 1850.

We have characterized this period as one of significantly increasing globalization of the European economy and we believe our hypothesis can be extended to the banking sector. Each of these countries has a central bank in place by the 1820s, depending of course on how one defines that concept, and each has strong growth both in the volume and the variety of banking services as suggested by our review of the types of institution that evolved in this period. Furthermore, unique to this set of countries in this period, but not to the British or anybody else in the world, was the development of banks that lent directly to industry (sometimes with a government mandate to do so). This approach was most obvious in Belgium in this period, but it had a foothold in Germany and France by the middle of the nineteenth century. We conclude that financial expansion was accompanying industrial and commercial expansion in this period and that financial innovation and financial integration were rapidly closing the gaps in the chain of substitutes for bank money. As a result, business firms and governments were increasingly able to tap into the broad European capital market. This development presages the remarkable integration after 1850, when the few core countries on the gold or silver standard evolved into a full-scale international gold standard that swept up these four countries, as well as much of the 'periphery' (as discussed in Chapter 9), in a rising tide of capital and product market integration.

6. GROWTH AND CYCLES

We now consider the data on overall growth. There are some GNP numbers for France before the post-Napoleonic period, but they are little more than educated guesses. Be that as it may, let us look briefly at the data reproduced in Price (1981).

	GNP (million 1905–13 Fr.)	Population (millions)	GNP (Per Capita)
1701–10	2818	20.0	141
1781–90	4760	26.8	178
1803–12	5693	29.0	196

The compound annual rate of growth over the first 80 years here is 0.66 per cent for the real income in the first column, and 0.29 for real GNP per capita. These numbers are not particularly reliable, of course, but in comparison with the equivalent British calculations available in various sources, they do suggest that there was comparable growth in the two countries over the first 80 years of the eighteenth century.

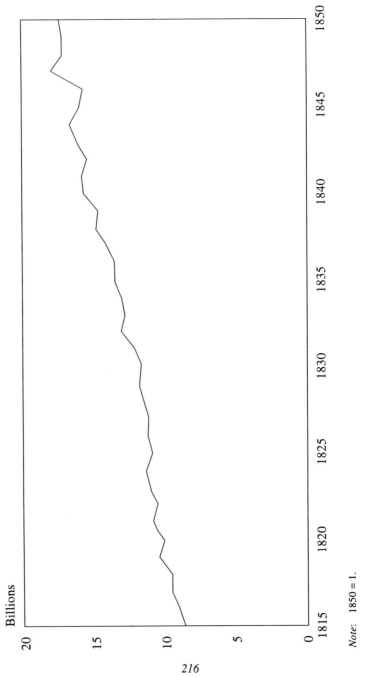

Note: 1850 = 1.

Figure 8.2 French real gross domestic product 1815–1850

The French data seem considerably more reliable from 1815 onward, as published by Toutain (1987). Figure 8.2 shows the level figures for real gross domestic product for the Toutain data for the period 1815 to 1850. Note, with respect to the following discussion, that the rates of change of these data appear in Table 8.10 below, in our discussion of business cycles.

Several things stand out in the figure. For one thing, the growth rate of real GDP looks to be fairly constant over this period. In fact, breaking this sample in half, arbitrarily, the annual growth rate from 1815 to 1833 is 2.29 per cent (1.66 per cent per capita), while from 1833 to 1850 it is 1.79 per cent (1.32 per cent per capita). While these rates were chosen to try to neutralize the effect of the business cycle on the data, it is obvious that the downturns of the 1840s also pushed the growth rate down. Note that we do not have either German or Belgian data to use to pursue the topic of overall (GNP) growth in those two countries before 1850.

Cycles 1750–1800

Given the nature of the political economy of Belgium and Germany during the late eighteenth century and the absence of the appropriate data from the same era, it is difficult to identify cyclical behavior. For Prussia, the aggregate would have been so dominated by agriculture that any sizeable failures in the agricultural sector could arguably be identified as downturns in the business cycle. At that time Belgium was part of the United Provinces, and although a substantial part of its non-agricultural economy would still have been tied to the Antwerp markets, a growing share of overall economic activity was being generated in the industrial areas of Liège and Namur. Still, we hesitate to offer a quantitative assessment of the business cycle in these regions.

For *France*, however, for the period from 1760 to 1800, we do have a reasonably good record of events. For the identification of downturns, we turn largely to Cullen (1993). He argues that, despite the unsuccessful war with Britain, the 1760s did not see a recession. In 1763 there was a financial crisis, but this does not seem to have been associated with a real downturn in France; there were some difficulties in Britain that year and they extended into 1764, as we noted in Chapter 7. There was a worldwide recession in textiles in 1768, but France's involvement in textiles was relatively small (compared to its agricultural sector) and the French did not have a recession that year. The British may well have had a recession that year, however, again as indicated in Chapter 7. In France, 1769 marks the beginning of a series of agricultural problems, related to cold weather and thus the wheat crop, that produced serious difficulties nationwide by 1771–2. In fact, Cullen refers to a business crisis in 1771–2, with 1772 being a recession year. Indeed, he argues, the crisis was 'spread over 1773 and 1774' (p. 641) and notes that this was the only real economic crisis in the global sense that affected France in this period. (Britain is involved in this event, as well.)

The years 1789 and 1790 are often mentioned as crisis/recession years in France. Part of this has to do with the collapse of the existing banking system, such as it was; part is the result of the evident fiscal crisis associated with the demise of the *ancien régime*; and part is the result of interpreting the rapid inflation as a sign of a real event. Cullen (1993) argues that there was indeed a recession, but that the major causes were agricultural (again, bad weather). Even so, there was a financial crisis in late 1787, with high short-term interest rates and, as just noted, this extended into 1789. In Britain, of these years, only 1789 seems one of possible recession, so this particular event seems peculiar to France. Finally, there was a financial crisis in 1793, but we have, as yet, no confirming real data on which to certify that event as a recession.

Cycles 1800–1850

In this section we will present our material country-by-country and then do a cross-country comparison keyed to British cycles. We are, of course, on the track of common business cycles that might have been spread by the increasing integration (and industrialization) of these four economies. After all, if a world economy was visible to Karl Marx by 1848, we ought to see it in the phenomenon of the business cycle that he stressed in his denunciation of capitalism. The problem, as we shall point out, is that agriculture, and not the collapse of speculative booms, provides the proximate cause for many of the downturns of this period and these agricultural crises are inevitably linked to the weather, which tended to be more severe locally or regionally rather than globally. Even so, these events produce some evidence of integration and, further, there are actually some industrially-oriented world events in this period as well. Here we will introduce an approach that focuses on all phases of the business cycle rather than just on recessions. The scarcity of data makes our efforts in this chapter somewhat limited in this respect, but in Chapter 12 we will find the technique addresses the question of integration quite nicely in the years after 1850.

In Table 8.10 we list the macroeconomic data that we have been able to put together for *France*. While the period we are considering begins in 1800, the data begin in 1815. We will, however, discuss the events in the first 15 years of the century, but without the aid of much data. One thing stands out in the table. There is visibly a strong relation between the growth rate of real GDP and the agricultural production index. In fact, the simple correlation coefficient between the two series is 0.96, while it is only 0.01 between real growth

Table 8.10   French cyclical data 1816–1850

Date	GDP Growth	Industry Growth	Agric. Growth	Agric. Prices	Inflation Rate	Long Rate	Short Rate	Bankrupt
1816	3.77	9.95	3.06		14.97			
1817	6.71	3.11	9.09		10.80			
1818	0.00	8.79	–3.01		–10.20			
1819	8.70	–0.93	12.50		–16.15			
1820	–2.82	8.15	–7.40	86	3.88			1,200
1821	7.85	7.53	9.68	85	–4.53	0.24	0.17	1,340
1822	–3.84	6.25	–8.44	78	1.42	–0.58	–1.03	1,340
1823	6.45	0.00	9.20	78	4.39	0.06	0.20	1,730
1824	1.82	2.25	2.04	76	–4.48	–0.33	–0.04	1,290
1825	–4.43	2.92	–9.60	78	8.42	–0.30	0.01	1,390
1826	3.34	4.22	3.37	78	–2.69	0.24	0.47	2,160
1827	–0.36	1.37	–0.98	83	1.96	–0.32	–0.12	1,910
1828	2.53	–2.76	3.67	76	–2.06	–0.12	–0.21	2,230
1829	2.82	4.78	3.17	82	4.74	–0.04	–0.65	1,890
1830	–0.70	–0.67	–2.23	88	1.57	0.14	0.46	2,080
1831	3.77	–0.67	3.87	85	–6.79	0.58	0.24	2,440
1832	7.46	1.34	10.30	88	–3.06	–0.47	–1.45	1,350
1833	–1.89	10.14	–6.92	87	0.67	–0.36	–0.38	1,120
1834	1.89	4.13	0.17	74	–0.66	–0.21	0.25	1,250
1835	3.38	5.07	3.26	76	1.79	0.05	–0.13	1,430
1836	0.30	7.41	–4.85	77	1.77	0.14	0.97	1,760
1837	3.55	2.02	3.83	80	–7.53	0.00	–0.21	2,120
1838	5.65	8.16	4.50	84	2.02	–0.08	0.15	1,990
1839	–0.83	–0.93	–2.98	86	–2.11	–0.12	0.55	2,820
1840	6.44	5.43	7.60	86	0.64	0.02	–0.76	2,800
1841	1.03	2.61	0.16	77	3.34	–0.12	–0.19	2,650
1842	–2.34	0.85	–4.29	77	0.02	–0.09	–0.15	2,410
1843	4.38	2.94	6.14	84	–5.35	–0.12	–0.15	2,880
1844	2.98	0.82	5.50	81	–1.13	–0.03	–0.21	3,040
1845	–4.24	2.03	–9.55	86	5.30	0.05	–0.28	3,490
1846	–1.28	2.38	–3.23	98	7.59	0.24	0.08	3,830
1847	13.06	–3.19	23.72	104	2.01	0.02	1.48	4,810
1848	–4.88	–14.34	–2.76	69	–24.06	1.77	0.86	3,580
1849	0.47	11.05	–3.94	66	7.62	–0.46	–0.28	3,260
1850	0.94	2.89	0.00	64	0.41	–0.22	–1.15	2,210

Sources: Columns 1–3, 5: Toutain (1987); Columns 6, 7: Homer and Sylla (1991); Columns 4, 8 Levy-Leboyer and Bourguignon.

and industrial production, in Column 2. In a nutshell, if the real GDP numbers are at all accurate as an indicator of the French cycle, then the French cycle from 1815 to 1850 is an agricultural one. One reason, therefore, that cycles might be shared across nations in this period would be because the weather is shared. Another is that bad weather in France, for example, could be exported to other countries in the form of higher food prices and a smaller demand for foreign products. The latter situation allows for integrated product markets to work their effect, but the day of large-scale industrial crises, associated with rising inventories and subsequent lay-offs, had clearly not arrived by 1850, on the strength of these simple correlations.

The other series of some general interest in the table is that on inflation. What is immediately obvious about these numbers is that inflation in this period appears to be mean-reverting, just as it was in the British case. Again, by 'mean-reverting' we mean that inflation and deflation alternate around either a constant or a trend. In contrast, Marczewski (1988) has identified two long periods of falling prices in this period, from 1815 to 1824 and 1826 to 1844. The data for the real GDP deflator really do not confirm this. That is, 1815 and 1824 have an index number of 0.816 and 0.817 respectively, while between 1826 and 1936 prices are unchanged on average, only falling somewhat thereafter; some of this can be seen in Table 8.10.

Marczewski is, however, right on the main point of his paper: there are quite a few years of *stagflation* (rising prices and falling real GDP at the same time). In Table 8.10, of the 11 downturns in real GDP in the entire period, 9 show rising prices in the same year! Marczewski has a complicated explanation of this, involving agricultural production (if agricultural production falls, GDP falls and agricultural prices rise) and, separately, he invokes the quantity theory of money. Unfortunately, changes in agricultural production are not highly (negatively) correlated with inflation rates; this puts more weight on the behavior of changes in the money stock, where, we believe, the weight probably belongs.[13]

The standard literature on French business cycles makes much of the financial crises that sometimes accompanied these events, and these, as it turns out, have a more international flavor than we have described to this point. Before our data begin, there obviously were some recessions. In 1806–7, for example, the imposition of the Continental System must have had some effect on French businessmen whose contacts exceeded the Continental boundaries. A recession was likely at that point. The year 1815 is also very probably one of recession, due to bad harvests, considering the relative extent of the agricultural sector at this time. The year 1817, on the other hand, is alleged to have been a 'classic subsistence crisis' (Caron, 1979), but it was unaccompanied by a major downturn in real GDP; furthermore, agricultural production rose that year, so we do not agree with Caron. In 1820 and 1822 there were declines in agricultural production and in GDP of 2.8 and 3.8 per cent respectively, but this seems to have provoked no comment in the literature. We note that bankruptcies rose slightly in 1821–2 and then sharply in 1823. This is possibly a lagged effect on firms weakened by what might have been a 'double-dip recession'. In 1825, on the other hand, the agricultural decline was slightly larger, as was the decline in real GDP and so the year is generally described as one of recession. There was a financial crisis in 1829–30, involving the failure of all of the newly formed English-style iron-making companies, but this is only associated with a mild decline in real GDP (and agricultural production, really, seems to be the culprit in the recession).[14] Bankruptcies were up in 1828, when industrial production declined, and again sharply in 1832, again suggesting the lagged effect of the recession on business profits.

The 1830s showed only minor declines in real GDP and the agricultural production figures also fluctuated somewhat less violently. In 1839 there was a minor industrial event, involving mainly the railroads, but, again, the minor downturn in real GDP probably owes more to the decline in agricultural production than to events in the industrial sector. There was, though, a sharp rise in bankruptcies in 1839 and the larger total was sustained into 1840.

Harvests were poor in 1845–6, apparently, and the real GDP numbers in Table 8.10 confirm that those two years were recession years. Furthermore, bankruptcies jumped in 1846 and 1847, again possibly lagging behind the recession itself. There were disastrous harvests in 1847–8 (say Levy-Leboyer and Bourguignon, 1990), but 1847 is actually a very good year, at least in terms of agricultural production. In fact, 1847 is the middle of what is called a 'scissors' in the literature on the French economy. The general idea (LLB) is that bad harvests, which cause agricultural prices to rise sharply (1846 and 1847), hurt the economy, while abundant harvests (1847) hurt the farmer (actually in 1848). This would be one way to pull together the data that we have on inflation, agricultural prices, bankruptcies and agricultural production in this period. Bankruptcies rose in 1847 and were still relatively high in 1848. In any case, a recession is not in doubt in this period, since 1848 shows the largest absolute and relative decline in real GDP in the entire period studied in this section.

More to the point, however, this period features an international financial crisis (in 1848) and a domestic financial crisis (which wiped out the newly formed *caisse* style of banks). Industry was also involved in the 1848 collapse significantly, as indicated in Table 8.10, but rebounded sharply in 1849. The industrial decline was echoed in other European countries (for which we have firm data), and so depression, agricultural decline and, as it turns out, revolution, was spread pretty widely around Europe at that time. This event might not qualify as the first major post-industrial revolution crisis (1837–41 having a claim as well), but it certainly has all of the flavor of one of those complicated (international) events.

In the French data, then, the broad upward trend in real product at a comfortable rate (1 to 2 per cent) and the apparent instability (in terms of frequent and sometimes deep recessions) seem to stand out. The trend in real growth is the result of the industrial revolution, of course, while developments in the agricultural sector provide the cause of many of the downturns in the 90 years for which we have data. Finally, we note that much of the evidence assembled in this and previous sections implies that growth was relatively persistent over the period. On the whole these results corroborate the contention of our earlier discussion that growth was self-sustaining over much of this century and that the industrial revolution (or some sort of self-sustaining transformation, at least) may well have been in place in France by 1820. This is, of course, a contested view.

Since we do not have data for Belgium and Germany that can match those reported for France in Table 8.10, we must be, shall we say, a little more imaginative in identifying cycles in those countries after 1800. What we have for *Belgium*, are wheat prices from Mitchell (1978); real per capita consumption of meat, fish, grains for bread and gin in Antwerp from Lis and Soly (1977); trade data on iron from Fremdling (1991); and bond prices from Homer and Sylla (1991). Because any particular real series might be affected by short-term fluctuations in relative prices as well as long-run trends, generally speaking we looked for downturns in three or more of these real series as indicators of a recession.

All three of the series for which we have data before 1820 (meat, fish, and gin consumption) show a downturn in 1818 and fish and gin consumption fell, along with imports, in 1822; so we identify these as recessions. In fact these downturns seem to be simultaneous deviations from a downward trend in per capita consumption that left consumption of all three commodities substantially lower in 1822 than they were at the time of Waterloo; while the idiosyncratic nature of these series leads us to be cautious about stating our conclusions too strongly, these series are consistent with a general continental downturn resulting from the combination of demobilization and the end of the Continental System and the return of competition with British industry.

The next recession year, by our definition at least, seems to be 1828 when the same three series (fish and gin consumption and imports) all declined. This recession was followed by one in 1831 and it appears to have been the worst year between the end of the Napoleonic Wars and the general world crisis of the late 1830s. All four of the real consumption series declined and meat, fish, and bread consumption all fell dramatically. In addition, the import figures fell that year. The years after 1831 were generally good ones, but then Belgium seems to have been caught in the world downturn of 1837–38. Here, for the first time, we also see falling prices accompanied by rising bond yields. In a world in which monies are tied to a commodity standard, we interpret this confluence of events as consistent with an economic downturn.

The Belgian economy recovered after 1838, but from 1842 to 1850 there are only two years in which only one of the real series did not decline. In terms of recession, however, before the crisis of 1848–49, the primary candidates would appear to be 1842, when fish, bread and gin consumption all declined in a year that also shows falling prices, and 1845 when fish consumption, bond prices and exports all declined. As we saw in France and the United Kingdom, the political turmoil of 1848 was accompanied by economic downturn and Belgium was no different. Indeed, in terms of the breadth of the crisis, 1848 was the worst year in Belgium to that date, with every series showing a decline. This downturn worsened the following year when every series but meat and fish consumption declined further, and meat and fish consumption increased by only small amounts.

For *Germany*, we have price data from Mitchell (1978); iron import and production data from Fremdling (1991); and bond prices from Homer and Sylla (1991). As we noted above, during this period we generally interpret falling prices and rising bond yields as an indication of an economic downturn and using this criterion 1818 appears to be the first post-Waterloo recession in Germany. Although our real series do not begin until after this date, the narrative evidence provided in, for example, Kitchen (1978) is consistent with a real downturn resulting largely from the removal of protection from British competition. In the case of Prussia, Kitchen reports a bad crop year in 1816–17. From our data we see falling prices and rising yields in three years (1821, 1826, and 1832) and imports fell with bond prices in 1831. While imports fell again in 1836 and 1838, in Germany we do not see the kind of problems associated with the Atlantic economies during the late 1830s.

As with Belgium and France, however, Germany seems to have been caught in the general downturn of the late 1840s. There seems to have been a mild recession in 1845 with imports falling and yields rising, but in 1848 every real series declined along with commodity prices and bond prices and in the following year only the bond market recovered. Again, at least in breadth, the late 1840s would seem to have been worse than the late 1830s, at least on the continent.

In terms of a 'continental cycle', our tabulations suggest that the years 1818, 1825–26, 1837–38, 1842 saw recessions in at least two of the three continental economies and the years 1821–22, 1831–32, 1845–46, and 1848–49 saw recessions in all three. This is strong evidence of an international cycle in this period, as Karl Marx argued in 1848. We also think this evidence suggests that there was a great deal of integration of these economies, even though two of the three were still heavily agricultural.

7. CONCLUSIONS

We began this chapter with a discussion of the demographic developments of three major continental economies between 1750 and 1850. Perhaps the most striking aspect of that discussion was the general acceleration after 1800 of the growth of urban areas in each of the countries. In fact, in each country urban areas were growing substantially faster than overall population, which was growing relatively rapidly in two of the three countries. France, to be sure, had the lowest urban growth rate after 1800 (0.96 per cent per annum), but that rate was three times what it had been during the previous half century and it was still roughly twice as rapid as overall population growth. We argued that the urbanization rates are important because they are indicators of modernization in general and industrialization in particular.

Turning to the industrial figures themselves, we see that in terms of the leading manufacturing industries of the day – coal, iron and cotton textiles – output after 1815 grew at rates (aggregate and per capita) that were rapid by just about any standard other than that established by the British. Furthermore, in terms of overall industrial production, the growth rates were accelerating after 1800 and in every case the per capita growth rates exceeded one per cent per annum. Again excluding the British figures as the standard, this must be recognized as an outstanding economic achievement, and this early growth created industrial sectors upon which these countries were able to launch full-blown industrialization a generation later.

No discussion of European industrialization would be complete without touching on the changes in the countryside in general and agricultural production in particular. French agricultural production was growing rapidly by historical comparison after 1800 (1.56 per cent per annum). Although this figure falls below that of the growth of industrial production (which was 1.77 per cent) as one might reasonably expect, it still puts per capita agricultural growth above 1 per cent per annum. Although we do not have a comparable index for Germany, the evidence on output per worker and yields suggests that German agriculture was converging on that of France from below, which would further suggest that advances were fairly robust in Germany as well. Underlying these quantitative changes in agriculture were the liberation of the peasantry and the enclosure of open fields. Although linking the contribution of these changes to the increase in output is controversial, it is still hard to imagine the subsequent developments in European agriculture if ties to feudalism had been maintained in the countryside.

In some ways, perhaps our most interesting contribution to the historiography of this era is the discovery of a surprisingly common business cycle among these countries. Between 1815 and 1850 there were four episodes of one or two years in which at least two of the three continental nations experienced strong indications of a recession and there were four episodes in which all three were in recession. Looked at another way, there was only one downturn in which only one country participated; this was Belgium in 1828. On the whole, then, we feel that the evidence suggests an emerging globalization of the European landscape, a globalization that becomes very obvious after 1850, as we shall emphasize in Chapters 10 through 12.

NOTES

1. The linen industry provides an excellent example, possibly employing a quarter of a million workers in the growing of flax (50,000) and manufacturing of the final product (200,000) in 1765.
2. Note that in 1750 the two largest cities in Belgium were Brussels and Liège. The latter is especially noted for its early industrial development.
3. See the survey of this literature in Goldsmith (1984).
4. See Weber (1976) and, especially, Braudel (1967) for contrasting views.
5. Note that the details of these indices – as growth rates – appear in Table 8.10 in our discussion of French business cycles.
6. The situation is one of high labor densities in the context of a system of property rights that held labor in the countryside and depressed the rate of capital accumulation in agriculture. Even so 'In the livestock sector or the cultivation of industrial crops there is no evidence of French backwardness' (Newell, 1973, p. 137).
7. As we have noted elsewhere, U.K. production of pig iron was relatively large compared to the sum of production of the other countries. In this case, the row sum for 1850 in Table 8.5 is 761,000 metric tons; this amount is 33.3% of the British production of 2,285,000 metric tons that year. Growth-rate comparisons show the globalization, while absolute production figures do not.
8. We put the matter this way merely to warn the reader that these are very rough estimates. As noted, Bairoch refers to his measure of the level of industrial production as 'potential industrial production'.
9. We suspect that the German figure for 1860 in Table 8.9 is incorrect. The tables for coal, pig iron, cotton and railroads earlier in this chapter suggest an absolute growth rate in Germany possibly in excess of those for Belgium and France.
10. The Bank of France replaced an earlier bank, the Caisse de Comptes Courants, which had been founded in 1796. Note that much of the following discussion is drawn from Cameron (1967), but amended as noted.
11. The first of these savings banks dates to 1818; by 1845 there were more than 350 of them, not, apparently, serving the workers.
12. The first of these was Jacques Lafitte's Caisse Général du Commerce.
13. Two further comments should be made. (1) There are money stock data available for the French data (in St. Marc, 1983), but these data appear to us to be unreliable for this period. (2) In modern times the inflation rate is a lagging indicator of the business cycle (and changes in the money stock are a leading indicator). This would suggest that the price effects of a particular real decline might occur, for example, in the year after the decline in real GDP On this basis, for the French data, there are only five such episodes (in 1822, 1839, 1845, 1846 and 1848). Again, the argument is that the effects of the recession (or whatever caused it) are lagged with respect to the inflation rate. Stagflation, if it is a meaningful concept and not just a statistical coincidence, would be of interest if there were a causal link between the two.
14. They were English-style in that they used coke and a considerably more capital-intensive technology. Firms employing charcoal-based smelting technologies fared much better. It

is, of course, possible that these firms succumbed because they did not have sufficient time to get established. The effect of this may have been in 1828 rather than 1829–30, on the basis of the data shown in Table 8.10.

9. The development of the 'peripheral' countries 1750–1850

1. INTRODUCTION

In this chapter we continue to explore the issues of growth and integration before 1850, just as we did in Chapters 7 and 8; however, the countries studied here followed different paths from those of the countries covered above. In particular, the countries in this chapter cannot be said to have made any *substantial* progress toward industrialization by 1850, with the notable exceptions of the Netherlands and specific regions of Austria–Hungary. At the same time, all of these countries except those on the Iberian peninsula were part of the growing European industrial community in important ways. In any case, we identify the growth, cycles and integration of these countries both in their own right and with respect to the rest of Europe. We note that this evidence calls into question the use of the term 'periphery' that is so often used in this context. In a way, this is obvious, for the growth, development and integration in the century after 1750 surely paved the way for what were sometimes spectacular changes in the decades leading up to 1914, as we shall see in Chapters 10 to 12.

Section 2 contains the population data, including urbanization rates. Generally speaking, the population figures are the most reliable and comprehensive data available, even though they shed no light on cycles, so we must once again use population figures aggressively to establish orders of magnitude of the growth rates of the economies of these countries. We also go into considerable detail about early industrialization in these countries. This material, which is covered in Section 3, leads to some conjectures about growth, but we have no annual indices of any sort for any of these countries – no estimates of industrial or agricultural production, only scattered information on price levels and, of course, no data on any economic aggregates; thus, we will have to lean heavily on a more disaggregated discussion to squeeze out any generalizations about this set of countries.

One sector that does get some coverage in the literature, although generally without particularly good data, is banking. Since banks actually developed alongside the modern economy, we will be able, in Section 4, to expand the discussion of growth a little further to include the financial sector, but there are huge gaps in the quantitative records of these countries. Furthermore, there is only very scattered evidence on business cycles, so we will not be able to pursue our interest in identifying any events that might be common to a larger set of countries than we covered in Chapters 7 and 8. We will, though, review the available data in Section 5, and these data reveal the possible existence of a 'common' European cycle in, at least, some cases. Our conclusions in Section 6 will be appropriately brief.

Despite the absence of data, taken together the material in this chapter yields a rather fair cross-country comparison of a set of countries that were developing fairly rapidly by historical standards; however they were not developing rapidly in per capita output nor were they industrializing at anything like the rates of the countries we discussed earlier. We think, in addition, that goods and technology were crossing borders relatively freely in this century (1750–1850), and with them came the stirrings of international business cycles, although the empirical evidence is certainly muted in this set of largely agricultural economies.

2.   POPULATION ESTIMATES, 1750–1850

Population data for most of the countries studied in this chapter are generally as reliable as those we reviewed in Chapter 8 for the more economically advanced countries of the time. First, we review the overall population figures for the set of nine countries that we are studying here; they appear in Table 9.1.

Rather surprisingly, the rates of growth of population in both sub-periods for most of these countries are quite comparable to the rates achieved by the more industrially-advanced countries studied in Chapter 8, putting aside the rather remarkable Dutch figures from 1750–1800. Although none of the countries in Table 9.1 had much of an industrial base before 1800, their overall growth rates were sufficient and their economies were adequately linked to the agricultural changes taking place throughout Europe, to produce larger incomes and rising populations. It seems clear that an important step toward industrialization was being taken by these countries in this period, mainly in the building of an economic infrastructure, if nothing else.

It also seems clear that every country for which comparisons can be made – except the Iberian countries – shows an accelerated population growth after 1800. Following our discussion in Chapter 3, the growth of population during this period reflects a combination of the agricultural progress and continuing improvement in (average) standards of health. In this period only the Italian and Iberian population growth rates are lower than the French, who were noted for their early transition to low birth rates, while the other growth rates

Table 9.1   Population levels and annual growth rates 1750–1850 (millions)

Country	Population			Growth Rates	
	1750	1800	1850	1750–1800	1800–1850
Aus.–Hun.–Cz.	10.685	14.051		0.55	
Denmark	0.820[a]	1.030[b]	1.420	0.41	0.92
Italy	15.511	18.539	24.080	0.36	0.52
Netherlands	2.479	2.141	3.000	−0.29	0.67
Norway	0.620	0.885	1.390	0.71	0.90
Portugal	2.457	3.092	3.846[c]	0.46	0.40
Spain	9.579	13.026	15.455[d]	0.61	0.30
Sweden	1.770	2.350	3.460	0.57	0.77
Switzerland	1.299	1.594	2.379	0.41	0.80

Notes:
[a]   1760.
[b]   1815.
[c]   1854.
[d]   1857.

Sources: 1750 and 1800 were derived from Bairoch et al. (1988), except for Denmark in 1760, which is from Maddison (1991) and Sweden and Norway, which are from Mitchell (1992), The Italian and Swiss figures for 1850 are from Madison, while the Netherlands 1850 figure is from Mitchell (1992).

compare favorably with those achieved in Belgium and Germany, as discussed in Chapter 8. We submit that the situation for the Mediterranean-based economies is not particularly surprising given their economic histories and we offer more details below in our country-by-country comparisons.

Further insights can be gleaned from the urbanization rates of these countries. The most obvious thing that appears in Table 9.2 is that for every country in the table except Norway, Denmark and the conglomerate of Austria, Hungary and Czechoslovakia, urbanization *decreased* from 1750 to 1800. These countries thus join Belgium, which Table 8.2 shows also had a declining percentage of its population living in urban areas. Belgium, though, was industrializing rapidly in this period, while none of the countries in Table 9.2 were. This observation allows us to make a very sharp distinction between the countries discussed in Chapters 7 and 8 and those presently studied, since the first set (again save Belgium) had a rising urbanization rate and the second set (save Austria–Hungary and the sparsely populated countries of Norway and Denmark) had a declining rate.[1] Thus, while in terms of agricultural output and productivity one might speak of convergence, one is almost inclined to speak of divergence in terms of the industrial achievements of the two sets of countries, at least to the extent that urbanization corresponds with industrialization. This observation surely helps to justify our division of countries between these two chapters. However, in terms of the level of urbanization, some of these countries compare favorably with those in Chapter 8.

Table 9.2　Urbanization in nine countries 1750–1850 (millions)

Country	Urban Population			Urbanization Rate		
	1750	1800	1850	1750	1800	1850
Aus.-Hun.-Cz.	0.78	1.11	1.88	7.3	7.9	
Denmark*	0.08	0.12	0.18	10.4	11.2	11.2
Italy	3.49	4.06	5.80	22.5	21.9	24.9
Netherlands	0.69	0.73	1.03	36.3	34.1	34.3
Norway	0.04	0.05	0.10	5.2	5.5	7.4
Portugal	0.43	0.47	0.55	17.5	15.2	14.3
Spain	2.05	2.54	3.74	21.4	19.5	24.2
Sweden	0.10	0.13	0.21	5.3	5.0	6.1
Switzerland	0.10	0.11	0.32	7.7	6.9	13.5

Note: Portugal's last population figure is for 1854; Spain's is for 1857. Denmark's first two population numbers are for 1760 and 1815.

Sources: See Table 9.1.

Before proceeding to the material on industrial production, we consider the patterns of urban growth. Some of the countries listed in Table 9.2 had one or at most two large cities and the rest of the population resided in communities that were little more than country towns, which was no doubt related to the narrowness of the commercial and industrial development in these countries. Even in 1850, Copenhagen had 73 per cent of Denmark's urban population and, while this financial and commercial center did grow in the period from 1815 to 1850, its rate of growth was relatively slow, falling below the population growth rate in Denmark as a whole. In 1850, Bergen and Oslo had 52 per cent of Norway's urban population; these were commercial centers that actually doubled in population in the first half of the nineteenth century, but they were involved in fishing and timber, with very little industrial activity taking place. In 1850, Stockholm had 43 per cent of Sweden's urban population; in this case there was some notable early industrial activity, but the rate of growth of Stockholm grew by only 22 per cent over the previous 50 years, a fact that attests to the modest beginnings of industrialization before 1850. Stockholm, of course, was a capital city and the financial center of Sweden.

In southern Europe a different pattern emerged, although low rates of urbanization were still typical. Spain, for example, had a large number of moderately sized cities. In 1850 there were 37 cities of over 20,000 inhabitants, while in all of Scandinavia (including Finland) there were only six. While some of these Spanish cities prospered in this period, Madrid and Barcelona clearly stand out (with half a million inhabitants between them in 1850). From 1750 to 1800, Madrid grew by only 5 per cent while Barcelona doubled; both accelerated in the next fifty years, with Madrid growing 67 per cent and Barcelona 120 per cent. These are respectable rates of growth and compare favorably with those of countries experiencing an industrial revolution, but these two cities account for 25 per cent of Spain's urban growth in the period. Spain's growth, too, was concentrated mainly in commercial activities, although by the urbanization indicator a broader growth was present, particularly in the capital city and along the Mediterranean coast. Italy was in a similar situation, with 55 cities of over 20,000 inhabitants in 1850. What is different about Italy from 1800 to 1850, when one looks at the detailed figures, is that, while many of the major cities grew slowly (Rome 14 per cent, Bologna 9 per cent, and Florence 16 per cent) or declined (Naples and Venice), there was vigorous growth in the north, in Genoa (42 per cent), Milan (55 per cent) and Turin (60 per cent). It was in this region, by no coincidence, that the industrial revolution first took hold in Italy, and, for that matter, this is the area that subsequently produced the impetus for the political unification of Italy.

The other three countries in our set do not have such a clear pattern. Portugal had only two cities with more than 20,000 inhabitants in 1850, Porto and Lisbon. These two had 57 per cent of the urban population. Collectively these two cities grew 32 per cent from 1800 to 1850; both were commercial centers, one in the north of the country and one in the middle, and marine and agricultural products were the mainstays of their economic activity.

Switzerland, in 1800, showed little sign of its future as a commercial center. The four leading cities in 1800 (Geneva, Basel, Bern and Zurich) had a combined population of 61,000 inhabitants at that time. In the next fifty years, however, these cities grew, collectively, by 175 per cent. While still not large by European standards in 1850, these four cities had clearly begun their rise to prominence (in finance and commerce) that is certainly much more noticeable in the next century.

Finally, the Netherlands constitutes yet another special case. Amsterdam, the largest city and the financial and commercial capital of the country, grew very slowly (7 per cent) over the entire 100-year period; in contrast, Rotterdam, the largest port in the Netherlands, grew by 104 per cent. Rotterdam, sitting on the delta of the Rhine, shared in Europe's growth at the time; Amsterdam's slow growth, even to 1850, reflects the industrial situation in the Netherlands more accurately, but one should emphasize that throughout the period 1750 to 1850 the Netherlands was the most urbanized country in Europe (including Great Britain). In this sense, most other countries, mainly in northern Europe, were converging on the Netherlands, with industrial and commercial activities leading the way in some of those countries. In what follows, the Netherlands continues to be a special case, as the broader story of growth and cycles is continued in this chapter.

3. INDUSTRIALIZATION AND ECONOMIC GROWTH: SOME PRELIMINARY GENERALIZATIONS

Because industrialization had only a limited beginning in most of the countries we are discussing in this chapter, it is not possible to construct anything like the detailed tables on specific industrial activities that we were able to put together for the countries in Chapters 7 and 8. In Table 9.3 we report the available industry-by-industry data for the industrialization of the nine countries we are considering in this chapter; these data are from Mitchell (1978 and 1992). Here Austria–Hungary clearly stands out. With the largest amount of track laid (the system was started in 1837 and reached 473 kilometers by 1844), the lead in pig iron and coal production and the largest cotton industry, Austria–Hungary is clearly a member of the industrial community in 1850, but, even so, in 1850 France had 2,915 km of track laid while Germany had 5,856. Pig-iron production and cotton and coal consumption were all larger in those countries than in Austria–Hungary. In fact, the real industrial spurt, such as it was, in Austria–Hungary was at the end of the nineteenth century.

The indicators of industrial activity in Table 9.3 show that all but three countries had launched their rail systems by 1850, and the other three had done so by 1856. Other than Austria/Hungary, only Italy stands out with enough of a system in place in 1850 (at 620 km of track laid) to significantly affect – and reflect – the pace of industrialization. Turning to other industries, in 1850, Switzerland and Austria/Hungary had significant cotton industries and Spain, whose railway system had already been started, also had a presence in cotton textile production. Sweden, which had no domestic coal industry, produced high-quality pig iron mostly from charcoal. Although much of its output was subsequently exported, Sweden maintained a specialty iron and steel industry in the period (Adamson, 1991). In the next sixty years, this sector turned out to be the leader in an explosion of growth comparable to (if not greater than) that which occurred in Germany. Finally, one notices the Netherlands' large coal imports. This figure reflects the lack of coal and a

Table 9.3   Industrialization of nine European countries 1850

	Austria/Hungary	Denmark	Italy	Netherlands	Norway	Portugal	Spain	Sweden	Switzerland
Railway	1357	30	620	176	–	–	28	–	25
Pig Iron	195							142	
Iron Ore								322	
Coal Imports		128		1182					
Coal Prod.	877				52				
Cotton Cons.	2.9			–0.2			16	2	
Cotton Spind.	1400[b]								900[b]
Flax/Hemp	158[a]								

Notes:
[a] 1851.
[b] 1852.

Source: Mitchell (1978, 1992). Railway is km of track open, cotton spindles are in thousands. All other figures are in thousands of metric tons.

relatively large urbanization, rather than industrialization *per se*, although there certainly were a number of expanding, albeit traditional, industrial activities in the Netherlands at the time; these included brewing, sugar-refining, pottery, glass-making and paper production (Griffiths, 1979).

We continue our discussion of individual country performance with some data on overall industrial production from the leaders among the peripheral countries; they appear in Table 9.4.

Table 9.4   Industrial production in the periphery

	Industrial Potential			Per Capita Output		
	1750	1800	1860	1750	1800	1860
Austria/Hung.	3.7	4.8	9.5	7	7	11
Italy	3.1	3.7	5.7	8	8	10
Spain	1.6	2.1	4.0	7	7	11
Sweden	0.3	0.5	1.4	7	8	15
Switzerland	0.2	0.4	0.8	7	10	26
United Kingdom	2.4	6.2	45.0	10	16	64

Note: United Kingdom in 1900 = 100.

Source: Bairoch (1982).

Table 9.3 shows negligible industrial activity in Denmark, the Netherlands, Norway and Portugal in 1850; accordingly, they are left out of Table 9.4. What remains, then, are the five countries that did have a *relatively* rapidly growing industrial base, particularly after 1800 (see, especially, the per capita figures), but none of these countries was converging on the United Kingdom in either industrial 'potential' or per capita output, at least by the indicators displayed in Table 9.4. The four omitted countries are clearly in the periphery, but so too, by any relative standard, are the others, although, again, Austria–Hungary, a populous country, does have a respectable amount of industrial production in 1850 (their overall industrial potential was exceeded only by that in France, Germany and, of course, the United Kingdom). The five countries in Table 9.4, having laid the foundation in the 1800–1860 period, began to converge on the United Kingdom in the next fifty to sixty years, as we shall describe in Chapters 10 to 12.

The figures in Table 9.4 are not for gross national output, of course, and the reader is surely aware that the agricultural sectors of even the more advanced countries are in the neighborhood of 60–90 per cent of gross domestic product even as late as 1850. Still, what should be clear is that by the standard of economic development of the previous fifteen centuries or so, industrial progress is quite remarkable and, as we shall relate, it is even evident in the countries that do not appear in Table 9.4. Furthermore, we cannot restate the point firmly enough that the classification of these countries as peripheral or backwards is really only relative to Britain.

We do have some national product figures for the last 30 years of the period in question, for all of the countries in our set. These are decennial figures only, as published by Bairoch (1976) and are, surely, both suggestive and only roughly comparable, because some estimates apparently have very wide 'confidence' intervals. In Table 9.5 we show index numbers for both real GNP and per capita real GNP for 1840 and 1850, with 1830 = 1. The four countries of Belgium, France, Germany and the United Kingdom were discussed in detail in Chapters 7 and 8, while the remaining nine are the business of the present chapter.

The safest generalization from Table 9.5 is that all of the countries grew in real terms for each of the two decades, whether this calculation is in real

Table 9.5 The growth of real GNP in Europe

	Real GNP			Per Capita Real GNP		
	1840	1850	Rank	1840	1850	Rank
Austria/Hung.	1.153	1.275	12	1.064	1.132	10
Belgium	1.272	1.648	1	1.169	1.393	2
Denmark	1.141	1.410	7	1.082	1.231	7
France	1.204	1.383	8	1.144	1.261	4
Germany	1.150	1.437	6	1.090	1.257	5
Italy	1.068	1.120	13	1.019	1.045	12
Netherlands	1.210	1.444	5	1.101	1.230	8
Norway	1.196	1.551	3	1.089	1.250	6
Portugal	1.099	1.145	11	1.020	1.040	13
Spain	1.153	1.306	10	1.095	1.190	9
Sweden	1.108	1.309	9	1.021	1.088	11
Switzerland	1.207	1.603	2	1.141	1.417	1
United Kingdom	1.265	1.527	4	1.139	1.324	3

Notes:
1830–1850 (1830 = 1).
Rank is in 1850 units of currency.

Source: Bairoch (1976).

aggregate figures or in real per capita ones. Indeed, the ranks obtained for the two sets of figures are closely correlated, with the rank correlation coefficient of 0.85. We believe this is a fact that ought to be emphasized about the growth of the European economy in this period, if only because it implies that, with the exception of Portugal and Italy, at some point during the period there is an historical turning point at which all of the countries in western and central Europe experienced modern economic growth.

Of course individual countries had different experiences, many of which have provoked much discussion in both the narrative literature and in the political arena at the time. Even here, however, regional generalizations muffle many of the nationalistic themes that dominate this literature, since it is more a question of being Mediterranean and/or heavily agricultural than it is in being 'behind the times' or without 'visionary entrepreneurs' *per se*. Thus Italy, Spain and Portugal fight for the bottom position, while Belgium, the United Kingdom, France, Norway and Germany are typically near the top. Aside from Norway and Switzerland, which were small economies in the aggregate, these are the major economic players in an industrial sense, and their fortunes seem related to the progress of their heavy industries for the most part.

4.   INDUSTRIALIZATION, 1750–1850

In this section we provide some background to our overview of the European periphery, especially with regard to its industrialization. Because our interest is macroeconomic, we would normally lean on aggregate data, but in view of the general absence of such data, we will rely more on narrative accounts of specific industrial activities to construct an outline of the resulting growth. Rather surprisingly, a common pattern emerges, even across countries as diverse as those studied in this chapter. The first, and most obvious, feature of this pattern is that every one of these countries had an industrial base by 1800 and in several cases this base can be traced back before 1750. The second feature is an increase in industrialization in the 1750 to 1800 period, although the literature has typically tended to put this down as 'development' rather than 'growth'. The third and final feature on which we comment here is that both in terms of data availability and growth rates the 1815–1850 period outperforms the 1750–1800 one. We argue that this acceleration indicates that all of these countries were on their way toward industrialization by 1850 and it suggests a degree of integration. This observation further emerges from the industrial record presented in the remainder of Section 9.4 and our discussion of the banking sector in Section 9.5.

Turning to the discussion of individual countries, we begin with the *Netherlands*. The general view is that the Dutch industrial sector was competitive in the early days of the industrial revolution, say from 1750 to 1795, with many of its main industrial activities – paper, soap, calico printing, tobacco, brewing and distilling – based on a combination of imported raw materials, Dutch trading and financial capital and know-how and a relatively large urban-based proto-industrial work force (Mokyr, 1976; van Houtte, 1977). The Dutch also possessed a nascent cotton industry, based on English technology (from 1776), with finishing and spinning equipment and the waterframe (around 1780), and with steam engines introduced in 1797 (Dhondt and Bruwier, 1976). Putting aside comments in the literature about the inability of Dutch entrepreneurs to move with the times, the main event of the period seems to be the unique effect of the Napoleonic wars on the Netherlands. Specifically, the Dutch had maintained no political allies in the trade wars and the maritime blockades dating back to Dutch independence, and a 20-year 'decline' of the external-and-finance-based Dutch economy ran from 1795 to around 1815.[2] Perhaps no other country in our sample experienced such economic displacement as the Netherlands at this time, and this event surely attests to the potential costs of war to those literally caught in the middle. It was probably the loss of the Baltic trade that the Dutch felt most keenly.

After 1815, of course, one might have expected the Dutch to prosper, but it appears that a combination of lost markets, industrial backwardness and poor resource endowments (neither coal nor iron, for example) prevented the Dutch from developing an industrial base comparable to their neighbors. Again one reads of entrepreneurial failure, but such a claim simultaneously explains too much and not enough. Dhondt and Bruwier (1976) mention a strong start before 1830 (a more traditional date since that was when the modern Netherlands emerged from the union with Belgium). There was a steamship industry (from 1823), spinning jennies and mules (widespread by 1819) and steam power in textile mills (1818). The textile industry was fully rooted by 1830. This is not to say that 1830 to 1850 did not show more rapid technological change. Drawing on figures from Craig and Fisher (1997, p. 44), we find that in 1820 the Dutch ranked eighth among 12 European countries in output per capita. Those ranked lower were Austria–Hungary, Sweden, Portugal and Italy. Since the Dutch were probably no worse than third in 1750, the potential cost of the Napoleonic wars is obvious, but from 1820 to 1870, a period in which few credit the Dutch with much in the way of industrialization, the Dutch moved to fifth in per capita output on a 1.47 per cent per year growth rate per capita. The evidence suggests that this growth was based on the same advantages the Dutch had in 1750 for the most part, and that the slowdown in growth between 1795 and 1815 resulted more from exogenous international affairs than a fundamental flaw in the Dutch economy.

In *Austria and Hungary* in the last half of the eighteenth century, the government was involved in policies designed to enhance economic progress.[3]

These policies included no internal tariffs (from 1775 in Austria and 1784 in Hungary) and a strong mercantilist subsidy, government ownership and import substitution policy that predated the period.[4] Austria had most of the early industry in this period, and there was a nascent cotton textile industry as early as 1724; while linen, wool and cotton flourished in Bohemia and Moravia in the latter half of the eighteenth century. Other industrial activities included porcelain, glass, mining and smelting, although most of this was not based on the factory system, and urban populations were relatively small and showed almost no gain from 1750 to 1800.

This is not to say that there were no factories in the Empire, because there certainly were. The largest factory (possibly in Europe) was the Linz woolen fabrics factory established in 1672. (It was stated-owned in 1754.) There were also other textile factories, a needle factory and porcelain factories in Austria in this period. Rather, we note that relative to the leading industrializers, Austria–Hungary lagged substantially in the share of its commodity production conducted in factories.

In contrast to the Netherlands, the Habsburg Empire was in a favorable position during the Napoleonic Wars. In fact, during the Wars, mechanized cotton mills spread over the area and a domestic engineering industry developed. After the Wars, Austria–Hungary continued to grow, and, believe it or not, the Budweis–Linz railroad line, in 1832, was the longest Continental line in existence at the time (at 130 km). Data on coal production, beginning in 1819, show an output of 95,000 metric tons in that year and 877,000 in 1850, yielding a healthy annual compounded rate of growth of 7.17 per cent; coal consumption followed suit, roughly, since little coal was imported (see Gross, 1971). Even granted that output in Austria–Hungary was *much* less than in Belgium, France, German and, especially, the United Kingdom, comparable figures on growth attest to the catching-up of Austria–Hungary:

		Growth Rate of Coal Output %
Austria–Hungary	(1819–1850)	7.17
Belgium	(1831–1850)	4.88
France	(1820–1850)	4.66
Germany	(1819–1850)	4.82
United Kingdom	(1820–1850)	3.47

We would argue that in fact in this period Austria–Hungary was near the middle of the European countries in terms of its overall growth and development as well as in its industrialization. Comparisons using per capita data drawn from the entire Empire, which after all included the most economically backward regions of Europe, tend to disguise this fact. Indeed, in some respects, it would be similar to including the East Indies in the Dutch figures. Given the composition of the Empire, the invidious comparisons with what was going on in Germany (and even Great Britain) at the time, seem irrelevant. Austria started its industrial transformation at roughly the same time as the other continental countries and the process developed, undramatically but steadily, throughout the period. The acceleration that occurred after the Napoleonic Wars was also shared by the other countries examined here, at different rates of growth, to be sure.[5]

After a fashion, then, we are moving down the industrial ladder, and we must point out that the next country, *Italy*, falls somewhat in the same category as Austria–Hungary for the same reason: per capita calculations tend to disguise the progress that was actually made because, like Austria–Hungary, the regions that ultimately composed the nation state of Italy included some of the poorest in Europe. Still, Italy was definitely on a lower economic rung than Austria–Hungary in this period. There were several potential sources of Italy's relative backwardness, not the least of which was its resource base. For the leading technologies and industries of this particular period the resources of northern Europe were a real advantage – coal and iron ore being the most conspicuous – and not only was the coal well placed in the north, but water transportation was relatively easy to improve. On this point, Italy had a further disadvantage in its poor river transportation; indeed, Clough (1964) emphasizes the lack of canal construction over the entire period. Although Clough blames this on the failure of venture capital in Italy, there was actually some early canal construction in the Piedmont after 1800, spreading to Lombardy and the Veneto. Still, one must consider what failure might mean in this context. Capital will seek the highest (risk-adjusted) rate of return; it may simply have been the case the such returns were available elsewhere in Europe.

According to Clough, there was intense interest in official circles in Italian development by 1750 and a number of projects were undertaken in the next half century, especially in the agricultural sector. After 1750, agriculture in the Italian north was producing for national and international markets on a relatively large scale. Furthermore, beginning in 1770, the medieval guilds were abolished, further opening up markets to entrepreneurs. With respect to industrialization, the first flying-shuttle appeared in Venice in 1738 and the establishment in which it was utilized ultimately employed 500 workers (some on a 'putting-out' basis). The silk industry in the North grew from 126 reels in 1730 to 272 in 1787, and at this time the cotton industry was firmly established in Milan. There was also a widespread wool industry in the Piedmont and Lombardy, the origins of which actually predate the 1750–1850 period. Indeed, in Tuscany there were blast furnaces before 1750 and there was a pottery industry established in 1738. By the end of the eighteenth century, glass, metalworking and sugar refining were all established, as was a paper industry, all indications that, at least qualitatively, the northern regions of Italy were well along the industrial path by the early nineteenth century.

Italy was affected by the Napoleonic occupation in a somewhat mixed way. Obviously the French had a hand in the establishment of a strong anti-Austrian nationalism and an interest in using Italian resources. In addition, as was the case elsewhere in Napoleonic Europe, political structures were liberalized during this period; on the other hand, the Continental System was also costly to the Italians. Still on balance, it appears, Italian development continued during the war period.

After the Napoleonic wars, there is a noticeable acceleration in growth and development in Italy that we believe was generally experienced by the countries we are discussing in this section. Agriculture continued to employ new machinery and the cotton industry was well established by 1830. The silk industry also continued its growth, as did machine tools, an industry that (by 1860) was producing many of the devices of an industrial economy, including jennies, printing presses, waterwheels, railway cars and armaments, to name only the more glamorous. In fact, in our earlier tabulation (Craig and Fisher, 1997), Italy moved from 11th to 9th (of 13 European countries) in output per capita, from 1820 to 1870. We do not want to exaggerate, and we do not want to advance the claim that per capita output rose sharply over this half century, since it did not, but it surely rose significantly in the birthplace of Italy's industrialization, that is, in the North. It also rose in at least part of the South, especially in the Kingdom of Naples in the 1820–50 period, where, aided by a strongly protectionist tariff policy, wool, machine tools, linen and cotton were established around the commercial and financial center of the city of Naples (which was Italy's largest city at the time). Although this overview of Italy is not really novel, we feel it does shift the emphasis from Italy as a laggard nation, or even an economically stagnant one, to Italy as a developing country and, more important, one that was developing in the same way as other European countries, on the backs of entrepreneurs in the new and leading industries of the day.[6]

In 1750, *Sweden* had a traditional cast-iron industry that was based on its high-grade ores and timber resources. In the 1760s, attempts were made to import British technology (using imported coal) and success was achieved on a limited scale by 1766 with workers smuggled in from England. The first effort was at Göteborg (Gothenburg), while the first English-style operation arrived in Stockholm in 1771 at the Bergsand foundry; this firm evolved and expanded and became a leading engineering works. It was not alone, of course, and Swedish iron and copper work were world-famous. Furthermore, eighteenth-century Swedish chemists, physicists and botanists made significant contributions to the world's stock of technical knowledge. However, as the iron and steel markets expanded, Sweden's lack of coal was a tremendous disadvantage, but, until the metallurgy was better understood, producing quality steel and iron from coal remained problematic everywhere and Sweden's pig iron producers found a niche in the market for high-quality pig iron produced with charcoal.

The most significant transportation scheme in Sweden during this period was the Göta canal which ran right across the country; this project had been proposed as early as the sixteenth century. A start was made in 1752 to link Göteborg to iron and charcoal supplies, but the canal itself was started in 1810 and was completed (to Stockholm) in 1832, just in time to welcome the railway age! Understandably, it was never much of an economic factor.

As we have indicated in Table 9.3, Sweden had a small cotton textile industry by 1850. But in 1850, in spite of full participation in industrialization from 1750 and some overall economic growth, Sweden had the lowest rate of urbanization (at 6.15 per cent) of any country in our survey and was the lowest in industrial potential (see Table 9.4). Furthermore, Swedish economic development only looks good in the per capita figures when compared with the Mediterranean countries (again in Table 9.4). Still it is important, in thinking about Sweden's relative position in 1850, also to note its variety of banking services, its European-leading level of education and its long tradition of high-quality metalworking (see Sandberg, 1978, 1979). Together these characteristics clearly put Sweden in a good position to accelerate its economic growth towards the end of the nineteenth century.

In our general discussion around Tables 9.1 to 9.5, we have noted that *Spain* and *Portugal* grew relatively slowly in this period, with a slowdown of population growth in the 1800–1850 period (compared with 1750–1800). Furthermore, both countries had decreasing urbanization rates in the 1750–1800 period, but in 1800–1850 Spain diverged from Portugal in that its urbanization rate increased substantially; indeed Spain was a fairly urbanized country by European standards in 1850. The figures in Table 9.3 do not indicate much industrial development in Spain by 1850 and none in Portugal at that date, but in Table 9.4 we saw that Spanish per capita industrial output was comparable to that of all of the other major 'peripheral' industrializers in 1750 and 1800; furthermore, it grew, by this indicator, as rapidly as Austria–Hungary and Italy in the 1800–1860 period. The rate of growth of 'industrial potential', on the basis of some very crude numbers, was 1.07 per cent per year over the 1800–1860 period. This figure may come as a surprise to some, but of course we can identify only a relatively small base for this calculation and the level was still very low by European standards. Evidently, in what follows, we are looking for the details of the Spanish acceleration toward a more industrialized economy, albeit again from a low level, while Portugal advanced so slowly that it appears to diverge even from the path of modest growth of the southern European (peripheral) countries.

The analysis of *Spanish* development prior to 1850 is influenced by the extreme pessimism of Nadal (for example, 1970). Rather than repeat that story or enter into that debate, we glean from the literature the details that support the data shown in Tables 9.1 to 9.4. Speaking first of agriculture and the transportation infrastructure, we note that Sarrion (1995) argues that drainage, irrigation, canal- and road-building projects accelerated in the second half of the eighteenth century, especially after 1766. There was a Canal Imperial, including the Canal di Castilla and the Canal Imperial di Agagona (on the Ebro), especially around Saragossa. The latter was built on an earlier canal, which was constructed during the sixteenth century. The major construction period for the canal on the Ebro was 1785–88; it was financed by government debt, and there were numerous navigation and irrigation canals built in the same period. The debt was floated in Amsterdam for the most part and, along with war deficits, posed a significant burden for the narrow tax base of the Spanish government. The purposes of these projects were apparently to meet the demands of a growing population and to service growing agricultural markets (in grain, wine and olive oil), some of them being for export. Indeed, there was a grand design to link the Atlantic to the Mediterranean by waterways, a sea-to-sea proposal that other countries attempted (especially the French and the Swedes, the one earlier than the Spanish and the other later).

In spite of the general view to the contrary, industry had a foothold in Spain even before 1750 and continued to grow in the next century. There was for example, a growing industrial sector in Cuenca between 1724 and 1771, with a broad spectrum of activities involved (including metallurgy, construction and woodworking but, interestingly, not textiles). Similarly, and more generally, Fernandez de Pinedo (1988) documents technological change in Spanish iron-making from 1650. He remarks that water-powered tilt-hammers, probably imported from Italy, were used as early as 1550 and that by the middle of the seventeenth century, an iron industry was well established in northern Spain. Fernandez also notes that in the next century a substantial number of (charcoal) bloomeries were operating in the north and they increased in number and size over the period. The government attempted to introduce newer northern European methods in the mid-to-late eighteenth century; while this approach was generally unsuccessful, output expanded all along the northern coast and into Catalonia. Suggestive of progress, charcoal supplies ran down and, by 1760, coal had been introduced. Case-hardened steel was produced by 1784 and a blast furnace had been established in Galicia in 1791.

After the Napoleonic Wars, there was an iron-making boom, not in the north but in the southeast. The funds for this boom (in Malaga) were originally derived from agriculture and shipping, but local entrepreneurs also moved into lead and graphite from 1801, amassing the capital that later funded the iron industry; even so, the precipitating event may have been the removal of government controls on mineral production after 1817. The rise of the iron industry was founded on British methods from the 1820s and on local ore (and new sources of charcoal). Soap, textiles and chemicals were included in the southern boom by the 1840s. Some of this may have to do with the relative decline of the north of Spain, but new methods were the mainstay of this activity. There is no doubt, in sum, that there was a Spanish iron-making industry throughout the 1500–1850 period and, although it was on a relatively small scale by European standards, it grew and progressed technically. In fact, new developments in the West quickly reached Spain. Fernandez reminds us that even so, traditional methods were (*ex post*) economically efficient in Spain, an argument more acceptable to economists than to historians and politicians.

In *Portugal*, the roots of modern expansion are seen even before 1750 (Pedreira, 1990). Recall from Chapter 2 that, in some respects, Portugal was, along with Spain, arguably the first modern state. In 1680 there was in place a northern linen and lace industry, exporting to Spain and the colonies, and there was also a traditional woolen industry in the northwest (Minho) as well as in the south-central area near Lisbon. The north was (and is) a densely populated area with good water resources and a flourishing agriculture, while the south was poorer, with farm families producing woolens on their handlooms in the off-season. By the early nineteenth century there were textile factories in the Serra de Estrela (north central). But the industrial presence in Portugal remained on a narrow base, in scattered locations, and was technologically backward even as late as the nineteenth century. It did exist, however, and in the next half century there were ceramics (Mafra), leather goods (Alcanena and Guimaraes), nail-making, hats (Braga), silk spinning and weaving (Cinta) as well as the linen and woolens already mentioned. However, modern factories were not well established in Portugal by 1850, even though a thriving proto-industrial sector remained in place. The factories that did exist were in the northeast, where there were cotton mills (1840s) in Negrelos and in Minho. There were also woolen mills in the Serra de Estrela in the 1840s, again founded on a base that went back centuries.

While we do not have the types of aggregate industrial data for Portugal as we reported earlier for other countries, we do have the annual real GDP estimates of Nunes, Mata and Valerio (1989) that show 415,000 contes in 1833, rising to 467,000 in 1844 and declining again to 367,000 in 1850 (a year of recession). While the growth from 1833 to 1844 was promising, and Portuguese entrepreneurs seemed aware of world technology throughout the period, a combination of rural dispersion and slow population growth, along with an unfavorable distribution of resources, combined to keep

Portugal on the back burner of European industrialization to 1850. There was development, indeed there was considerable development by the standards of earlier centuries (Pedreira, 1990), but little or no growth in per capita industrial output in the period (1750–1850). But recall that in our earlier estimates of per capita output in Section 9.3, we found a rise from 1830 to 1850. This actually compares favorably with growth in Italy. Also Portugal's per capita output was 67 per cent of that of Spain in 1850, and the descriptions of Portugal's industrial activity would seem to corroborate this figure.

This section has covered a wide range of countries, but several things are obvious to us. For one, all of these countries were participating in the new industrial activities of the time by the beginning of the nineteenth century, and by 1850 these industries were developing rapidly. Even so, the extent of industrialization in 1800, or 1850, differed widely among the countries considered in this section. We think the correct conclusion is that the *process* of industrialization was underway in *all* of these countries, but that local economic conditions, and not politics or government involvement in the process, generally drove the extent of this activity. Hampered by weaker capital markets, relatively small proto-industrial workforces, relatively poor transportation facilities, relatively backward agricultural sectors and lesser development of their often spartan mineral resources, Italy, Spain, Portugal and parts of Austria–Hungary lagged behind either parts of their own country or the more rapidly industrializing North. These are all economic disadvantages, but none was intrinsically structural, as we believe history was already demonstrating by 1850.

5.   BANKING IN THE PERIPHERY

In order to guide the review of some very fragmentary material, we begin our discussion of banking in these countries with some generalizations. Our general hypothesis in this study is that the banking and financial markets followed the development of each economy, arising as the demand for financial products increased and this development helped produce a convergence and integration of European financial markets. Of course, this statement does not mean to suggest that there were no significant financial innovations in the period we are discussing; rather it simply implies that innovations in the financial sector were neither as extensive nor as dramatic as those in the industrial sector, which witnessed a plethora of inventions and innovations and an increasingly rapid technology transfer in the period. Of course capital markets were international to some degree at this time, even in the periphery, and this fact, too, needs to be appreciated on a country-by-country survey. It is worth mentioning that in the literature there appears to be a tendency to regard financial systems as 'retarded' in some sense if they do not lend to industry on a large scale. Typically, *credit mobilier* style banks are perceived to be the solution to this problem but they do not emerge on any substantial scale until after 1850. We classify this argument with another one frequently put forward with respect to industry in these countries: No measurable progress will be achieved until government provides significant financial assistance in terms of, say, tariff protection or through the direct issue of government-secured debt for what were essentially private ventures. We believe these ideas are not supported by the detailed historical arguments and that 'peripheral' development, like that in the other countries we have already studied, was not necessarily assisted by such devices, which are mostly mercantilistic and, hence, more likely to create rents than to assist in development. In our story the banking sector is not very different from the industrial sector in terms of its development during this period, which is to say that it developed from a system largely designed to discount notes drawn against mercantile activity in 1750 to one increasingly prepared to finance industrial activities by 1850, without much input from the government or even by means of special lending arrangements whose time had not yet come.

As might be expected given its location and history, banking in the *Netherlands* was relatively advanced in 1750, and so we begin this section with a discussion of the subsequent financial development there. After some years of failure, silver coinage was re-established in 1755 and between 1749 and 1779 the per capita money stock in the Netherlands nearly doubled. The Bank of Amsterdam was still one of the dominant financial institutions in all of Europe in 1750 and it created demand deposits, as did the private banks in Amsterdam and elsewhere in the Netherlands (these others were the so-called *wisselbanken*). There were also merchant banks, dealing in precious metals, coins and discounts, and bankers' acceptances were in common use by 1750. With the exception of the general crisis of 1763 and the problems associated with the Fourth Anglo-Dutch War, banking and financial intermediation expanded rapidly between 1750 and 1795.

The Dutch banks suffered the fate of their customers – whose fortunes were largely tied to trade – in the 1795 to 1815 period and there were numerous closures and forced refinancings. Even so, there must have been a relatively rapid expansion of the money supply in this period, since wholesale prices, drawn from van Stuijvenberg and de Vrijer (1982), increased dramatically. Our source lists only five-year averages, but from an index number of 72 in 1750–54 and 107 in 1785–89, at the peak wholesale prices were 255 in the 1810–14 period (with 1905 = 100). It is certainly true that some of the inflation (which was much more rapid than in either England or France) was the result of a slowed economy compared to the money growth rate. This conclusion follows from the equation of exchange (MV = Py). No doubt, also, some inflation could be attributed to supply shocks in key sectors, if only because a fixed-base-weight index, such as the one discussed here, would produce spurious readings of inflation as a result of such changes in relative prices.

Although the crises of the late eighteenth century had already shaken the foundations of Dutch finance, it is generally accepted that the Dutch failed to recover their place at the top of European finance after the Napoleonic Wars (Homer and Sylla, 1991; Kindleberger, 1993), though the reasons typically given for this relative decline are somewhat less than acceptable. Among the explanations offered are the rise of the British, an increasing tendency of the Dutch to become *rentiers*, the decline of empire and so forth. These are closer to descriptions of what happened rather than explanations of why. With the loss of much of her international trading empire, the share of trade passing through Dutch ports on Dutch ships declined. At the same time the post-Napoleonic Dutch regime resorted to mercantilist policies, which the regime was ill-prepared to defend and which only exacerbated the declining Dutch fortunes. Furthermore, the large government debt led to high tax rates *and* government borrowing (Griffiths, 1979, Chap. 3), which together tended to make the Netherlands a less rewarding place to invest; thus, the demand for financial intermediation, beyond placing the government debt, seems to have diminished.

With respect to government debt, the yields on Dutch government debt peaked in 1814, the year the Bank of the Netherlands was founded, and it dominated Dutch finance from that date. Of course, the Bank specialized in government debt and over the long run the state's finances improved, with the benchmark securities circulating near par by the end of the century. Even with this recovery of Dutch state finances, by the end of the century the Bank of the Netherlands was three times as large as the rest of the country's banks combined!

In 1816, following the Napoleonic Wars, the *Austrian* National Bank was established. It served as the central bank, at least in the nineteenth-century sense of the term, and it possessed a monopoly of the note issue. It served primarily as a discount house for the government and the large private banks; the latter, in turn, served the nobility and other 'most respected clients' – to borrow Good's (1984) term – for the most part this state of affairs dates back to the eighteenth century. Although the number and geographical dispersion of small-scale savings banks expanded during this period, both Good (1984) and Rudolph (1972) argue that there was little banking development prior to 1850.

Following our main theme, one cannot separate the evolution of banking from the evolution of industry. On this point, Rudolph is generally pessimistic about the *level* of industrial development before 1850, though his annual per capita growth rate of 2.6 per cent for industrial production from 1830 to 1850 surely suggests rapid growth (Rudolph, 1972) and, in fact, the smaller banking houses were often tied to commercial and industrial activities even in the second half of the eighteenth century. The impression that there was financial intermediation of any importance arises from the perceived necessity of a link between the industrial and financial sectors. Finding a relatively low level of industrial development and no major direct links between the two sectors in Austria–Hungary before 1850, one is tempted to conclude that Austrian finance was in some sense retarded or backward; however, we would argue that the admittedly conservative and small-scale nature of those activities simply reflected the domestic investment opportunities faced by Austrian entrepreneurs.

In the nation that in earlier days had been a pioneer in international banking and once had networks of early 'banks' over much of western and central Europe, the admission that in 1750 *Italy* was not well endowed with banking resources seems to require some explanation. What the politically and economically fragmented region had, in the 1750–1815 period, was a similarly fragmented banking community, with different coinages and different (private) banks or bankers, involved mainly in deposit maintenance and short-term lending, in the style of banks elsewhere. Genoa was particularly well stocked with bankers throughout the 1750–1850 period, and Genoese capital played an important role in European capital markets. Turin, also, had a vigorous banking community throughout this period.

The Napoleonic period brought a uniform currency, French, to be sure, but it was a 'paper and specie' currency and was in any case dispensed with after Napoleon's downfall. What survived was a considerable number of coinages (based on local mints) that gave an apparently chaotic character to Italian banking; it also provided for arbitrage opportunities. In the North, as already noted, the established towns had major banking institutions, some of which dated from the Renaissance, and in 1845, the Bank of Genoa (a joint-stock bank) was formed. There was also a Bank of Turin. In fact, the two were merged in 1849, into the Banca Nazionale Sarda, which became the Banca d'Italia after unification. In the South there was a bank in Sicily that dated from 1808, and in the Kingdom of Naples, the Cassa di Sconto was established in 1818 to lend to the government, but its lending powers were broadened in the 1820s to include industrial firms. This provision was eliminated after the crash of 1834. There were also savings banks in Italy – the *casse di risparmio* – that grew rapidly after 1823 – that is, after the founding of one in Milan. Furthermore, there were, in this period, banks that dealt in commercial loans and insurance companies were another source of capital from 1826.

The lack of comprehensive data here should not obscure the fact that a substantial banking community still existed in 1750, that it grew until the late

1790s, when it was confronted with the mixed blessing of the Napoleonic incursion, and that it expanded with the Italian economy from 1815 to 1850, with *crédit-mobilier*-style banks emerging shortly thereafter. On net then, we think, Italian banking flourished in the capital cities and in the financial and industrial ones, and it would be more appropriate to speak of a high level of banking deposits than the converse. The fact that they did not lend to industry in any volume is neither surprising nor a relative disadvantage before 1850.

From 1625 until the early eighteenth century, *Sweden* was on a silver and copper standard, guided by the Riksbank. A paper currency, dominated by notes issued by the Riksbank, was gradually developed, and in 1745 Sweden went entirely on a paper standard, mainly because of the need to finance the Russian wars of 1741–3 by borrowing from the Riksbank. This standard lasted until 1789, when two new banknotes, one of which was redeemable in silver, were introduced; this issue, too, was inspired by the financial needs of another Russian war (1788–90). Following a currency conversion and return to silver in 1802, stability lasted until yet another Russian war in 1809. Sweden returned to silver in 1834 following the subsequent devaluation. In the earlier period, in addition to the Riksbank, there were also public and private discount houses (established in 1773, 1787 and 1797) and payment notes were also drawn on balances with merchant houses and traders.

Modern Swedish commercial banks were first established in the 1830s. Indeed, these *enskilda* banks began to issue currency, and by 1859 had over 43 per cent of the total note issue. But these banks had unlimited liability, regulated interest rates and, accordingly, they had relatively small deposit businesses. Nonetheless, this system was arguably adequate for the task at hand, given Sweden's relatively low level of industrial development; this task was to service a small country growing on the fringe of the Industrial Revolution.

In our discussion of *Spain*'s industrial development above, we noted the Spanish government's debt-financing of canals and other activities in Castille; this activity produced at least one bank (to manage mostly public affairs), the Banco Nacional de San Carlos (1783). Although engaged in public business, it was actually under private control. There were also, according to Sarrion (1995), a set of individuals actively engaged in banking in Madrid and Cadiz at the same time. These would have been banking families with links to the merchant banking tradition, the likes of which could be found in all of the financial centers of Europe. Similarly, throughout Europe, their business was mainly commercial and short term at this time. However, capital, mainly in the more industrial north, was raised in other European markets – especially in Paris, London and Amsterdam.

Most accounts of Spanish banking simply ignore these and other early efforts and begin their story with the joint-stock bank of San Fernando in

Madrid. It was founded in 1829, following the revision of the Commercial Code in that year, and it eventually blossomed into the Bank of Spain with a monopoly of the note issue (from 1874). There was also a stock exchange in Madrid from 1831. In 1844 there were two new banks of issue, the most important being the Bank of Barcelona, in the industrial center of Spain. The only other joint stock banks of this period were the Bank of Isabella II in Madrid (1844) and the Bank of Cadiz (1846), the latter actually created when the Bank of Isabella II was partly merged with the Bank of San Fernando and partly separated (in Cadiz). The development of Spanish banking, not unlike that of Austria–Hungary, reflects the relatively small scale of Spanish industry and commerce until the 1820s, when new industrial and commercial enterprises and changes in government regulations inspired a strong move toward modern banking and toward central banking – again, in the nineteenth-century sense. We see no reason to suppose that banking in Spain was either retrograde or a drag on Spanish development, which itself proceeded, as we have already noted, at a pace that reflected Spain's position in the changing world economy, given her resource endowment, public policies and so forth.

6. BUSINESS CYCLES IN THE PERIPHERY

We do not have data to conduct time-series analysis for any of the countries we are studying in this chapter. The literature, obsessed with either very long-run trends or short-term financial crises, is also incomplete by almost any standard. What we have decided to do, under the circumstances, is to summarize the cyclical information in Chapters 7 and 8 and then look for echoes in the literature describing the economies of the periphery. In short, we will assume the existence of a cyclically interactive European economy and then look to see if it extended beyond the four major economies for which reasonably good and relatively extensive data do exist. We will, of course, forswear any attempt to construct cyclical dating for any of these countries by themselves, although for the period from 1830 to 1850, a little more precision is possible.

In Table 9.6, we show the dating of the major cycles in the United Kingdom, France, Belgium and Germany. Thus for global events, albeit on this rather meager evidence, the following years might produce echoes in other countries:

1762–63	1772–74	1793–94		
1806–08	1815–16	1818–19	1821–22	1825–26
1831–32	1837–38	1840–42	1845	1848–49

Table 9.6   Declines in the United Kingdom and France 1750–1850

United Kingdom	France	Belgium	Germany
1754			
1756			
1762	1763		
1765			
1768			
1773–74	1772–74		
1778–79			
1785			
	1789–90		
1793–94	1793		
1797			
1801			
1808	1806–07		
1812			
1816	1815		
1819	1820	1818	1818
	1822	1822	1821
1826	1825	1828	1826
1832	1832	1831	1831–32
1837		1837–38	
	1839		
1840–42	1842	1842	
	1845–46	1845	1845
1848	1848	1848–49	1848–49

This is 13 events in 90 years and is quite possibly as close to the identification of the major 'European' recessions as we can get. Now we will search for echoes in the periphery.

For *Austria–Hungary* we were unable to locate any information before the 1830s. In the coal production figures in Mitchell (1992) we note significant declines in production in 1831, 1833 and 1843. In the consumption of coal figures, the years of sharp decline were 1833 and 1843 (we could not make a comparison for 1831). The two events, in any case, certainly follow by one year international events on which we have already remarked; furthermore, the coal industry is one especially apt to show cyclical influences.

For the *Netherlands*, there was a stock exchange crisis in 1763, following a drop of prices upon the ending of the Seven Years War. At this time two banks failed as did some 30 banking and merchant houses, but the recession, if there was one, was over by the end of the year. For 1772 the Dutch literature ties a recession that began around Christmas (and lasted until 1774) to bankruptcies in England. Both of these events appear to be part of the international cycle. The War of 1780–4 hindered trade and produced a crisis on the Amsterdam stock market, and together these developments may have resulted in a recession that is not echoed elsewhere in the literature. In 1789 the Dutch East India Company failed and its collapse involved the Amsterdam banks.

In *Italy*, the Naples 'share' market crashed in 1834; the usual explanation of this is that it was a bubble produced by the over-expansion of the textile industry. The financial side of this event, which may actually have had an international dimension, was that the Cassa di Sconto, a bank that had been lending to industry up until that point, ceased to do so after the crash.

In *Portugal*, real GDP fell drastically in 1834–5, 1838–41 and in 1850. Aside from 1838–41, these are not the exact years of the international events, but if there were a lag in effect, from the leaders to the periphery, then this, too, would be mild evidence of the effects of the international cycle. In *Spain*, there was a financial panic in 1847–8, involving one bank and two credit companies. Indeed, the entire financial community shrank from seven to four institutions during this crisis. No doubt this is also a recession and, one notes, this is a year of the international cycle.

In *Denmark*, industrial production declined sharply in 1819–22, 1833–4, 1841–2 and 1848–50 (Hansen, 1974). These are almost perfectly mirrored in the cycles listed above, with perhaps a slight lag that seems characteristic of the periphery. There was also a mild decline in 1828–9 in industrial production; this was also at the time of our international reference cycle dating of Table 9.6. In *Sweden*, Jonung (1976) notes that there was a policy-induced decline in the money stock and the price level following the Seven Years War that produced a recession in 1764. Jonung seems to think the recession ran until 1768, but this might have been a 'financial' rather than a real recession in its later years.

How might we summarize this section? For the period before 1815, it is likely that there were recessions after the Seven Years War; during the general financial problems of 1773–4; possibly something in the early to mid-1780s; a full-blown recession in some countries in 1789–90; another international event in 1793–4; and recessions at the points of severest strain during the Napoleonic Wars, probably in 1803, 1806 and 1812.

The 1816 recession seems to have been shared by everyone, and there is widespread agreement, even in the periphery, that 1819–20, 1825–6, and 1828–9 were recession years for many (if not most) countries. We have established similar information for 1832–3 (or 1834), 1839–42, and 1848–49, but we have some even more intriguing information bearing on this later period in the Western European Gross National Product figures put together by Bairoch (1982). In his tabulation, there are significant declines in this aggregate in

    1833   1836   1839   1846   1848

These dates correspond well with what we have described above both in terms of the major economies and the countries on the periphery.

7. CONCLUSIONS

We have, following the literature, used the term 'periphery' to describe the countries we discussed in this chapter. In our case, we mean simply that these countries did not industrialize as rapidly as did the four leaders that we discussed in Chapters 7 and 8. We have documented that all countries, including the Iberian ones, had 'modern' textile operations soon after the British, and all were developing their iron industries and their economic infrastructures. There appears to us to have been an industrial 'process' at work at the time, one that was shared internationally at rates and times that are surely country-specific. Perhaps this is what most writers on the subject are saying, or trying to say but we resist the temptation to identify the countries lower on the scale than France and Germany as laggards in any negative sense. Just as development within a modern country is uneven from region to region, so, too, was it uneven in the European setting. In fact, it was very uneven, but all countries, right down to the bottom of the table, were experiencing economic and population growth rates that were uniquely rapid for any sustained period in their history, putting aside the lucky winners of the international plundering fraternity.

The impression from looking at the details of industrialization is strengthened, we feel, with reference to financial development. Surely each of these countries had parallel development of its banking sector – parallel, that is to say, with whatever rate of industrialization and growth it was achieving. The literature, perhaps dipping into anachronism, often seems to search for more, in particular, chiding the financial industry and even the government for providing so little financial assistance to the budding entrepreneurs of the periphery. Certainly capital is the life-blood of the industrial revolution, but we feel that a successful device of later times (the *crédit mobilier*) is not a relevant choice in the century before its appearance and, in fact, financial firms did spring up in the wake of economic and industrial progress, without (in the fashion of the time) heavy direct involvement in the industrial process.

Business cycles are easier to document, of course, as the data get better as they do over time. We do have some figures for the eighteenth century for the leaders, but for the periphery there is no time-series data and, for that matter, little interest in the literature in securing a reference cycle dating for these countries individually or collectively. We have attempted to do so using our preliminary estimates of the international cycle as a kind of reference cycle and then checking through a sparse literature mostly devoted to other topics for echoes of these reference cycles. This works to some extent prior to 1816, but after that we can report very strong echoes in the periphery of the already established international cycle. Of course these echoes are mostly in the industrial sector, and this sector is relatively small in these countries, to put it mildly, but this is the information that we have and it is the industrial sector that can be expected to produce this sort of evidence, so we are not in any sense apologizing for our emphasis.

NOTES

1. Note that much of the Austrian result comes from the behavior of the population in just one city, Vienna.
2. According to Mokyr (1976), among the leading industries only the rural textile industries, which served local markets primarily, did well in this period.
3. Good (1984) argues that the government involvement in economic activity was largely the result of military and political competition with Prussia.
4. See the discussion in Gross (1976) and Freudenberger (1983).
5. In Craig and Fisher (1997), we show that Austria-Hungary ranked last (13th) in per capita industrial output in both 1820 and 1870. In terms of what we have just pointed out, this means simply that it did not alter its relative position. It is, of course, the fact that this figure includes large, relatively stagnant, agricultural areas, that is largely responsible for this result.
6. We did not say 'its' entrepreneurs, for throughout the period much entrepreneurial capital was provided by German and Swiss industrialists, with the former more important in the North and the latter in the Kingdom of Naples.

PART IV

The Maturing of the Industrial Revolution
1850–1913

10. Population and overall economic growth 1850–1913

1. INTRODUCTION

During the period from 1850 to 1913, the industrial revolution entered a new phase, one in which first iron, coal and then the railroad supplemented textiles as the most conspicuous industries across Europe; later these industries were joined by newer ones, including steel, machine tools, chemicals and electrical power, and, at the end of the period, the automobile. The growth of these new industries was accompanied by the proliferation of large-scale manufacturing operations. One of the reasons that we have selected 1850 as a starting point for this last unit is that it is a point at which economic agents in Europe – including national governments – can be said to have been fully conscious of the existing dimensions of the industrial revolution. In fact, not only were the economic agents in each country aware of the industrial transformation taking place elsewhere, but they also conducted real and financial transactions in ways that built virtually unbreakable economic ties; the resulting economic integration benefited all the countries that participated in it. Trade, real capital flows, migration, technology transfer and the growth of the international financial community were the key aspects to this integration, as they are today.

For this part of the study, per capita measures of real income or output provide an important view of the actual performance of the European economies over time. In this chapter, we relate the rate of economic growth during the period 1850 to 1913 in each country to the structure of its economy. In doing so we show how and explain why some countries were able to stay ahead, some were able to catch up, while others either fell behind or fell further behind. As the leading industries changed over time, for example, some countries were able to increase their participation in those activities through natural advantages based on resource endowments, by means of comparative advantages in the trade of manufactured products and of institutional (often legal) changes that permitted entrepreneurs to take advantage of the new economic situation. That is, catching the wave of economic change required some combination of political support, a conducive institutional structure and aggressive behavior by key economic agents. Our objective is to illustrate the degree to which these factors produced an historically remarkable 'convergence' in the sense that the set of European economies looked more like one another at the end of the period than at the beginning. Our level of illustration continues to be macroeconomic as much as is possible.

In Section 2 we review the population trends and urbanization in the European countries. Although each of these countries was undergoing a demographic transition from high to low fertility and mortality rates, in general the mortality rates either fell earlier and/or faster than the fertility rates, resulting in fairly robust population growth rates throughout the period. We then turn to measures of overall economic performance (Section 3). Here we see that the growth in output per capita accelerated after 1850. We follow the discussion of overall output growth by focusing on the performance across sectors (Section 4). Specifically, we look at industrial production, the trends in specific industries, and the growth of manufacturing relative to agriculture. One of the keys to the growth we discuss in Sections 3 and 4 is the expansion of international trade, which we review in Section 5. We conclude this chapter with a brief summary.

2.   POPULATION GROWTH

The first topic, as in the other units in this study, is that of the growth of population. During the nineteenth century, all of the countries listed in Table 10.1 experienced what demographers often refer to as 'the demographic transition' – the movement from historically high birth and death rates to considerably lower levels of each. Although the timing of the transition differs from country to country, by the end of the period they had all moved from crude birthrates in the neighborhood of 45–50 per thousand to rates around 20 per thousand. Crude death rates fell as well and, in addition, all European countries experienced considerable emigration – much of it to the United States. This multi-faceted transition clearly had effects on the labor supply, although it is beyond the scope of this study to document this (see Williamson, 1996 and 1998; and O'Rourke et al., 1994).

Table 10.1 shows the size and the growth rates of the populations of these countries from 1850 to 1913. Note that the French figures are unusual, possibly because France was the first country to experience the 'demographic transition'. Even so, the differences among the remaining nations are often remarkable. At the low end of the distribution are Italy and Spain; these two agriculturally-dominated countries are at the low end of per capita output as well, as we shall see. At the high end of the distribution are Germany, Denmark and the Netherlands; Germany and Denmark also grew rapidly as measured by output per capita.

Table 10.1   The population of selected European countries 1850–1913 ('000s)

Country	Base Year	Base Year Population	Population 1870	1913	Growth Rates Overall	1870–13
Austria	1850	17,490	20,320	28,850	0.79	0.82
Belgium	1850	4,414	5,056	7,605	0.87	0.95
Denmark	1850	1,424	1,793	2,833	1.10	1.06
France	1850	35,630	38,330	39,771	0.17	0.09
Germany	1850	35,312	40,805	66,978	1.02	1.15
Hungary	1852	12,500	13,600	18,660	0.66	0.74
Italy	1861	24,971	26,526	35,192	0.66	0.66
Netherlands	1850	3,057	3,618	6,213	0.86	1.26
Norway	1850	1,390	1,735	2,447	0.55	0.80
Portugal	1850	3,850	4,366	6,004	0.71	0.74
Spain	1858	15,530	16,200	20,200	0.48	0.51
Sweden	1861	3,889	4,162	5,622	0.71	0.70
U.K.	1850	27,550	31,260	45,650	0.80	0.88

Note: The compound growth rates use the end points of each period.

Sources: Austria, Hungary, Norway, Spain, U.K. (Mitchell, 1992); Belgium, Italy (Maddison, 1991); Denmark (Hansen, 1974), France (Toutain, 1987); Germany (Hoffmann, 1965); Netherlands (van Stuijvenberg and de Vrijer, 1982); Portugal (Nunes, et al., 1989); Sweden (Krantz and Nilsson, 1975).

In earlier chapters we have used growth rates of urbanization to supplement our rather meager data on the actual growth rates of the European economies. There is no need to do that here, in view of much more adequate data, but we still think the urbanization numbers are interesting, particularly as they seem to suggest rather more strongly than anything else we will see in this chapter how these economies were becoming more alike.

One way to see what was going on is to look at a 'short list' of the major European cities (Table 10.2). In the absolute numbers, one is struck by how large many cities became, especially in the 1850–1910 period, when the 'second' industrial revolution was spreading. In most cases, at least as many people were added to the cities from 1850 to 1910 as resided in the same cities in 1850. This was the case in 45 of the 51 possible cases listed, and in every city, at least of those listed, for Germany. In the last part of the 'first' industrial revolution, from 1800 to 1850, the growth of U.K. cities stands out. Of the 12 cases when cities grew faster than 2 per cent per year for the 50 years, 7 were in the United Kingdom. On the other hand, in the

Table 10.2   Population of selected European cities 1800–1910 ('000s)

| Country | City | 1800 | 1850 | 1910 | Annual Growth Rates | |
					1800–1850	1850–1910
Austria	Budapest	54	178	880	2.38	2.66
Hungary	Prague	75	118	224	0.91	1.07
	Vienna	247	444	2031	1.17	2.53
Belgium	Antwerp	62	88	302	0.70	2.06
	Brussels	66	251	720	2.67	1.76*
Denmark	Copenhagen	101	129	559	0.49	2.44
France	Bordeaux	91	131	262	0.73	1.16
	Lyon	110	177	460	0.95	1.59
	Marseille	111	194	551	1.12	1.74
	Paris	581	1053	2888	1.19	1.68
Germany	Berlin	172	419	2017	1.78	2.66
	Bremen	40	53	247	0.56	2.56
	Cologne	50	97	517	1.32	2.79
	Dortmund	4	11	214	2.02	4.95
	Dresden	60	97	548	0.96	2.88
	Essen	4	9	295	1.62	5.82
	Frankfurt	48	65	415	0.61	3.09
	Hamburg	130	132	931	0.03	3.26
	Hanover	18	29	302	0.95	3.90
	Munich	40	110	596	2.02	2.82
	Nuremberg	30	54	333	1.18	3.03
	Stuttgart	18	47	286	1.92	3.01
Italy	Florence	78	106	233	0.61	1.31
	Genoa	91	120	272	0.55	1.36
	Milan	135	242	579	1.17	1.45
	Naples	427	449	723	0.10	0.79
	Palermo	139	180	342	0.52	1.07
	Rome	163	175	542	0.14	1.88
	Turin	78	135	427	1.10	1.92
Netherlands	Amsterdam	217	224	574	0.06	1.57
	The Hague	38	72	281	1.28	2.27
	Rotterdam	53	90	427	1.06	2.60
Norway	Oslo	10	28	243	2.06	3.60
Portugal	Lisbon	180	240	435	0.57	0.99
Spain	Barcelona	115	175	587	0.84	2.02
	Madrid	160	281	600	1.13	1.26
	Valencia	80	90	233	0.24	1.58

Table 10.2   (continued)

| Country | City | 1800 | 1850 | 1910 | Annual Growth Rates | |
					1800–1850	1850–1910
Sweden	Stockholm	76	93	342	0.40	2.17
Switz.	Zurich	12	17	191	0.70	4.03
U.K.	Belfast	37	103	387	2.05	2.21
	Birmingham	74	233	840	2.29	2.14*
	Bradford	13	104	288	4.16	1.70*
	Bristol	64	137	357	1.52	1.60
	Dublin	165	272	305	1.00	0.19*
	Edinburgh	83	202	401	1.78	1.14*
	Glasgow	77	357	1000	3.07	1.72*
	Leeds	53	72	453	0.61	3.06
	Liverpool	80	376	753	3.10	1.16*
	London	1117	2685	7256	1.75	1.66*
	Manchester	90	303	714	2.43	1.43*
	Sheffield	31	135	465	2.94	2.06*

Note: The * indicates slower growth, 1850–1910.

Source: Mitchell (1992).

period of convergence (1850–1910), while many U.K. cities continued to grow rapidly, fewer U.K. cities grew faster than 2 per cent per year and 9 of the 12 cities grew less rapidly in 1850–1910 than in 1800–1850; these are marked with an asterisk. Indeed, these are 9 of the 10 cities reported in Table 10.2 that showed lower growth in the 1850 to 1910 period (Brussels being the other). Furthermore, the German cities, only average performers in the earlier period, exploded in this period, with all 12 listed having growth rates in excess of 2.5 per cent per year. All of this is very strong evidence, we feel, of the changing dynamics of the ongoing industrialization of Europe.

A more general way we can look at the numbers, repeating the discussion of earlier chapters, is through overall urbanization rates. These data, collected in Table 10.3, are not as comprehensive as those used in other parts of our population surveys, and they reflect different sources, as noted in the table.

All of these countries urbanized rapidly in this period, and it is within reason to again conclude that these figures, producing growth rates in excess of population growth rates, *suggest* the relative growth rates of per capita income. We will not perform these calculations here, but we again note the

Table 10.3   Percentage of the population residing in urban areas in Europe 1850–1910

Country	1850	1860	1870	1880	1890	1900	1910
Austria–Hungary[a]	9.0	10.2	10.9	13.7	16.0	–	–
Belgium[b]	32.6	34.8	36.9	43.1	47.7	–	–
Denmark	20.9	23.4	24.9	28.1	33.2	38.2	40.3
France	25.5	28.9	31.1	34.8	37.4	40.9	44.2
Germany[c]	26.8	29.4	32.5	35.6	39.4	–	60.0
Italy[d]	–	25.2	24.9	27.0	–	–	–
Netherlands[e]	29.0	–	–	–	43.0	–	–
Norway	12.3	19.8	25.7	18.3	23.7	–	–
Spain[e]	–	16.2	–	–	29.6	–	–
Sweden	10.1	11.3	13.0	15.1	18.8	21.5	24.8
U.K.[f]	50.2	54.6	61.8	67.9	72.0	77.0	78.1

Notes:
In cases where no data were available for the years listed at the head of the column we have reported figures for the next closest year.
[a] The urban population for Austria is cities with 10,000 or more inhabitants; for Hungary it includes 'free' and 'small' cities.
[b] The urban population includes cities with 5,000 or more inhabitants.
[c] The 1910 figure comes from Trebilcock (1981, p. 54).
[d] The urban population includes cities with 6,000 or more inhabitants.
[e] The urban population includes cities with 10,000 or more inhabitants.
[f] The figures for the United Kingdom include England and Wales only.

Sources: Austria–Hungary, Germany, Italy, Netherlands, Norway and Spain (Weber, 1899, p. 82, 95, 101, 111, 115, 116, 118, 119); Denmark, France, Sweden and the United Kingdom (Berry and Horton, 1970, p. 75).

strong growth of German urban population after 1890 and the relatively slow growth rates in France and the United Kingdom in the same period. To see the resulting convergence in quantitative terms, consider that the overall coefficient of variation (the standard deviation divided by the mean) fell by more than 10 per cent between 1850 and 1890. This is as far as we can go with the figures containing so many gaps.

While it should be clear that population growth in this period caused both aggregate demand and aggregate supply to grow, the debate that has arisen concerns whether it also caused per capita income to grow. Largely, this is a question of what happens to savings and investment on the demand side and on the nature of the supply-side effects of population growth. That is, population growth surely provides more labor ultimately, but the question is whether there are independent supply-side effects – most notably in the form of increasing skills and technological change, that is to say, productivity growth – that provide the per capita growth. In fact, for the period and place that we are considering, the rate of technological change was quite rapid by historical comparison, so that any possible negative effects of population growth (demand outstripping supply, for example) were negated for all of these countries; that is, we will see in the next section that all of these economies experienced per capita growth in this period. Indeed, we have shown elsewhere (Craig and Fisher, 1997) that there is a positive correlation between per capita growth and population growth across these countries during this period. Although why this might be the case generally has been debated a great deal in the literature, Boserup's (1965) work on the relationship between population growth and economic development suggests that the former leads to the latter through scale economies in social overhead capital (i.e. infrastructure) and technological change. In any case, a detailed investigation of the specific circumstances of each country would be warranted on this point.

One final topic concerns the integration of European labor markets in this period. While not exactly a neglected topic, with the exception of the work summarized by Williamson (1996), one rarely finds this subject incorporated into discussions of the European macroeconomy. The basic firding is that European populations moved across borders more than in any previous period in modern times. These were not forced moves (economic 'forces' aside) but were directed primarily by individual decisions to locate in what were expected to be more favorable labor markets than those abandoned. The decision was sometimes prompted by difficulties in the home country (e.g. agricultural problems in Ireland and Sweden) and sometimes by the special lure of America, but often, especially for the intra-Europe migration, there were specific situations that came and went over time. There is a large literature that has grappled with the causes of this phenomenon, but we will forbear. What is important is the increasing evidence that workers were willing to move to obtain higher wages. These movements tended to assist the economic integration that was evident in product and capital markets.

The population movement that has gained the most attention in the literature is that from Europe to the rest of the world (mainly America). Some recent calculations of these flows appear in Mitchell (1992) as reported in Table 10.4. Here, while the figures fluctuate a great deal from country to country, we find very rapid growth in population movements out of Europe, with Italy and the United Kingdom leading the way in volume. The annual rate of increase of the total in the table in 60 years is 2.6 per cent, which is well above all the national rates of population growth at the time (see Table 10.1).

This section on population contains evidence that a broad set of European countries actually had common growth experiences in this period. All but

Table 10.4   Emigration from Europe 1850–1910 ('000s)

Country	1851–60	1861–70	1871–80	1881–90	1891–00	1900–10
Austria-Hun.	31	40	46	248	440	1,111
Belgium	1	2	2	21	16	30
Denmark	–	8	39	82	51	73
France	27	36	66	119	51	53
Germany	671	779	626	1,342	527	274
Italy	5	27	168	992	1,580	3,615
Netherlands	16	20	17	52	24	28
Norway	36	98	85	187	95	191
Portugal	45	79	131	185	266	324
Spain	3	7	13	572	791	1,091
Sweden	17	122	103	327	205	324
U.K.	1,313	1,572	1,849	3,259	2,149	3,150
Total	2,171	2,805	3,013	7,497	6,230	10,301

Source: Mitchell (1992).

France had historically rapid population growth rates, and for every country but the United Kingdom urbanization accelerated in the second half of the nineteenth century. We do need to point out, before moving on, that some countries urbanized relatively rapidly without seeing much in the way of industrial catching-up (e.g. Spain), while others were transformed into industrial states while maintaining relatively low levels of urbanization (e.g. Sweden). Thus, at a general level it is probably best just to underscore the contributions that historically rapid-growing populations and urbanization made to the basic growth rates (via positive effects on both aggregate demand and aggregate supply) and avoid further generalizations.

3.   THE GROWTH OF REAL PER CAPITA OUTPUT

Although we have argued above and elsewhere (Craig and Fisher, 1997) that the notion of convergence should be considered broadly, ultimately most discussions of the topic, for better or worse, focus on per capita output (see for example, Barro and Sala-i-Martin, 1992). To give the reader an idea of the relative economic performance of these countries during this period of growth and integration, we begin with Table 10.5. It needs to be emphasized, at the outset, that the nations at the lower end of the scale had large, in some areas

Table 10.5   Growth rates of per capita national output in Europe 1850–1913

Country	Base Year	Growth 1870–1913	Growth 1890–1913	Growth Overall	Output* 1870	Output* 1913
Aus.–Hun.	1867	1.40	1.13	1.22	28.1	29.5
Belgium	1850	1.04	0.90	1.04	95.0	95.0
Denmark	1850	1.67	1.93	1.87	51.8	75.2
France	1850	1.43	1.67	1.35	68.4	79.0
Germany	1850	1.59	1.43	1.59	59.4	74.3
Italy	1861	0.79	1.29	0.66	42.4	35.1
Netherl.	1850	0.80	0.77	0.73	64.2	60.0
Norway	1865	1.36	1.56	1.33	57.7	70.2
Portugal	1850	0.72	0.16	0.79	30.7	25.1
Spain	1860	–	0.38	0.97	40.0	26.4
Sweden	1861	2.03	2.54	2.03	41.8	60.1
U.K.	1850	0.84	1.00	1.20	100.0	100.0

Note: * Based on 1913 £ (see Craig and Fisher, 1997), U.K. = 100, in each case. Note that there are slight differences in the growth rates between the two sets of figures, attributable to the different methods of calculation. Note that the Spanish GDP estimates are available only for 1860, 1890 and 1910. All growth rates are compound rates calculated from the end points of the data.

Sources: Austria/Hungary – GNP (Komlos, 1990); Belgium – GDP (Maddison, 1991); Denmark – GDP (Hansen, 1974); France – GDP (Toutain, 1987); Germany – NNP (Mitchell, 1978); Italy – GNP (ISTAT, 1957); Netherlands – NI (van Stuijvenberg and de Vrijer, 1982); Norway – GDP (Mitchell, 1992); Portugal – GDP (Nunes, et al., 1989); Spain – GDP (Molinas and Prados de la Escosura, 1989); Sweden – GDP (Krantz and Nilsson, 1975); U.K. – GDP (Mitchell, 1992).

near-subsistence, agricultural sectors that tend to obscure the relative performances of their industrial sectors. Austria–Hungary, Italy and Spain are the most conspicuous examples of these 'dual economies', and the first two mentioned did, indeed, have strong industrial sectors.

For these European countries, the figures in the last two columns of Table 10.5 show that the United Kingdom was the leader in terms of output per capita throughout the period (they led in 1850, as well). Belgium was not far behind at all times, attesting to its complete absorption into the international industrial community. France, Germany, the Netherlands and Norway were all between 57 per cent and two-thirds of the U.K. total in 1870 and all but the Netherlands closed the gap substantially in the next 43 years, as they approached the U.K. standard. Denmark and Sweden, two much more agriculturally-oriented countries in 1870, virtually exploded in the same period, showing the highest overall growth rates. In addition to the Netherlands, three countries with dominant agricultural sectors actually diverged from the United Kingdom; these were the southern European countries of Italy, Portugal and Spain. Each had some industrialization, as we shall see shortly, but they were dragged down, in the per capita calculations, by their large (and partly subsistence) agricultural sectors. Austria–Hungary, which did keep pace with the United Kingdom, was affected by the same phenomenon.

Turning then to the growth rates of actual real national product in the first part of Table 10.5, we note again that for the period 1870–1913 the growth rates in general conform to the convergence hypothesis. Even though there are several countries below the two leaders – the United Kingdom and Belgium – in terms of their per capita growth rates, most of the industrializing countries were gaining on the leaders and some were doing so quite rapidly. In the 1870–1913 period, Italy, the Netherlands, Portugal and Spain are the only countries that grew more slowly than the United Kingdom, while Belgium maintained its position relative to the United Kingdom. In the boom period of 1890–1913, the impression of convergence is even stronger, with Italy joining the converging countries (and the Netherlands, Spain and Portugal continuing to lag). We attribute an important part of the convergence to the continuing spread of the industrial revolution to the converging countries.

One thing we might expect to see among these countries is some connection between growth rates (of their national product) and investment ratios. This is actually a prediction of the 'demand-side' Harrod–Domar growth model, for example, but it is certainly not a controversial insight. Quite simply, the shifting of resources from the consumer sector to the capital goods sector (relatively), when technological change was presenting entrepreneurs with more efficient methods, certainly implies that countries with higher investment ratios would grow more rapidly than those with low ratios. As Table 10.6 suggests, there is indeed some such relation.[1]

Table 10.6   Growth and investment for seven European countries 1870–1913

Country	Growth Rate	Investment Ratio
Denmark	3.20	10.7
France	1.52	6.6
Germany	2.74	13.2
Italy	1.44	11.0
Norway	2.16	16.3
Sweden	2.73	10.4
U.K.	2.06	7.3

Here four of the five countries with annual growth rates over 2 per cent per year show average investment ratios over 10 per cent of national product, while France, near the bottom of the table in growth, has the lowest average investment ratio. Italy, with slow growth and a relatively large investment ratio, and the United Kingdom, with respectable growth and a low investment ratio, are clearly exceptions. We remind the reader that the expected relationship, which is actually pretty strong in the table, holds *ceteris paribus*; the major omitted influential factor, in the Harrod–Domar model at any rate, is the rate of technological change. For the United Kingdom, this is probably relatively slow, if much of the extensive literature on the 'relative decline' of the United Kingdom economy is correct (see McCloskey, 1971), while for the slowly growing country of Italy, the inefficient sectors (notably agriculture) were clearly undermining the gains in productivity of the industrial sector in this overall calculation.

This overview of the aggregate economic growth of the European states between 1850 and 1913 indicates that by the end of the period all of them except for Portugal and Spain had achieved levels of output and growth rates that were consistent with modern economic growth. Between 1870 and 1913 there were four countries – Italy, the Netherlands, Portugal and Spain – that experienced a real growth rate of less than 1 per cent per year. These economies, except for the Netherlands, were dominated by their agricultural sectors, so that, even though their industrial sectors were growing (and the Italian industrial sector actually was growing quite rapidly), the day was yet to come when they would show up well against the leaders.

In closing this section, we think it is useful to look at a graph of the situation. In Figure 10.1, we present per capita real national product statistics from 1850 to 1913 for the European countries for which such calculations could be made. Note that these figures are normalized in order to facilitate comparisons. The normalization involves dividing each series by its mean; this produces, in effect, differently-based index numbers (they are unity at the (different) points of the mean) and facilitates comparisons of growth rates.

There are a few outliers in the graph, to be sure, but the overwhelming impression one gets is that there is a common path that these countries followed. Note that the United Kingdom, which is identified with a solid line in the graph, is actually near the bottom of the series up to 1865 and near the middle at the end. This also illustrates some degree of convergence of growth rates in this period. While countries are moving upward at different rates – and all are moving upward – it is clear that many are gaining on the United Kingdom; on the other hand, some (again, Spain, Italy, Portugal, and the Netherlands) are not. Even so, what we wanted to show in Figure 10.1 is more subjective: there seems to be a normalized 'path' of growth rates for these countries in this period, clustered around the British rate of growth.

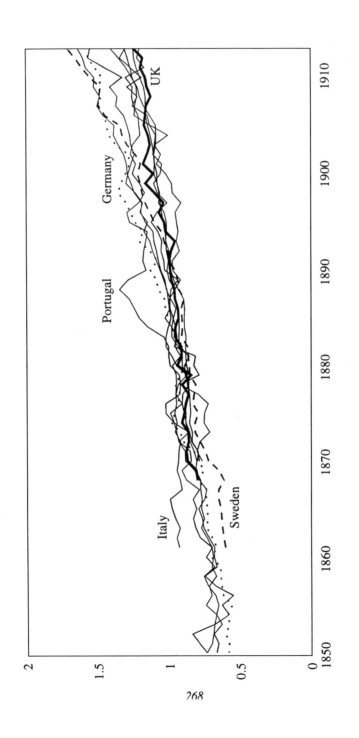

Figure 10.1   Normalized national products 1850–1913

During this period, then, we have found some evidence of convergence of national products, measured on a per capita basis; this, however, is conditioned by many country-specific factors that tend to obscure the basic drive to convergence. We have much more to say about convergence in the remainder of this chapter, and, for that matter, in the remainder of this study. Recall that to this point we also have found that all of these countries had growing populations, and many had significant emigration either to other European countries or out of Europe entirely. Furthermore, all of these countries were urbanizing rapidly, as their commercial industrial and service sectors expanded, and this is another way they were converging on the European leader (the United Kingdom) in this respect. However, we are only part way along in our summary of the economic characteristics of the European countries; the next section considers the details of changes in the agricultural and manufacturing sectors. This will add considerably to the impression of convergence, even for some of the outliers already noticed in the more comprehensive national product statistics.

4.   SECTORAL GROWTH

In 1850, the economic development of Europe followed a roughly geographical line, with England at the head of the list, and the Balkans (and Iberia) at the end. Industrialization, urbanization, the extent of the middle class, the volume of savings, the percentage of resources in the agricultural sector and the development of the banking system more or less followed this pattern, which flowed from northwest to the south and southeast, approximately. What happened over the next 63 years is quite remarkable: many of the other countries in Europe converged on the leader in one or more respects and all, even Spain, were experiencing a profound change in their economic make-up. Let us look at some of the details.

The manufacturing sector offered higher wages and higher rates of return on capital throughout the period; thus, capital and labor were attracted to manufacturing, leading to growth rates in industrial production that were greater in each country than those for the economy as a whole. This sector, thus, led the way toward a converging economic landscape in Europe. Since industrialization is the key to the economic transformation of Europe, broad figures on the entire industrial sector are a good place to begin. In fact, we have production indices for eight of the European nations that we are considering and so we present those numbers in Table 10.7. The figures in the table are annual growth rates of industrial production and we have singled out 1890–1913 in order to isolate some interesting cases in the last 20 years or so of the period.

Table 10.7   Annual growth rates of industrial production 1850–1913

Country	Base Year	Overall (%)	1890–1913 (%)
Austria	1867	2.82	2.72
Denmark	1872	5.22	4.98*
France	1850	2.50	2.48
Germany	1850	3.74	3.98
Hungary	1867	3.12	3.69
Italy	1861	3.43	4.29
Spain	1850	2.50	2.04
Sweden	1861	3.65	3.98
U.K.	1850	2.02	1.99

Note: * (1905–1913).

Sources: Austria, Hungary (Komlos, 1990); Denmark (Kristensen, 1989); Germany, Sweden, U.K. (Mitchell, 1978); France (Toutain, 1987); Italy (Fenoaltea (1988); Spain (Carreras, 1987).

The industrial production figures in Table 10.7 show the process of convergence rather more clearly than the broader figures of Section 3. Here the United Kingdom has the slowest growth in both periods (although it still has the largest manufacturing economy in 1913) so that all the nations in the table (even Spain!) are converging on it. The results for Germany and Sweden are not unexpected, considering that we have already shown rapid per capita growth for those two countries. Interestingly, Denmark had the most rapid growth of industrial output during the period. Of more interest, in some ways, are the spurts in industrial activity in Italy and Hungary, two of the economies that are still dominated by their agricultural sectors in 1913. Spain is also interesting. From 1850 to 1880, the Spanish industrial sector grew at 2.76 per cent, which put it in the same league as Austria and France and ahead of the United Kingdom during that period. But from 1890 to 1913, Spain 'only' managed to keep up with the United Kingdom's growth rate; it was still converging, to be sure, but it was so far behind (in Table 10.5) that the Spanish per capita national product was but 26 per cent of that in the United Kingdom. This appears to be a critical period in Spanish history, although the roots of the industrial problem may well lie somewhere in the 100 years before 1890.

We could argue that countries are solidly in a period of modern economic growth when the long-run trend of average living standards, as measured by per capita output, is not only upward but temporary downturns in the levels are made up relatively quickly. Further, the key factor may well be the shift of capital and labor from agriculture to manufacturing and services. Because this shift of resources is to the more productive sector – that is, the sector with the greatest value of output added per unit of input – real per-capita output grew faster, as a result of the reallocation of resources from agriculture to manufacturing. It was sustained growth simply because the output of manufactured products continued to grow and to outpace that of agricultural products. The period from 1850 to 1913 saw quite a few European countries transforming in this way, with the rest, for the most part, firmly on the same path, even if some distance behind.

A dramatic way to visualize the change wrought in this manner is to look at yet another measure of structure, the ratio of agriculture to manufacturing in the national products of these economies. Each of these countries was experiencing a 'relative decline' of its agricultural sector in this period, although we are not in a position to document this completely. We do have appropriate numbers for seven countries, though; Figure 10.2 presents the results for the 1850 to 1913 period. What is in the table is the ratio of industrial to agricultural output. This graph illustrates the early lead and continuing shift out of agriculture by the United Kingdom. One tends to think of the rapid transformation of other countries in this period, but the changing structure of the U.K. economy is the most impressive thing about Figure 10.2.

Berend and Ranki (1982) discuss the possibility that international trade patterns had something to do with the rate of change of the industrial-agricultural mix. Indeed, trade grew rapidly, and many European countries saw the terms of trade improve for their agricultural and extractive products, a result that could, paradoxically, slow down the rate of industrialization by diverting capital and entrepreneurial energy to the agricultural sector. However, generalizations are hard to achieve here since some countries had strong growth and favorable terms of trade (notably Sweden and Denmark) while others had agricultural sectors (notably involving grain) that actually suffered deteriorating terms of trade. France is an example of the latter. Of course improvements in the transportation infrastructure also helped the relatively bulky agricultural products of all countries that had substantial agricultural sectors.

In fact, during this period, many countries made comparable strides toward industrialization, and some of them did so over short periods of time. These results are lost in the relative scaling of Figure 10.2. To demonstrate this phenomenon, we have constructed a table of these numbers at various points in the period, beginning with 1867, because that is the date at which the sample is complete. The results appear in Table 10.8.

Here we see that in 1913 five of the seven countries had manufacturing sectors that clearly dominated the agricultural sector (in contributing to na-

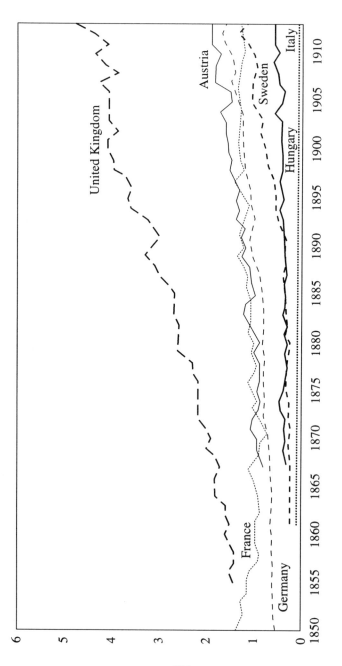

Figure 10.2   Ratio of industrial to agricultural production 1850–1913

Table 10.8   *Ratio of manufacturing to agriculture in national output 1870–1913*

Country	1867	1890	1913	Percentage Change	
				1867–1890	1890–1913
Austria	0.788	1.200	1.930	52.28	60.83*
France	1.123	1.218	1.298	8.46	6.57
Germany	0.651	1.055	1.628	62.06	54.31
Hungary	0.316	0.369	0.612	16.77	65.85*
Italy	0.060	0.062	0.098	3.33	58.06*
Sweden	0.215	0.354	1.200	64.65	228.98*
U.K.	1.700	3.200	4.800	88.23	50.00

Note: * indicates larger percentage change 1890–1913.

Sources: Austria and Hungary (Komlos, 1990), France (Toutain, 1987), Germany (Hoffmann, 1965), Italy (ISTAT, 1957), Sweden (Krantz and Nilsson, 1975) and U.K. (Feinstein, 1972).

tional product); in 1870 only the United Kingdom and France (and probably Belgium) was in such a position. This period is obviously one of profound change in the structure of many European countries. Lost in Figure 10.2, then, is the fact that Italy was moving rapidly toward industrialization (up 58.06 per cent in the last 23 years of the period). Of course, the Italian ratio is still very low compared to the other countries (in 1913). Sweden's performance is also remarkable in the same period, for its astronomical percentage change (1890–1913). Further, we should note yet again that all but France converged on the United Kingdom in the 1890 to 1913 period, in the sense that the percentage changes in the ratio in all but France were larger than for the United Kingdom. In effect, then, two more countries had joined the 'league of industrial nations' by 1913, and the laggards were moving relatively rapidly toward that status.

As important as the shift out of agriculture was, changes in the composition of industrial output were clearly of special importance in this period. During the early days of the industrial revolution, the technological innovations in textile production made the greatest contribution to overall industrial progress. The mechanization of the spinning, weaving and fulling of cotton and wool made textiles the first modern industry, and nowhere did textile production grow as fast (or as early) as in the United Kingdom. Almost simultaneously there sprang up a machine-tool industry to construct the instruments of the newly-mechanized industry. These machines were made at least partly of iron and later driven by steam; thus, textile production contributed to the growth of the iron, coal and the machine-tool industry. Similarly, the expansion of the coal industry led to the search for better steam engines, which in turn led to the demand for better metallurgy, and so forth. Later railroads were built to haul both the inputs and outputs of this process; this in turn further increased the demand for iron and coal. In this way Britain became the first industrial nation.

In order to show what happened to the industrial structures of these nations in the 1850–1913 period, we have chosen seven major industries to illustrate our points. The data for these appear in Table 10.9. Growth rates for these industries, where we have data, exceeded national growth rates, sometimes considerably so. For cotton use (in the textiles industry), all countries grew faster than the British in the 1850 to 1913 period. This was also true of pig iron, except for Norway which had a small industry. For coal production, those countries that produced it again outperformed the British, except for the other leading nation in 1850, Belgium. Railroad track construction tells the same story. Thus it is pretty clear that there was strong convergence on the leaders (Belgium and the United Kingdom) in the traditional smokestack industries in this period.

For the newer industries, rather remarkably, the U.K. economy is again at the bottom of the table in terms of growth (except for electric power in Spain). This is an aspect of the British 'relative decline' that has often been remarked upon (and chemicals, as suggested by the decline of the sulfuric acid industry, has sometimes been selected as the clearest relative failure of all). In any case, the converging countries found the new industries growing very rapidly in this period; even for these industries there is convergence toward the United Kingdom, which at one time had the second largest per capita production both of steel (in 1870) and the largest of sulfuric acid (in 1880) in Europe. This table, while not very detailed in a time-series sense, establishes a clear picture of the convergence we are trying to establish.

To see the effect of a shifting composition on overall output, consider the case of France, a relatively early industrializer and a country universally considered to be at the 'core' of the European economy. Tables 10.1 and 10.5 put France's average annual rate of overall economic growth in the neighborhood of 1.75 per cent after 1850 and adjusting this number upwards by as much as 50 per cent would not substantially alter the point we are about to make (and lowering it by a like amount would only strengthen our case.) Yet Crouzet (1970, p. 217) shows that in the leading industries of the day (including mining, metallurgy, metal fabrication, and chemicals) average annual growth exceeded 3.4 per cent *after 1815*! No wonder they are typically called 'leading' industries.

In order to focus even more on the issue of convergence, we have calculated the per capita growth rates of the same industries for the 1890 to 1913

Table 10.9 Industrial activity in Europe – per 1,000 capita 1850–1913

	Cotton Consumption (tons)			Pig Iron Production (tons)			Coal Production (tons)			Railroad Track (km)			Steel Production (tons)			Sulfuric Acid Production (tons)			Electric Power (gwh)		
	1850	1913	%	1850	1913	%	1850	1913	%	1870	1913	%	1880	1913	%	1900	1913	%	1900	1913	%
Aus./Hun.	1.08	4.49	2.44	6.55	48.14	3.44	53.15	1095.18	5.26	45.20	485.29	4.11	1.10	54.22	9.98	0.65	7.37	7.18			
Belgium	2.17	18.01	3.40	32.85	302.24	3.64	1318.76	3252.79	1.47	193.48	621.15	1.90	14.68	306.88	8.81	5.55	55.26	6.79			
France	1.76	6.71	2.22	12.80	122.75	3.78	128.71	1018.07	3.45	91.39	1026.69	4.05	2.67	108.78	9.47	5.38	22.63	4.19	0.97	3.79	14.56
Germany	1.67	7.16	2.78	6.64	232.64	6.00	220.83	3865.39	4.80	174.14	947.65	2.82	3.72	243.00	10.73	2.08	25.78	7.46	2.16	10.77	15.71
Italy	0.24	5.02	6.96	1.06	10.57	4.71	1.50	18.32	5.14	127.30	532.80	2.90	0.08	24.65	20.21	1.91	18.32	11.97	0.38	5.05	26.27
Netherl.	0.32	5.44	4.77				9.24	276.29	5.73	56.52	531.41	3.74									
Norway				3.46	2.89	−0.40	10.85			45.95	1273.13	6.00									
Spain	1.33	4.50	2.29	4.18	20.55	3.17	22.97	204.32	4.38	53.93	746.29	4.99	1.91	14.88	8.21		1.02		0.73	2.29	10.93
Sweden	0.83	3.82	3.11	47.09	123.16	1.94	7.78	61.85	4.23	210.36	2537.44	5.11	2.94	94.13	8.82	2.11	14.94	7.82	1.94	20.57	23.95
U.K.	10.94	20.66	1.05	91.42	212.61	1.39	1.822	6.397	1.97	370.80	712.17	1.08	13.92	155.86	6.23	25.99	23.70	−0.28	1.20	5.13	14.10

Notes: Starting points when not as indicated by column head: Austria–Hungary (1852); Belgium: steel (1875); Germany: cotton (1858); Italy: cotton (1861), steel (1880); Netherlands: coal (1870); Norway: pig iron (1866), coal (1907); Spain: pig iron and coal (1860), steel (1885); Sweden: sulfuric acid (1887).

Sources: Industrial data (Mitchell, 1978); population (see Table 10.1).

period. During this time, many nations substantially accelerated in their industrial development and so this calculation goes part way toward capturing the end-of-period dynamics of the era.

While incompleteness of the data is somewhat of a problem in Table 10.10, it is very clear that the United Kingdom experienced the slowest per capita growth rates in all categories of industrial production, including the new industries (except in comparison with Spanish electrical power generation). In the cotton industry, Belgium, the Netherlands and France were growing the most rapidly, while in iron and steel it is France, Germany and Italy that dominate. For the last of the traditional sectors – railroads – the only signs of rapid growth are in the Scandinavian countries; these countries had incomplete systems in 1890. For the new industries in the last three columns, as noted, the United Kingdom does less well, especially in sulfuric acid and steel. Sulfuric acid, in a way, is a bellwether sector for the United Kingdom, since in 1890 total production in the United Kingdom was greater than in all other European countries combined. In 1913, on the other hand, Germany was well ahead of the United Kingdom and France was closing rapidly.

Table 10.10   Major industries in Europe per capita growth rates 1890–1913

Country	Cotton	Iron	Coal	Rail	Steel	Sulfuric Acid	Electric Power
Aus./Hun.	2.14	3.05	2.07				
Austria		3.35	1.70			7.64	
Belgium	4.05	2.63	−1.58	−2.22		7.36	
Denmark				1.72			
France	3.20	4.09	1.80		8.22	3.44	13.39
Germany	1.90	4.78	3.59	0.36	7.84	4.81	13.50
Hungary		2.31	4.12				
Italy	2.31	14.22	2.05	0.76	8.72		21.95
Netherl.	3.43			−0.31			
Norway		26.51		2.08			
Spain	1.36			1.23			6.92
Sweden	1.58	1.34		1.83	4.76	6.25	21.96
U.K.	0.31	0.28	0.61	−0.17	2.56	0.09	12.18

Note: Electricity is for 1900 to 1913. Italian sulfuric acid begins in 1893.

Thus, while these tables show the convergence of many countries toward the per capita levels of the leaders, they also suggest that there are economy-specific factors that need to be considered. For one thing, while the major industrializing economies each had a full range of smoke-stack industries, there were many cases when this was driven by coal imports rather than domestic coal production; this clearly affected the industrial mix. For another, many of these countries were still dominated by their agricultural sectors in 1913, even though the transformation to industrialization was well on its way. This would have produced differences in tariff policy, for example, and, for that matter, in the business cycle experiences of these countries. Finally, we should note that the relative situation of the United Kingdom may have involved more than just a market-driven convergence. In particular, it has been argued that a sort of a malaise overcame British entrepreneurs and this sickness stifled growth in the United Kingdom so that 'convergence' toward the United Kingdom, as we are defining the concept, could be exaggerated. The relative performance of the sulfuric acid industry that we have noted several times is one such example of what is sometimes called the 'British disease' in the literature.

We hesitate to enter this debate here, but the point we have been trying to make since Chapter 1 is that economic agents seek the highest return on the capital (human, physical, and financial), given their endowments and risk preferences and the constraints and relative prices they face. Thus, the British followed a path that was profitable for them. To adopt the latest technologies was not a cost-free decision, given that the British had substantial investments in already profitable enterprises. In general our sympathies lie with the view expressed by Harley (1980, p. 42) who notes that 'To suggest that the British economy would have been better off if it could have adjusted without cost is hardly a useful analytic contribution'.

5.   THE FOREIGN SECTOR: THE GROWTH OF EXPORTS

We begin by presenting the basic data for real exports for this period. We are interested in the volume of exports, since this would provide evidence of the basic linkages of the commodity sectors across nations. Recall that we have repeatedly explained how commodity flows provide the main international links driving nations together after 1500. We have argued that the industrial revolution, as it spread across Europe, drew these countries together in the sense just described. If so, it is the behavior of exports (and imports for that matter) that would show this, since it is by trade (and capital and labor flows, of course) that the process would spread.

There are a few real series for exports available, but most collections of national accounts do not produce such real numbers, leaving us little choice but to attempt crude measures of real exports for these countries. The obvious thing to do is to take wholesale prices, and use these as deflators for nominal exports. The idea is that wholesale prices at this time are generally for commodities that are traded internationally. Table 10.11 reports the results of calculating the growth rates in real exports and comparing these figures with growth rates of real national product. In this exercise, we used only the nominal exports (and deflated them, as noted), even when actual real data were available, to maintain comparability across countries.[2]

Table 10.11   Growth rates of real exports and real national product 1850–1913

Country	Real Output			Real Exports		
	1850–70	1870–90	1890–1913	1850–70	1870–90	1890–1913
Aus/Hun.	–	2.38	2.01	–0.44	4.58	1.49
Belgium	2.35	2.09	1.90	4.18	4.11	3.48
Denmark	1.59	2.35	3.07	–	2.51	4.93
France	1.55	1.17	1.82	3.92	2.88	2.87
Germany	2.30	2.71	2.77	–	1.38	4.19
Italy	0.70	0.86	1.95	6.16	0.91	3.88
Netherlands	1.43	1.99	2.11	4.47	6.18	4.11
Norway	1.57	1.84	2.44	7.25	2.43	3.45
Portugal	1.58	2.14	0.86	5.25	–0.28	1.32
Spain	–	–	–	4.13	5.18	–0.36
Sweden	2.77	2.14	3.25	6.43	4.04	1.65
U.K.	2.61	1.56	1.86	4.09	2.71	2.48

Notes: For Real Output, Belgium begins in 1860, Italy in 1861, Norway in 1865 and Sweden in 1861. For Real Exports, Austria–Hungary begins in 1867, Germany in 1880, Italy in 1861, Norway in 1865, Portugal in 1865 and the United Kingdom in 1851.

As noted, for purposes of comparison, Table 10.11 also shows real output patterns among these countries. Of the ten possible comparisons, only three countries, the United Kingdom, Belgium and Portugal, showed a lower rate of output growth in the last period (1890–1913) than in the first one (1850–1970); two of these (the United Kingdom and Belgium) were the leaders in Europe in 1850. In the first period, only Sweden had a more rapid growth than these two leading countries; in the last period, the two leading countries had lower growth rates than all but Portugal and France. One also notices that a number of countries accelerated from the first to the second to the third period; these were Denmark, Germany, Italy, the Netherlands and Norway. This is another dimension of the convergence toward the leaders that is so obvious here and in earlier tables.

The real export figures show several additional aspects of the convergence to which we have referred so often. For one thing, exports generally grow faster than real output, establishing in a very obvious way how increasing interactions among these nations contributed to their economic convergence. Of the 30 possible cases where we could make such calculations, 26 show export growth exceeding national output growth. Furthermore, figures reported by Berend and Ranki (1980, p. 546) for the period 1860 to 1910 show that the so-called 'peripheral' countries saw their exports grow faster than the European average.

There is an important qualification however, and that is that of the nine possible cases where such a comparison can be made, all nine show lower rates of growth of exports in the 1890–1913 period than in the 1850–1870 period. This is the result of several major factors. First, the earlier period reflects the very rapid development of railway systems throughout Europe, but particularly where coal and iron (and finished railroad products) were being transported. Second, the decline of the agricultural exports of many of these nations and the growth of exports by others, including those not in the tables – for example, Russia, the United States and Argentina – is surely a major factor in this result. Third, we note that as nations grow alike, there are fewer absolute advantages to exploit in trade. Trade, at any time will be based on both absolute and comparative advantage. A nation without a domestic iron industry – but with industries that rely on iron, such as the railroad – will be forced to import iron; this would be the exploitation of an absolute disadvantage. As the nation develops its own iron industry, this source of exports (from the perspective of the iron-exporting country) will dry up. The result is that trade, in this period, becomes more and more a matter of comparative advantage, as these nations became more alike. This, possibly, was not as powerful a factor as the absolute advantages of the earlier period. Finally, we note that the middle third of the century represented a period of free trade. The resulting gains from trade were myriad (see for example Berend and Ranki (1982) and Nye (1991) for discussions of this effect). However, tariffs were often raised in the 1890–1913 period, and in some cases, such as the famous alliance of iron and rye in Germany, even earlier, although not in all countries. This, too, is surely a factor in the relative decline of exports.

We conclude, then, by emphasizing again how decisive the results of this section are. The trade figures identify the leaders in 1850 and they show how the relative position of these leaders slipped over time. The trade figures also suggest how important trade itself was to this convergence, if only because trade outpaced the growth of all of these countries. This is not really surprising, and we have suggested earlier at various places that trade played the same role throughout the 1500–1913 period. Here, though, there is much more complete evidence available.

6. CONCLUSIONS

It is our contention that the integration of the European economy that was in place during this period explains the timing and the course of the catching-up that occurred among the later industrializing countries. The technological structure of the leading industries of the late nineteenth century differed from the earlier (1750–1850) leading industries in one of two ways and sometimes both. The scale of production was larger and/or their production involved relatively complex technical characteristics absent from the early leading industries. Together these two characteristics of late-nineteenth-century industrialism rewarded the capacity to attract or supply financial and human capital on an unprecedented scale, the former to finance the scale of production and the latter to organize it.

Here then were the returns to an integrated international economy. Surely the United Kingdom had a great deal of financial and human capital, both absolutely and relative to latecomers like Austria–Hungary or even to a continental economic power like Germany, but the United Kingdom also had a great deal of capital sunk in older technologies. At the margin British capitalists would not have found it profitable to scrap entire industries to create new ones. Once an innovation occurred, however, the entrepreneurs, financiers and politicians in countries like Germany – which had lagged behind in the development of the earlier industries – learned how economic agents in other countries had prospered from earlier innovations and were now themselves in a position to capitalize on the new opportunities. Most important, it was the integration of the European economic order that made these opportunities possible. Without the transfer of technology and access to capital the latecomers would have been non-comers at this time.

There is another intriguing question that we might as well address at this point. What can we say, after going through the exercise here, about the state of European integration in 1913? That is, is Europe an early version of the global economy that we see at the end of the twentieth century, or are countries too different to make such a generalization valid? We are going to say more about important aspects of this question in the rest of this study, but here we should note that surely the notion of a global economy, with technology-transfer, financial interaction and commodity market interaction, applies to the northern European countries in 1913, without exception. Outside the realm, but moving quickly in, is Italy, while Spain and Portugal are only inching along. This is close enough, we feel, to make such a claim interesting, since Spain and Portugal still (at the end of the twentieth century) represent challenges to the European Community.

There are other countries in the network in 1913, of course. The United States, Canada, Australia and Japan leap to mind. What happened over the next eighty years, after the disintegration of the two world wars, the Depression and the Cold War were disposed of, is that one by one, countries were attached to the global economy that was in place in 1913. It is as if an economic centrifugal force was established that gradually sucked in nations as they acquired the physical, human and financial infrastructure to participate in the global economy. At the end of the twentieth century, we are witness to the possible absorption of the vast non-market economies (of Russia, China and their allies). This too, fits the pattern.

NOTES

1. Note that these growth rates are domestic rates that have not been converted to a common currency, such as the pound; therefore the rates differ from those in Table 10.5.
2. We also looked at nominal exports (and imports) and achieved broadly similar conclusions with those, probably because of the low rates of inflation these countries generally experienced in this period.

11. Financial factors in European growth and integration 1850–1913

1. INTRODUCTION

During the period 1850 to 1913, the banking systems of Europe grew very rapidly by almost any standard. The typical pattern was for the money stock to grow considerably faster than nominal national product, as we illustrate below, for all countries but the United Kingdom. Because price levels did not change much, this means that velocity – that is, the average number of times a unit of domestic currency changed hands – fell substantially over the period 1850–1913. With growth rates of money much in excess of the rates of inflation, this would surely suggest that the rapidly expanding banking systems of Europe were providing new financial services at unprecedented rates as industrialization progressed.

We begin our work in this chapter in Section 2, by describing the data for the money stocks, inflation rates and the velocity of money for each country. The objective here is to see just how alike, in a macroeconomic sense, these countries became during this period. In Section 3 we discuss the interactions among the financial variables of the 13 European countries that we are examining in this study. We expect a lot of interaction, of course, since from the 1870s many of these countries were on the gold standard; indeed, even before that date gold often served as the primary international reserve even when countries were not firmly committed to the standard. An immediate implication is that there would be considerable monetary cohesion among nations adhering to the gold standard. The fact is, while the inflation rates of these countries appear synchronous, as the 'law of one price (level)' in a gold standard world implies, there is a surprising lack of correlation of money-growth rates across countries. This is documented in Section 3. This leaves us with a puzzle which, we believe, is resolved with reference to an explanation based on what is known as the 'monetary approach to the balance of payments'. In this theory, also as explained in Section 3, goods flows and changes in the demand for money take the place of the automatic adjustment of gold stocks across nations maintaining the gold standard. While no direct tests have ever been conducted with respect to this possibility, it seems clear that this is one way to resolve the disparate behavior of money growth rates and inflation rates that we have observed.

In Section 4 we discuss the institutional development of European banking systems. This material spells out the details of the expansion of financial services, going country-by-country. Although we distinguish considerable differences in the initial institutional structure and path of financial growth among these countries, by the end of the period we identify what appears to have been a surprising degree of similarity in the banking systems of the countries in question. In short, we find that by 1914 every European country had a 'mixed' banking sector with institutions that accepted deposits that could be drawn upon, discounted notes and provided long-term credit (or underwriting) for industrial and commercial activities. That is, each country had growing supplies of what are typically called savings, merchant, commercial and investment banking services.

In Section 4, we also consider central banking. By 1850, most countries had central banks in some form, and in most countries adherence to the international gold standard was the major objective of the monetary authorities. Gradually, other central banking functions – such as the lender of last resort and firm control over the money supply – spread across these countries and by 1914, every one in our set of countries was in a position to operate an independent monetary policy. That is exactly what they did in 1914, as the gold standard was abandoned in the face of the unusually large demands for public finance at the start of the First World War.

2.   MONEY, PRICES, AND NATIONAL INCOME

In this section we review the data on money growth rates and inflation for these countries. Table 11.1 summarizes the data for two sub-periods between 1850 and 1913; note that there are real growth rate figures included here for purposes of comparison. We should warn the reader that these data are from a variety of sources, are not all dated the same and often refer to different aggregate measures, across countries. Note, also, that as far as possible, the data periods have been set to match the dates of the money-stock series, since it is the behavior of the money stock that is our prime interest in this discussion.

Several things stand out in this tabulation. Most obviously, the money growth rates are considerably faster than the inflation rates; indeed, the latter are close to zero for these countries, whatever period one chooses. The money growth rates are also faster than the real-income growth rates and, for that matter, faster than growth rates for nominal income (which can be inferred from the table). Furthermore, the inflation rates and the money growth rates appear to grow more slowly in the 1870 to 1913 period than in the overall period, especially in the cases where there is a long run of data to

Table 11.1   Growth rates of money, prices and real income, various dates to 1913

		Date to 1913			1870 to 1913		
Country	Date (M)	Money	Prices	Real Income	Money	Prices	Real Income
Aus./Hun.	1867	5.69	–0.05	1.97	5.09	0.22	2.18
Denmark	1870	5.39	0.11	2.62	5.39	–0.24	2.74
France	1850	2.47	0.61	1.52	2.39	0.23	1.52
Germany	1850	5.01	1.45	2.60	5.18	0.83	2.74
Italy	1861	4.44	0.38	1.58	3.68	0.40	1.44
Norway	1865	5.49	0.63	2.10	4.93	0.63	2.16
Spain	1874	1.98	0.64	–	1.98	0.70	–
Sweden	1861	5.89	0.63	2.74	6.17	0.47	2.73
U.K.	1871	1.72	0.00	1.72	1.71	–0.00	1.72

Note: The dates for all series are established for the beginning of the money stock series, except that those for Norway start in 1865 and for Sweden in 1861 because those are the dates when the real product series begin.

Sources: *Output*: Table 10.2. *Prices*: (consumer prices for all but Spain (wholesale prices): Germany, Sweden, Spain and U.K. (Mitchell, 1992); Austria/Hungary (Komlos, 1990); Denmark (Hansen, 1982 and Maddison, 1982, spliced); France (Levy-Leboyer/Bourguignon, 1987); Italy (Fratianni and Spinelli, 1984); Norway (Bordo and Jonung, 1987). *Money*: Austria-Hungary (Komlos, 1990); Denmark (Bordo and Jonung, 1987); France (St. Marc, 1983); Germany (Sprenger, 1982); Italy (Fratianni and Spinelli, 1984); Norway (Klovland, 1987); Spain (Acena, 1990); Sweden (Jonung, 1975); U.K. (Capie and Webber, 1985).

look at. Since the later period is, roughly, that of the gold standard, this suggests one obvious way the gold standard might have affected these economies: it lowered money growth and inflation. More obvious, however, is the fact that inflation rates are absolutely very low (by any standard); this also has to be counted as a possible effect of the gold standard, at least at first glance.

Looking at the standard deviations of the data provides yet another way to illustrate the possible influence of the gold standard. In Table 11.2 we illustrate the standard deviations of the first differences (of the logarithms) of the data on money stocks and consumer prices. This set of results presents overwhelming evidence in favor of something widely thought to be true about the operation of the gold standard, namely that countries were required to keep their inflation rates low and relatively constant, in order to maintain their parity with gold (or with the British pound). The lower standard devia-

Table 11.2   Standard deviations of money growth and inflation 1850–1913

	Overall	1870–1913	Data Period
Money Growth			
Austria–Hungary	0.049	0.025*	1867–1913
Denmark	0.054	0.048*	1870–1913
France	0.038	0.034*	1850–1913
Germany	0.038	0.031*	1850–1913
Italy	0.054	0.029*	1861–1913
Norway	0.039	0.030*	1850–1913
Spain	0.058	0.058	1874–1913
Sweden	0.086	0.055*	1850–1913
U.K.	0.017*	0.022	1871–1913
Consumer Price Inflation			
Austria	0.030	0.030	1867–1913
Belgium	0.052	0.049*	1850–1913
Denmark	0.035	0.028*	1850–1913
France	0.049	0.036*	1850–1913
Germany	0.066	0.039*	1850–1913
Italy	0.037	0.040	1861–1913
Netherlands	0.053	0.053	1871–1913
Norway	0.038	0.038	1870–1913
Portugal	0.087	0.075*	1850–1913
Spain	0.065	0.045*	1850–1913
Sweden	0.042	0.035*	1850–1913
Switzerland	0.053	0.047*	1850–1913
U.K.	0.032	0.027*	1850–1913

Notes: Lowest value comparing the two periods is denoted by *. The Spanish and Swiss inflation rates are computed from the wholesale price level.

Sources: See Table 11.1. Additional prices used here are as follows: Belgium (Mitchell, 1992); Netherlands (van Stuijvenberg and de Vrijer, 1982); Portugal (Nunes et al., 1989); Switzerland (Mitchell, 1992).

tions, comparing the overall period with 1870–1913 are marked with asterisks in the table.

In Table 11.1, employing the equation of exchange ($MV = Py$) in its dynamic form, the rate of change of the income velocity of money would be the residual. Clearly, to reconcile the figures, velocity must be falling – and falling pretty substantially – for all countries except the United Kingdom. Is this an exception to the quantity theory of money? We think not, since, as explained by Friedman (1956), while the quantity theory of money is certainly obtainable in a world with constant real income and constant velocity, that is not the essence of the theory, which actually holds *ceteris paribus*. Indeed, according to Friedman, what is important to establish, to underscore the relevance of the theory, is the stability of the demand for money (or of a 'velocity function') for each country.[1] In fact, the finding of a declining velocity is perfectly acceptable to the quantity theory of money.

In modern times, velocity often rises, and we think this is due, among other things, to the invention of new forms of money, new ways to purchase goods and services (such as with credit cards) and the relaxation of restrictions on interest rates on the components of the money stock. In the period we are examining, however, we generally see velocity declining, not rising, and, we suspect, the effect of the invention of monetary substitutes is not very important in this period. In fact, one thing is very clear, and this is that the use of money was extended dramatically through the significant extension of both specific financial instruments and the geographical territory receiving up-to-date banking services in all cases except for the United Kingdom, which was already quite sophisticated in its development of financial services as the period began. Table 11.3 lists the velocity figures, at arbitrary five-year intervals.

In Figure 11.1, we plot the velocities for the seven countries listed in Table 11.3. Here we see a useful characteristic of the velocity numbers: since velocity is essentially unit-free, direct comparisons can be made across countries. Of course both monetary and nominal income figures are not produced by similar procedures in each case, so one should not expect this compilation to provide more than a general picture of this phenomenon.

What we see in either Table 11.3 or Figure 11.1, is the convergence of all countries toward the level of velocity that remains roughly constant for the United Kingdom for the entire period. Indeed, the decline of velocity toward the U.K. level is part of the catching-up of each these countries to the most advanced country in terms of its banking structure. By 1913 most had caught up or gone ahead of the United Kingdom in terms of the index; so this is yet another way that the economies of these countries converged in this period, becoming much more similar to each other in terms of the shape of their financial systems, at least as judged in this aggregate fashion.

In their study of the behavior of velocity, Bordo and Jonung (1987) argue that the period of declining velocity after 1914 is the result of the monetization process, whereas the period of rising velocity is the result of increasing financial sophistication. 'Financial sophistication', as Bordo and Jonung use the term, is defined as *both* the emergence of a large number of substitutes for money and the development of various methods of economizing on money

Table 11.3   The velocity of money in Europe 1851–1913

Date	Denmark	France	Germany	Italy	Norway	Sweden	United Kingdom
1851	–	2.48	3.39	–	–	–	–
1856	–	3.28	3.92	–	–	–	–
1861	–	2.83	3.02	5.21	–	9.41	–
1866	–	2.88	2.77	3.69	3.80	9.77	–
1871	3.33	2.28	2.90	3.06	3.46	6.07	1.97
1876	2.36	2.02	2.62	2.57	3.52	4.45	1.82
1881	1.83	1.93	2.24	2.28	2.85	3.89	1.98
1886	1.49	1.83	2.01	2.11	2.24	3.03	1.84
1891	1.46	2.13	1.96	2.16	2.28	3.11	1.88
1896	1.19	1.92	1.78	1.91	2.06	2.96	1.78
1901	1.33	1.78	1.54	1.89	1.74	2.15	1.91
1906	1.15	1.71	1.34	1.62	1.54	2.05	1.99
1913	1.19	1.83	1.20	1.59	1.50	1.97	2.01

Note: Annual Growth Rates, 1871–1913:

	−2.45	−0.52	−2.10	−1.56	−1.99	−2.68	0.05.

Sources: See Tables 10.2, 11.1 and 11.2.

balances. In fact, monetization itself is a form of growing financial sophistication and, in any case, we are studying only the period of declining velocity. Even so, there are other forms of money in this period. For example, the use of commercial bills was certainly increasing in this period, although in the absence of really good figures on their volume it is not possible to offer more than the conjecture that their use does not seriously alter the trends in monetary usage we have identified.[2]

From the figures provided, France actually shows only a modest decline in velocity over the period, with the bulk of the effect completed by 1886. Thus, the subsequent convergence of the French toward the U.K. standard is not as remarkable as it is for most of the other countries, attesting to the relatively advanced financial development of the French system throughout the period. The Germans show less financial development in 1850 than do the French, since their velocity is higher, but they catch up rapidly. Indeed, by 1890 the Germans have surged ahead and finish (along with Denmark) with the lowest velocity among the country in the sample. This finding of greater financial development in Germany is somewhat surprising, but, as we shall discuss in Section 4, it can be explained partly in terms of the large compensating balances that the German banks required of their large corporate customers,

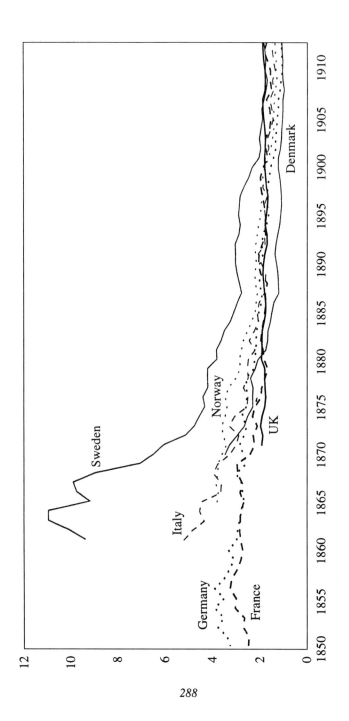

Figure 11.1   The velocity of money in Europe 1850–1913

allowing the banks to expand their liabilities accordingly. A further factor was the lending policies of the Reichsbank, practices which were quite liberal by the standards of the day. We shall also comment in that section on the Danish (and Norwegian) financial sectors.

Across these nations, then, while neither measures of money nor measures of national income are strictly comparable, velocity calculations suggest another way countries grew together in this period. Indeed, as Figure 11.1 shows rather dramatically, all countries converged on the United Kingdom in the first part of this period, with all but the relatively developed French more than doubling their use of banking and monetary services as a percentage of income, and with all countries ultimately moving ahead of the United Kingdom. The main point, though, is that financial services relative to income grew substantially in all countries but the leader, and at rates suggested by how far behind the leader they were in 1850. We feel, on balance, that an important aspect of the pan-European economy – comparably sophisticated banking systems – was in place by the beginning of the twentieth century.

3.   CROSS-COUNTRY CORRELATIONS: AN EXPLANATION

The next task is to extend the search for financial integration to the data on inflation rates and money growth rates of the individual countries. We will take the approach of employing correlation analysis on these variables. The most important variable at which one could look, to see the effect of the system, is the inflation rate. A general prediction, for a set of countries on the gold standard, is that inflation rates will be correlated across countries, with the system providing discipline both for those with overly rapid inflation and for those with price levels that grow more slowly than their competitors. This expectation is realized since the inflation rates are closely correlated, as demonstrated in Table 11.4, particularly in comparison with the rates of growth of the money stock.

The most surprising thing in Table 11.4 is the result for very low correlations for money growth rates. This is quite decisive and somewhat unexpected in view of the closer correlations among the inflation rates. To make this clear, we have marked with an asterisk those cases in which the inflation correlation is higher than the money growth rate one; note that this is only possible for the nine countries for which we have both money and price data. This comparison shows 24 cases when inflation was more closely correlated than money and only 2 when it was not.

Even though the inflation and money growth series do not all refer to the same countries, it is possible to look at all of them together in order to see if

Table 11.4 Correlations among inflation rates and money growth rates 1850–1913

Money Growth

	Denmark	France	Germany	Italy	Norway	Spain	Sweden	U.K.
AH	0.113	0.184	0.052	0.021	0.059	-0.109	0.146	-0.254
De	–	-0.185	0.407	0.090	0.315	-0.068	0.479	0.238
Fr		–	-0.059	0.260	-0.047	-0.046	0.226	-0.189
Ge			–	0.215	0.237	0.020	0.359	0.376
It				–	0.104	-0.028	0.111	0.113
No					–	0.357	0.461	0.412
Sp						–	0.266	0.204
Sw							–	0.420

	Bel	Den	Fra	Ger	Ita	Neth	Nor	Por	Sp.	Swe	Swi	U.K.

Consumer Price Growth

	Bel	Den	Fra	Ger	Ita	Neth	Nor	Por	Sp.	Swe	Swi	U.K.
Au	0.285	0.149*	0.351*	0.319*	0.254*	0.249	0.417*	0.090	0.384*	0.250*	0.431	0.443*
Be	–	0.539	0.462	0.507	0.313	0.202	0.400	0.436	0.245	0.506	0.376	0.386
De		–	0.472*	0.531*	0.131*	0.266	0.600	0.378	0.214*	0.696*	0.062	0.583*
Fr			–	0.630*	0.406	0.176	0.227	0.352	0.285*	0.481*	0.134	0.488*
Ge				–	0.338	0.344	0.536	0.350	0.272*	0.523	0.108	0.361
It					–	0.275	0.495*	0.196	0.392*	0.387*	0.496	0.306
Ne						–	0.408	0.005	0.340	0.436	0.142	0.292
No							–	0.197	0.319	0.837*	0.432	0.651
Po								–	0.200	0.378	0.462	0.445*
Sp									–	0.387	0.150	0.360
Sw										–	0.349	0.515
Su											–	0.570

Sources: See Table 11.1.

the differences narrow over time, as the operation of the classical (post-1870) gold standard suggests might be the case. These plots appear in Figures 11.2 and 11.3, with money growth rates in 11.2 and consumer price inflation rates summarized in 11.3. While the data are somewhat sparser in the early parts of these graphs, it seems clear that for both collections there are wider fluctuations before 1870 than after. Furthermore, as one might have expected from the data discussed to this point, the coincidence of the series is greater for inflation rates than it is for money growth rates. Both series show slight upward trends from 1870 to 1913, and the money growth rates are more rapid in all periods. Note that the outliers identified in the money growth rates do not involve the largest economies (of France, Germany and the United Kingdom). Also note that we have not identified individual countries in the inflation series primarily because of the remarkable uniformity of these numbers.

The first thought one might have is that the quantity theory of money was suspended in this period, since not only are the growth rates of money and prices dissimilar, but the money growth rates are not highly correlated across countries (while inflation rates are).[3] These results, particularly those for 1870 to 1913, come from a period when the gold standard was in operation. Under the specie-flow mechanism, what is supposed to happen in such a world is that gold moves from high-inflation to low-inflation countries as a result of equilibrating the balance of payments. These gold flows enter the monetary base, expanding the money supply and bringing higher price levels in the low-inflation country. Actually, as seen in Table 11.1, countries do experience similar inflation rates in both periods, with a rather narrower distribution of inflation rates in the 1890 to 1913 period than overall. But why are inflation rates so low compared with money growth rates and why are money growth rates not closely correlated across countries, while inflation rates are? We continue with what is called the 'monetary approach' to this problem.

We may use the word 'arbitrage' to describe the process that links prices across countries. Of course, arbitrage really exists in single product lines rather than in price indices and, equally necessarily, arbitrage is weakened by transactions and transportation costs, tariffs and limited by the state of information available to individuals. Nevertheless, the process of arbitrage, product-by-product, will go into action as soon as the average of prices (or the interest rate) in one country is out of line with that of its trading competitors and will continue until the difference is eliminated. It is important to emphasize that we are speaking of arbitrage at the relative *money* prices of commodities, not at relative prices *per se* here, for what drives both the monetary approach and the specie-flow approach under the gold standard is the quantity theory of money.

To see the role information might play in the process we have been describing, consider the following from McCloskey and Zecher (1981, p. 189),

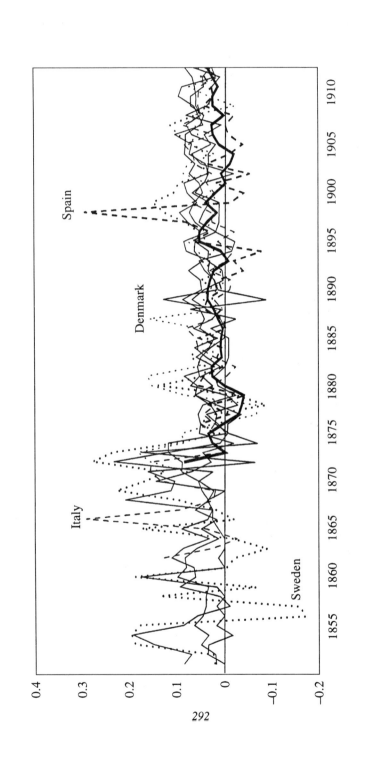

Figure 11.2 Money growth rates 1850–1913

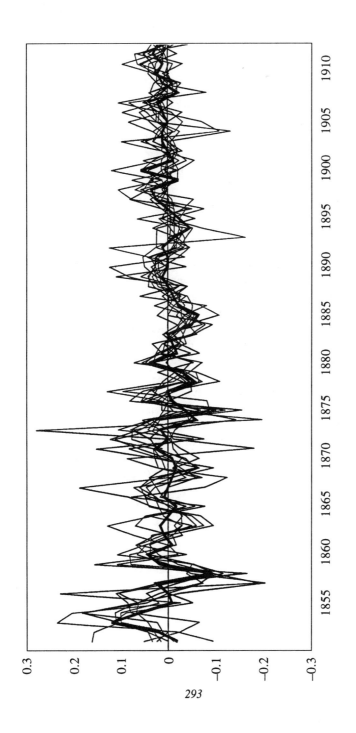

Figure 11.3   Inflation 1850–1913

> A flow of gold is by no means a necessary part of this process of arbitrage. In fact, the mere *threat* of arbitrage may be sufficient to bring a nation's prices and interest rates into line with the world's, without flows of anything.

That is, economic agents in one country, upon receiving information that their money prices are out of line, and knowing that exchange rates cannot adjust to validate their prices (under the gold standard), will quickly react to adjust their prices. In so doing, they alter the domestic price level which in turn induces a change in the domestic demand for money. This is either accommodated by the monetary authorities or supplied from the world's stock of money (see also McCloskey and Zecher, 1984). The operation of this mechanism is indirectly supported by recent empirical work on business cycles by Basu and Taylor (1999).

One thing that is different about this explanation, compared to the usual specie-flow mechanism, is that it argues that (international) prices drive domestic prices directly and, through money demand, domestic money stocks. In the usual specie-flow theory, it is money entering the monetary base that drives the domestic monetary base, the domestic money stock, and, ultimately, the domestic price level. For another, and here we return to our seemingly anomalous results for money and prices, the monetary approach implies that the domestic demand for money operates as a filter for this effect, transmitting a different effect to the domestic money supply depending on the nature of money demand. For the specie-flow mechanism, on the other hand, the money-demand function filters money stock changes on their way to changes in the price level.

To explain further, note that the demand for money is also a function of real income (and interest rates), and a combination of differences in the income elasticity of money demand and different variances and rates of growth of income would cause the money-demand filter to disturb either the monetary or price data (or both). Under the monetary approach, it is monetary quantities that are affected, especially in the short run (the context of the correlation tests reported above). Price levels, of course, would be correlated, since that result is achieved by either direct arbitrage in international commodity markets or the threat of arbitrage.[4] Under the specie-flow mechanism, on the other hand, the demand for money filters the effect of changes in the monetary base on money and prices. The latter might be expected to have roughly the same pattern internationally; this is not what we have observed. We think this experience, and these data, provide a promising test of the 'monetary approach'. Unfortunately, it seems to be most useful in a world that is no longer with us.

4. THE EVOLUTION OF BANKING

In this section we discuss the institutional development of the financial sectors of 12 European countries. For any nation, the money supply, defined as specie in circulation, bank notes and bank deposits, is determined jointly by the decisions of commercial bankers (when they determined the quantity of reserves they held against their notes and deposits), by the actions of individuals (when they determined the quantity of gold and currency they held relative to their bank deposits), and by the portfolio decisions of the central bank. Of course all of these are influenced or shaped by the evolving institutional structure of the country's financial system.

We begin our survey with the United Kingdom, which by all accounts had the most sophisticated financial system in the world in 1850. The other countries we consider, in order, are France, Germany, the Netherlands, Belgium, Austria and Hungary, Sweden, Denmark, Norway, Italy, Spain and Portugal.

United Kingdom

The United Kingdom was on the gold standard throughout the period and, because of its economic and military dominance, sterling was also the dominant international currency. As long as foreign bankers and policy makers believed that the Bank of England could and would maintain convertibility, sterling was 'as good as gold'. Domestically, the United Kingdom's currency supply was relatively inflexible, partly on account of the restrictions of the Bank Charter Act of 1844, which also divided the Bank of England into two departments: an Issue Department and a Banking Department. Following the arguments of the currency school, which greatly influenced the Cabinet at that time, the Issue Department maintained a 100 per cent reserve against all notes above a small initial volume that was backed by government securities. These restrictions, at least in part, contributed to liquidity crises – and bank failures – in 1847, 1857, and 1866.

While Bloomfield (1959) does not give high marks to the Bank of England for its adherence to the gold standard rules, studies of interest rate policy by Dutton (1984) and Goodhart (1984) suggest pretty strongly that the Bank's responses were stabilizing with respect to the gold standard and (even) destabilizing with respect to the domestic economy on occasion. At times, however, there was direct intervention by the Bank of England in domestic financial markets. In 1857 and 1858, for example, there was a business downturn that put considerable pressure on the banking system. Apparently, the Bank of England almost exhausted its reserves as it expanded its lending, with the consequence that the defined limits on the Bank's note issue embodied in the Bank Charter Act of 1844 ultimately had to be suspended. This example illustrates the Bank's willingness to provide, when called upon, an 'elastic' currency in the presence of a liquidity crisis. An intervention occurred again in May 1866, upon the failure of the prominent brokerage firm of Overend Gurney; this time the Bank Charter Act was suspended immediately. Again, in November 1890, the Bank of England led a consortium of London banks in providing liquidity in the face of the possible collapse of the Baring Brothers investment firm. We can see, then, that during this period the Bank of England sometimes took on the role of a central bank in the modern sense of the term, as the lender of last resort and controller of the money supply.

The U.K. banking sector from 1850 consisted of a wide variety of institutions in addition to the dominant joint-stock banks (London and provincial). The list includes building societies, merchant banks, savings banks, discount houses and foreign banks. Collectively, they participated in all banking activities, including in some cases the issuance of bank notes, though this practice was restricted over time and prohibited to all new banks after the Bank Act of 1844. The service of clearing and discounting of bills was crucial to the development of Western trading, and London eventually became the center of these activities.

At the same time, it is clear that U.K. banks did not take as active a role in lending to industry as did banks in many other countries, as we shall see below. For example, Kindleberger (1993) suggests that a typical U.K. bank held only 20 per cent of its assets in loans and advances to the industrial sector in the nineteenth century; in Germany, France and Italy the proportion was higher, especially towards the end of the period. Of course, it is likely that the U.K. industrialists could and frequently did 'roll over' their short-term bills as they came due (see Mathias, 1983), and that the banks tacitly agreed to convert these ostensibly short-term loans into long-term ones, so that they could be used for fixed-capital projects. It is also a fact that other sources of funds were more readily available to industrialists, in view of the much more extensive and sophisticated U.K. capital markets. There is also an issue of control. In at least some countries, banks controlled industrial firms much more than they did in the United Kingdom. In a sense, this is more a matter of the avenue through which funds flowed, from savers to investors, rather than a better strategy for investment. Even less can be said in favor of the beneficial effects of having governments attempt to regulate the direction or volume of this flow, although a large literature disagrees with our position on this issue.

We can summarize the evolution of the U.K. banking sector during the period from 1850 to 1913 as follows. First, British banking was evolving over time and the technology of banking from the middle of the century and later differed from that found earlier in England, just as the leading industries and scale of operations were changing over time. Second, both despite and because of Parliamentary regulations, the banking system developed as a widespread and diversified financial system that included a number of characteristics that typify banking to this day, including building societies, deposit banking and check-writing on a large scale. Finally, the Bank of England occasionally served as a central bank in the modern sense of the term – that is, it controlled the money supply and served as a lender of last resort. Indeed, mostly because of the successful maintenance of the pound sterling–gold price, the Bank of England, and its relatively inflexible monetary policy became the model for late-nineteenth-century European central banks.

France

Modern banking in France began with the Bank of France, which began operations in February 1800, in order to discount bills of exchange for, and make advances to, the government. From 1848, the Bank of France had the national monopoly of note issue, and it was, by far, the dominant bank in the country, partly because most other banks failed in that revolutionary year. With respect to the other functions of a central bank, it seems clear that the Bank of France followed a conservative discount policy. While the Bank expanded throughout the period, reaching 60 branches by 1870 and 411 by 1900, because of its conservative policy and the recourse of French businessmen to other sources of funds, the Bank of France seems to have played a lesser role than the Bank of England in regulating the money supply and in mitigating financial panics during the nineteenth century, though by the end of the period the Bank of France was acting as a lender of last resort, at least at times.

Prior to the Franco-Prussian War, France, as a founding member of the Latin Monetary Union of 1865, was on a bimetallic standard.[5] During the period immediately after the Franco-Prussian War, silver began to flow into France (and other silver or bimetallic countries as well) at the same time gold was flowing out to pay the war indemnity. As a result France limited its silver coinage in 1874 and suspended it in 1878. A financial collapse in 1882 severely weakened the Bank of France, and numerous (newly created) banks failed. In this situation, the Bank found it impossible to simultaneously loosen credit and maintain convertibility. This is not unusual, of course, but the Bank was itself heavily committed to its own discounts and so it was severely restricted in its ability to act as a lender of last resort. Otherwise, there is nothing remarkable to report about the performance of the Bank of France in this period.

In all likelihood the French money stock was relatively inflexible (inelastic) in the face of cyclical and/or sudden changes in the demand for money.

With reference to particular cycles, Marczewski (1988) argues that the inflexibility of the money supply was responsible for repeated episodes of 'stagflation' – meaning falling real output and a (moderately) rising price level – in France; this occurred in 1853, 1859, 1870–71, 1900–02. This stagflation presumably occurred because the money stock did not, in these periods, decline along with its demand. The opposite, presumably, happened frequently during expansions.

With respect to private banks, after 1851 the French government created several new financial institutions. In 1852, a nationwide mortgage bank (Crédit Foncier de France) and the famous Crédit Mobilier were founded. The latter, which itself was modeled on Belgian investment banks, became in some respects a prototype for many subsequent ventures in investment banking in Europe. The Crédit Mobilier sold bonds and granted loans primarily for public projects, especially railroads. Interestingly, the Crédit Mobilier did not provide capital directly to the manufacturing sector, though many of its imitators in other countries did; it was eventually forced to liquidate in 1867 on account of an unsuccessful venture into real estate loans. In addition to the mortgage and public works financing of the Crédit Foncier and the Crédit Mobilier, in 1860 the former was directed to extend its lending into agriculture, and to do so it created the Société de Crédit Agricole.

The government was hostile to English-style deposit banking after 1851 and, while prior to the early 1860s other banks were also founded, checkwriting, a specialty of English banks, was slow to develop, being legalized only in 1865. The discount banks filled the gaps, for the most part. Three banks which countered this trend were the Crédit Industriel et Commercial (founded in 1859), the Crédit Lyonnais (1863), and the Société Générale (1864). Each was national in scope and offered demand-deposit accounts. Although each of these banks did some lending to the manufacturing sector, particularly during their early years, their lending functions were concentrated in short-term securities – typically either high-grade government bonds or commercial bills secured by commodities – rather than long-term capital projects.

We can summarize the evolution of the French banking sector during this era with three observations. First, the French were slower than the British in developing widespread deposit banking, and this probably had some, albeit small, effect on French financial development. Second, the French developed the joint-stock investment bank earlier than and to a greater extent than all European countries except Belgium, though with respect to both deposit and investment banking France and the United Kingdom were much more similar by the end of the period than at its beginning. Finally, the Bank of France had a monopoly of the note issue and it also served as a lender of last resort on occasion, but, like European central banks of this period, it did so only in a limited fashion. Its main policy objective, again like other European central banks, was to maintain the exchange rate.

Germany

Following the Seven Years War, in 1765 the Prussian government established the predecessor of the Royal Bank of Prussia. In 1846 this bank was reorganized as the Prussian Bank, which took over the assets and liabilities of the Royal Bank. Although the Prussian Bank was privately owned, the government exerted considerable control over its operation. At this time it did not possess a monopoly of note issue, though by 1865 the Bank's note circulation dominated, reaching 40 per cent of the total in the country. In 1875, four years after final unification, the Prussian Bank became the Reichsbank – like the Banks of England and France, a private bank with public duties. At that time 33 other banks maintained the right of note issue; as they went out of business or surrendered that right, no new note-issuing banks were chartered.

With political unification came monetary unification as well, and in 1871 the new German Empire went on the gold standard, defining the mark in terms of gold and thus converting the German states from silver to gold. Bloomfield (1959) claims that subsequently the Reichsbank did not play by the rules of the gold standard system, but, according to Sommariva and Tullio (1987, 1988), the evidence actually suggests that the German central bank did. Indeed, McGouldrick (1984) argues that while gold inflows were actually cyclically neutral in Germany the Reichsbank stabilized gold inflows in this period by means of bill-discount rate policy.

With the possible exceptions of the Bank of England and on a smaller scale the National Bank of Belgium, the Reichsbank came the closest of the nineteenth-century central banks to a modern central bank. At one time or another it used all of the tools available to control the money supply and smooth economic activity. Most important, Germany had a relatively flexible money supply due to the laws regulating the Reichsbank note issue. This was limited to three times the value of its specie reserve, with the provision that the value of uncovered notes should not exceed 250 million marks. When the bank wanted to exceed this limit, during a crisis for example, rather than requiring legislation or executive permission – as was required of the Bank of England – it could do so by paying a 5 per cent tax on the subsequent note issue.

In addition to issuing notes, the Reichsbank, like any large financial institution that deals with smaller ones, used *moral suasion* to encourage 'responsible' behavior on the part of its customers (Bloomfield, 1959, p. 45). It also served as a lender of last resort both on a day-to-day basis (Tilly, 1991,

p. 183) and by rescuing major commercial banks during financial crises, (as in 1901 when it rescued the Leipziger Bank). Finally, just after the turn of the century the Reichsbank was engaged in the most conspicuous activity of modern central banks – namely, open market operations. On at least four occasions between 1901 and 1910 the bank sold bills in the open market to raise interest rates and stifle inflationary pressures. Thus by the end of the period the three largest economies in Europe – Britain, France, and Germany – had central banks whose operations had converged towards a common standard that corresponded roughly with the modern conception of a central bank.

Private banks were the dominant form of banking enterprise in Germany, and they were ubiquitous throughout the period. In Prussia alone there were 642 of these by 1861 (Tilly, 1967, p. 161). These banks did not issue notes but they did considerable business in banker's acceptances and discounts. They also dealt with the government, some times on a very large scale (e.g. the Rothschilds of Frankfurt). The banks that did lend to industry were the Kreditbanken, the first of which was the Schaaffhausen'schen Bankverein in Cologne (1848). Subsequently, attempts to emulate the early success of the French Crédit Mobilier motivated growth in this type of bank after 1852, and their growth in the 1860s was quite rapid. By 1865 there were 14 such Kreditbanken in north Germany, and they controlled more than 20 per cent of all joint-stock bank assets (Tilly, 1967, p. 164).

The passage of an act of general incorporation in 1870 led to tremendous growth in both the role and the concentration of universal or 'mixed' banks. These banks derived their name from their combination of investment banking – that is, underwriting – and commercial banking. Tilly (1986) argues that the German mixed banks evolved naturally from financial institutions that handled almost exclusively a small number of large state accounts into ones that handled large industrial accounts. German bankers guided (or even controlled) the finances of many major enterprises, in some cases explicitly involving themselves in capital projects, and in return they demanded that the enterprises maintain relatively large balances in the banks. This practice, we feel, accounts for the unusually large decline in velocity in Germany noted in Figure 11.1 and Table 11.3.

Belgium

As we have already noted in passing, Belgium was the first country to develop the investment bank, and both its central bank and its banking system in general were quite advanced compared to its European counterparts. Further, alone of all the European central banks we review in this chapter, the Banque Nationale de Belgique (National Bank of Belgium) was explicitly chartered to conduct all the functions of a modern central bank. Founded in 1850, the National Bank was privately owned, but the government appointed the Bank's governor and a special commissioner to oversee the Bank's operations and to report to the finance minister. Belgium had followed the French monetary system since 1832 and was a charter member of the Latin Monetary Union. Like France, Belgium was bimetallic until the suspension of silver coinage in 1878 placed it *de facto* on gold, and it remained on gold throughout the rest of the period.

From its founding, the National Bank of Belgium handled the government's accounts, possessed a monopoly of note issue, and served as a lender of last resort. The Bank also stood ready to purchase high quality bills from the Belgian banking system and to provide the day-to-day credit needs of the financial system; like the Reichsbank, it did not ration credit to the extent that most other central banks did.[6] In addition, Bloomfield (1959) notes that the Bank planned to use open market operations – that is, it intended to sell bills from its portfolio in order to raise interest rates, presumably to slow down economic expansion and thus smooth output over the business cycle – but that it never did so in practice. There is no evidence relating the Bank's behavior to particular episodes or financial crises during this era, but it may well be that the efficient operation of the Bank throughout the period actually resulted in the dearth of such crises in Belgium.

In 1822 the Dutch government chartered the Société Générale de Belgique. This institution was the world's first joint-stock investment bank; indeed, its charter gave it the ability to perform every major banking service. It could discount bills of exchange, issue notes, accept deposits, make loans (personal, industrial and real estate), manage royal estates and sell bonds to finance industrial investment. In short the Société was the first of the great mixed banks.

With the passage of a law of general incorporation, in 1873, the number of banks grew rapidly. According to Cameron (1967), the number of joint stock banks grew from 4 in 1850 to 21 in 1870 and 47 in 1875, and the per capita assets of those banks grew by a factor of five between 1850 and 1875. With respect to the growth of mixed banks in particular, Van der Wee and Goosens (1991) claim that in 1870 six were of the mixed type, and by 1913 at least 30 of Belgium's 250 to 300 financial institutions could be considered mixed banks. These institutions focused on industrial development, both at home and abroad, and were led by the Société Générale, which by 1879 held almost 50 per cent of its assets in coal and metals (Van der Wee and Goosens, 1991), industries in which Belgium was a world leader.

In addition to its well-deserved reputation as a leader in industrial finance, Belgium had an assortment of other financial institutions that provided financial services to smaller-scale savers and borrowers. These included mortgage banks, savings banks and mutual credit societies. In short, Belgium had a relatively sophisticated banking system earlier than many other countries, with a modern central bank at its head, a number of large mixed banks and a diversified set of smaller institutions.

Netherlands

While the Bank of the Netherlands was founded in 1814, as late as 1896 the Bank did not possess a monopoly over the note issue in the Netherlands, although nearly two-thirds of all the notes in circulation were Bank of Netherlands notes. There were no restrictions on the volume of the Bank's note issue; however, 40 per cent of the combination of its notes and deposit liabilities had to be backed by gold or silver. The Netherlands was on a silver standard in 1850 (since 1847), which it retained until 1875, when it returned to a bimetallic standard; this only lasted until 1877. In 1883–4 the Bank was threatened with suspension as its gold reserves fell perilously low, but it survived. In terms of the Bank of the Netherlands' behavior as a lender of last resort, no direct evidence is available, though Bloomfield (1959) argues that it was performing the two primary duties of a central bank by the end of the nineteenth century.

For a country that had been among the leaders of early modern finance, the Netherlands had a surprisingly undeveloped banking sector. Except for Spain and Portugal, the Netherlands had the lowest ratio of assets held by financial institutions to national product of any of the European countries we are studying, and the growth of total assets was quite low as well (see Craig and Fisher, 1997). Furthermore, there were only 13 banks in the Netherlands in 1896 with a capital of 7 million florins. At contemporary exchange rates that was less than one-thirteenth the value of Belgian bank capital (according to Muhleman, 1896). One reason for this may well have been that Dutch firms relied on the banks of other countries in this period, but it is an unusual finding, nevertheless.

Austria–Hungary

Given its early start at political integration (see Chapter 2), it is not surprising to learn that the Austro-Hungarian Empire also had one of the earliest starts at central banking, a unified currency being one of the economic advantages of political integration. The Austrian National Bank (later the Österreichisch-ungarische Bank) was established in 1816. Although privately owned, the Bank maintained state loans (repayable on demand) on its balance sheet and handled Imperial accounts. In return it was granted the note-issuing monopoly from the date of its charter, making it among the earliest of all European central banks to have such a monopoly.

The Empire was on a silver standard from 1857, but the currency was never strictly convertible, and the world financial crisis of 1873 precipitated a permanent suspension of silver redemption. By the end of the decade, paper money was circulating at par due to the decline in the world price of silver (Hawtrey, 1931), and silver ceased to be coined, except on government account, after 1879. In 1892, Austria–Hungary formally joined the gold standard countries, although full convertibility was not achieved until 1900. Interestingly, the movement to gold was financed by a foreign loan handled by private Austrian banks rather than by the central bank (Kindleberger, 1993).

Little has been written about the performance of the Austrian National Bank as a lender of last resort, probably because it did not fulfill this role to any large extent. This cannot be attributed to any technical limitations since the National Bank had the potential to deliver a relatively elastic currency, and the renewal of its charter in 1887 was accompanied by the establishment of a fractional reserve system similar to that governing the German Reichsbank. Instead, the Bank's performance reflects more the conservative policies of its directors.

Following the revolution of 1848, the state decided to accelerate its investment in railroad construction. Accordingly, it chartered three joint-stock credit institutions: the Niederösterreichische Escomptegesellschaft (1853), the Banca Commerciale Triestina (1854) and the Creditanstalt für Handel and Gewerbe (1855). The first two were traditional merchant or commercial banks, specializing in short-term credit on trade. The esteemed Creditanstalt was Austria's first mixed bank, performing traditional discounting services while also serving as a 'mobilier' style investment bank. By 1883 there were 13 such banks in the Empire. Between the founding of the Creditanstalt and the Crash of 1873, more than a thousand joint-stock companies were chartered, and the investment banks played an important role in providing short-term credit, long-term capital financing and in some cases outright ownership of the new industrial ventures. In the decades that followed, however, new industrial and financial firms were not founded at anything like this rate; indeed, by 1907, Germany had eight times as many joint-stock companies as the Austro–Hungarian Empire (Rudolph, 1972), many more than mere size would have suggested.

While it has often been alleged that the banking system of Austria–Hungary failed to promote economic growth adequately, this is not entirely clear. Although its central bank served neither as a lender of last resort nor as a promoter of economic growth, the investment, commercial and mortgage banks of the empire were modern and by most accounts competent financial intermediaries. In fact, considerable capital flowed into the country (and into the banking system) from abroad (Trebilcock, 1981) a fact that could be compared favorably, for example, with the United States in this period. That is, in an international capital market, there is less need to develop domestic institutions if foreign ones will do the job; indeed, the attraction of foreign capital during the early stages of industrialization has often been a positive rather than a negative influence on growth, and this was probably the case in Austria.

Scandinavia

Sweden has the world's oldest continuing central bank, the Riksbank, which was founded in 1656 and taken over by the State in 1668. The other two Scandinavian countries, Norway and Denmark, founded central banks in 1816 (the Norwegian Centralbanken or Norges Bank) and 1818 (the Nationalbank of Denmark). Sweden and Denmark went on the gold standard in 1873, and in 1875 they were joined by Norway; the three of them formed the Scandinavian Monetary Union based on the krone. This confederation of countries remained successfully on the gold standard until 1914 and there was a good deal of financial integration, as well. From the 1870s, for example, the Riksbank accepted the notes of the Danish and Norwegian central banks, and in 1901 the three formally agreed to reciprocate the arrangement. Although the explicit role of the state in the ownership of the central bank differed in each country – in Sweden the state owned 100 per cent of the stock, in Norway a majority, and in Denmark none – by the end of the period each was performing as a modern central bank, possessing a monopoly of note issue and serving as a lender of last resort.

The Swedish Riksbank assumed lender of last resort functions in the 1890s, making it a central bank in the modern sense of the term. It did so for three reasons. First, the legislated limits on note issue were raised over time and never became a binding constraint; thus, the Bank could easily accommodate fluctuations in the demand for its liabilities. Second, the rapid economic growth of Sweden during this period made the Bank a good credit risk, and the Bank managed its gold reserves by borrowing in foreign markets. Finally, due to the stable political climate and the country's rapid and stable economic growth, the Swedish banking system was never confronted with a financial panic during this period, though of course this may have been an endogenous characteristic that itself was partially a result of the strong banking system.

The experience of central banking in *Denmark* was similar to that of Sweden in most important respects: in particular, the Nationalbank handled the Danish state accounts; Denmark decided to go off silver and on to gold at the same time as Sweden; the Nationalbank had a monopoly of note issue throughout the era – even before the Riksbank; the government lifted the restrictions on note issue over time, so that the Nationalbank was easily able to meet sudden increases in the demand for liquid funds; and by the end of the period it was consciously acting as a lender of last resort, most notably by rescuing the commercial banking sector during the international crisis of 1907–08.

The *Norwegian* central bank possessed a monopoly of note issue from its founding, and it dominated Norwegian banking until mid-century. From the 1850s the growth of other commercial banks reduced its influence in the Norwegian capital market. Egge (1983) claims that as late as 1895 the Bank operated largely as a commercial bank in competition with the newly-established private commercial banks and did little central banking. After that date, however, the Bank increasingly behaved like a central bank with a larger discount business, and even like a lender of last resort during crises, but it continued its commercial lending in competition with other banks, and as a result a number of private and foreign banks created the Centralbanken for Norge, a private central bank, to provide discounting and lender-of-last-resort services. This bank quickly became the largest one in the country, and in 1907 this resulted in a conflict between the Norges Bank and the private banks over the latter's submission of monthly reports to the Norges Bank. After that time, the Norges Bank gave up its commercial banking activities and served solely as a central bank.

In 1850, *Sweden* had in place a financial system that featured most of the technology of modern banking of the time, although it was geographically concentrated and small on a per capita basis. In 1834, private (*enskilda*) banks began to issue currency and these issues grew to 43.2 per cent of the total note issue by 1859. In 1863 the Bank Reform Act established private banking on the joint-stock principle and permitted banks to lend at market interest rates. While a number of banks continued to issue notes, others turned to deposit banking; thus, in 1864 there were 24 unlimited liability or note-issuing banks and 4 limited joint-stock banks. A decade later there were 27 note-issuing and 8 limited liability banks; by 1895 there were 45 banks of both types; and by 1908 there were 83 (Lundstrom, 1991). In addition to these institutions, there were 300 savings banks, more than 40 mortgage companies and numerous other financial institutions.

By most empirical measures *Denmark* and *Norway* were financially developed by 1870 and became increasingly so over the next 40 years. By 1900 these two countries had the highest ratios of assets held by financial institutions to national product of any European country. Besides their national banks, Norway had 36 incorporated banks in 1896 and a single large mortgage bank, while Denmark had 18 banks in 1870, 40 in 1896, and 140 in 1913/14. Despite a relatively large number of institutions in the *Danish* financial system, most were quite small and the banking sector was actually quite concentrated, with roughly half of the balances held in three institutions: the Privat bank, an investment bank founded in 1857; the Landsmanbank, a mixed bank founded in 1872, that had both a traditional commercial division and rural mortgage division; and the Handelsbank, a merchant bank founded in 1873 (Johansen, 1991). In addition there were a number of credit associations and building societies in Denmark. Between 1850 and 1895 the value of assets held by Norwegian financial institutions increased by a factor of eight. While the growth experienced by the Norwegian financial sector was rapid relative to much of the rest of Europe, Norway's financial growth was slower than either Sweden's or Denmark's. Egge argues that Norway's geography played a large role in this outcome. Specifically, its capital markets were poorly integrated, due, at least partly to the sheer cost of transacting between locations, and its economy was poorly suited to take advantage of the sweeping economic changes of the time.

Italy

As mentioned in Chapter 2, the Italian state was formed in 1861 – although its modern borders were not established for another decade – and had at that time an elected Parliament that oversaw monetary matters. In 1862, the lira was established as legal tender and in 1863 the official exchange rate of the lira with the British pound was set at 25.3. This rate ruled during the intervals in which Italy had a fixed exchange rate in the succeeding fifty years. In 1865 Italy joined the Latin Monetary Union and adopted the coinage convention of the Union, but in the following year Italy went to war with Austria over control of Venice, and from that time until 1884, the lira was inconvertible.

Italy was on the gold standard from 1884 to 1893 and again after 1902. It was a financial crisis (in 1893–4) that disrupted this arrangement and, not coincidentally, the Bank of Italy was founded at that time. This bank was actually a consolidation of the Banca Nazionale nel Regno, Banca Nazionale Toscana, Banca Toscana di Credito e d'Industria, and the Banca Romana. The new Bank of Italy did not possess a monopoly of note issue, rendering its control over the money stock somewhat tenuous; even so, the Italian government may well have attempted to adhere to the rules of the international gold standard through legislation and treasury operations. It has been claimed (Cohen, 1967, 1972) that the Banca d'Italia supplied the banking system with a true lender of last resort by the end of the period. Indeed, according to Cohen, the Banca was an effective central bank from its inception, providing day-to-day credit for the other joint-stock banks and responding to financial crises by direct lending or by the creation of consortia to provide funds (in 1907 and 1911). This safety net allowed the leading commercial and investment banks to follow the German practice of lending for long-term industrial activities.

Prior to the unification of Italy in 1861, each of the major constituent states of the country had a central bank of issue; indeed, some had other banks of issue and there were numerous discount houses and other lending institutions. After unification there were five banks of issue in Italy and a sixth was added when the Papal States joined the Union in 1870. This number was subsequently reduced to three with the formation of the central bank in 1894. After unification there were three non-note issuing joint stock banks, which grew to 13 in the following five years. Most of these were started with foreign capital. Among the most notable of these were Credito Mobiliare and the Credito Italiano, both of which were started with French funds; the latter was eventually taken over by the former. In 1871 came the Banca Generale, which was partly financed with German capital. These *mobilier*-type banks did not lend directly to Italian manufacturing industries, but primarily invested in railroads, canals and state securities. Both the Credito Mobiliare and the Banca Generale failed in the crisis of 1893. They were replaced by two German- (and Swiss-) financed and managed institutions, the Banca Commerciale and a new Credito Italiano. These firms operated along the lines of the German mixed banks described above.

Including the major institutions mentioned above, in 1880–84 there were 115 commercial and industrial banks that performed the roles of discounting and underwriting; 190 savings banks, which were restricted in the amount of commercial and underwriting they could perform; and 217 cooperative lending institutions (credit unions, as we would call them now). By 1910–14, these had grown in number to 126, 186, and 377, respectively. Their assets grew even more rapidly, from 12 billion lire in 1880 to 40 billion lire in 1910–14.[7]

In the two decades following unification, Italy had, with the exception of Spain and Portugal, the most backward financial sector in Europe. After 1900, however, Italy's banking sector was growing faster than that of any other European country, at least as measured by financial assets. In addition, whereas in 1880 Italy's share of financial assets to national product was the second lowest in Europe (again, Spain had the lowest ratio), and less than half that of Britain and Germany, by 1913 it had almost caught up with both the latter.

Spain and Portugal

To finance its alliance with France against Britain during the American War of Independence, the Spanish Crown created the Banco Nacional de San Carlos. In 1829 this bank was reorganized as the Banco Español de San Fernando, commonly referred to as the Bank of Spain, though it did not formally take this name until 1856. While the Bank was privately owned, the government appointed its governor and two sub-governors, and in return for a monopoly of the note issue granted in 1874, the Bank was rechartered with a capital of 100 million pesetas, granted a note issue of up to five times that amount, and it in turn granted the government a 125 million peseta loan.

Although never formally a member of the Latin Monetary Union, in 1868 Spain adopted the Union's monetary standards, substituting the peseta for the franc; however, like the other countries in the Union, Spain ceased coining silver in 1878, except on government account. With a large public debt, the interest on which was paid in gold, and a balance of payments deficit during this period, Spain found it difficult to maintain convertibility. In 1883 the Bank of Spain suspended the convertibility of its notes into specie. Convertibility was not resumed for the rest of the century, and the value of the peseta steadily eroded relative to the other major currencies. By the end of the century the peseta had fallen to half its original buying power in terms of the pound (Vicens Vives, 1969, p. 719). During the 1890s, the Bank's most noticeable role was its monetization of the government's debt, which was incurred fighting colonial wars, the most disastrous of which was that against the United States. Furthermore, it has been argued (Tortella, 1977) that the Bank's behavior in domestic markets was often destabilizing in the sense of deflating during monetary crises. Overall, then, we must conclude that the Bank of Spain was one of the few nineteenth-century European central banks which was not functioning as a modern central bank by World War I.

Following the revolution of 1820 *Portugal* adopted a constitution in 1822. That same year the Bank of Portugal was created to handle the finances of the new political regime. Although the Bank did not have a monopoly of note issue (as late as 1896 there were seven other banks issuing notes), its notes alone were accepted for payments of public debts. In 1854 Portugal went on the gold standard, making it one of the earliest states to do so. This was abandoned, however, in 1890 and Portugal did not return to the standard. Furthermore, there is no strong evidence that the Bank intervened in domestic financial affairs in this period. Thus, while Portugal had a central bank in the sense that the Bank of Portugal served as the financial agent of the state, it did not perform the tasks of a modern central bank.

The key to the *Spanish* banking system was the Bank of Spain. As late as 1843 it was the only joint-stock financial institution in the country! The liberalization of Spanish policy during the 1850s and 1860s led to considerable growth in the banking sector, and by 1873 there were 16 banks of issue and 17 other joint-stock credit institutions (Tortella, 1972). In the following year the Bank of Spain was granted the note-issuing monopoly in return for loans to the government and 11 other note-issuing banks merged with the Bank of Spain. This led to a concentration of financial control in the hands of an institution that was itself a tool of the state. Consider that as late as 1900 the Bank of Spain held more than two-thirds of the assets held in Spanish financial institutions (Anes, 1974), and at the same time the ratio of the Bank's public to private assets was four to one (Trebilcock, 1981).

As already noted, *Portugal*'s banking system was dominated by its central bank, the Bank of Portugal. Although in 1896 there were seven banks of issue other than the Bank of Portugal, and 30 other non-issuing banks as well, the Bank of Portugal's capital was almost twice that of all other banks combined (Muhleman, 1896, pp. 119–20). Compare this to a country like Sweden, one of Europe's poorer states, where the ratio was almost exactly reversed (p. 112) or even Austria–Hungary, where the capital of other banks was six times that of the central bank, and one sees the potential effect of concentrating credit in one government-controlled institution.

Private banking in Spain and Portugal clearly did not measure up to the European standard of the time. This seems to have been partly because few worthwhile proposals were put before the banks and partly the result of very strict laws of incorporation. In both Spain and Portugal the laws against incorporation and the heavy borrowing by the state (that ended up on the books of the banking sector) surely impeded (crowded out) the financial sector's support for private activities. While government borrowing in and of itself is not necessarily good or bad, and could even be very important for relatively backward countries like Spain and Portugal, it seems there was both waste and an excessive amount of money spent on maintaining antiquated empires and in funding railroad projects that did not pay off. Even without the crowding out, however, it is not likely that either country would have challenged the European leaders at this time, and, further, there is little likelihood that the Iberian banks would have broken the mold and led the way if there had been a different political/financial system in place.

5. CONCLUSIONS

Taken together, the findings discussed in this chapter lead us to two broad conclusions. First, despite differences in the initial conditions and the different evolution of the banking system within each country, increasing financial development was a pervasive and international phenomenon that helped produce what we could refer to as an increasingly *common* 'industrial-financial system' across these countries. Second, the gold standard did not 'work', in the way the classical price-specie-flow mechanism predicts; instead, as an international currency, gold flows equalized any balance of payments deficits or surpluses, while domestic price levels but not money stocks were highly correlated across countries.

We began this chapter with a discussion of the definition and potential role of financial development in economic growth. Our measure of this – the behavior of the velocity of money – in fact indicates the extent to which economic activity in a country is monetized, at least in the absence of a substantial growth of other financial intermediaries. Clearly, the financial development of a country is determined to a large extent by the institutional structure of its banking sector. Over time, as the banking sectors of the European economies converged toward a mixed system, the velocities converged as well.

Finally, with respect to the banking sectors of the European countries, three general statements can be made. First, at the beginning of the period, the extent and type of banks and banking services offered varied greatly from country to country. As time passed, this diversity narrowed considerably, by a kind of financial (technological) transfer. Second, by the end of the period, every country had a mixed banking system, even though the means by which the various banking activities were carried out still differed considerably among countries. All had central banks, as well. Finally, the path to this convergence varied across countries. While the British led the way in discounting bills, the Belgians and French pioneered the joint-stock investment bank and the Germans and Austrians developed the mixed bank.

NOTES

1. Evidence suggesting that this is so for these countries is presented in Craig and Fisher (1997).
2. As noted, the United Kingdom comes across as the only country in the sample that does not show a decline in its velocity figures. In fact, as measured by this index, in the United Kingdom monetary and banking services were added at the same rate as the economy expanded from 1870 to 1913. This finding is hardly surprising, really, because the United Kingdom had the most advanced financial sector in 1850. But it may also suggest a growing use of money substitutes in the United Kingdom, since the growth of commercial bank liabilities in this period (at least to 1880) was also very rapid. In this case the index would be misleading, as it would be when velocity increases occur, later in the twentieth century.
3. As shown in Craig, Fisher and Spencer (1995), this pattern actually holds up for all other measures of prices available (also see Craig and Fisher, 1997).
4. In the long run we would expect the money stock to show a closer relationship across countries, at least if there are infrequent shocks to the system (such as those coming from new gold discoveries). See Craig and Fisher (1997).
5. In addition to France, the original members of the Latin Monetary Union were Belgium, Italy and Switzerland, with Greece joining in 1867.
6. The Bank could issue notes at its discretion with the provision that all issues above a fixed amount (275 million francs) were taxed at a rate of 6 per cent. Note the similarity to the regulations concerning the Reichbank's note issue.
7. The figures cited here are annual averages from Cohen (1972).

12. European business cycles in the Victorian era

1. INTRODUCTION

There appears to be a strong tradition in the literature on European business cycles that by the beginning of the twentieth century these events are quite closely correlated across countries. The most prominent lines of influence mentioned in the literature are either real (with either foreign trade or capital markets serving as the avenue of transmission) or nominal (with the gold standard serving in the same capacity). Most studies deal with a particular country, and the result is that what we could call the 'pan-European cycle' is hard to pin down, even though many of the parts to the puzzle exist. To gain this perspective, then, we propose to look at a large number of countries, with the object being a closer identification of the *common* cyclical influences in this period.

Beginning with the financial variables discussed in Chapter 11, we note that there is a strong tradition in the literature that financial crises in one European economy spread to others, producing roughly simultaneous financial and real contractions for a number of countries. What we showed in Chapter 11 was that while inflation rates were closely related across countries, money growth rates were not. Our explanation of the failure of money to fit into the pattern – as predicted by the 'specie-flow mechanism' of the gold standard – is that adjustment was actually by means of a mechanism described by the 'monetary approach' to the balance of payments so that international financial equilibrium was achieved through trade and capital flows rather than direct monetary adjustment. This result implies that in all likelihood the money stock would not serve in its traditional role as a leading indicator in the domestic economy, while price levels and interest rates, being determined internationally, would offer little assistance in identifying cycles *within* each country.

In this chapter we take a close look at real variables that can serve as *indicators* of the state of the economy. We begin in Section 2 with real GDP (or GNP) for ten countries; these data provide what we think is an effective quantitative picture of the magnitude and timing of these events in Europe. Since business cycles are more than just fluctuations in real GDP – and because the national product data for these countries are often suspect – we will add (also in Section 2) the results of tests using industrial production and imports. These are coincident indicators of the state of the economy that have enjoyed considerable success in modern times. Our results, using a 'phase coincidence' procedure, indicate close *and increasing* integration of the business cycle among these countries.

In the remainder of the chapter we look at both the narrative and empirical record for eleven European nations, searching for common recessions. In Section 3 we look at cycles in the United Kingdom because those data are the best we have and because of the possibility that U.K. recessions are exported to other countries via trade and capital flows. In Section 4, then, we will look at a set of four countries for which a reasonably complete (common) cyclical pattern can be discerned. This framework is then applied (in Section 5) to the remaining six countries to see how they fit the recession pattern of the five (more advanced) industrial economies. They do fit well, and in our conclusions in Section 6, we set down the common cycles that we think we have identified for this broad sample of European countries.

2.   INTERACTION AMONG COINCIDENT INDICATORS

The main way we would normally want to identify the cycle for each country is by means of the behavior of real national product. We have useful data for ten countries for, as noted, somewhat different time periods. Because of the non-stationarity of the log-level figures on real national product, a comparison of correlation coefficients across countries would not be especially interesting; on the other hand, correlations of the first differences of these series rarely turn up anything; that is, most such correlations across countries are not very large in absolute terms. While this is not especially favorable for the hypothesis of the pan-European cycle, we do have an alternative, as employed both by Friedman and Schwartz (1982) and Ford (1981). This alternative involves counting the percentage of the years in which these economies were in the same phase of the business cycle (expansion or contraction), where the phases are identified by the sign of the changes in the level figures. What is useful about this technique, which ignores magnitudes, of course, is that expansion years are treated equally with contraction years. It is the fashion in the literature to look mainly at the timing of contractions, as if all we cared about with respect to cycles were the downturns. We believe the 'phase-coincidence' approach just described provides a useful alternative.

Table 12.1 contains the results of calculating the percentage of the years when these economies were in the same cyclical phase as identified by the sign of the change in real GDP. We look at the entire period (which is defined for each country in the footnote) in the top of the table (Part A) and the sub-period 1890 to 1913, in Part B.

For the entire period, the average of these figures (unweighted) is .669, indicating coincident phases in two out of every three years. For the 1890 to 1913 period, the average of the figures (in Part B of Table 12. 1) is higher, at .709. For the major industrial economies (Belgium, France, Germany, Sweden and the United Kingdom), the comparable figures are .705 for the overall period and .746 for 1890–1913; these are noticeably higher and indicate that the correspondence of cyclical phases for these countries had reached three out of every four years by 1913. We conjecture that the widening of international product and capital markets and the shrinking of the volatile (and often out of phase) agricultural sectors of these countries are the principal factors involved here. Notice, in this connection, that Italy and Portugal, two economies for which the agricultural cycle dominates to the end of the period, are on the low end of these comparisons. Indeed, Portugal actually shows decreasing phase coincidence over the period. These numbers, at any rate, provide evidence of considerable and increasing coincidence throughout the period.

We also have a set of *industrial production* indices for seven European countries for this period. Industrial production is an important part of GNP, of course, but it is generally more volatile than GNP. We have already argued that the increasing coincidence of business cycles across countries is partly the result of industrial activity replacing agriculture as the main component of national product, as this period wanes. The reasons for this are that the industrial sectors of these nations were knit more closely together to begin with and that, as time passed, this integration increased. This situation was a result of the growth of what was traded internationally, in the first instance, although it also reflects agricultural protection in some cases. In present-day studies, one typically finds that industrial production is a coincident and pro-cyclical variable. It is certainly a pro-cyclical variable in this period, with very high correlations with GNP.

A phase-coincidence tabulation, done in the same way as Table 12.1, reveals a pattern remarkably similar to that for real national product. The results, which are the relative incidence of the first differences of the data showing the same sign, are shown in Table 12.2. These numbers are lower than the real national product numbers, we believe, because of the narrower base of the industrial production figures (and because the series are more volatile, as already noted). Even so, only four of the relationships (of 21 possible) show lower coincidence of phases in the 1890 to 1913 period than overall. These results are similar to those for real national product. Similar, too, is the difference in the averages, with the entire period showing an average coincidence of 0.660, while the 1890 to 1913 period shows an

Table 12.1 Integration of business cycles: frequencies

	Belgium	Denmark	France	Germany	Italy	Norway	Portugal	Sweden	U.K.
A. 1850–1913									
Aus.–Hun.	0.630	0.696	0.609	0.565	0.674*	0.609	0.609	0.522	0.674
Belgium	–	0.887	0.623	0.774	0.654	0.854	0.717*	0.904	0.774*
Denmark		–	0.540	0.603	0.654	0.792	0.651*	0.827	0.682
France			–	0.651	0.596	0.604	0.540*	0.635	0.635
Germany				–	0.577	0.667	0.603*	0.769	0.635*
Italy					–	0.625	0.596*	0.558	0.635
Norway						–	0.625	0.833	0.667
Portugal							–	0.692*	0.619*
Sweden								–	0.654
U.K.									–

	Belgium	Denmark	France	Germany	Italy	Norway	Portugal	Sweden	U.K.
B. 1890–1913									
Aus.-Hun.	0.708	0.750	0.708	0.583	0.667	0.750	0.625	0.667	0.708
Belgium	–	0.958	0.667	0.792	0.708	0.958	0.583	0.958	0.750
Denmark		–	0.708	0.750	0.750	0.917	0.542	0.917	0.792
France			–	0.708	0.708	0.625	0.500	0.750	0.667
Germany				–	0.667	0.750	0.542	0.833	0.625
Italy					–	0.667	0.542	0.667	0.708
Norway						–	0.625	0.917	0.792
Portugal							–	0.625	0.500
Sweden								–	0.708
U.K.									–

Notes:
* Indicates total period has a larger frequency of similar phases than 1890–1913.
Beginning dates: all are 1850 except Belgium (1860), Italy (1861), Norway (1865), and Sweden (1861).

Sources: Belgium (GDP) from Maddison (1991); Denmark (GDP) from Hansen (1974); France (GDP) from Toutain (1987); Germany (GDP) from Mitchell (1978, 1992); Italy (GNP) from ISTAT (1957); Norway (GDP) from Mitchell (1978, 1992); Portugal (GDP) from Molinas and Prados de la Escosura (1989); Sweden (Real DP) from Krantz and Nilsson (1975); and the United Kingdom (GNP) from Mitchell (1992).

Table 12.2   Industrial production: phase coincidence

	Austria–Hungary	France	Germany	Italy	Spain	Sweden	U.K.
A. 1850–1913							
Aus./Hung.	–	0.635	0.651	0.558	0.571	0.538	0.541
France		–	0.619	0.635*	0.587	0.731	0.619
Germany			–	0.788*	0.698*	0.769	0.712
Italy				–	0.615	0.750	0.692
Spain					–	0.750	0.651*
Sweden						–	0.712
B. 1890–1913							
Aus./Hung.	–	0.750	0.667	0.583	0.708	0.667	0.667
France		–	0.708	0.583	0.625	0.750	0.667
Germany			–	0.750	0.625	0.833	0.833
Italy				–	0.625	0.750	0.750
Spain					–	0.792	0.625
Sweden						–	0.750
U.K.							–

Note: * Indicates more frequent coincidence in the entire period than in the 1890–1913 period.

Sources: Germany, Italy, Sweden and the United Kingdom from Mitchell (1978, 1992); Austria-Hungary is calculated from data provided in Komlos (1983); France from Toutain (1987); and Spain from Carreras (1987).

average coincidence of 0.700. This finding supports our argument that increasing industrialization is one major reason why cycles grew together during this period.[1]

The last coincident indicator we have is the volume of *real imports*. We prefer imports to exports in this role because we are trying to measure cycles within each country and imports are a component of national demand that would be driven by domestic real incomes. The results of a phase-coincidence tabulation appear in Table 12.3; they are achieved by comparing the signs of changes in real imports across countries (as a percentage of the total possible in each case). Again the coincidence is higher in the second period than in the entire one. This is especially noticeable among the major European economies, since 12 of the 17 exceptions (marked with an asterisk in the table) involve Portugal and Spain (there are 66 cases in all). Dropping these three countries, we get an overall average of 0.714 for the 1890 to 1913 period; this compares with 0.640 for the entire period. If we also dropped Italy (an agricultural country), we would find coincidence near 80 per cent for the major European industrial economies in the 1890–1913 period.

We conclude, then, that contemporaneous, real variables appear to draw together over this period, with rather high associations occurring for all variables and most countries in the 1890 to 1913 period. Of course economic integration continues to occur in Europe but we believe we are looking at an especially important period here, since it is the rapid growth (and rapid relative growth) of the industrial sector that seems 'proximately' responsible for much of the interaction we have observed. We also note that, since these are cyclically coincident variables, we have a strong indication, on balance, that cycles are becoming more closely integrated by the end of the period. We will continue to look at this matter in the next section, where we use the variables just identified and other evidence to try to pin down the cyclical turning points within countries.

3. BUSINESS CYCLES IN THE UNITED KINGDOM

In Table 12.4 we illustrate the behavior of six indicators of the business cycle in the United Kingdom. Except for unemployment, the numbers provided are annual growth rates of the data. We have listed observations for what we believe are the recession years in this period. Our selection is based on the numbers in the table as well as an inspection of the large literature on U.K. business cycles.

Looking at real GNP first, we note that negative changes in this aggregate occur at a relatively high level in 1879, 1892 and 1908, and, as we will see, the literature concurs in the view that these are years of recession. Lesser downturns occur in 1866, 1872, 1881, 1884–5, 1893 and 1902–3, so these years, too, could be added to the list of recession years for this period. (Note that we only include recession years in the tables in this and subsequent sections.) Over the entire sample, then, there are 11 years of GNP-recession out of the 58 possible between 1855 and 1913; this yields, on average, four years of upturn for each year of downturn in this period. Cycles in real GNP, presumably, are slightly over five years in duration.

There are some unemployment figures for the 1855–1910 period in the United Kingdom, as produced by Feinstein (1972). In Table 12.4 we reproduce these numbers. There appears to be remarkable coincidence of this series with that for GNP cycles in that unemployment often rises above 5 per cent the same year that GNP growth dips significantly. But there is a difference with the unemployment numbers, since unemployment often remains high after the GNP downturn disappears; this happens in 1868–9, 1880, 1887, 1894, 1895, 1904, 1905 and 1909. This very modern phenomenon is

Table 12.3 Real imports: phase coincidence

	Belgium	Denmark	France	Germany	Italy	Netherlands	Norway	Portugal	Spain	Sweden	U.K.
Entire Period											
AH	0.690	0.750	0.667	0.667	0.524	0.571	0.643	0.522*	0.619*	0.595	0.595
BE	–	0.659	0.682	0.444	0.577	0.641	0.614	0.438	0.619*	0.571	0.682
DA		–	0.614	0.889	0.614	0.659	0.841	0.591*	0.636*	0.795*	0.750*
FR			–	0.556	0.461*	0.635	0.604	0.375*	0.714*	0.635	0.587
GE				–	0.556	0.556	0.728	0.728	0.556	0.778	0.556
IT					–	0.596	0.542	0.625	0.385*	0.635*	0.654
NE						–	0.614	0.562	0.619	0.651*	0.635
NO							–	0.500*	0.583	0.646	0.667
PO								–	0.500	0.521*	0.604*
SP									–	0.476	0.492
SW										–	0.746
U.K.											–

1890–1913

	Belgium	Denmark	France	Germany	Italy	Netherlands	Norway	Portugal	Spain	Sweden	U.K.
AH	0.850	0.800	0.750	0.800	0.650	0.650	0.750	0.300*	0.600*	0.650	0.600
BE	–	0.917	0.750	0.833	0.667	0.833	0.875	0.458	0.542*	0.708	0.792
DA		–	0.750	0.917	0.667	0.750	0.875	0.458*	0.542*	0.792	0.708
FR			–	0.667	0.417	0.667	0.792	0.208*	0.625*	0.708	0.625
GE				–	0.750	0.750	0.792	0.458	0.458	0.708	0.792
IT					–	0.667	0.542	0.708	0.292	0.625	0.708
NE						–	0.708	0.542*	0.667	0.625	0.708
NO							–	0.333*	0.667	0.667	0.667
PO								–	0.500	0.417	0.583
SP									–	0.500	0.500
SW										–	0.792
U.K.											–

Note: * Indicates cases in which the overall period has the higher coincidence. Data.

Sources: All data come from Mitchell (1978, 1992) except those for Portugal, which are from Nunes, Mata and Valerio (1989).

Table 12.4   Unemployment rates and growth rates of various indicators in the United Kingdom 1855–1913

	GNP	Unemployment	Ind. Prod.	Imports	Investment	Exports
1858	0.66	7.30	–2.08	–3.76	2.67	5.10
1866	–0.11	2.60	3.68	7.66	–11.33	12.15
1867	1.36	6.30	–6.13	–7.02	12.78	–4.32
1873	0.00	1.10	1.11	2.76	–4.94	–2.04
1878	0.69	6.20	–0.21	–0.94	–5.13	2.55
1879	–1.86	10.70	–3.66	1.29	–15.12	2.41
1884	–0.62	8.10	–3.79	–4.04	–3.81	2.07
1885	–0.21	9.30	–4.32	1.39	–12.39	–2.59
1886	1.10	10.20	–2.13	–3.60	–9.20	2.22
1892	–1.51	6.30	–4.96	–3.68	4.48	–9.56
1893	–0.49	7.50	–1.65	–3.47	–0.88	–2.93
1902	–0.71	4.00	1.73	1.14	0.00	1.07
1903	–0.05	4.70	–2.10	1.70	0.51	1.68
1908	–3.09	7.80	8.36	–6.43	–15.86	–10.09

Sources: Unemployment comes from Feinstein (1972); all other data come from Mitchell (1978, 1992).

especially noticeable for those times when GNP growth is actually negative (1872 and 1900 being the only exceptions). In any event, aside from the 1870s, the unemployment datings confirm the GNP datings pretty well, on the whole.

Of the six sets of data for the United Kingdom in Table 12.4, five of them are *coincident indicators* of the U.K. cycle, and one (unemployment) is sometimes a coincident and sometimes a lagging indicator. This gives us a fair macroeconomic picture of the annual cycle. What we now propose to do is put these data together and attempt a cycle dating mainly on these six series. We believe these are likely to be the major items in any compilation that would be attempted anyway, so this exercise should produce a reasonable cycle dating, accepting, of course, that the data are sufficiently reliable.

The year 1858 was selected because of slow growth, a decline in industrial production and imports and unemployment over 7 per cent; in this case, unemployment was treated as a coincident indicator, which it sometimes appears to be. As we noted in Chapter 4, there was a financial panic at this time (in October 1857) that began in the United States. There was also a financial panic in May 1866, and in 1866 real GNP declined and so did investment, rather dramatically. We are designating this a recession year, in rough agreement with the literature on the foregoing numbers and on the behavior of unemployment (in 1867); this is an example of using unemployment as a lagging indicator. The year 1867 gave us a problem since GNP grew that year (1.37 per cent), but the lagging unemployment indicator and all of the other contemporaneous indicators clearly signaled a recession. Again this conclusion is in agreement with the literature. These two events, though, mark the end of the 'financial panic – recession' syndrome that occurs much more frequently in the explanations of cycles in other countries at this time.

In 1872 and 1873 there were signs of recession in the GNP figures, especially with zero growth in 1873. Only investment, of the other indicators, showed recession, although industrial production also grew rather slowly that year. In any case, difficulties were reported in most of the other countries in our study, and the United States suffered a financial panic along with the collapse of its railroad boom at this time. Indeed, indicating the international dimensions of this event, the real export figures decline (in 1873). The year 1874, though, is too good to indicate as one of recession, and we believe the same can be said for 1875 and 1876. Possibly the next downturn started in 1877, but the evidence for designating that year a recession year from the coincident indicators was not convincing. The year 1878, at least, had significant unemployment and a drop in all of the other indicators (except GNP). There was a financial panic in the countryside in 1878, and a much publicized failure of the City of Glasgow Bank in that year, but there was no general panic (and none in London). The year 1879, though, was also a clear case. Unemployment continued high after this event, as it frequently does in this period, again fulfilling its role as coincident indicator.

At least some of the reference cycle literature generally finds a turning point for the next recession in 1883, and we think this is a likely date. We have designated 1884, 1885 and 1886 as recession years, and, from the data, this appears to be the most serious and longest-lived event in this period. While GNP growth is stagnant at this time, taking the three years as a whole, we note that unemployment was high for four years (again showing a lagging pattern in 1889). The other indicators also offered considerable support for this choice. This recession was arguably the worst of the period, but it has no strongly certified causes other than that of a collapse of an investment boom.

In 1892 and 1893 there are very strong signs of recession from all of the indicators (except investment in 1892). The year 1894 is such a strong year in all but the lagging indicator that it is clearly not a year of recession, although part of it could have been, which is how one might interpret the designation in the reference cycle literature. There were financial panics in other countries at this time (including the United States), and most countries had recessions at this time; signs of an international crisis occur in the export figures for the United Kingdom, which are very bad for the three year period from 1891–1893. This is possibly the clearest example of an export-led recession in the period, especially in view of the failure of other indicators to provide any assistance in explaining the event.

The years 1902 and 1903 show small declines in real GNP and here we have used the fall in GNP, as well as the weak performance of the coincident indicators for our designation. The year 1904 could also have been included, but we feel GNP growth is just too rapid for a recession. Clearly the lower turning point of the 1902–03 downturn is sometime in 1904, while the previous upper turning point may well be in 1901, as at least some of the literature suggests. International events are again suggested for this episode, although the end of the Boer War (in 1902) is sometimes mentioned. There is a decline in exports in 1901, but it is a modest one; more convincing, for the international explanation, is simply the fact that many other countries had recessions at this point. Finally, 1908 is a clear case in all respects, with unemployment performing clearly as a lagging indicator.

The literature for U.K. cycles is too large for us to condense to fit the small space we have available, but we can certainly attempt to characterize it. One thing that immediately strikes one is that the cycles are relatively long *in the literature* on the United Kingdom. To convey this information, we have compiled a subset of the cyclical datings from two of the better-known sources in the literature, in Table 12.5. While the methodology differs across these efforts, as we shall indicate, a somewhat longer cycle seems pretty well entrenched in this literature, with many downturns of three or more years indicated (in parentheses) in the table.

In the first two columns of the table we list the cycle dates established by Rostow in 1948; this study employs the 'reference cycle' approach of the National Bureau of Economic Research in the United States.[2] A more recent attempt, with even longer downturns, is by Capie and Mills (1991) who find different (earlier) dates for the peak in four of the five cycles they identify in 1871–1913.

One thing that immediately strikes us about these results is that the level of real GNP in the trough of the cycle is frequently higher than it was in the previous peak. Now this can happen because the table identifies 'turning points' rather than years of recession (so that the later year is typically a year of growth), but we think this does not resolve the problem since there are

Table 12.5   *Reference cycle turning points in the United Kingdom 1854–1913*

Rostow (1948)		Capie/Mills (1991)	
Peak	Trough	Peak	Trough
1854			
	1855 (1)		
1857			
	1858 (1)		
1860			
	1862 (2)		
1866			
	1868 (2)		
1873		1871	
	1879 (5)		1879 (8)
1883		1882	
	1886 (3)		1886 (4)
1890		1889	
	1894 (4)		1893 (4)
1900		1899	
	1904 (4)		1904 (5)
1907		1907	
	1908 (1)		1908 (1)
1913			

years of substantial growth *within* most of the recessions identified in Table 12.5. For the long 'recession' in the 1870s, for example, the economy grew substantially, at modest unemployment, in 1874, 1875 and 1876. While the 1883 to 1886 downturn seems reasonable (in the reference cycles of Rostow), the Capie and Mills determination, covering 1882 to 1886, is for a period showing some growth (at 4.6 per cent). The depression from 1890 to 1894 also shows substantial growth in real GNP (of 6.7 per cent) as does the alternative dating of 1889 to 1893 (of 2.8 per cent). The problem, again, is that 1891 was a year of rapid growth. Finally, the identified recession from either 1899 or 1900 to 1904 has to deal with the problem that the only years of declining GNP in this period are 1902 and 1903. In sum, while the turning points in the literature seem well established, we believe there are both contractions and expansions within these depressions (at least in the sense we would use the term today).

There is also the idea of a Great Depression in Europe between 1873 and 1896. If by 'depression' is meant 'stagnation', then this does occur, but not in the United Kingdom, although this was once thought to be the case. (See Saul (1985) and Capie, Mills and Wood (1991) for recent discussions.) The problem is, basically, that output figures do not show such a result, as already discussed in the text. Similarly, the popular idea of a Great Victorian Boom, running from 1850 to 1873, has run into difficulties, as explained in general terms by Church (1975) and in terms of a new industrial production index by Crafts, Leybourne and Mills (1989). The basic problem is the failure to find broad data that make this period look very different from either an immediately earlier or an immediately later period.

The upshot of all this is that the shocks appear to come from four sources: international, where the contact is through both the financial and the commodities markets; domestic financial disruptions (at least early on); special cases (e.g. war or its abrupt end) and lower investment in the classic sense of the term. All of this suggests that a single-theory methodology would not work particularly well in the British case, at least over the entire period.

France

In Table 12.6 we show the years that we believe indicate recessions in the French economy. There are 25 such years (out of the 63 possible) which indicates a higher frequency of recessions than in the United Kingdom. A major reason for this is that the much more agricultural French economy received some massive agricultural shocks, mostly in the form of large declines in agricultural product; in fact, for every downturn except those noted with an asterisk in the table, the agricultural decline was larger (in percentage) than the decline in real GDP. It is also noticeable that most of the really large swings in agriculture occurred before 1880, with the exception being the unusual event in 1910. The 1910 recession, of agricultural origin, was the last of its type in French history. Nothing like this happened in the United Kingdom during this period.

We have five indicators of French cycles available in Table 12.6, but we lack unemployment data. Unfortunately, the French data on investment growth are nominal, which makes them considerably less useful, depending on what was happening to the prices of investment goods, than the British figures. What we have done, bearing in mind that the agricultural contribution is already embedded in the real GDP figures, is use industrial production, real imports and nominal investment as indicators of the cycle. The years with substantial declines in GDP cannot be ignored, of course, and many of the years with declines in at least three of the four indicators, similarly, would seem to be clear cases. The latter are 1851, 1865, 1878, 1893, 1895, 1901,

Table 12.6   Business cycle indicators for France – growth rates

	GDP	Industrial Production	Imports	Investment	Agricultural Production
1851	−1.67	−1.23	−2.44	9.07	−3.09
1853	−8.25	7.60	3.47	33.70	−19.35
1855	−2.80	7.08	17.03	13.26	−8.04
1859	−10.04	−2.73	4.87	−11.78	−15.55
1861	−3.58	10.13	26.65	5.94	−12.86
1865	−2.51	−0.51	11.01	−0.30	−5.44
1867	−5.24	1.58	10.27	−1.39	−13.27
1870	−7.79	−17.22	−11.79	−40.10	−5.48*
1871	−4.77	−6.98	18.16	−28.99	−5.55*
1873	−7.39	−1.10	−0.42	6.48	−14.06
1876	−8.45	0.81	11.25	6.06	−18.81
1878	−1.27	−0.58	21.41	−8.64	−3.37
1879	−6.44	0.58	12.09	11.54	−16.05
1883	0.29	−0.79	3.20	−10.64	0.47*
1884	−1.16	−3.38	−1.55	−10.52	0.12*
1885	−1.76	−3.84	−4.05	−19.40	−1.55*
1886	1.61	5.63	7.02	−19.57	−2.31*
1893	1.68	−0.55	−7.25	−5.23	3.54*
1895	−2.12	−1.74	−1.11	6.34	−4.80
1900	−1.10	−8.40	−2.34	11.14	5.49*
1901	−1.57	1.44	−3.14	−15.05	−5.80
1902	−1.71	−0.84	1.63	−16.23	−4.74
1904	0.78	−2.95	−4.35	−8.68	5.31*
1908	−0.51	−1.30	−2.21	3.87	−0.67
1910	−6.26	−2.88	7.15	22.00	−16.84

Sources: GDP and imports are from Mitchell (1978, 1992); agricultural and industrial production are from Toutain (1987); investment is from Levy-Leboyeur and Bourguignon (1990)

1902, 1904 and 1908. In 1893 and 1904, in this set, real GDP actually increased, so this is far from a certain designation. Finally, 1855, 1861 and 1897 remain undecided in our view, although we are inclined to treat the first two, at least, as years of recession on the basis of the GDP figures alone.

There is a literature on the Great Depression in France for this period. Price (1981, p. 225) takes this view: 'Along with other industrialising countries, France experienced a long period of economic depression and crisis. The period c.1880–c.1914 is characterised by this ...'. Note that this is not the same timing as in other countries (it is usually 1873–1896). Also note that in 1913, French real GDP was 75 per cent higher than it was in 1880! Cameron (1961) also refers to a Great Depression in France, but his runs from the peak in 1882 to the recovery in 1897–8. He allows that there was a temporary recovery in 1887–9, but that financial disruption, industrial stagnation and a stagnant international trade were the principal agents of this depression. Even so, we note that GDP in the recession year of 1897 was 18 per cent above GDP in 1882 (and 21.5 per cent above 1885, a recession year in our tabulation above). Again we would argue that these long periods are punctuated by shorter cycles.

The literature on French cycles makes much of the financial crises that sometimes accompanied these events, and these have a partly international flavor. The contractions of the 1850s and 1860s all show very sharp agricultural declines and two of these years (1853 and 1861) actually exhibit perversely strong gains in the industrial sector. Henderson (1961) locates a recession in 1863–4, perhaps related to trade difficulties brought on by the American Civil War; below, we will argue that 1865 is a better choice for this event, at least in the annual data. The decline in 1867 was coincident with the collapse of the Crédit Mobilier and Henderson refers to this as a commercial crisis that severely affected railroad construction, but there was also a harvest failure at this time. According to Price (1981), this is the last of the general agriculturally-induced downturns in this period.

International events are more important – and agricultural events less so – as we consider the last forty years of the data. The military disaster in 1870 produced considerable financial pressure (including a sizeable indemnity) and thus the industrial collapse of 1870–1 hardly needs further explanation. The international financial crisis of 1873 does not seem as important in France as the agricultural decline of that year (of 13.1 per cent); nevertheless, that was a year of recession in France. The sharp downturns in 1876 and 1878–9 seem agricultural, primarily, although Levy-Leboyer and Bourguingon (1990) note that the investment market 'toppled' in 1876, suggesting that they believe a financial event might have precipitated the first of these downturns. Henderson (1961) notes that there were railroad failures in 1878 as well as a failure of the grain harvest (and the dreaded phylloxera!). From 1878, there was apparently a financial and speculative boom – as well as a rather steady industrial expansion. Another financial collapse began with bank failure in January 1882; this distress is associated with a recession in 1883–5 that probably began in 1882. The expansion itself may have got out of hand (in the traditional over-investment sense); evidence for this exists in the rise of investment as a percentage of nominal GDP to 9.1 per cent in 1882, and then an abrupt decline to 6.3 per cent, thereafter. In fact, these events occurred alongside an international financial crisis that 'lastingly weakened the Banque de France and brought about the collapse of the main banks in the Lyons market in January 1882' (Levy-Leboyer and Bourguignon, 1990, p. 83; and Henderson, 1961). As if this were not enough to think about, Caron (1979) and Marczewski (1988) argue that sharpened international competition in the agricultural markets (especially floods of American and Russian wheat) also undermined the French agricultural sector. That is, 1884 provides a peak in agricultural output so that the decline of agricultural production in 1885 helped prolong that particular recession.

The international financial crises of the 1890s seem to have bypassed France and, in particular, French downturns in the period (in 1893 and 1895) were relatively mild ones. An industrial decline in 1900 did contribute to a general decline (the agricultural contribution here was also considerable) but we note that quite a few other economies were in a recession at this time. Recessions in 1904 and 1908 are also echoed around the world, but 1910 seems to be specific to the French economy. The last cited was a full-blown agricultural event, however, the last of its kind in modern French history.

We conclude that while the detailed evidence suggests that the French shared in world cycles for many of these events – and the industrial sector exhibits an increasing influence – a largely independent agricultural cycle is still a major part of the French cyclical experience even at the end of the period. War was also important in the French case, and mention is often made of the influence of foreign competition, especially in the 1880s. As we will see later in this section, the French are a lot like the Italians in having their cycles so related to agricultural events.

Germany

In Table 12.7 we show complete data for four indicators of German business recessions for the years we think that such a designation is warranted. There are 18 years out of the possible 63 years that we reviewed, beginning in 1851. This is slightly more than one out of four years that the German economy was in recession. Most of the years selected showed declines in real NNP; indeed *all* of the years showing declines in real NNP are shown in Table 12.7.

It is easy to see recessions in 1853 and 1855 just on the basis of the NNP growth rates. In 1853, both industrial production and investment declined sharply; in 1855, however, industrial production actually increased; the culprit in that recession was an agricultural collapse (agricultural income and employment both fell sharply that year); they also fell in 1853, for that

Table 12.7 Business cycle indicators for Germany, growth rates of the data, 1851–1913

	NNP	Industrial Production	Import	Investment	Agricultural Income	Employment	Unemployment Rate (%)
1853	-4.51	-1.01		-77.32	-1.77		
1855	-6.06	3.05		-91.09	-6.74		
1857	2.50	8.70		-56.80	5.06		
1861	-4.52	0.00		-54.18	-6.98		
1867	0.01	0.00		-31.08	-2.85		
1869	-5.95	5.41		-68.88	-4.11		
1873	3.26	8.00		-14.06	1.41		
1875	-1.16	0.00		-21.30	-0.66		
1876	-0.86	3.64		6.77	-3.64		
1877	-0.89	-3.64		-20.51	-0.60		
1879	-2.84	-3.64		-23.84	-6.87		
1880	-2.95	-3.77		2.17	-0.02		
1882	-0.84	0.00	9.34	-2.34	2.64	0.43	
1891	-3.42	2.47	0.32	-33.40	-6.20	1.07	4.20
1894	-1.35	4.55	4.83	-9.51	-1.36	0.50	3.30
1900	-1.07	5.04	-2.65	-12.01	3.37	1.44	2.25
1901	-0.74	-3.33	1.88	-17.60	-6.06	1.84	6.95
1908	0.49	-1.27	-5.72	-25.13	5.24	0.27	2.90
						0.65	

Sources: NNP, industrial production, imports and investment are from Mitchell (1978, 1992); all other data are from Hoffmann (1965).

328

matter. We believe the literature (see below) has established the existence of a recession in 1857 as well, although it may have lasted less than a year. The next significant decline in NNP was in 1861; that year investment also fell sharply while industrial production was level; agriculture was also important in this event, with agricultural income falling 6.74 per cent (agricultural employment that year was slightly up, though). NNP growth was slow in 1864 and industrial production was stagnant (and industrial employment fell slightly); agriculture expanded in 1864, however. The conclusion we draw about these early cycles is that they appear to be dominated by events in the agricultural sector, whether due to domestic scarcity or foreign abundance.

In the 1870s, most countries experienced slow growth, especially after 1873, and some accounts for some countries show an extremely long contraction running from 1873–4 to 1878–9. This is also discernible in the German NNP data, with 1875, 1876, 1877 and 1879 all showing declines. Industrial production shows somewhat the same pattern, with significant declines in 1877 and 1879. Actually, both series declined sharply in 1879 and 1880. The investment figures provided in Table 12.7 show sharp declines in 1873, 1875, 1877, and 1879. The year 1879 clearly was a difficult one by all standards. Note that one can see a dampening of the amplitude of German cycles in this period, compared to the 1851–1870 period.

There appears to have been a mild downturn in Germany in 1882, in NNP; this downturn is echoed in the production and investment figures in Table 12.7, as well. In 1885 there was a sharp drop in imports, but all of the other figures were up strongly that year, and the next overall downturn actually was not until 1891. In 1891, when NNP fell 3.41 per cent, we see a rise in industrial production, but a sharp decline in investment and a rise in unemployment to 4.20 per cent (from 2.4 per cent the previous year). The proximate cause here is once again agricultural, although the investment swing is also important; in this year agricultural incomes fell by 6.01 per cent.[3] The year 1894 also shows a recession rather clearly, using unemployment, investment and NNP data as the basis for this judgment.

NNP declined in 1900 and 1901, while unemployment exceeded 3 per cent in 1901 and 1902; if the latter is playing the role of a lagging indicator, then this suggests that 1900 and 1901 are recession years. In 1900, industrial production was up sharply, while investment and imports were down; since agricultural incomes were also up, it isn't obvious which sector led the way in this particular event. It is, however, a sharp enough decline to be recorded as a recession. The year 1901 shows a general decline as suggested by several series. The year 1908, when NNP actually rose a little, seems a good bet for a short recession, since unemployment was up significantly over the previous year. This year also showed declines in all of the other figures that appear in

Table 12.7. We are listing it as a recession year in spite of the slight growth in GNP, somewhat tentatively.

By and large, the German literature agrees with our quantitative description of German cycles, but there are some differences to consider. We begin with the detailed survey of the German economy in this period by Kitchen (1978). Kitchen identifies the period 1857 to 1861 as a depression and emphasizes that it was international in scope, having begun (possibly) in the American agricultural sector, where a production boom in 1857 produced falling prices worldwide. He argues that domestic (German) overinvestment in the boom from 1850 to 1857 produced an overheated (p. 96), undercapitalized economy that was vulnerable to shocks. Henderson (1975) agrees and singles out the recession in the United States as the shock in this case. The cause, he says, was a bumper wheat crop. In Germany, then, it was the export-import firms and their banks that were hardest hit. However, Kitchen's claim for a four-year recession seems wrong, on the evidence, for the only year in which real net national product declined in the 'depression' was in 1861; indeed, real net national product was 9.8 per cent *higher* in 1861 than it was in 1857, but it is certainly true that real investment fell sharply in 1857, more than recovered by 1860, and then fell sharply again in 1861. We suspect this might be two cyclical events, with the more serious recession occurring in 1861.

Kitchen notes that there was a financial panic in 1866, partly caused by unease concerning the war between Prussia and Austria. There was, in fact, a stock market crash in that year, and there were falling prices in some sectors, but the fact is that in 1866 and 1867, real NNP *rose*. Indeed, a failure of the harvest was the principal reason for the very slow growth of the German economy at this time, although the war (and what Henderson (1975) describes as a civil war in June 1867) surely took a toll. Henderson does not mention a recession here, however.

From 1870 to 1873, Kitchen argues, another investment boom occurred, with an accompanying expansion of the banking sector (Borchardt (1976), says roughly the same thing). The crash in 1873, to Kitchen, ushers in the Great Depression, the first signs of which were price declines and the collapse of the stock market in Vienna in May 1873. Henderson argues that the collapse was of a 'speculative mania' that was partly based on the easy finance that resulted from the large French indemnity payments. He calls it (p. 164) 'a wild orgy of speculation'. By the end of 1874, the iron trade was in trouble and the difficulties for the German economy continued even through 1880, says Kitchen. Here it is worth noting that NNP in 1880 was 4.1 per cent higher than it was in 1873 (the peak!). But it is certainly likely that 1875, 1877, 1879 and 1880 were years of recession (in terms of declines in real NNP). Possibly we could agree on the proposition that the period from 1873 to 1880 was one of stagnation for Germany, as it was for quite a few countries worldwide in this period but, contrary to Kitchen's implication and Borchardt's (1976) explicit claim to the contrary, the stagnation was over after 1880, with only mild downturns in 1891 and 1894. Finally, Kitchen describes a recession that ran from 1901 to 1903/4. This event he appears to attribute to financial market difficulties. We note, yet again, that the real NNP of Germany (as measured by Hoffmann, of course) was 11 per cent higher in 1903 than it was in 1901. Indeed, going solely by real NNP, the period of 1898–1902 is more a period of stagnation, again, although we argue that 1900 and 1901 were the actual recession years in this period.

As already noted, our review yields 18 years of decline in the 63 possible in Germany, which is fewer recessions than shown in the French case. We also note that agriculture is actually more dominant in the German case than might have been expected in view of the strength of industrial growth in Germany throughout the period. That is, the downturns in 1855, 1861, 1869 and 1891 were all fairly severe and in all but one of these industrial activity actually expanded rapidly, as revealed by the percentage changes in the industrial production index, while agricultural production invariably declined in these recession years. But Germany shared many of its cycles with the United Kingdom and France, a fact that we will document later in this chapter.

Italy

To begin, as with the other countries, we will look at the downturns in the Italian real GNP data of this period. There are, indeed, numerous downturns in these data, with 17 of the 52 possible years showing recessions in GNP – meaning that the typical pattern was roughly for one lean year to be followed by two years of growth. This is shown in the first column of Table 12.8. While the more severe downturns were scattered over the entire period, there is a slight tendency for the Italian business cycles actually to get worse over the period. This is a pattern unlike that in the three other European countries we have looked at so far.

In Table 12.8 we list five cyclical indicators for Italy for the 1861 to 1913 period, although the obvious smoothing of the production index and the rather large fluctuations of the real investment figures suggest that there might be problems with the data. There are quite a few downturns in the annual real GNP figures, but not all of these are echoed in the other indicators. Using the GNP figures mainly, there appear to be major downturns in 1867, 1881, 1888–9, 1892, 1897 and 1910. On the basis of the figures provided by ISTAT (1957), there were substantial agricultural declines in 1881 (20 per cent), 1888–9 (11 per cent), 1892 (10 per cent), 1897 (14 per cent) and 1910 (17 per cent). Some

Table 12.8   Business cycle indicators for Italy, growth rates of the data,
1851–1913

	GNP	Industrial Production	Imports	Investment	Agricultural Production
1863	−1.86	0.00	12.83	−16.99	−3.55
1867	−8.45	5.26	1.21	−27.16	0.16
1870	−0.58	4.88	−3.55	−26.10	−0.71
1872	−0.58	2.35	12.52	−1.89	−2.84
1874	−0.82	2.20	2.92	−33.64	−1.40
1876	−0.89	0.00	11.10	−37.08	−2.93
1878	0.06	0.00	−4.02	2.55	−1.62
1881	−5.66	7.28	11.06	−84.32	−20.46
1883	−0.93	6.35	11.37	−19.69	−5.21
1888	−3.39	0.00	−32.86	−10.94	−2.19
1889	−3.57	−2.30	11.23	−49.10	−8.96
1892	−4.84	−5.64	9.08	−46.07	−10.07
1894	−0.79	5.41	−5.45	−32.88	−8.02
1897	−3.93	3.73	2.99	−56.58	−13.56
1902	−2.13	2.93	3.68	−32.86	−9.96
1904	−0.34	5.17	8.09	−11.51	−3.29
1908	−2.11	13.06	3.81	−23.43	−6.52
1910	−7.37	3.86	4.10	−34.08	−17.31

Sources: GNP is from Fratianni and Spinelli (1984); investment and agricultural production are from ISTAT (1957); industrial production is from Mitchell (1978, 1992).

of this was related to the tariff war with France (1888–1898), but in any case, the agricultural nature of most of these severe declines seems well established. There are also recession–level declines of GNP in 1863 (1.86 per cent), 1902 (2.13 per cent) and 1908 (2.11 per cent) and there is some support from the investment figures for these events; again, agricultural production declined in each of these years (4 per cent, 10 per cent and 7 per cent, respectively). We can add 1870 and 1894 to the list, since four of the five indicators were down in these years. We also note that 1872, 1874, 1876, 1878, 1883 and 1904 may well represent milder recessions.

We have remarked in previous sub-sections on theories of long waves and of a Great Depression in the last quarter of the nineteenth century, and now it is time to do the same for Italy. Gerschenkron (1962), basing his work mostly on industrial figures, argues that long cycles dominated short ones in this period. For the period 1881 to 1913, he identifies only one cycle, with 1881–88 and 1896–1913 being periods of growth and the downturn being 1888–96 (he actually calls it a period of stagnation). He does, however, identify mild downturns (and upturns) in several years within his long wave. Another writer favoring a long cycle (a 'Kuznets cycle') in construction, migration and capital flows at least, is Fenoaltea (1988). In his view, this cycle had peaks in the 1870s, late 1880s and just before World War I. While his explanation favors international factors (resource flows), it is worth noting that neither Gerschenkron nor Fenoaltea refer to the overall business cycle exactly.

An early and influential discussion of Italian downturns is by Clough (1964). He identifies an agricultural crisis in 1853–4 and what he calls 'deep depressions' in 1865–6, 1874–9, 1888–93 and 1906–8.[4] The 1865–6 event he regards as having originated in America. He mentions the recovery of the cotton industry and the fall of American demand because of demobilization from the Civil War; this scenario, he says, coincided with a peak in railroad construction in Italy and with a widespread over-extension of credit there. In fact, there was a banking panic in 1866, and we can see the outlines of a recession in 1867 (preceded by a sharp decline of imports in 1866). Thus, it is likely that the event began in 1866 and that 1867 is the year of recession; it is also likely that the causes mentioned by Clough were an important part of the story. Clough refers, next, to a 'Western Civilization-wide economic crisis which began in 1873' that hit Italy in 1874. This event, too, was international in scope (originating, possibly, in U.S. railroads), although Toniolo (1990) suggests that it started with a financial crisis in Berlin. While Clough has the depression lasting the entire period, we feel that the time is really one of stagnation (since real GNP declined in only two of the five years). Indeed, real GNP in 1879, in the trough, was 1 per cent higher than in 1874, the peak!

Clough refers to another deep depression (or crisis) from 1888 to 1893 that he believes originated in the tariff war with France that ran from 1888 to 1898. Cafagna (1976, p. 294) says 'The years between 1889 and 1896 were the darkest years of the great depression in the international sphere and bore especially heavily on the Italian economy'. He also discusses the banking crisis, which, he says, began in 1889. Indeed, the loss of both exports and imports (look at the disastrous import figures for 1888 in Table 12.8) appear to have undermined the Italian banking structure and produced, as a result, the 1893–4 crisis in banking that resulted in a major overhaul of the banking system (see Chapter 11). Again Clough mentions the over-extension of credit and investment in non-profitable enterprises by the banks, and there was (Zamagni, 1993) a withdrawal of foreign capital that led to a drain of gold reserves. In fact, the numbers in Table 12.8 support the idea of recessions in 1888–9, 1892 and 1894, and growth was quite modest in 1891. But we again note that real GNP in 1894 (the trough) was larger than in 1887 (the peak). Luzzato (1963), as described by Toniolo (1990), refers to the period from 1884 to 1894 as the 'blackest' for the new Italian Kingdom in this period, but Toniolo's discussion of the numbers follows ours, essentially; he says (p. 87), 'if we accept the existing estimates, it is likely that the 'blackest years' were not seen as such by the great mass of Italians'. Toniolo also notes, correctly we feel, that the entire period from 1861 to 1896 shows no appreciable growth in per capita Gross Domestic Product in Italy. Thus one might refer to this period as the Great Stagnation. The stagnation, then, appears to have lasted longer in Italy than in the other countries we have examined. Quite possibly this is just because the Italian economy was more agricultural than the others in this period; in general, these were not good years for European agriculture.

Clough, finally, identifies 1907 and 1908 as a depression, although he does not indicate what the cause might be. Toniolo (1990), though, mentions an investment boom that had a temporary interruption in those years; cotton, machine tools and machinery stand out in his summary. He also mentions a stock market collapse in 1906 and a general financial crisis in 1907. Clough, in turn, regards the declines in real national income in 1897, 1902, 1908 and 1910 as slight. These are also years we will designate as ones of recession below (with real GNP declining by more than 2 per cent in each case). It seems, then, that Clough is emphasizing downturns that were international in scope, as well as ones that feature a domestic financial aspect. This somewhat exaggerates Italy's place in the international cycle, in our opinion; we also think it overly emphasizes the influence of financial problems. However, we do not disagree in substance with Clough's determination of the dates of Italian cycles, putting aside his belief in longer cycles than we can see.

Italy, then, shows an international dimension to its cycles, but this differs from the countries we have been studying to this point in being tied somewhat more to international agricultural events. Furthermore, Italy does not appear to show either fewer or less severe cycles over the period and this, too, we attribute to the stronger influence of the agricultural sector. There are occasional problems in the financial sector, as our review of the literature suggests, and some of this may be related to Italy's part-time participation in the gold standard in the period, but for the most part, in Italy it seems that financial collapse followed agricultural disarray, rather than the converse.

Sweden

The last of the industrial economies that we plan to treat as a separate case is Sweden. Sweden is unusual in having the most rapid per capita growth of any of these countries in the late nineteenth and early twentieth centuries. Sweden in 1850 was dominated by its agricultural sector, but by 1910 the industrial sector passed it (as a percentage of GDP), and was moving very rapidly in terms of its relative contribution to national product. Sweden does not show the cyclical patterns of other countries in its real GDP series, partly because of the rapid growth rate and perhaps, no doubt, partly because of the smoothing of the data (see Sheffrin, 1988). In any case, we exhibit the Swedish indicators in Table 12.9.

Table 12.9 Business cycle indicators for Sweden, growth rates of the data, 1851–1913

	GDP	Industrial Production	Imports	Investment	Agricultural Production
1868	−5.55	10.54	−2.72	−44.35	−12.93
1875	−1.98	4.26	−11.86	8.05	−5.64
1878	−0.36	−4.08	−19.11	−10.18	−3.25
1887	−1.43	6.06	2.38	−29.19	−2.57
1901	−1.11	2.90	−11.03	−4.93	2.24
1908	0.39	−2.20	−14.11	−12.58	3.42

Sources: GDP, investment and agricultural production are from Krantz and Nilsson (1975); all other data are from Mitchell (1978, 1992).

The literature on the Swedish cycle tends to concentrate on the role of export fluctuations in temporarily undermining the Swedish economy; this seems appropriate in view of the importance of exports to Sweden's rate of growth. The literature also emphasizes the fact that Sweden's downturns throughout the period are tied to the international cycle, as might be anticipated. Heckscher (1963), for instance, argues that this begins with the recession of 1857 and, while smaller in amplitude (in Sweden), Sweden is generally not omitted from the 'global' recessions. He specifically mentions the collapse of export markets that deal in industrial materials (iron ore and timber, presumably). The banking system, he feels, weathered these storms very well, perhaps because the downturns were so mild.

Jorberg (1961) compiles a set of reference cycles for Sweden based, he says, on the examination of between 96 and 180 individual series, some monthly. He establishes lower turning points in 1869, 1879, 1887, 1893, 1901 and 1909 but allows that the 1869 and 1893 dates could be set a year earlier on the basis of the annual data alone. Putting aside the trough in 1869, then, his reference cycles are as follows

Peak	Trough	Duration	Change in GDP
		(Peak to Trough)	
1875	1879	4 years	+12.4%
1884	1887	3	+ 1.1
1890	1893	3	+8.5
1900	1901	1	−1.1
1907	1909	2	+0.6

We have calculated the duration of the recessions in the tabulation assuming that the downturn in the cycle runs from (e.g.) mid-1875 to mid-1879. While Table 12.9 notes downturns in real domestic product in 1875 and 1878, 1887 and 1901, we think Jorberg's cycles are too long to fit the annual series. In particular, the annual figures from which those in Table 12.9 were derived show that Swedish real domestic product was generally higher at the trough than at the peak, as noted in the last column of the tabulation; the only exception is the 1-year recession at the turn of the century.

We do agree, however, that the emphasis of both Heckscher and Jorberg on the international origins of Sweden's downturns seems largely correct. For one thing, as we note below, the years of Sweden's cycles are the same as those of the majority of the major industrial economies in this period, with the exception of the downturn in 1868. For another, Sweden's real exports seem an unusually volatile coincident indicator of the cycle, as the following suggests.[5]

Peak	Trough	Export Decline
	(Peak to Trough)	
1855	1858	60.7%
1867	1868	11.4
1874	1875	9.1
1877	1878	9.3
1885	1886	2.4
1900	1901	8.1
1907	1908	11.3

Thus, with the exception of 1885–6, these recession years are all years of substantial decline in real export volume. Note that iron ore exports (not shown) were particularly volatile in this period, declining 40 per cent in 1867, 80 per cent in 1876, 37 per cent in 1886 and 14 per cent in 1909.

The years of decline in real domestic product, in the 53 that are available, number only 6, and of these, only 1868 represents anything like a major downturn. Of the 6, only the declines in 1868 and 1875 are clearly recessions. In both of these events, agricultural production declined sharply – 12.9 per cent and 5.6 per cent respectively – as noted in the table. In fact, the agricultural sector dominated the overall cycle in four of six cases, while the industrial sector did so in only one, the very mild downturn in 1878.

Looking for overwhelming evidence of recession and recalling our discussion of the literature, we think that the following were the years of downturn in this period.

1857–8 1868 1875 1878 1887
1901 1908

We have selected most of these downturns as obvious from the GDP and indicator results, and have added 1908 because of the decisive declines of the three other indicators in Table 12.9 (and the very small growth in real GDP). Recall that these are annual numbers and that they are far from definitive, so that there very well could have been a recession in 1908. There are also two years that are doubtful, in our opinion. These are 1877, where there was a very small decline in GDP (but imports and investment grew) and 1909, in this case a year of small GDP growth, but with sharp declines in industrial production and investment. Finally, we note that 1857–8 should be added to our list of downturns, after reviewing the literature.

6. INTERNATIONAL DIMENSIONS OF CYCLES: FURTHER RESULTS

There are two remaining tasks in the analysis of the data bearing on the international cycle in this period. One of these is to draw together the cyclical results for the five countries we have studied in detail here and the other is to extend the results to the other (more peripheral) countries we have discussed in this study, insofar as the data can bear the load. We note that the latter task should not be expected to reveal much about the international cycle in this period, mainly because those other economies appear less integrated with the international economy than the ones just considered. In particular, while they could be expected to show some signs of the international cycle (as identified in the other results), they have their own cycles, often tied to events in their agricultural sectors.

For the five major economies analysed in detail, the data in Table 12.10 represent an attempt to line up the dates of downturn, as indicated by our earlier work. What we have done here is to attempt to locate periods in which most of these countries were in recession at approximately the same time. Within these periods, the years 1867–8, 1878–9, 1901–2 and 1908 stand out as representing the pan-European cycle, with the number of countries involved noted in a separate column. In our compilation, in any event, a good case could be made for two international downturns in the 1850s, one in the 1860s, and three in the 1870s. In the 1880s only one recession stands out and the same is true of the 1890s. There appear to be at least two international recessions in the first decade of the 20th century.

Table 12.10 *The international business cycle among five major European economies 1851–1913*

Date	Number	Countries
1853–4	3	France, Germany, Italy
1857–9	4	France, Germany, Sweden, U.K.
1867–8	5	France, Germany, Italy, Sweden, U.K.
1873–4	4	France, Germany, Italy, U.K.
1875–6	4	France, Germany, Italy, Sweden
1878–9	5	France, Germany, Italy, Sweden, U.K.
1882–4	4	France, Germany, Italy, U.K.
1893–4	4	France, Germany, Italy, U.K.
1901–2	5	France, Germany, Italy, Sweden, U.K.
1903–4	3	France, Italy, U.K.
1908	5	France, Germany, Italy, Sweden, U.K.

Several notes need to be added to this compilation. First, the period of 'stagnation' in Europe in the 1870s, stands out in this summary, with most countries in recession in each of the (arbitrary) 2-year periods between 1873 and 1879. Indeed, only Sweden had as few as two bad years out of the seven, and Germany was in recession for five years. Second, judged somewhat casually, it is easy to see how a believer in the international cycle might notice something like a 10-year cycle in the data. This would show recessions in at least four countries in 1857–9, 1867–8, 1873–9, 1882–4, 1893–4, 1901–2 and 1908. Only the twentieth century shows more than one event, counting 1873–9 as a single recession, as the literature is prone to do. These dates do encompass the downturns we feel were international in scope, but we must hasten to point out that individual countries experienced quite a few other downturns in the period that were not well coordinated internationally.

The way we are going to bring in the other countries in our sample is to take those with real national product declines that match recession years for the countries we have studied in detail. We do not have the space to do more than this, and we believe that this deals with an interesting question: is it possible to show that the international cycles (just identified) also affected the other (more peripheral) European countries? This exercise would establish an important dimension to the integration of the European economy in this period.

In Table 12.11 we list the growth rates of real national product for the six remaining countries in our sample. We do this only for the years that we have already identified for the five major countries that we have discussed in detail. The years listed on the left are groups of years in which the major countries generally showed some decline, as described in Table 12.10. While the table begins in 1853, we will begin our discussion in 1867–8, because that is the point at which we have data for at least five countries.

Counting the already identified recessions in which these peripheral countries also show declines in their national products after 1870, we see that Austria–Hungary, with six such events of any magnitude, seems most affected by the international cycle among these countries. Of the other countries, both Norway and Portugal show some reaction to international cycles and so does the Netherlands (in the twentieth century). On the other hand, Denmark shows little effect and Belgium, essentially, shows none.[6]

About these results, it should be emphasized that many of these countries have national products that are dominated by their agricultural sectors and so they might be expected to be out of phase with the industrial countries. Were we to try to identify cycles purely from the industrial production figures, as our work on industrial production indices above suggests, we would show much more integration (of industrial cycles). This conclusion makes an important point: Industrialization is one of the main mechanisms by which countries were brought into the European 'global' economy at this time (trade, capital flows and technology transfer are the others). Countries on the periphery were being brought into the European economy, but the signs of this in their overall product accounts are covered up by events in their large and relatively volatile agricultural sectors. We are not saying that there were not some integrating aspects to agricultural development, for there surely were. We are merely concentrating on the main forces that produced something we think was changing dramatically in Europe before 1914.

Table 12.11 The international business cycle among six other countries 1851–1913 (growth rates of national product)

Year	Aus./Hun.	Belgium	Denmark	Netherlands	Norway	Portugal
1853			−0.12			−20.67
1854			−0.96			−16.39
1857			0.04			21.01
1858			−6.43			11.55
1859			6.00			−10.97
1867		0.52	2.33		2.42	−1.22
1868	2.80	3.57	1.06		−0.16	7.53
1873	−8.63	0.66	2.97		2.39	2.21
1874	6.40	3.24	2.37		3.68	2.70
1875	0.33	−0.21	0.80		2.77	6.36
1876	−2.60	1.27	1.58		2.95	0.66
1878	16.38	2.87	1.52		−3.57	0.36
1879	−15.56	1.00	3.86		0.90	1.80
1882	18.20	3.33	9.87		−0.12	0.97
1883	−0.74	1.44	5.56		−0.37	4.25
1884	4.10	0.89	1.14		1.72	10.80
1893	0.49	1.50	2.31		2.65	−0.50
1894	3.47	1.48	1.59		0.60	−0.25
1901	0.03	0.90	1.70	−4.65	2.49	−1.02
1902	6.82	2.02	2.59	6.06	1.51	3.89
1903	−0.05	2.23	4.00	2.61	−0.58	−0.11
1904	−7.98	2.54	3.65	−1.96	0.17	−3.33
1908	−0.23	1.00	−0.06	2.87	3.16	1.69

Sources: Austria/Hungary – Komlos (1987); Belgium – Maddison (1991); Denmark – Hansen (1974); Netherlands – van Stuijvenberg and de Vrijer (1982); Norway – Mitchell (1978, 1992); Portugal – Molinas and Prados de la Escosura (1989).

7. CONCLUSIONS

There are at least four influences that we think lie behind the cyclical integration of the real sectors of the major economies in the late nineteenth century.

First, technological change in the production of basic commodities and manufactured goods and the growth of the transportation and communication networks provided the goods and the means of transporting them from one place to another; these factors are usually prerequisites for the growth of trade. Industrial production in all of these countries grew rapidly in this period; indeed, among the industrial products involved, coal, iron (and iron ore), textiles and crude steel stand out. Agricultural products also benefited from the same sort of improvements, and developments in international grain markets in particular are sometimes important in discussions of the business cycle in this period, as we have noted (especially in the 1880s).

Second, the growth in real incomes that was a result of the industrial revolution contributed to an increase in the demand for goods, many of which were not produced domestically. Between 1870 and 1910, real output per capita grew rapidly in most of these countries, and with it grew domestic demand. Though estimates of aggregate output become less reliable the further back one goes, recent calculations of earlier numbers suggest that these rates are considerably above those earlier in the century. We have discussed this elsewhere in this study.

Third, increases in the rate of capital accumulation facilitated the growth of output and real incomes; this new capital spilled across national borders. Taking some figures from Mitchell (1978), we note that the investment/output ratio (in real terms) often grew in this period. For Germany, the ratio went from 11.2 to 13.9 per cent; for Italy, from 7.8 to 14.4 per cent; and for Sweden, from 10.3 to 10.9 per cent. Only for the relatively mature economy of the United Kingdom did it decline (modestly). More directly to the point at hand, there was an unprecedented increase in foreign investment in these countries. Between 1870 and 1914, foreign investment by the United Kingdom grew from 4 to 7 per cent of gross national income; indeed, the three major European economies (of France, Germany and the United Kingdom) provided something like 75 per cent of the world's external investment over this period.

Finally, liberalization of the institutional arrangements for the exchange of goods and services was evident in the late nineteenth century. Though average tariff rates actually rose somewhat late in the century, and there were occasional tariff wars in the same period, tariffs were more normally employed as a means of raising government revenues than for protection. In fact, trade restrictions, quotas and tariffs as tools for the promotion of domestic industry were rare prior to the inter-war years (see Kenwood and Lougheed, 1983) except for the protection of the agricultural sector from the 1880s. With respect to the growth of trade itself, the ratio both of imports and exports to total output grew for most of the countries in our sample during the period (as discussed in Chapter 10). Perhaps more important, the largest trading partners of each of these countries were other European economies.[7]

In summary, we argue that because the period we have studied was marked by an integration of the real economies of the major economic powers in Western Europe, business cycles were similarly integrated. Though we have not offered much direct evidence concerning the mechanism for the transmission of specific supply or demand shocks between these countries, we hypothesize, being very general about it, that when there was a downturn in one country, it was passed on to others through price and quantity changes that were stimulated by either positive or negative supply or demand shocks. In any case, there was a thriving international economy in this period, and there was also an international real business cycle, at least among the largest players, by the late nineteenth century.

NOTES

1. Another coincident variable in modern studies of the business cycle is the level of *real investment*. We do not have as many of these series as we have for GNP and industrial production but the results still fit the pattern already revealed (see Craig and Fisher, 1997).
2. Friedman and Schwartz (1982) also use the NBER methodology in their dating (beginning in 1868). They only differ in listing the trough in 1893 instead of 1894.
3. Unemployment continued high; in fact it was not until 1896 that it dropped below 3 per cent. This pattern has a very modern sound to it, since we have often observed such behavior in the late twentieth century (and we saw this also in the U.K. data already discussed).
4. The outlines of Clough's short cycles between 1873 and 1896 are hard to see because of his evident belief in the existence of a Great Depression over that period. Like many early writers on the subject, he exhibits a tendency to confuse nominal with real events in this context.
5. There were also sharp declines in exports in 1860–1, 1880–1, 1893–4, 1897–8 and 1903–4. None of these appear to be associated with Swedish downturns, however. Note that we are thinking of exports as a potential causal factor here. Since they are (given imports) included in real domestic product, there is no need to list then in Table 12.9.
6. The latter result is not really credible. The problem is that there is only one year of decline in the entire run of Belgian data (in 1875).
7. For example, the United Kingdom and Germany were the two largest trading partners of France by 1910. The United Kingdom was the largest trading partner of Germany, and only Russia and the Austro-Hungarian empire had more trade with Germany than did France. After the United States, Germany and France were the largest trading partners of the United Kingdom.

13. Growth and cycles 1500–1913

1. INTRODUCTION

In this final chapter we consolidate our findings around the topics of growth and cycles. Because our presentation to this point has been conducted period-by-period and country-by-country, we have not been able to generate an overall view of the period from 1500 to 1914, an era which encompasses both 'early modern' and 'modern' times, after all. In the remainder of this volume, then, we draw together the threads presented in previous chapters, recalling the agenda that was set out in Chapter 1.

We address very general topics in Section 2. Specifically, we review our evidence concerning the economic development of Western Europe – that is, we review the political, social and broad economic characteristics of the remarkable changes that spread across Europe in these 413 years. Having done this, we again narrow our discussion to that of growth, in Section 3 and business cycles, in Section 4. In these two sections we document, from our earlier discussions, why we think both growth and cycles have a decidedly modern character, from the beginning of our story. This is not to say that growth rates then were as rapid as those now in this geographic area, but rather to say that in a fundamental economic sense, the *process* that drives these economies upward was essentially the same then as it is now. Cycles, also, have a modern tone to them, in amplitude and frequency. This is certainly not to say that the causes of cycles then are the same as now, but rather that the *processes* – of reaction to shock and transition – are not dramatically different. Section 5 contains some very brief concluding remarks.

2. DEVELOPMENT AND CHANGE IN WESTERN EUROPE

Europe of the early sixteenth century contained quite a few of what we think of as modern economic institutions. Markets were as global as possible, given the technology of shipping and costs of transacting, with overland and overseas travel as far as Asia and with an emerging transatlantic trade on the horizon. Men crowded themselves and their goods into sailing ships and sought their fortunes overseas, but by far the largest trade was local in character, involving the produce of the land and the town. Financial intermediation was available in 1500, and central banks were created in the following century, being first conceived for the purpose of facilitating and managing the Crown's finances. Roads existed throughout Europe, and ports were established, both on a scale more-or-less appropriate for the markets that existed. Private fortunes were made and lost in the traditional ways, and venture capital came from savers who were themselves either the owners of the venture or merely those who wished to share in the risks and returns, but not the burden of labor that went into speculative enterprises. Can anyone doubt that this paragraph would not also describe 1914, say from the perspective of the twenty-third century, save for the comment about central banking?

What were the broad changes then, that altered the economic landscape over this period? We think that the important changes that occurred were in all sectors of the economy and involved commerce, industry, agriculture and government. In the remainder of this section we will emphasize governments, because without nation-states based on the institution and protection of private property, it is unlikely that the West would have achieved anything like what it actually did achieve.

Take the monetary system as a case in point. From 1500, gold (and to a lesser extent silver) was the acknowledged basis of domestic money supplies, and European economies faced a constraint in the form of their inability to create additions to the monetary base (gold reserves) without aggressive mercantile policies. Thus, price levels were policed, in the long run, by the supplies of gold relative to the demands. If inflation (e.g. 1500–1618) or deflation (e.g. 1873–1896) occurred, it was because of an imbalance between the supply and demand for gold for monetary purposes, or because the governments of individual countries sought to achieve their objectives by abandoning gold and printing money (e.g. 1793–1815). Aside from the three episodes mentioned, there were no comparable global episodes of inflation or deflation, although there were plenty of countries that departed from the *de facto* standard at times. Thus the entire period we are studying has a very strong unifying characteristic: a metallic standard was the norm and, consequently, inflation rates normally were, in effect, mean-reverting around a value near zero. Earlier periods were like this, but those since 1914 have not been. Note that when countries began to sign onto the classical gold standard in a formal sense, existing practice became *de jure*. The heyday for this activity was between 1870 and 1914.

From our modern perspective, the arrival of central banks in the seventeenth century, particularly as they were required first of all in order to permit governments to raise funds for their projects, military and otherwise, might have been expected to produce general inflation from the outset. But such was the grip of the idea that currencies had to reflect the market value of gold or silver, that governments generally just dabbled in inflationary finance, always returning to the gold-backed alternative, usually at some pre-existing par, when possible. As time went on, of course, the financial industry developed new (and existing) products, such as bills of exchange, notes and bonds and, of course, currency and demand deposits. These devices lowered transactions costs, and thus were sought on both sides of the market, but both bills and currency came under heavy fire because of their apparent involvement in the many financial crises that emerged when these financial instruments became widespread. It was thought (by Adam Smith, for example) that if bills were drawn on real property and if currency were reasonably well backed by gold, then over-issue would be impossible. We think observers of this period, whether contemporary or modern, simply confused events caused by the collapse of speculative bubbles or by the effects of adverse selection, asymmetric information and moral hazard problems with the tendency of institutions to retain insufficient quantities of gold. In the event, governments generally took over the currency issue, without there being any obvious change in the frequency or severity of financial panics, and governments became increasingly firm in their control of the monetary base, mainly for the purpose of maintaining the external value of their currencies. This situation produced long-run stability of the price level, as we have already pointed out, although this was typically not the objective of the policy.

One good reason for starting our survey in 1500 is that by then quite a few European states were established in something resembling their modern forms. Having a nation-state of some durability, regardless of the ruling hierarchy, lent itself to the development of national objectives and national policies to achieve those objectives. Aside from the exchange rate policy already discussed, these objectives could not be described as 'macroeconomic' in any modern sense of that word, with a few exceptions, to be discussed in a moment. National governments were responsible for domestic security and justice, and for establishing and defending an international economic presence. These activities require real resources, of course, and the search for sources of revenue created interesting and sometimes long-lasting changes in the arsenal of fiscal weapons. Interestingly, the central bank, which in our time is the instrument of monetary policy, was one of those devices, although its use was constrained by the gold mentality of the time. What is most interesting about these early modern governments, we think, is that they controlled very close to the same percentage of GDP (3–7 per cent) for most of the period, reaching the upper-bound figure during times of war. Only as the twentieth century approached did we see the birth of the modern fiscal state, with some countries beginning social and even socialist schemes that, of course, required relatively larger expenditures.

We are a little less certain of the macroeconomic influence of some other developing characteristics of this era. Foremost among these is the general drift in the West toward more representative governments. We cannot really assert that just because one of the most democratic of governments, Great Britain, led the way in terms of economic development, that it follows *ipso facto* that broadening the political basis of nations necessarily improved their economic fortunes. Partly, our hesitation stems from the observation that it seems unlikely that economic agents would have substantially different opportunities in one regime than in another, aside from the scattered episodes when governments (such as the French with the Huguenots) shot themselves in the foot through persecution. After all, it is stability, security, and the protection of property that promote economic development, and these can be, and were, provided by a variety of governments. At the same time, if any important economic agents, such as laborers, are prevented from receiving their marginal products because of legal, social or political constraints, then such a system would be relatively inefficient. Such inefficiencies were surely smaller in 1914 than they were in 1500, but they were large enough in 1914 in the countries we are talking about to have inspired some very strong labor movements, with still unfinished agendas, at that date.

One aspect of public policy that is apparently both macroeconomic and geopolitical comes under the general heading of 'mercantilism'. Any government at any time will, by its nature, create rent-seeking opportunities that will attract the attention of economic agents. The idea here is that governments, in exchange for a share of the take, can easily be persuaded to create price controls, tariffs and subsidies, and to carve up markets to licensees who either pay for the service or who remit a percentage of the net returns. This was just as true in 1500 as in 1914 (or 1999), with the modern form being the protective tariff, a device that provides revenues to the firm, tax revenues and votes to the government, and wages to the workers, at the cost of manifest economic inefficiency. Modern governments (in 1914) were not 'residual claimants' in the sense that government officials directly profit from the activities of the government. In 1500, there were absolute monarchies, typically, in which case the crown, and anybody else related to the crown, was in fact a residual claimant. This transformation engineered a profound change in the nature of the economic rents created by governments, but the sort of rents created by mercantilist policies have not changed very much, involving, as we said, tariffs, quotas and the like. This picture, too, provides a continuity for our entire period.

Were there macroeconomic aspects to mercantilistic policy? Keynes thought so, and argued in the *General Theory* that in chronically underemployed economies like those of the pre-industrial revolution world, there was a deficiency of saving and hence considerable (probably disguised) unemployment. Mercantilist policies to enrich nations, thus, started with a correct manifesto and, indeed, some of their policies were applauded by Keynes, particularly the direct involvement by the government in private markets, and the tendency to attract gold in order to lower domestic interest rates.

However, our characterization of the entire period runs toward the interpretation that only during recessions did significant unemployment arise and then, depending upon the century in question, no stabilization policy was either feasible or desirable. Rather than being chronically underemployed, with inadequate saving, we think the history of the period shows that saving and employment were appropriate for the economies of the time. In other words, with slower productivity growth, higher transportation costs, poorer sources of information, lower human skills and narrower markets, the *equilibrium* growth rates of the sixteenth century would be less than those of the nineteenth century without reference to inadequate (but simply lower) savings rates. Indeed, in our view mercantilism had a role to play (albeit a small role) in that such policies surely did lower the risks of certain extremely risky activities, such as the global expansion of trade, the fruits of which were more apparent in the nineteenth century than they were in the sixteenth.

3. GROWTH RATES, 1500–1914

We can, of course, provide growth rates for most of the European countries in our sample, from the early to mid-nineteenth century. Some of these rates come from production indices; some come from estimates of (for example) gross domestic product, particularly at the end of the period; and some have significant gaps that we are unable to fill. The data for any period prior to 1750 simply do not exist, although there are estimates in the literature, if that is not misusing the word 'estimates'. This is not the place to apologize for our work or that of others on this subject, but to put down our best guesses as to growth rates, over the entire period, ignoring the source of our estimates which are discussed in earlier chapters. We will, though, return to the question of the accuracy of our estimates, since we should not produce estimates of an average growth rate without being as candid as possible about the associated variances.

In Table 13.1 we have collected our best guesses as to the growth rates in Western Europe, on a country-by-country basis. Here we divide the data into the three periods at which we have been looking: 1500–1750, 1750–1850 and 1850–1910. In the first set of figures we have used the population growth rate as the minimum and the rate of urbanization as the maximum. As can easily be verified, for all countries except Belgium, the latter is higher than the

Table 13.1 Annual (compounded) growth rates in Western Europe 1500–1914

Country	1500–1750 Minimum[a]	1500–1750 Maximum[b]	1750–1850 Minimum[a]	1750–1850 Urban	1850–1914 Minimum[a]	1850–1914 Actual[c]
Aus./Hung./Czech.	0.19	0.36				
Austria					0.79	1.94
Hungary					0.66	same
Belgium	0.24	0.15	0.53	0.78	0.87	1.52
France	0.15	0.29	0.52	0.64	0.17	2.61
Germany	0.17	0.29?	0.60	1.00	1.02	1.32
Italy	0.18	0.18	0.44	0.10	0.66	
Netherlands	0.28	0.36	0.19	−0.06	0.55	1.28
Portugal	0.29	0.35	0.43	−0.19	0.71	1.50
Scandinavia	0.28	0.70				
Denmark			0.55	0.08		
Norway			0.81	0.35		
Sweden			0.67	0.14		
Spain	0.10	0.16	0.45	0.11	0.71	2.74
Switzerland	0.32	0.37	0.60	0.56	0.48	1.45
United Kingdom	0.30	0.83	0.96	1.58	0.80	2.00

Notes:
[a] population growth rate.
[b] rate of urbanization.
[c] actual GDP growth rate.

former. We have argued that this suggests per capita growth in all countries except Belgium which, as we discussed earlier, is a special case.

Looking first at the period from 1500 to 1750, we find relatively rapid growth in (what became) the United Kingdom and in Scandinavia. The former is not surprising, while the latter may well be mainly the result of relatively rapid Swedish growth; after all, this is the period of the Swedish Empire. In the next set, at a real rate of growth of about one-third of 1 per cent, are the Dutch, the Portuguese, and the Swiss. Close behind, at roughly 0.25–0.30 per cent, are the French and the Germans. The Italians, Spanish and Belgians, in contrast, fall below even this range. We submit that none of this is unreasonable, as our survey of a considerable amount of other evidence suggests, although we would certainly not want to defend our 'maximum' rate of growth any further than that.

In the 1750 to 1850 period, our minimum growth rate (which is the population growth rate) still seems reasonable as a minimum, but for a number of countries there appears to be no good maximum rate. In any case, all we have, if we want to be consistent, is the rate of urbanization. It is probable that the countries that show the lowest urbanization rates – Italy, the Netherlands, Portugal, Spain and the Scandinavian countries – surely did grow more slowly than the countries with the highest urbanization rates – Belgium, France, Germany and the United Kingdom, where the industrial revolution was taking root. The Mediterranean countries in that list were also the victims of political shifts and in the move away from Mediterranean trade; they also had little more than a presence in industrialization in this period, although all were decidedly on their way (relatively speaking) by 1830 or so. Even so, we would clearly not want to use the rate of urbanization in this period as an actual measure of the overall growth rate, simply because it appears to be too slow, possibly, for any of the countries in the sample. Recall about this measure that, if the agricultural sector grows rapidly, as it was doing in this era of the 'agricultural revolution' (though that term has been used to characterize a number of eras), then urbanization figures would not correctly measure overall growth. Indeed, in many of these countries, agriculture was probably growing relatively rapidly, compared with industry and even commerce, and thus urbanization is a poor guide to progress. We think this is even a problem in the United Kingdom, where the agricultural sector was adding workers right up to 1850.

When we have real GDP data, as we do from 1850 to 1914, the third period we have featured in Table 13.1, we no longer need to guess at real rates of growth. By this time, Sweden and Germany were eclipsing the United Kingdom (in growth rates of real GDP), but every economy shows both accelerated growth (every country is over 1 per cent per year) and growth per capita. We no longer need a minimum growth rate for this period and have included the population growth rate merely to make the point about the real per capita growth rate (which is the difference between the two columns). While the rankings change as we move across the table, we note that the United Kingdom, France, Germany and even Austria–Hungary are generally near the top, while the Mediterranean countries are typically near the bottom. One could, therefore, generalize about this in an obvious way, bearing in mind that some other countries bounce around the rankings – notably Portugal, the Netherlands and Belgium – for both political and economic reasons.

We conclude, if it isn't obvious, that growth was endemic in this world and, for that matter, so was per capita growth, for some countries throughout the period and for others mainly between 1500 and 1750, and after 1850. Growth, therefore, is an important characteristic, if not a defining one, for the early modern and modern periods studied in this book. Our other conclusions about growth are country-specific and are discussed in other chapters.

4. THE BUSINESS CYCLE

We have adopted the shock-transmission theory of the business cycle for this study, and so we will begin this summary with a recapitulation of the theory. The general idea is that a shock (an unexpected event with serious repercussions) interrupts the general upward drift of economic output. We have avoided any involvement in currently fashionable theories, like the real business cycle theory, simply because the shocks in this period appear to be political, weather-related and sometimes financial, at least the shocks that we were able to identify. We are well aware of the fact that much of the literature focuses on the financial events, particularly when there are banking systems to blame, and we accept the warning of the real-business cycle point of view that many of these events are reactions rather than independent causes of the recessions in this period.

Financial panics and the like enter the story, then, as contributing factors in the transmission of shocks both to the economy and over time; however, we think the principal transmission mechanisms are put in place by economic agents as part of their optimizing strategy. The most important of these, then (1500) and now (1999), is probably what is known in the literature as 'consumption smoothing'. The general idea is that economic agents (consumers and firms) know that they live in a world where demand can dry up temporarily, for whatever reason. Accordingly, they prepare themselves for this by accumulating financial and real wealth, with some considerable part of this being either consumable or marketable. Portable human capital would also play a part in this effort. When the random event occurs, as it does for every country throughout this period and certainly in every decade as well – if not every five-year period – economic agents respond by drawing down their savings (real or financial) in order to smooth their consumption (or investment) expenditures. This action has the effect of bolstering current demand somewhat at the expense of future demand (if you dissave, you cannot consume as much in the future). Thus, current demand is lower because of the shock, and future demand is lower because some of the shock is eased by switching demand from the future to the present. We think this behavior is inevitable, rational and pervasive in the 1500 to 1914 period, with both the means to engage in it and the extent to which those means were exploited being significantly less at the beginning of the period than at the end.

Much of the modern literature since Keynes has also spoken of cumulative downward pressures on economies that occurs because falling effective demand breeds further falling effective demand as firms lay off workers. We think that this is a factor, of course, but we think there are strict limits to how far this can proceed (in this period) since (a) growth is endemic and (b) economic agents could not long exist in an inactive state in an agrarian economy in which 80 per cent or more of the labor force worked directly in the production of food and clothing. With endemic growth, economic agents would presumably be aware of it and would, consequently, expect the upward momentum to reassert itself after a relatively short period. It takes only a cursory knowledge of these cyclical events to realize that few of the downturns ever last more than two years throughout this period; economic agents would have this knowledge and they would have the incentive to exploit it. The academic literature, to be sure, speaks of very long downturns, some as long as a century, but we think this is a result of confusing growth with cycles, mis-measuring growth and, equally important, confusing nominal and real measures of growth.

Above, we mentioned financial factors in downturns and we need to say more about this issue, since financial factors loom so large in the literature. There were, in fact, famous financial collapses in this period that did not appear to be followed by (or even be associated with) downturns in real economic activity. A financial collapse, after all, merely affects the agents involved in the first place and, if they are speculators willingly taking risks, their losses do not translate into losses for the bulk of economic agents. Even in a financially diverse economy like the United States in 1987, we find that a catastrophic collapse of equity markets might well not produce a recession. Our modern estimates suggest that consumption might respond to a decline in stock prices by something like 2–4 per cent of the decline in stock prices. This is not zero, but is a small effect on consumption. In stock market crashes before 1914, those directly involved in the revaluation of their portfolio were generally the wealthy, and their propensity to consume was considerably less than that of the rest of their society. It would not be a presumption to argue that something like a 1–2 per cent effect would occur on consumption, an effect often too small to be counted on to produce a recession in and of itself

There were also waves of bank failures in the countries we are studying, and these became an important part of the economic landscape in some cases as early as 1750. By 1914 most countries had some form of institutional arrangement designed to ameliorate this source of instability, including defined policies of the central bank to operate as a lender of last resort. There was also a general movement in Western Europe toward concentrating the note issue in the central bank. It is well known that this did not stop the phenomenon and the reasons for this failure are equally familiar. It is certainly probable that occasionally a wave of bank failures was the first sign of a particular recession. More commonly, banks will fail when their customers fail, and when they do, other customers (their depositors) who were unable to withdraw their funds will also be liable to failure. Customers were understandably nervous about this possibility and so bank runs persisted beyond this period and indeed continue to this day whenever there is doubt concerning the ability of customers to extract their funds from the financial institution, or its insurers, in a timely way. The implication is that, as banking systems expanded as they did in this period, from virtually nothing to systems with hundreds of private banks, they became an increasingly important part of the transmission mechanism, often providing 'after-shocks' when they failed *en masse*. This, we feel, is what the history of this period tells us about the role of banks in the business cycle.

To this point our own research and our review of that of others points to an evolving business cycle, from an agricultural and (much less) trade-oriented event to a mostly trade/manufacturing event by the time we reach 1914, particularly for the industrial countries in our sample. Recessions were international in scope even at the beginning of the period, but over time they became more so, although our only clear proof of this proposition exists in our comparisons of cycles after 1850. Financial factors, also, played an increasingly important role in cycles, but generally, as we have pointed out, in extending and deepening recessions once they were under way. We also noted that typically recessions simply ended, with their downward forces sapped by the ever-present upward movement in these economies, noticeable from the beginning of the period. Indeed, it is the impetus of this upward movement that Kuznets characterized as 'modern' economic growth.

What can we say about the statistical properties of cycles, referring in this case, to the length and amplitude of recessions, and to their frequency? Speaking generally, first, we note that much of our review of European economic growth since 1500 bears on these issues. With respect to the length of the cycle, what we noted is that faster (endemic) growth rates will end recessions earlier, but that societies with substantial private banking systems often have longer recessions, due to financial after-shocks. In other words, these two factors move in opposite directions in this long period, as we have already pointed out. Then, too, societies with agricultural shocks might be expected to recover more quickly than industrial societies, simply because bad weather is rarely a recurring event; this would lead to shorter recessions in the earlier periods, on the whole. Because of consumption smoothing, which we feel exists throughout this period, recessions tend to be spread over time. But consumption smoothing is only possible if economic agents (consumers in this case) have substantial (and liquid) real and financial resources. Quite transparently, these resources are more considerable at the end of the period than at the beginning. Indeed, the awareness of the cycle as an important and pervasive economic phenomenon is certainly greater at the end of the period than at the beginning and this, too, would lead to a greater demand for appropriately liquid resources. Somewhat paradoxically, therefore, cycles would be longer at the end of the period than at the beginning, because economic agents could 'afford' them. Finally, we mentioned the possibility of cumulative failures of effective demand leading to a downward spiral, at least until the engine of growth started to assert itself again. This particular mechanism is associated with more urban economies, which concentrate on commerce and manufacturing and which are typically more engaged internationally; so this mechanism obviously tends to be more of a factor at the end of the period than at the beginning. Where does the balance fall? We do not know, but we note that for anything we have been able to measure, recessions are not distinctly longer at the end of the period than at the beginning.

With respect to amplitudes – that is, peak to trough declines – the evidence does seem to be a little bit clearer. Obviously the longer a recession, the better the chance that after-shocks will occur, and we all have the specter of the Great Depression to remind us of this possibility. It turns out that this information is not particularly helpful during this period, though, simply because we were not able to generalize about the length of recessions in view of the offsetting influences. By their nature, agricultural collapses seem capable of greater mischief than industrial and commercial mishaps, and we have noted in the data that in many countries with large agricultural sectors sizeable agricultural declines dragged GDP down disproportionately. The further back we go, the larger the share of total output emanating from the agricultural sector, on balance; so without much doubt it is likely that amplitudes were larger early on than later. Of course industrial and commercial economies tend to have greater interaction beyond their borders but, as we shall note, this observation has more bearing on the frequency of recessions (which are more easily transmitted) than on their severity. In fact, in a very obvious sense, if a society diversifies into industrial and commercial activities, then, since agricultural shocks and financial and industrial (technology) shocks are not necessarily closely correlated, it is likely that 'cyclical risk', to coin a term, is lowered by this diversification. This risk reduction occurs because the three sorts of activities are not perfectly correlated (to put it mildly) and, further, because there is considerably more diversification in the commercial and industrial sectors than in the agricultural one.

The next issue concerns the frequency of recessions. It would be nice if we could offer an answer to the big question – are they more or less frequent in Victorian times than they were 400 years earlier? – but that is not possible. Of course we could guesstimate how frequent the agricultural and disease shocks were in the early period, based on their frequency in agricultural economies of the nineteenth century. This calculation would be suggestive, but with broader world markets in more agricultural products in the later than in the earlier period and with better transportation to help ameliorate the effects of a purely local (meaning regional or country-wide) downturn, along with, presumably, more diversified agricultural sectors, one would naturally want to be cautious with such a guesstimate. Another factor, of even more influence, is the fact that more rapidly growing societies would have some would-be recessions swallowed up by the growth rate (we call these 'growth recessions' these days). This observation would hold good at any time, but, more important, some of the more agricultural economies of the Victorian era were growing faster than any economies 400 years earlier.

In Chapter 6 we offered some suggestions on the frequency of recessions, although always on a limited basis. For *Spain*, for example, we found 19 cycles in shipping tonnage (from Seville) between 1500 and 1580; there were also financial crises in 1557 and 1575. There was another financial crisis in 1596, and four sharp shipping tonnage cycles between 1600 and 1610. In *England*, the only other country with any early data worth mentioning, there were severe cycles in cloth production in the 1550s and 1560s, amounting to as many as four or five recessions, while during the period from 1520 to 1600, there were 12 harvest failures, amounting to a rate of 0.15 possible agricultural recessions per year. We would hesitate to draw any conclusions from this evidence alone, but we will still want to return to this information in a moment.

For the seventeenth century, with its slower or even negative growth rates, we anticipate that recessions would be more frequent (and harder to distinguish from longer-term movements in, for example, the patterns of world trade) and so we hesitate to make much out of our information. After 1750, however, for the United Kingdom, as discussed in Chapter 7, we found 12 recessions between 1750 and 1790 and 22 between 1790 and 1850. This works out to 0.3 of a recession per year (let us call this a 'recession rate') for the early period and a recession rate of 0.37 for the second. From 1850 to 1914, as reported in Chapter 12, there were 9 recessions (using Rostow's dates), for a recession rate of 0.18. Clearly, for the United Kingdom, the rate fell over time, at least comparing the two broad periods. For France, Chapter 8 indicates that there were 10 recessions between 1815 and 1850; this works out to a recession rate of 0.28. From 1851 to 1914, the rate rose, slightly, to 0.3 per year. Thus the more agricultural England of the 1750 to 1850 period and the more agricultural France yielded a rate somewhere around 0.3 a year, while the most industrial economy studied (the United Kingdom from 1850 to 1914) was down to a recession rate of 0.18.

In Chapter 12 we also looked at Germany, Italy and Sweden. Neglecting Sweden, because its data possibly contain anomalies (but it still fits the pattern), we find that Germany had 15 recessions between 1851 and 1914, for a recession rate of 0.23, while the much more agricultural Italy had a rate of 0.32 per year from 1861 to 1914. France, as already noted, also had a 0.3 rate for this period. If we graded the four economies mentioned for this later period, from industrial to agricultural, we would go – United Kingdom, Germany, France and Italy. This would be the same order as the calculation of the recession rate yielded.

We might speculate, then, that a recession rate somewhere around 0.3 might be a good guess for all of the countries studied for the longer period from 1500 to 1750. We could not prove this, of course, but these were agricultural economies with quite small industrial and commercial sectors. This is not to say that such calamities might not bunch up in particular periods, but just to go on record as the first to say that when the definitive work on recessions is published for that period, that is what we predict will be found. Incidentally, our brief survey of the 'evidence' from this period does not dramatically contradict this conjecture. We note, not that it has anything to do with what we are doing in this volume, that for the United States (and most other major countries) since 1950 (to 1998), there were 7 recessions (counting 1980 as a separate recession), which works out to a recession rate of 0.14. This, too, does not seem unreasonable from the longer perspective of our survey.

Our last topic concerns the international nature of the cycle. Our very reasonable proposition, almost certainly true for most countries most of the time, is that as time passed, 'international cycles' became more frequent. There are two things to look at here: the exact recessions that we think were shared by at least several countries; and the documentation of the drift toward the 'global recession'. Again, we have to be careful in our interpretation, since the earlier data are drawn from the narrative record, for the most part, while as time goes by the weight of the narrative record diminishes in the total determination of recession dating, while the frequency of international events increases. We say this simply because the narrative record often fails to distinguish between financial panic and recession, two different matters at any time, but especially relevant for a largely agricultural economy.

We simply cannot guess, on the evidence we have assembled, about the nature of the international cycle before 1700. For the sixteenth century we have actually little solid data on which to lean. For the seventeenth century, on the other hand, we proposed a number of years of recession for five major countries for which some data (imports, cloth production and agricultural prices) of an annual nature were available. The list is pretty scattered and does not bear repeating here, but four of the five countries might have had recessions in 1619–22, mainly reflecting trade and cloth production. Agricultural price increases suggest another possible European calamity around 1630–31, and the years that might stand up as showing international crises in the agricultural sector on the basis of price behavior in two or more countries are 1647, 1661, 1693 and 1697. But this is, at most, suggestive.

After 1750, we have more to go on, although not as much as we would like, clearly. In the following we repeat the list of the years of possible global recession that we have been able to identify for the individual countries studied in Chapters 7–9; these dates were reported in Chapter 9.

1762–3	1772–4	1793–4	
1806–8	1815–16	1819–20	1825–6
1832	1839–42	1848	

These are mostly years in which political events or their aftermath provide some approximation of a shock, although what we really see here are mostly commercial and industrial recessions, mixed with agricultural events in some cases (notably in 1815–16, 1839, and 1848). In this group of ten events, we think, are recessions that look a lot like modern global events; these are those from 1819 onward. If there is, then, a period of time that one might want to say contains the birth of the *modern* international cycle, it might be the period after the Napoleonic wars.

In Table 12.10 in Chapter 12, we produced global events for the last 64 years of the period studied. The dates selected were as follows.

1853–4	1857–9	1867–8	1873–4
1875–6	1878–9	1882–4	1893–4
1901–2	1903–4	1908	

In this case there are 11 such events in the 64 years, a rate arguably higher than in the preceding century. Although our lack of information prevents us from identifying international cycles as precisely in earlier periods, we think it is certainly reasonable to claim that what we have attests to the increasing globalization of European business cycles. In particular, the scattered, largely agricultural, events of the sixteenth and seventeenth centuries gradually gave way to commercial and trade-based cycles (sometimes merely the result of agricultural events, to be sure) after 1700, and, in turn, gave way to modern events following the Napoleonic wars. As trade and manufacturing became increasingly important in more economies, this globalization increased to the point, we think, that major recessions were generally shared by 1914, for all but the most agricultural of the European economies. In effect, we are saying that, while cycles were possibly no more numerous at any time in the sample, international cycles became a larger percentage of the total as time went on. What we have added to the debate is a measure of quantification (or documentation, at least).

5. CONCLUSIONS: DEVELOPMENT AND CHANGE ONCE AGAIN

While growth and cycles have been salient features of western economic development since 1500, the underlying structure of the economy – the tectonic plates, as we have referred to that structure elsewhere (Craig and Fisher, 1997) – and changes in that structure must also be considered, because inherent in our discussion of growth and cycles are the fundamental changes taking place in the economic structure. The most important of these was the relative decline of the agricultural sector, by which we mean agriculture's share of output and employment. Of course, the flip side of agriculture's decline is the rise of manufacturing, and in both cases the resulting changes were related to technological innovations.

We have employed the term *integration* to describe the process by which a *European* economy emerged from the fragmented economic and political units of the late Middle Ages. Whereas others have employed this term to mean something quite specific, typically associated with a statistical test designed to reject the null hypothesis of no integration, we have followed the lead of Alexander Gerschenkron in defining integration very broadly. Thus, in one sense integration involves access to standard technologies. This access tends to promote competition in comparable product lines. So, in many instances we see that over time one manifestation of integration is economic similitude. At the same time, the erosion of trade barriers – whether those barriers are associated with technological constraints, like shipping costs, or whether they involve contracting costs or government interference – facilitated the recognition of and recourse to comparative advantage, which would tend to promote diversity of product lines among trading partners. In either case we would expect to see integration in the financial sector, which facilitated the resulting transactions.

Underlying these processes of integration within particular countries was the emergence of what Simon Kuznets called 'modern' economic growth. We interpret this concept to mean that the long-run average compounded rate of growth was large enough that economic downturns were quickly overcome and as a result the standard of living, as measured by output per capita, would have been expected to increase substantially, say 25–50 per cent over the typical lifetime. Such a condition was probably unheard of for any extended period of time for any geographic region of note in Europe for the millennium from the fall of Rome to the Age of Discovery. Kuznets emphasized the sectoral shift of resources – primarily from agriculture to manufacturing – as the key to this process, but we view this sectoral shift as the middle link in a chain of economic causality that stretches both geographically across Europe and chronologically through time. The first link is the underlying technological and institutional change that shocks or disturbs the previous sectoral equilibria and the link that follows the resulting sectoral shift is the trans-regional and trans-national integration discussed above. Again, that integration in turn allows the regional or national economy either to develop new competing lines of production or to specialize and trade as dictated by comparative advantage, or both, and of course each of these links can be endogenous under certain conditions. In the end, we see technological innovation, modern economic growth, and economic integration and convergence as parts of the whole we call 'the integration of the European economy from 1500 to 1914'.

Bibliography

Abel, W. (1980), *Agricultural Fluctuations in Europe* (New York: St. Martins Press).

Abramovitz, M. (1986), 'Catching Up, Forgiveness, and Falling Behind', *Journal of Economic History* (June).

Abramovitz, M. (1993), 'The Search for the Sources of Growth', *Journal of Economic History* (June).

Acena, P.M. (1990), 'The Spanish Money Supply, 1874–1935', *Journal of European Economic History* (Spring).

Adamson, R. (1991), 'Borrowing and Adaptation of British Technology by the Swedish Iron Industry in the Early Nineteenth Century', in K. Bruland (ed.), *Technology Transfer and Scandinavian Industrialisation* (New York: Berg Publishers Ltd.).

Aldcroft, D.H. and P. Fearon (1972), *British Economic Fluctuations, 1790–1939* (London: Macmillan).

Allen, R.C. (1988), 'The Price of Freehold Land and the Interest Rate in the Seventeenth and Eighteenth Centuries', *Economic History Review* (February).

Allen, R.C. (1994), 'Agriculture During the Industrial Revolution', in R. Floud and D.N. McCloskey, *The Economics of Britain Since 1700*, Vol. 1, (2nd edn) (Cambridge: Cambridge University Press).

Allen, R.C. (1999), 'Tracking the Agricultural Revolution in England', *Economic History Review* (May).

Anderson, B.L. and P.W. Pilling (1990), 'Spanish Entrepreneurs and British Technology in Early XIXth Century Andalucia', *Journal of European Economic History* (Spring).

Anes, R. (1974), 'El Banco de Espana (1874–1914): un banco nacional', in P. Schwartz and G. Tortella (eds), *La Banca Espanola en la Restauracion* (Madrid: Servicio de Estudios del Banco de Espana).

Aoki, M. (1984), *The Cooperative Theory of the Firm* (Oxford: Clarendon Press).

Appleby, A.B. (1979), 'Grain Prices and Subsistence Crises in England and France, 1590–1740', *Journal of Economic History* (December).

Ashton, T.S. (1959), *Economic Fluctuations in England, 1700–1800* (Oxford: Clarendon Press).

Attman, A. (1986), 'American Bullion in the European World Trade, 1600–1800', *Acta* (Regiae Societatis Scientiarum et Literarum Gothoburgensis).

Azpilcueta de Navarro, M. (1556), *Commentario resolutorio de usuras* (Salamanca).

Bairoch, P. (1976), 'Europe's Gross National Product, 1800–1975', *Journal of European Economic History* (Fall).

Bairoch, P. (1982), 'International Industrialization Levels from 1750 to 1980', *Journal of European Economic History* (Spring).

Bairoch, P., J. Batou and P. Chevre (1988), *The Population of European Cities, 800–1850* (Geneva: Librairie Droz).

Barbour, V. (1963), *Capitalism in Amsterdam in the 17th Century* (Ann Arbor: University of Michigan Press).

Barro, R.J. (1987), 'Government Spending, Interest Rates, Prices and Budget Deficits in the United Kingdom', *Journal of Monetary Economics* (Sept.).

Barro, R.J. and X. Sala-I-Martin (1992), 'Convergence', *Journal of Political Economy* (April).

Basu, S. and A. Taylor (1999), 'Business Cycles in International Historical Perspective', *Journal of Economic Perspectives* (Spring).

Becker, G.S. and N. Tomes (1976), 'Child Endowments and the Quantity and Quality of Children', *Journal of Political Economy* (August).

Berend, I.T. and G. Ranki (1980), 'Foreign Trade and the Industrialization of the European Periphery in the XIXth Century', *Journal of European Economic History* (Winter).

Berend, I.T. and G. Ranki (1982), *The European Periphery and Industrialization, 1780–1914* (Cambridge: Cambridge University Press).

Berry, B.J.L. and F.E. Horton (1970), *Geographic Perspectives on Urban Systems* (Englewood Cliffs, NJ: Prentice-Hall).

Blaug, M. (1985), *Economic Theory in Retrospect*, (4th edn) (Cambridge: Cambridge University Press).

Bloomfield, A.I. (1959), *Monetary Policy under the International Gold Standard, 1880–1914* (New York: Federal Reserve Bank of New York).

Bog, I. (1961), 'Mercantilism in Germany', *Jahrbücher für Nationalökonomie und Statistik* (No. 2).

Borchardt, K. (1976), 'The Industrial Revolution in Germany, 1700–1914', in C. Cipolla (ed.), *The Emergence of Industrial Societies* (New York: Barnes and Noble).

Bordo, M.D. (1986), 'Explorations in Monetary History: A Survey', *Explorations in Economic History* (October).

Bordo, M.D. and L. Jonung (1987), *The Long-run Behavior of the Velocity of Circulation: The International Evidence* (Cambridge, MA: Harvard University Press).

Bordo, M.D. and E.N. White (1990), 'British and French Finance During the

Napoleonic Wars', Working Paper No. 3517, National Bureau of Economic Research (Nov.).

Boserup, E. (1965), *Conditions of Agricultural Growth* (London: Allen and Unwin).

Bowles, S. and H. Gintis (1993), 'The Revenge of Homo Economicus: Contested Exchange and the Revival of Political Economy', *Journal of Economic Perspectives* (Winter).

Braudel, F. (1967), *Capitalism and Material Life* (London: Weidenfeld and Nicolson).

Braudel, F.P. and F. Spooner (1967), 'Prices in Europe from 1450 to 1750', in M. Postan and H.J. Habakkuk (eds), *The Economy of Expanding Europe in the 16th and 17th Centuries, Cambridge Economic History of Europe*, vol. IV (Cambridge: Cambridge University Press).

Brenner, R. (1972), 'The Social Basis of English Commercial Expansion, 1550–1650', *Journal of Economic History* (March).

Cafagna, L. (1976), 'The Industrial Revolution in Italy, 1830-1914', in C. Cipolla (ed.), *The Emergence of Industrial Societies* (New York: Barnes and Noble).

Cameron, R.E. (1961), *France and the Economic Development of Europe, 1800–1914* (Princeton: Princeton University Press).

Cameron, R.E. (1967), *Banking in the Early Stages of Industrialization* (New York: Oxford University Press).

Cameron, R.E. (1989), *A Concise Economic History of the World: From Paleolithic Times to the Present* (New York: Oxford University Press).

Cameron, R.E. (1990), 'La revolution industrielle manquée', *Social Science History* (Winter).

Capie, F.H. (1992), 'British Economic Fluctuations in the Nineteenth Century: Is There a Role for Money?', in S.N. Broadberry and N.F.R. Crafts (eds), *Britain in the International Economy* (Cambridge: Cambridge University Press).

Capie, F.H. and T.C. Mills (1991), 'Money and Business Cycles in the U.S. and U.K., 1870–1913', *Manchester School* (V. 59, Supplement).

Capie, F.H., T.C. Mills, and G.E. Wood (1991), 'Money, Interest Rates and the Great Depression: Britain from 1870 to 1913', in J. Foreman-Peck (ed.), *New Perspectives on the Late Victorian Economy* (Cambridge: Cambridge University Press).

Capie, F.H. and A. Webber (1985), *A Monetary History of the United Kingdom*, Vol. I (London: Allen and Unwin).

Caron, F. (1979), *An Economic History of Modern France* (New York: Columbia University Press.

Carreras, A. (1987), 'An Annual Index of Spanish Industrial Output', in N.

Sanchez-Albornoz (ed.), *The Economic Modernization of Spain, 1830–1930* (New York: New York University Press).

Chambers, J.D. (1953), 'Enclosure and Labour Supply', *Economic History Review* (No. 3).

Chambers, J.D. and G.E. Mingay (1986), *The Agricultural Revolution, 1750–1880*. (London: Batsford).

Chaunu, P. and H. Chaunu, *Seville et l'Atlantique*, 11 vols. (Paris: A. Colin).

Chorley, G.P.H. (1981), 'The Agricultural Revolution in Northern Europe, 1750–1880: Nitrogen, Legumes, and Crop Productivity', *Economic History Review* (February).

Church, R.A. (1975), *The Great Victorian Boom, 1850–1873* (London: Macmillan).

Cipolla, C.M. (1972), 'The So-called "Price Revolution": Reflections on the Italian Situation', in P. Burke (ed.), *Economy and Society in Early Modern Europe* (New York: Harper and Row).

Clapham, J.H. (1949), *A Concise Economic History of Britain from the Earliest Times to 1750* (Cambridge: Cambridge University Press).

Clark, G. (1987), 'Productivity Growth without Technical Change: European Agriculture before 1850', *Journal of Economic History* (June).

Clark, G. (1989), 'Productivity Change without Technical Change: Reply to Komlos', *Journal of Economic History* (December).

Clark, G. (1991), 'Yields per acre in English Agriculture, 1250–1860: Evidence from Labour Inputs', *Economic History Review* (August).

Clark, G. (1992), 'The Economics of Exhaustion, the Postan Thesis, and the Agricultural Revolution', *Journal of Economic History* (March).

Clark, G. (1993), 'Agriculture and the Industrial Revolution, 1700–1850', in Joel Mokyr (ed.), *The British Industrial Revolution: An Economic Perspective* (Boulder, CO: Westview).

Clarkson, L. (1971), *The Pre-Industrial Economy in England, 1500–1750* (London: Batsford).

Clay, C.G.A. (1984), *Economic Expansion and Social Change: England, 1500–1700*, two vols, (Cambridge: Cambridge University Press).

Clough, S.B. (1964), *The Economic History of Modern Italy* (New York: Columbia University Press).

Clough, S.B. (1972), 'Retardative Factors in French Economic Growth at the End of the Ancien Régime and during the French Revolution and Napoleonic Periods', in M. Kooy (ed.), *Studies in Economics and Economic History* (Durham: Duke University Press).

Clough, S.B. and R.T. Rapp (1975), *European Economic History* (3rd edn) (New York: McGraw-Hill).

Cohen, J.S. (1967), 'Financing Industrialization in Italy, 1894–1914: The

Partial Transformation of a Late-Comer', *Journal of Economic History* (September).

Cohen, J.S. (1972), 'Italy, 1861–1914', in R. Cameron (ed.), *Banking and Economic Development: Some Lessons of History* (New York: Oxford University Press).

Cole, W.P. (1981), 'Agriculture, 1700–1800', in R. Floud and D.N. McCloskey (eds), *The Economic History of Britain Since 1700*, Vol. 1 (Cambridge: Cambridge University Press).

Coleman, D.C. (1977), *The Economy of England, 1450–1750* (London: Oxford University Press).

Collins, E.J.T. (1993) 'Why Wheat? Choice of Food Grains in Europe in the Nineteenth and Twentieth Centuries', *Journal of European Economic History* (Spring).

Collins, W.J. and J.G. Williamson (1999), 'Capital Goods Prices, Global Capital Markets and Accumulation: 1870–1950', National Bureau of Economic Research, Working Paper no. 7145, Cambridge, MA.

Crafts, N.F.R. (1977), 'Industrial Revolution in Britain and France: Some Thoughts on the Question "Why was England First?"', *Economic History Review* (August).

Crafts, N.F.R. (1978), 'Enclosure and Labor Supply Revisited', *Explorations in Economic History* (April).

Crafts, N.F.R. (1980), 'Income Elasticities of Demand and the Release of Labour by Agriculture during the British Industrial Revolution', *Journal of European Economic History* (Spring).

Crafts, N.F.R. (1985), *British Economic Growth During the Industrial Revolution* (Oxford: Oxford University Press).

Crafts, N.F.R. (1987), 'British Economic Growth, 1700–1850; Some Difficulties of Interpretation', *Explorations in Economic History* (July).

Crafts, N.F.R and C.K. Harley (1992), 'Output Growth and the British Industrial Revolution: A Restatement of the Crafts-Harley View', *Economic History Review* (November).

Crafts, N.F.R., S.J. Leybourne and T.C. Mills (1989), 'Trends and Cycles in British Industrial Production, 1700–1913', *Journal of the Royal Statistical Society* (A) (Part I).

Craig, L.A. and D. Fisher (1997), *The Integration of the European Economy, 1850–1913* (London: Macmillan).

Craig, L.A., D. Fisher, and T.A. Spencer (1995), 'Inflation and Money Growth under the International Gold Standard, 1850–1913', *Journal of Macroeconomics* (Spring).

Crouzet, F. (1970), 'An Annual Index of French Industrial Production in the 19th Century', *Annales* (Economies-Sociétés-Civilisations).

Cullen, L.M. (1993), 'History, Economic Crises, and Revolution: Understanding Eighteenth-Century France', *Economic History Review* (November).

Davis, R. (1954), 'English Foreign Trade, 1660–1700', *Economic History Review.*

Deane, P. (1979), *The First Industrial Revolution* (2nd edn) (Cambridge: Cambridge University Press).

Deane, P. and W.A. Cole (1962, 1967), *British Economic Growth, 1668–1959* (Cambridge: Cambridge University Press).

De Vries, J. (1976), *The Economy of Europe in the Age of Crisis* (Cambridge: Cambridge University Press).

De Vries, J. (1984) 'The Decline and Rise of the Dutch Economy, 1675–1900', *Research in Economic History* (Supplement 3).

De Vries, J. (1994), 'The Industrial Revolution and the Industrious Revolution', *Journal of Economic History* (June).

Dhondt, J. and M. Bruwier (1976), 'The Low Countries, 1700–1914', in C.M. Cipolla (ed.), *The Emergence of Industrial Societies* (New York: Barnes and Noble).

Dornbusch, R. and J.A. Frenkel (1984), 'The Gold Standard and the Bank of England in the Crisis of 1847', in M.D. Bordo and A.J. Schwartz (eds), *A Retrospective on the Classical Gold Standard* (Chicago: University of Chicago Press).

Doughty, R.A. (1975), 'Industrial Prices and Inflation in Southern England, 1401–1640', *Economic History Review* (April).

Dutton, J. (1984), 'The Bank of England and the Rules of the Game under the International Gold Standard: New Evidence', in Michael D. Bordo and Anna J. Schwartz (eds), *A Retrospective on the Classical Gold Standard, 1821–1931* (Chicago: University of Chicago Press).

Eichengreen, B. (1983), 'The Causes of British Business Cycles, 1833–1913', *Journal of European Economic History* (Spring).

Egge, A. (1983), 'Transformation of Bank Structures in the Industrial Period: The Case of Norway, 1830–1914', *Journal of European Economic History* (Fall).

Elsas, M.J. (1935), 'Price Data from Munich, 1500–1700', *Economic Journal* (February).

Engerman, S.L. (1994), 'Mercantilism and Overseas Trade, 1700–1800', in R. Floud and D.N. McCloskey, *The Economic History of Britain Since 1700*, Vol. 1 (2nd edn) (Cambridge: Cambridge University Press).

Feinstein, C.H. (1972), *National Income Expenditure and Output of the United Kingdom, 1855–1965* (Cambridge: Cambridge University Press).

Feinstein, C.H. (1978), 'Capital Formation in Great Britain' in P. Mathias and M.M. Postan (eds), *The Cambridge Economic History of Europe* (Vol. VII), (Cambridge: Cambridge University Press).

Feinstein, C.H. (1981), 'Capital Accumulation and the Industrial Revolution', in R. Floud and D.N. McCloskey (eds), *The Economic History of England Since 1700* (Vol. 1), (Cambridge: Cambridge University Press).

Fenoaltea, S. (1982), 'The Industrialization of Italy, 1861–1913', unpublished manuscript.

Fenoaltea, S. (1988), 'International Resource Flows and Construction Movements in the Atlantic Economy: The Kuznets Cycle in Italy, 1861–1913', *Journal of Economic History* (Sept.).

Fernandez de Pinedo, E. (1988), 'From the Bloomery to the Blast-Furnace: Technical Change in Spanish Iron-Making (1650–1822)', *Journal of European Economic History* (Spring).

Fisher, D. (1989), 'The Price Revolution: A Monetary Interpretation', *Journal of Economic History* (December).

Fisher, D. (1992), *The Industrial Revolution, A Macroeconomic Interpretation* (London: Macmillan).

Fisher, F.J. (1950), 'London's Export Trade in the Early Seventeenth Century', *Economic History Review* (No. 2).

Flinn, M.W. (1974), 'Trends in Real Wages, 1750–1850', *Economic History Review* (August).

Flinn, M.W. (1981), *The European Demographic System, 1500–1820*. (Baltimore: Johns Hopkins).

Floud, R. and B. Harris (1997), 'Health, Height, and Welfare: Britain, 1700–1980', in R. Steckel and R. Floud, *Health and Welfare During Industrialization* (Chicago: University of Chicago Press).

Flynn, D.O. (1978), 'A New Perspective on the Spanish Price Revolution: The Monetary Approach to the Balance of Payments', *Explorations in Economic History* (October).

Flynn, D.O. (1986), 'The Microeconomics of Silver and East-West Trade in the Early Modern Period', in W. Fisher, et al. (eds), *The Emerging World Economy, 1500-1914* (Wiesbaden).

Fogel, R. (1964), *Railroads and American Economic Growth* (Baltimore: Johns Hopkins).

Fohlen, C.B. (1961), 'The Industrial Revolution in France', *Studi Storici* (II).

Fohlen, C.B. (1970), 'France, 1700–1914' in C. Cipolla (ed.), *The Emergence of Industrial Societies* (New York: Barnes and Noble).

Ford, A.G. (1981), 'The Trade Cycle in Britain, 1860–1914', in R.C. Floud and D.N. McCloskey (eds), *The Economic History of Britain Since 1700*, Vol. 2 (Cambridge: Cambridge University Press).

Fratianni, M. and F. Spinelli (1984), 'Italy in the Gold Standard Period, 1861–1914', in M.D. Bordo and A.J. Schwartz (eds), *A Retrospective on the Classical Gold Standard* (Chicago: University of Chicago Press).

Fremdling, R. (1991), 'Foreign Competition and Technological Change: British Exports and the Modernisation of the German Iron Industry from the 1820s to the 1860s', in W.R. Lee (ed.), *German Industry and German Industrialisation* (London: Routledge).

Freudenberger, H. (1983), 'An Industrial Momentum Achieved in the Habsburg Monarchy', *Journal of European Economic History* (Fall).

Friedman, M. (1956), 'The Quantity Theory of Money, A Restatement', in M. Friedman (ed.), *Studies in the Quantity Theory of Money* (Chicago: University of Chicago Press).

Friedman, M. and A.J. Schwartz (1982), *Monetary Trends in the United States and the United Kingdom, 1867–1975* (Chicago: University of Chicago Press).

Gayer, A.D., W.W. Rostow and A.J. Schwartz (1953), *The Growth and Fluctuation of the British Economy, 1790–1850* (Oxford: Clarendon Press).

Gerschenkron, A. (1962), *Economic Backwardness in Historical Perspective* (Cambridge, MA: Harvard University Press).

Gerschenkron, A. (1970), *Europe in a Russian Mirror, Four Lectures in Economic History* (Cambridge: Cambridge University Press).

Gilboy, E.W. (1932), 'Demand as a Factor in the Industrial Revolution', in A.H. Cole (ed.), *Facts and Factors in Economic History* (New York: Kelley (1967)).

Glassman, D. and A. Redish (1985), 'New Estimates of the Money Stock in France, 1493–1680', *Journal of Economic History* (March).

Goldsmith, J.L. (1984), 'The Agrarian History of Preindustrial France: Where Do We Go from Here?', *Journal of European Economic History* (Spring).

Goldstone, J.A. (1984), 'Urbanization and Inflation: Lessons from the English Price Revolution of the Sixteenth and Seventeenth Centuries', *American Journal of Sociology* (March).

Good, D.F. (1984), *The Economic Rise of the Habsburg Empire, 1750–1914* (Berkeley, CA: University of California Press).

Goodhart, C.A.E. (1984), 'Comment', in M.D. Bordo and A.J. Schwartz (eds), *A Retrospective on the Classical Gold Standard, 1821–1931* (Chicago: University of Chicago Press).

Gould, J.D. (1964), 'The Price Revolution Reconsidered', *Economic History Review* (December).

Grantham, G.M. (1993), 'Divisions of Labour: Agricultural Productivity and Occupational Specialization in Pre-Industrial France', *Economic History Review* (August).

Grice-Hutchinson, M. (1952), *The School of Salamanca: Readings in Spanish Monetary Theory, 1544–1605* (Oxford: Clarendon Press).

Griffiths, R. (1979), *Industrial Retardation in the Netherlands, 1830–1850* (Den Haag: Nijhoff).

Gross, N.T. (1971), 'Economic Growth and the Consumption of Coal in Austria and Hungary, 1831–1913', *Journal of Economic History*.

Gross, N.T. (1976), 'The Industrial Revolution in the Habsburg Monarchy, 1750–1914', in C. Cipolla (ed.), *The Emergence of Industrial Societies* (New York: Barnes and Noble).

Guy, J. (1984), 'The Tudor Age,' in K.O. Morgan (ed.), *The Oxford History of Britain* (New York: Oxford University Press).

Hamilton, E.J. (1929), 'American Treasure and the Rise of Capitalism,' *Economica*, (November).

Hamilton, E.J. (1934), *American Treasure and the Price Revolution in Spain, 1501–1650* (Cambridge, MA: Harvard University Press).

Hammarström, I. (1957), 'The "Price Revolution" of the Sixteenth Century: Some Swedish Evidence', *Scandinavian Economic History Review* (No. 2).

Hansen, S.A. (1982), *Okonomisk Vaekst i Danmark* (Bind II), (Copenhagen, University of Copenhagen, Institute for Economic History, No. 6).

Harley, C.K. (1980), 'Transportation, the World Wheat Trade, and the Kuznets Cycle, 1850–1913', *Exporations in Economic History, 1850–1913* (July).

Harrison, J. (1978), *An Economic History of Modern Spain* (New York: Holmes and Meier).

Hartwell, R.M. (1990), 'Was there an Industrial Revolution?', *Social Science History* (Winter).

Hawtrey, R.G. (1931), *The Gold Standard in Theory and Practice* (London: Longmans, Green)

Heckscher, E.F. (1935), *Mercantilism* (London: G. Allen).

Heckscher, E.F. (1963), *An Economic History of Sweden* (Cambridge, MA: Harvard University Press).

Heim, C.E. and P. Mirowski (1987), 'Interest Rates and Crowding-Out During Britain's Industrialization', *Journal of Economic History* (March).

Henderson, W.O. (1961), *The Industrial Revolution on the Continent* (London: Frank Cass).

Henderson, W.O. (1975), *The Rise of German Industrial Power, 1834–1914* (Berkeley: University of California Press).

Hicks, J.R. (1946), *Value and Capital* (Oxford: Oxford University Press).

Hicks, J.R. (1969), *A Theory of Economic History* (Oxford: University Press).

Hill, C. (1968), *Reformation to Industrial Revolution: The Making of Modern English Society, 1530–1780* (London: Pantheon).

Hobsbawm, E.H. (1954), 'The General Crisis of the European Economy in the Seventeenth Century', *Past and Present* (May).

Hoffmann, W.G. (1955), *British Industry, 1770–1950*, trans. W.O. Henderson and W.H. Chalconer (Oxford: Oxford University Press).

Hoffmann, W.G. (1965), *Das Wachstum der Deutschen Wirtschaft seit der Mitte des 19 Jahrhunderts* (Berlin: Springer-Verlag).

Homer, S. and R. Sylla (1991), *A History of Interest Rates* (3rd edn) (New Brunswick: Rutgers University Press).

Hoppit, J. (1986), 'Financial Crises in Eighteenth-Century England', *Economic History Review* (February).

van Houtte, LA. (1977), *An Economic History of the Low Countries, 800–1800* (New York: St. Martin's Press).

Hoyle, R.W. (1990), 'Tenure and the Land Market in Early Modern England: Or a Late Contribution to the Brenner Debate', *Economic History Review* (February).

Huck, P.F. (1992), *Infant Mortality and the Standard of Living During the Industrial Revolution*, Ph.D. dissertation, Northwestern University, Evanston, IL.

Israel, J.I. (1989), *Dutch Primacy in World Trade, 1585–1740* (Oxford: Clarendon Press).

ISTAT (1957), *Indagine Statistica Sullo Sviluppo del Reddito Nazionale dell'Italia del 1861 al 1956*, Annali de Statisica Serie 8, Vol. 9 (Rome: Instituto Poligrafica di Stato).

Jackson, R.V. (1985), 'Growth and Deceleration in English Agriculture, 1660–1790', *Economic History Review* (August).

Jackson, R.V. (1992), 'Rates of Industrial Growth During the Industrial Revolution', *Economic History Review* (February).

Johansen, H.C. (1991), 'Banking and Finance in the Danish Economy', in R. Cameron and V.I. Bovykin (eds), *International Banking, 1870–1914* (New York: Oxford, University Press).

Jones, E.L. (1981) 'Agriculture, 1700–80', in R. Floud and D.N. McCloskey (eds), *The Economic History of Britain Since 1700*, Vol. 1 (1st edn) (Cambridge: Cambridge University Press).

Jonung, L. (1975), *Studies in the Monetary History of Sweden*, Ph.D. Dissertation, University of California (Los Angeles).

Jonung, L. (1976), 'Money and Prices in Sweden, 1732–1972, *Scandinavian Journal of Economics* (#1).

Jorberg, L. (1961), *The Growth and Fluctuations of Swedish Industry, 1869–1912* (Stockholm: Almqvist and Wiksel).

Kennedy, P. (1987), *The Rise and Fall of the Great Powers: Economic Change and Military Conflict from 1500 to 2000* (New York: Random House).

Kenwood, A.C. and A.L. Lougheed (1983), *The Growth of the International Economy, 1820–1980* (London: George Allen and Unwin).

Kerridge, E. (1967), *The Agricultural Revolution* (London: Allen and Unwin).

Keynes, J.M. (1930), *A Treatise on Money* (two vols) (London: Macmillan and Company).

Keynes, J.M. (1936), *The General Theory of Employment, Interest, and Money* (London: Macmillan).

Kindleberger, C.P. (1964), *The Economic Growth of France and Britain, 1851–1950* (New York: Simon and Schuster).

Kindleberger, C.P. (1982), *Financial Crises: Theory, History and Policy* (Cambridge: Cambridge University Press).

Kindleberger, C.P. (1989), *Manias, Panics, and Crashes: A History of Financial Crises* (rev. edn) (New York: Basic Books).

Kindleberger, C.P. (1991), 'The Economic Crisis of 1619 to 1623', *Journal of Economic History* (March).

Kindleberger, C.P. (1993), *A Financial History of Western Europe* (2nd edn) (New York: Oxford University Press).

Kitchen, M. (1978), *The Political Economy of Germany, 1815–1914* (London: Croom Helm).

Klein, J. (1920), *The Mesta: A Study in Spanish Economic History, 1273–1836* (Port Washington, NY: Kennikat Press [1964]).

Klovland, J.T. (1987), 'The Demand for Money in the United Kingdom, 1875–1913', *Oxford Bulletin of Economics and Statistics* (August).

Komlos, J. (1983), *The Habsburg Monarchy as a Customs Union* (Princeton: University Press).

Komlos, J. (1987, 1990), 'Financial Innovation and the Demand for Money in Austria–Hungary, 1867–1913', *Journal of European Economic History* (Spring) and reprinted in J. Komlos (ed.), *Economic Development in the Habsburg Monarchy and in the Successor States* (1990), (New York: Columbia University Press).

Krantz, O. and C. Nilsson (1975), *Swedish National Product, 1861–1970* (Lund: CWK Gleerup).

Kriedt, P., H. Medick and J. Schlumbohn (1981), *Industrialization before Industrialization: Rural Industry in the Genesis of Capitalism* (Cambridge: Cambridge University Press).

Kristensen, N.B. (1989), 'Industrial Growth in Denmark, 1872–1913: In Relation to the Debate on an Industrial Breakthrough', *Scandinavian Economic History Review* (1).

Kunitz, S.J. (1983), 'Speculations on the European Mortality Decline', *Economic History Review* (August).

Landes, D.S. (1994), 'What Room for Economic History?: Explaining Big Changes by Small Events', *Economic History Review* (November).

Lane, F.C. and J.C. Riemersma (1953), *Enterprise and Secular Change* (Homewood, IL: Richard D. Irwin).

Lee, R.D. (1973), 'Population in Preindustrial England: An Econometric Analysis', *Quarterly Journal of Economics* (November).

Levy-Leboyer, M. and F. Bourguignon (1990), *The French Economy in the Nineteenth Century* (Cambridge: Cambridge University Press).

Lindert, P.H. (1985), 'English Population, Wages, and Prices, 1541–1913', *Journal of Interdisciplinary History* (Spring).

Lindert, P.H. and J.G. Williamson (1983), 'English Workers' Living Standards During the Industrial Revolution: A New Look', *Economic History Review* (February).

Lis, C. and H. Soly (1977), 'Food Consumption in Antwerp between 1807 and 1859: A Contribution to the Standard of Living Debate', *Economic History Review* (August).

Loschky, D. (1980), 'Seven Centuries of Real Income per Wage Earner Reconsidered', *Economica* (November).

Lydall, H.F. and E.H. Phelps Brown (1982), 'Seven Centuries of Real Income per Wage-Earner Reconsidered: A Note', *Economica* (May).

Lundström, R. (1991), 'Sweden', in R. Cameron and V.I. Bovykin (eds), *International Banking, 1870–1914* (New York: Oxford University Press).

Luzzato, G. (1963), *L'economia Italiana dal 1861 al 1914* (Milan: Banca Commerciale Italiana).

Maddison, A. (1982), *Phases of Capitalist Development* (Oxford: Oxford University Press).

Maddison, A. (1991), *Dynamic Forces in Capitalist Development* (Oxford: Oxford University Press).

Magnusson, L. (1987), 'Mercantilism and "Reform" Mercantilism: The Rise of Economic Discourse in Sweden During the Eighteenth Century', *History of Political Economy* (Fall).

Malthus, T.R. (1826 [1951]), *Principles of Political Economy* (2nd edn) (New York: Augustus Kelley).

de Malynes, G. (1601), *A Treatise of the Canker of England's Commonwealth* (London).

de Malynes, G. (1603), *England's View, in the unmasking of two paradoxes; with a replication unto the answer of Maister Jean Bodine* (London).

Mantoux, P. (1928), *The Industrial Revolution in the Eighteenth Century* (London: Macmillan, 1983).

Marczewski, J. (1988), 'Economic Fluctuations in France, 1815–1938', *Journal of European Economic History* (Fall).

Martín-Aceña, P. (1994), 'Spain during the Classical Gold Standard' in M.D. Bordo and F. Capie (eds), *Monetary Regimes in Transition* (Cambridge: Cambridge University Press).

Mathias, P. (1983), *The First Industrial Nation*, (2nd edn), (London: Methuen).

McCloskey, D.N. (ed.) (1971), *Essays on a Mature Economy* (Princeton: University Press).

McCloskey, D.N. (1972), 'The enclosure of Open Fields: Preface to a Study of Its Impact on the Efficiency of English Agriculture in the Eighteenth Century', *Journal of Economic History* (March).

McCloskey, D.N. (1975), 'The Economics of Enclosure: A Market Analysis' in W.N. Parker and E.L. Jones (eds), *European Peasants and Their Markets* (Princeton: University Press).

McCloskey, D. (1976), 'English Open Fields as a Behavior Towards Risk', in P. Uselding (ed.), *Research in Economic History*, vol. I.

McCloskey, D.N. and J.R. Zecher (1981), 'How the Gold Standard Worked, 1880–1913', in Donald N. McCloskey (ed.), *Enterprise and Trade in Victorian Britain* (London: George Allen and Unwin).

McCloskey, D.N. and J.R. Zecher (1984), 'The Success of Purchasing Power Parity: Historical Evidence and Its Implications for Macroeconomics', in M.D. Bordo and A.J. Schwartz (eds), *A Retrospective on the Classical Gold Standard, 1821–1931* (Chicago: University of Chicago Press).

McGouldrick, P. (1984), 'Operations of the German Central Bank and the Rules of the Game, 1879–1913', in M.D. Bordo and A.J. Schwartz (eds), *A Retrospective on the Classical Gold Standard, 1821–1931* (Chicago: University of Chicago Press).

McNeill, W.H. (1976), *Plagues and Peoples* (Garden City, NY: Anchor Press).

Mendels, F.F. (1972), 'Proto-Industrialization: The First Phase of the Industrialization Process', *Journal of Economic History* (March).

Milward, A. and S.B. Saul (1973), *The Economic Development of Continental Europe, 1780–1870* (London: Rowman and Littlefield).

Minchinton, W.E. (1969), 'Editor's Introduction', in W.E. Minchinton (ed.), *The Growth of English Overseas Trade in the Seventeenth and Eighteenth Centuries* (London: Methuen).

Mirowski, P. (1981), 'The Rise (and Retreat) of a Market: English Joint Stock Shares in the Eighteenth Century', *Journal of Economic History* (September).

Mirowski, P. (1985), *The Birth of the Business Cycle* (New York: Garland).

Miskimin, H.A. (1975), 'Population Growth and the Price Revolution in England', *Journal of European Economic History* (Spring).

Mitchell, B.R. (1978), *European Historical Statistics, 1750–1970* (New York: Columbia University Press).

Mitchell, B.R. (1992), *International Historical Statistics: Europe, 1750–1988* (New York: Stockton Press).

Mokyr, J. (1976), *Industrialization in the Low Countries, 1795–1850* (New Haven: Yale University Press).

Mokyr, J. (1987), 'Has the Industrial Revolution Been Crowded Out?', *Explorations in Economic History* (July).

Mokyr, J. (1990), *The Lever of Riches: Technological Creativity and Economic Progress* (New York: Oxford University Press).

Mokyr, J. (1993), 'Editor's Introduction: The New Economic History and the Industrial Revolution', in J. Mokyr (ed.), *The British Industrial Revolution: An Economic Perspective* (Boulder: Westview).

Molinas, C. and L. Prados de la Escosura (1989), 'Was Spain Different? Spanish Historical Backwardness Revisited', *Explorations in Economic History* (October).

Morineau, M. (1970), 'Was There an Agricultural Revolution in 18th Century France?', in R. Cameron (ed.), *Essays in French Economic History* (Homewood, IL: Irwin).

Muhleman, M.L. (1896), *Monetary Systems of the World* (New York: Charles H. Nicoll).

Nadal, J. (1970), 'The Failure of the Industrial Revolution in Spain, 1830–1914', in C.M. Cipolla (ed.), *The Emergence of Industrial Societies* (New York: Barnes and Noble).

Neal, L. (1994), 'The Finance of Business During the Industrial Revolution', in R. Floud and D. McCloskey (eds), *The Economic History of Britain Since 1700*, Vol. 1 (2nd edn) (Cambridge: Cambridge University Press).

Neal, L.T. (1991), *The Rise of Financial Capitalism* (Cambridge: Cambridge University Press).

Nef, J.U. (1937), 'Prices and Industrial Capitalism in France and England, 1540–1640', *Economic History Review* (May).

Nef, J.U. (1964), *The Conquest of the Material World* (Chicago: University of Chicago Press).

Newell, W.H. (1973), 'The Agricultural Revolution in Nineteenth Century France', *Journal of Economic History* (December).

North, D.C. (1981), *Structure and Change in Economic History* (New York: W.W. Norton).

Norwich, J.J. (1996), *Byzantium: The Decline and Fall* (New York: Alfred A. Knopf).

Nugent, J.B. and N. Sanchez (1989), 'The Efficiency of the Mesta: A Parable', *Explorations in Economic History* (July).

Nunes, A., E. Mata and N. Valerio (1989), 'Portuguese Economic Growth, 1833–1985', *Journal of European Economic History* (Fall).

Nye, J.V. (1991), 'The Myth of Free-Trade Britain and Fortress France: Tariffs and Trade in the Nineteenth Century', *Journal of Economic History* (March).

O'Brien, P. (1982), 'European Economic Development: The Contribution of the Periphery', *Economic History Review* (February).

O'Brien, P. and C. Keyder (1978), *Economic Growth in Britain and France, 1780–1914: Two Paths to the Twentieth Century* (London: George Allen & Unwin).

O'Rourke, K.H. and J.G. Williamson (1994), 'Late Nineteenth-Century Anglo-

American Factor Price Convergence: Were Heckscher and Ohlin Right?',
Journal of Economic History (December).

O'Rourke, K.H., J.G. Williamson and T.J. Hatton (1994), 'Mass Migration,
Commodity Market Integration, and Real Wage Convergence', in T.J. Hatton
and J.G. Williamson (eds), *Migration and the International Labor Market*
(London: Routledge).

Outhwaite, R.B. (1982), *Inflation in Tudor and Early Stuart England* (London: Macmillan).

Outhwaite, R.B. (1986), 'Progress and Backwardness in English Agriculture,
1500–1650', *Economic History Review* (February).

Overton, M. (1984), 'Agricultural Productivity in Eighteenth-Century England: Some Further Speculations', *Economic History Review* (May).

Overton, M. (1990), 'Re-estimating Crop Yields from Probate Inventories: A
Comment', *Journal of Economic History* (December).

Parker, G. (1987), *The Thirty Years War* (London: Routledge).

Pedreira, J.M. (1990), 'Social Structure and the Persistence of Rural Domestic Industry in Nineteenth Century Portugal', *Journal of European Economic
History* (Winter).

Perkins, J.A. (1981), 'The Agricultural Revolution in Germany, 1850–1914',
Journal of European Economic History (Spring).

Phelps, E. (1966), *Golden Rules of Economic Growth* (New York: Norton).

Phelps Brown, E.H. and S.V. Hopkins (1956), 'Seven Centuries of the Prices
of Consumables, Compared with Builders' Wage-rates', *Economica* (November).

Phelps Brown, E.H. and S.V. Hopkins (1957), 'Wage Rates and Prices: Evidence for Population Pressure in the Sixteenth Century', *Economica*
(November).

Phelps Brown, E.H. and S.V. Hopkins (1959), 'Builders' Wage-rates, Prices
and Population: Some Further Evidence', *Economica* (February).

Philpot, G. (1975), 'Enclosures and Population Growth in Eighteenth-Century
England', *Explorations in Economic History* (January).

Post, J.D. (1974), 'A Study in Meteorological and Trade Cycle History: The
Economic Crisis Following the Napoleonic Wars', *Journal of Economic
History* (June).

Post, J.D. (1984), 'Climatic Variability and the European Mortality Wave of
the Early 1740s', *Journal of Interdisciplinary History* (Summer).

Postan, M.M. (1959), 'Money, Population, and Economic Change in Late
Medieval Europe: A Note', *Economic History Review* (August).

Price, R. (1981), *An Economic History of Modern France, 1730–1914* (London: Macmillan).

Ramsey, G.D. (1957), *English Overseas Trade During the Centuries of Emergence* (London: Macmillan).

Ramsey, P.H. (1963), *Tudor Economic Problems* (London: V. Gollancz).

Rapp, R.T. (1975), 'The Unmaking of the Mediterranean Trade Hegemony: International Trade Rivalry and the Commercial Revolution', *Journal of Economic History* (September).

Rapp, R.T. (1979), 'Real Estate and Rational Investment in Early Modern Venice', *Journal of European Economic History* (Fall).

Reed, C. (1973), 'Transactions Costs and Differential Growth in Seventeenth Century Western Europe', *Journal of Economic History* (March).

Roehl, R. (1976), 'French Industrialization: A Reconsideration', *Explorations in Economic History* (July).

Romani, M.A. (1994), 'Regions in Italian History (XVth–XVIIIth Centuries)', *Journal of European Economic History* (Spring).

Romano, R. (1974), 'Italy in the Crisis of the Seventeenth Century', in Peter Earle (ed.), Essays *in European Economic History, 1500–1800* (Oxford: Clarendon Press).

de Roover, R. (1953), 'The Commercial Revolution of the Thirteenth Century', in F.C. Lane and J.C. Riemersma (eds), *Enterprise and Secular Change* (Homewood, IL: Richard D. Irwin).

Rostow, W.W. (1948), *The British Economy of the 19th Century* (Oxford: Oxford University Press).

Rostow, W.W. (1962), *The Stages of Economic Growth* (Cambridge: Cambridge University Press).

Rudolph, R.L. (1972), 'Austria, 1800–1914', in R. Cameron (ed.), *Banking and Economic Development: Some Lessons of History* (New York: Oxford University Press).

St. Marc, M. (1983), *Histoire Monétaire de la France, 1800–1908* (Paris: Presses Universitaires de France).

Sandberg, L.G. (1978), 'Banking and Economic Growth in Sweden before World War I', *Journal of Economic History* (September).

Sandberg, L.G. (1979), 'The Case of the Impoverished Sophisticate: Human Capital and Swedish Economic Growth before World War I', *Journal of Economic History* (March).

Sarrion, G.P. (1995), 'Hydraulic and Irrigation Works in Spain in the Second Half of the Eighteenth-Century', *Journal of European Economic History* (Spring).

Saul, S.B. (1985), *The Myth of the Great Depression, 1873–1896* (London: Macmillan).

Sheffrin, S.M. (1988), 'Have Economic Fluctuations been Dampened? A Look at Evidence Outside the United States', *Journal of Monetary Economics* (March).

Slicher van Bath, B.H. (1977), 'Agriculture and the Vital Revolution', *Cam-*

bridge Economic History of Europe (Vol. V), (Cambridge: Cambridge University Press).

Smith, A. (1776), *The Wealth of Nations* (New York: Random House, 1937).

Solomou, S. (1987), *Phases of Economic Growth, 1850–1973* (Cambridge: Cambridge University Press).

Sommariva, A. and G. Tullio (1987), *German Macroeconomic History, 1880–1979* (London: Macmillan).

Sommariva, A. and G. Tullio (1988), 'International Gold Flows in Gold Standard Germany: A Test of the Monetary Approach to the Balance of Payments, 1880–1911', *Journal of Money, Credit, and Banking* (Feb.).

Spooner, F. (1972), *The International Economy and Monetary Movements in France, 1493–1725* (Cambridge: Cambridge University Press).

Sprenger, B. (1982), 'Geldmengenanderungen in Deutschland in Zeitalter der Industrialisierung (1835 bis 1913)', *Kölner Vortrage und Abhandlungen zur Sozial- und Wirtschaftsgeschichte* (Heft 36).

Steckel, R.H. (1995), 'Stature and the Standard of Living', *Journal of Economic Literature* (December).

Steckel, R. and R. Floud (1997), *Health and Welfare During Industrialization* (Chicago: University of Chicago Press).

Sullivan, R.J. (1985), 'The Timing and Pattern of Technological Development in English Agriculture, 1611–1850', *Journal of Economic History* (June).

van Stuijvenberg, J. and J. de Vrijer (1982), 'Prices, Population and National Income in the Netherlands, 1620–1978', *Journal of European Economic History* (Winter).

Tilly, R.H. (1967), 'Germany, 1815–1870', in R. Cameron (ed.), *Banking in the Early Stages of Industrialization* (New York: Oxford University Press).

Tilly, R.H. (1986). 'German Banking, 1850–1914: Development Assistance for the Strong', *Journal of European Economic History* (Spring).

Tilly, R.H. (1991), 'International Aspects of the Development of German Banking', in R. Cameron and V.I. Bovykin (eds), *International Banking, 1870–1914* (New York: Oxford University Press).

Toniolo, G. (1990), *An Economic History of Liberal Italy, 1850–1918* (London: Routledge).

Tortella, G. (1972), 'Spain, 1829–1874', in R. Cameron (ed.), *Banking and Economic Development: Some Lessons of History* (New York: Oxford University Press).

Tortella, G. (1977), *Banking, Railroads, and Industry in Spain, 1829–1874* (New York: Arno Press).

Tortella, G. (1994), 'Patterns of Economic Retardation and Recovery in South-western Europe in the Nineteenth and Twentieth Centuries', *Economic History Review*.

Toutain, J.-C. (1987), 'Le Produit Intérieur Brut de la France de 1789 a 1982', *Économies et Sociétés* (No. 15).

Trebilcock, C. (1981), *The Industrialization of the Continental Powers, 1780–1914* (London: Longman).

Turner, M. (1976), 'Parliamentary Enclosure and Population Change in England', *Explorations in Economic History* (October).

Turner, M. (1982), 'Agricultural Productivity in England in the Eighteenth Century: Evidence from Crop Yields', *Economic History Review* (November).

Turner, M. (1986), 'English Open Fields and Enclosures: Retardation or Productivity Improvements', *Journal of Economic History* (September).

Van der Wee, H. and M. Goosens (1991), 'Belgium', in R. Cameron and V.I. Bovykin (eds), *International Banking, 1870–1914* (New York: Oxford University Press).

Verlinden, C., J. Craeybeckx, and E. Scholliers (1972), 'Price and Wage Movements in Belgium in the Sixteenth Century' in P. Burke (ed.), *Economy and Society in Early Modern Europe* (New York: Harper and Row).

Vicens Vives, J. (1969), *An Economic History of Spain* (Princeton: Princeton University Press).

Vilar, P. (1977), *Spain, A Brief History* (Oxford: Pergamon Press).

Weber, A. (1899), *Growth of Cities in the Nineteenth Century* (New York: Macmillan).

Weber, E. (1976), *Peasants Into Frenchmen* (Stanford: Stanford University Press).

Weir, D.R. (1984), 'Life Under Pressure: France and England, 1670–1870', *Journal of Economic History* (March).

Weisser, M.R. (1982), 'The Agrarian Depression in Seventeenth-Century Spain,' *Journal of Economic History* (March).

Weisser, M.R. (1987), 'Rural Crisis and Rural Credit in XVIIth-Century Castile,' *Journal of European Economic History* (Fall).

White, E.N. (1989), 'Was There a Solution to the Ancien Régime's Financial Dilemma?', *Journal of Economic History* (September).

White, E.N. (1990), 'Free Banking during the French Revolution', *Explorations in Economic History* (July).

Williamson, J.G. (1982), 'The Structure of Pay in Britain, 1710–1911', *Research in Economic History* (Volume 7).

Williamson, J.G. (1987a), 'Has Crowding Out Really Been Given a Fair Test? A Comment', *Journal of Economic History* (March).

Williamson, J.G. (1987b), 'Debating the Industrial Revolution', *Explorations in Economic History* (July).

Williamson, J.G. (1996), 'Globalization, Convergence, and History', *Journal of Economic History* (June).

Williamson, J.G. (1998), 'Globalization, Labor Markets and Policy Backlash in the Past', *Journal of Economic Perspectives* (Fall).

Wordie, J.R. (1983), 'The Chronology of English Enclosure, 1500–1914', *Economic History Review* (November).

Wrigley, E.A. and R.S. Schofield (1981), *The Population History of England, 1541–1871: A Reconstruction* (Cambridge, Mass: Harvard University Press).

Zamagni, V. (1993), *The Economic History of Italy, 1860–1990* (Oxford: Clarendon Press).

Index